EVIL PARADISES

WITHDRAWN

EVIL PARADISES

Dreamworlds of Neoliberalism

Edited by Mike Davis
and Daniel Bertrand Monk

THE NEW PRESS

NEW YORK
LONDON

Requests for permission to reproduce selections from this book should be mailed to:
Permissions Department, The New Press, 38 Greene Street, New York, NY 10013.

Published in the United States by The New Press, New York, 2007
Distributed by Perseus Distribution

ISBN 978-1-59558-076-4 (hc)
ISBN 978-1-59558-392-5 (pb)
CIP data available

The New Press was established in 1990 as a not-for-profit alternative to the large,
commercial publishing houses currently dominating the book publishing industry.
The New Press operates in the public interest rather than for private gain, and is committed
to publishing, in innovative ways, works of educational, cultural, and community value
that are often deemed insufficiently profitable.

www.thenewpress.com

Composition by NK Graphics, a Black Dot Group Company
Photograph of Michael Sorkin courtesy of Michael Sorkin Studio

Printed in the United States of America

4   6   8   10   9   7   5   3

MIX
Paper from
responsible sources
FSC® C068106

Evil Paradises revisits, now on a global canvas, many of the concerns of *Variations on a Theme Park,* the prophetic 1991 symposium on the future of American urbanism edited and inspired by Michael Sorkin. As practicing architect, critic, and theorist, Sorkin has become the most seminal, consistently creative presence in the contemporary urban studies scene. His twenty or so books (published or in press) include some of the toughest-minded architectural criticism ever written (*Exquisite Corpses*) as well as radical exposés of the politics of walls, borders, globalization, 9/11 monuments, and architectural counterterrorism (*Giving Ground, Against the Wall, After the World Trade Center,* and *Indefensible Space*). But Sorkin also sustains the utopian spirit in contemporary urban design, exploring the ecologies of communal self-organization (*Local Code*) and proposing breathtaking schemes for sustainable cities (*Eutopia* and the forthcoming *New York City* [*Steady*] *State*). He refreshes his extraordinary vision of global urbanism with constant fieldwork: Kumasi, Hanoi, Vienna, Johannesburg, Bangalore, Abu Dhabi, Taiwan, Jerusalem, and, most recently, New Orleans. Yet—as director of the Urban Design Program at City College of New York Graduate Center—he remains a militant New Yorker, deeply involved in local struggles for social justice and affordable housing.

The editors' accumulated debts to Sorkin's intellectual generosity exceed any simple accounting. All the greater, then, the pleasure we take in dedicating *Evil Paradises* to our gadfly, comrade, and chief instigator.

April 2007

Contents

Introduction

A Brechtian maxim: take your cue not from the good old things, but
from the bad new ones.
  —Walter Benjamin, diary entries, 1938[1]

Evil Paradises addresses a simple but epochal question: "Toward what kind of future are we being led by savage, fanatical capitalism?" Or, to frame the same question in a different way, "What do contemporary 'dreamworlds' of consumption,
property, and power tell us about the fate of human solidarity?" These case studies explore the new geographies of exclusion and landscapes of wealth that have
arisen during the long "globalization" boom since 1991. We focus, especially, on
those instances—ranging from Arizona to Afghanistan—where the *Atlas Shrugged*,
winner-take-all ethos is unfettered by any remnant of social contract and undisturbed by any ghost of the labor movement, where the rich can walk like gods in
the nightmare gardens of their deepest and most secret desires.

   Such places are now surprisingly common (if you can pay the membership fee),
and utopian greed—shades of Paris Hilton, Bernie Ebbers, and Donald Trump—
saturates popular culture and the electronic media. No one is surprised to read
about millionaires spending $50,000 to clone their pet cats or a billionaire who
pays $20 million for a brief vacation in space. And if a London hairdresser has
clients happy to spend $1,500 for haircuts, then why shouldn't a beach house
in the Hamptons sell for $90 million or Lawrence Ellison, CEO of Oracle, earn

$340,000 an hour in 2001? Indeed, so much hyperbole is depleted in the coverage of the lifestyles of billionaires and celebrities that little awe remains to greet the truly extraordinary statistics, like the recent disclosure that the richest 1 percent of Americans spend as much as the poorest 60 million; or that 22 million factory jobs in the twenty major economies were sacrificed to the gods of globalization between 1995 and 2002; or that rich individuals currently shelter a staggering $11.5 trillion (ten times the annual GDP of the UK) in offshore tax havens.[2]

It is now customary, except perhaps in the pages of the *Wall Street Journal*, to refer to this new and greatest gilded age—the outgrowth of the global counter-revolution against social citizenship unleashed by Margaret Thatcher, Ronald Reagan, and Deng Xiaoping in the early 1980s, and continued by Tony Blair, Bill Clinton, Boris Yeltsin, and Li Peng during the 1990s—as the reign of "neoliberalism." Resurgent late capitalism, we are told, has succeeded, where all the great world religions have failed in finally unifying all of humanity in a single imaginary body: the global marketplace. History ends and the realm of (personal, not collective) freedom begins—or does it? Neoliberalism, as Pierre Bourdieu eloquently warned us, is actually an authoritarian utopia that is nothing less than "a program of the methodical destruction of collectives," from trade unions and mill towns to families and small nations.[3]

Further, as Timothy Mitchell shows in the stunning essay on Egypt's supposed "free-market miracle" that opens this volume, the hegemony of neoliberal policies has little to do with self-regulating markets, supply and demand, or even the "economic" as an autonomous category. Neoliberalism is not the *Wealth of Nations* 2.0; nor is it latter-day Cobdenism, healing the world's wounds through peaceful free trade; and, most certainly, it isn't the advent of the stateless market utopia romanticized by Friedrich von Hayek and Robert Nozick. On the contrary, what has characterized the long boom since 1991 (or 1981, if you prefer) has been the massive, naked application of state power to raise the rate of profit for crony groups, billionaire gangsters, and the rich in general. As one of us wrote about Reagan's economic program more than a generation ago:

Although the rhetoric of the various campaigns and tax rebellions that paved Reagan's road to power was vigorously anti-statist, the real programmatic intention was towards a restructuring, rather than diminution, of state spending and intervention in order to expand the frontiers of entrepreneurial and rentier opportunity. Typical explicit or underlying demands included: accelerated depreciation allowances, unfettered speculative real estate markets and rampant condominiumization, subcontracting of public services, transfer of tax resources from public to private education, lowering of minimum wages, abolition of health and safety standards for small businesses, and so on.[4]

The central role of state power, rather than free markets, in the neoliberal program ironically finds its most dramatic expression in the massive privatization of public assets, the subcontracting of public employment (which now includes even the waging of war), and the deregulation of financial markets. Economic textbooks can drone on forever about profit-driven technological innovation and the invisible hand of trade, but, as David Harvey has rightly insisted, the "main achievements of neoliberalism have been redistributive rather than generative."[5] It has been corrupt insider political power, nothing less, that has given away the global commons to a plunderbund that includes Dick Cheney's Halliburton, Boeing, Blackwater, Carlos Slim's Telmex, Yukos, the Abramovich empire, Larry Rong Zhijian's China International Tourist and Investment Corporation, Silvio Berlusconi's Fininvest, and Rupert Murdoch's News Corporation. This cold fusion of crime, dirty politics, and capital is fittingly celebrated in the rise of such former mob hideouts as Dubai, Las Vegas, Miami, and even Medellín (see Forrest Hylton's essay) as global icons of the new capitalism.

Dynamic, ever-growing social inequality, moreover, is the very engine of the contemporary economy, not just its inadvertent consequence. The classic "Fordist" mass-consumption economies of the 1950s and 1960s, regulated by collective bargaining and a stable division of productivity gains between capital and labor, have been replaced (at least in the Anglo-Saxon countries) by what a team of Citigroup researchers call *plutonomies*: where the rich are the "dominant drivers of demand," skimming the cream off productivity surges and technology monopolies, then spending their increasing share of national wealth as fast as possible on luxury goods and services. The champaign days of the Great Gatsby have returned with a vengeance. As the national income share of the top 1 percent of Americans, for instance, soared from 8 percent in 1964 to 17 percent in 1999, their savings rate plunged (from 8 percent in 1992 to *negative* 2 percent in 2000)—meaning that they were consuming "a larger fraction of their bloated, very large share of the economy."[6]

Internationally, this spending spree by high-net-worth individuals has replaced market deepening (the expansion of mass-consumption entitlements) as the principal piston of economic expansion. Those elite firms who have traditionally scratched the itch of the very rich—Porsche, Bulgari, Polo Ralph Lauren, Tiffany, Hermes, Sotheby's, and so on—cannot open new branches fast enough in Shanghai, Dubai, and Bangalore. At the same time, staggering amounts of Third World rapine are converted into Manhattan townhouses, London squares, Key Biscayne yacht slips, and Irish country estates. As the Citigroup analysts emphasize: "The emerging market entrepreneurs/plutocrats (Russian oligarchs, Chinese real-estate/manufacturing tycoons, Indian software moguls, Latin American oil/agriculture barons) benefiting disproportionately from globalization are logically diversifying into the asset markets of the developed plutonomies." They have helped inflate the $30 trillion real-estate bubble, centered in the more neoliberal countries, that represents the most massive and dangerous accumulation of nonproductive, "fictional" capital in world history. "The earth," thus conclude the Citigroup researchers, "is being held by the muscular arms of its entrepreneur-plutocrats, like it, or not." Moreover, the rich will keep getting richer "because the globalized pool of [low-priced] labor keeps wage inflation in check."[7]

Who are these "muscular" plutonomic heroes? The Citigroup team reproduces a devastating table (compounded out of their own research and Survey of Consumer Finance data) that depicts the return to a robber baron–era topography of economic inequality.[8]

U. S. Mean Annual Income (families)
2004

top 10%	$302,100
next 10%	106,000
next 20%	69,100
next 20%	43,400
bottom 40%	18,500

Globally, the *World Wealth Report (2005)* from Merrill Lynch & Company reveals that nearly one thousand billionaires and almost *10 million* millionaires (net worth, exclusive of real estate) dominate the social pyramid and by 2009 will dispose of an estimated $42.2 trillion in assets. They generate the market for *uber*-toys like $1.25 million Buggati Veyrons (ironically made by Volkswagen) and two-hundred-foot-long super yachts. Although the largest group of high-net-worth households still resides in North America (some 3 million millionaires), the Chinese followers of Deng Xiaoping's "To Get Rich Is Glorious" are now the third-largest segment of the luxury market (about 11 percent) and are predicted to surpass the conspicuous consumption of wealthy Americans and Japanese by 2014.[9] (Air China's in-flight magazine is famously chockablock with glamorous ads for "Vienna Forest Villas," "Pure Beautiful Golf Villas," "Mediterranean-charm Villas," and even an "intellectual villa" designed by a Canadian architect.) Russia's new wannabe Romanoffs, meanwhile, queue up outside St. Petersburg to bid on "fifty miniature palaces, each modeled on a famous residence of British, French, and Russian monarchs." (A similar nostalgia for the Hapsburgs, according to Judit Bodnar, drives the Hungarian neoliberal rich back into the gloom of Edwardian *haute bourgeois* décor.)

But most of the world watches the great binge only on television: modern wealth and luxury consumption are more enwalled and socially enclaved than at any time since the 1890s. As our case studies repeatedly underline, the spatial logic of neoliberalism (*cum* plutonomy) revives the most extreme colonial patterns of residential segregation and zoned consumption. Everywhere, the rich and near rich are retreating into sumptuary compounds, leisure cities, and gated replicas of imaginary California suburbs (see chapters by Marina Forti, Laura Ruggeri, Rebecca Schoenkopf, Marco d'Eramo, and Anne-Marie Broudehoux). The "Off Worlds" advertised in the apocalyptic skies of *Blade Runner*'s Los Angeles are now open and ready for occupancy from Montana to China. Meanwhile, a demonized criminal underclass—as Patrick Bond explains in his essay on Johannesburg—everywhere stands outside the gate (although sometimes as little more than symbolic lawn jockeys), providing a self-serving justification for the withdrawal and fortification of luxury lifestyles.

This unprecedented spatial and moral secession of the wealthy from the rest of humanity also expresses itself in current fads for high-end monasticism (Sara Lipton), floating city-states (China Miéville), space tourism, private islands, restored monarchies, and techo-murder at a distance (Dan Monk). The super-rich can also retreat, self-deified but not yet dead, into their marble mausoleums (see Joe Day on personal museums), or buy up to 2 million acres of ranchland and singlehandedly "save Nature" (see Jon Wiener on Ted Turner's bison). Where the rich lack requisite power and numbers to create new luxury cities (as at Arg-e Jadid in Iran) or gentrify wholesale old capitals (like London or Paris), they can nonetheless "disembed" themselves from the matrix of popular urban life through the creation of separate transportation and security systems (as in Managua, discussed by Dennis Rodgers) or by the radical disfranchisement of poor people's right to unconditional use of public streets (as in the U.S. Supreme Court ruling in the case of Hicks, described by Don Mitchell). In post-Taliban Kabul (described by Anthony Fontenot and Ajmal Maiwandi), they simply evict the poor to build their palaces: an exhibitionist narco-warlord architecture that quotes both Walt Disney and Genghis Khan.

This is nothing less than a utopian frenzy, and the early twenty-first century, with its global vogue for evil paradises (of which Dubai may be both the most remarkable and sinister) recapitulates many of the same mythic, impossible longings that Walter Benjamin discovered in his famous excavation of Baudelaire's Paris. With Marx's theory of commodity fetishism as his Rosetta stone, Benjamin unraveled the mystery of the bewitched capitalist city where human collectivity, overwhelmed by its own colossal productive powers, hallucinates its social being as a swirling "dream-life of objects." But the inverted realities and false consciousness of the Victorian era have now grown to Himalayan, life-threatening proportions. If the iron-and-glass arcades of the 1850s were the enchanted forests of early consumer capitalism, today's luxury-themed environments—including city-sized supermalls, artificial island suburbs, and faux downtown "lifestyle centers"—function as alternative universes for privileged forms of human life. On a planet where more than 2 billion people subsist on two dollars or less a day, these dream-worlds enflame desires—for infinite consumption, total social exclusion and physical security, and architectural monumentality—that are clearly incompatible with the ecological and moral survival of humanity.

Monstrous paradises, indeed, presume sulfurous antipodes. In his dense, almost brutal critique of the 1935 second draft of Benjamin's *Arcades Project* (the exposé known as "Paris, the Capital of the Nineteenth Century"), Theodor Adorno chastised Benjamin for "discarding the category of hell found in the first sketch." "Hell," emphasized Adorno, was key both to the "luster" and "dialectical coherence" of Benjamin's analysis. "To revert to the language of the splendid first sketch of the Arcades," Adorno scolded, "if the dialectical image is nothing but the mode of apprehension of the fetish character in the collective consciousness, then the Saint-Simonian conception of the commodified world as utopia might well be disclosed, but not its obverse—the dialectical image of the nineteenth century as hell. But only the latter could put the image of the Golden Age in its proper place. . . ."[10]

The same dialectical injunction applies to the paradises of our new Golden Age. Brecht, "contemplating Hell" (in the tradition of Shelley confronted with the staggering wealth and squalor of London) decided that Hell "must be even more like Los Angeles." Many of the "dreamlands" described in the pages that follow are, in fact, iterations of Los Angeles, or at least "California lifestyle," as a global phantasmagoric ideal, which the nouveaux riches pursue with the same desperate zeal in the desert of Iran and the hills of Kabul as they do in the gated suburbs of Cairo, Johannesburg, and Beijing. But, as in autochthonic Los Angeles, Hell and the Mall are never more than a freeway drive apart. Thus *The Real Housewives of Orange County*, like their counterparts in Hong Kong's tony-phony

"Palm Springs" or Budapest's neo-Hapsburg gated communities, exploit the labor of maids who themselves live in slums or even chicken coops on the roofs of mansions. The *Metropolis*-like phantasmagoria of Dubai's super-skyscrapers or the Olympic megastructures in Beijing arise from the toil of migrant workers whose own homes are fetid barracks and desolate encampments. In the larger perspective, the bright archipelagos of utopian luxury and "supreme lifestyles" are mere parasites on a "planet of slums."

And precisely because the price of "paradise" is human catastrophe, we can share little of Benjamin's optimism about historical redemption through the "genuine" utopian aspects of such fantasies. Let's not kid ourselves: these studies map terminal, not anticipatory, stages in the history of late modernity. They expand our understanding of what Luxemburg and Trotsky had in mind when they warned of "Socialism or Barbarism." Indeed, viewed as an ensemble, these idle redoubts stand as testaments to the resignation with which humanity squanders the borrowed time on which it now lives. If Benjamin evoked a society that "dreamed itself waking," these gilded dreamworlds have no alarm clocks; they are willful, narcissistic withdrawals from the tragedies overtaking the planet. The rich will simply hide out in their castles and television sets, desperately trying to consume all the good things of the earth in their lifetimes. Indeed, by their very existence, the indoor ski slopes of Dubai and private bison herds of Ted Turner represent that ruse of reason by which the neoliberal order both acknowledges and dismisses the fact that the current trajectory of human existence is unsustainable.

Mike Davis
Daniel Bertrand Monk
April 2007

1

Dreamland

Timothy Mitchell

During the second half of the twentieth century, economics established its claim to be the true political science. The idea of "the economy" provided a mode of seeing and a way of organizing the world that could diagnose a country's fundamental condition, frame the terms of its public debate, picture its collective growth or decline, and propose remedies for its improvement, all in terms of what seemed a legible series of measurements, goals, and comparisons. In the closing decade of the century, after the collapse of state socialism in the Soviet Union and Eastern Europe, the authority of economic science seemed stronger than ever.[1] Employing the language and charisma of neoclassical economics, the programs of economic reform and structural adjustment advocated in Washington by the International Monetary Fund, the World Bank, and the United States government could judge the condition of a nation and its collective well-being by simply measuring its monetary and fiscal balance-sheets.

In Egypt, according to these ways of thinking, the 1990s was a decade of remarkable success that vindicated the principles of neoliberalism. After the government agreed to an IMF reform program, fiscal and monetary discipline brought the inflation rate below 5 percent and reduced the budget deficit from 15 percent of the country's gross domestic product (GDP) to less than 3 percent and for some years less than 1 percent, among the lowest levels in the world. The economy was said to be growing at more than 5 percent a year, and a revitalized private capitalism now accounted for two-thirds of domestic investment. The value of the Egyptian pound was pegged to the U.S. dollar, supported by hard currency reserves of more than $18 billion. These iconic statistics, repeated countless times in government newspapers and television bulletins and in publications of the IMF, constituted proof of the "remarkable turnaround in Egypt's macroeconomic fortunes" in the final years of the century.[2]

Pathological Exuberance

Yet if one looked beyond the official figures, even elsewhere in the same newspapers and television programs, other developments seemed to contradict this rosy view. Accompanying the picture of monetary control and fiscal discipline was a contrasting image of uncontrolled expansion and limitless dreams. The most dramatic example was the country's rapidly expanding capital city. While government budgets were contracting, Cairo was exploding.

"Dreamland," the TV commercials for the most ambitious of the new developments promised, "is the world's first electronic city." Buyers were invited to sign up now for luxury fiber-optic-wired villas, as shopping malls and theme park, golf course and polo grounds, sprouted out of the desert west of the Giza pyramids—but only minutes from central Cairo on the newly built ring road. Or one could take the ring road the other way, east of the Muqattam Hills, to the desert of "New Cairo," where speculators were marketing apartment blocks to expatriate workers in the Gulf saving for their futures at home. "Sign now for a future value beyond any dreams," prospective buyers were told, "Before it is too late." Purchasers could start payments immediately (no deposit was required) at agencies in Jeddah and Dubai. "No factories, no pollution, no problems" was the advertisement's promise, accompanied by the developer's slogan, "The Egypt of My Desires."[3] The development tracts stretched out across the fields and deserts around Greater Cairo represented the largest real-estate explosion Egypt had ever seen. Within the second half of the 1990s the area of its capital city was purported to have doubled.

The exuberance of the private developers was matched by the state's. While speculative builders were doubling the size of Cairo, the government was proposing to duplicate the Nile River. In October 1996, President Hosni Mubarak announced the revival of plans from the 1950s to construct a parallel river by pumping water up out of the lake behind the Aswan High Dam in the south into a canal running northwards that would eventually irrigate two million acres of the Western Desert.[4] Unable to persuade the World Bank or commercial investors that the Toshka scheme, as it was known, was feasible, the government proceeded with building the pumping station and an initial seventy kilometers of the canal, broadcasting daily television pictures of Caterpillar earthmovers toiling in the desert.[5] It allocated the first 100,000 acres of future farmland to a man described as the world's second-richest person, the Saudi financier Prince al-Walid bin Talal, whose Kingdom Agricultural Development Company appointed a California agribusiness, Sun World, to develop and manage what would become the world's single largest farm, consuming by itself 1 percent of the waters of the Nile.[6]

Sun World specialized in growing grapes and other table fruits on irrigated lands, and owned the global patents on more than fifty commercial varieties of fruit cultivar. In the excitement of the government's announcement that the project had found an American partner, the reason for this went unnoticed: Sun World had no money. The corporation was another failure of the U.S. farm industry, and had recently gone bankrupt. A second struggling California agribusiness, Cadiz Inc., had taken over Sun World, planning to pay off its debts by transforming it from a company producing crops into a marketing business that would sell its patents and trademarks, including the flagship brand, Superior Seedless grapes, around the world. Unable to make money growing and selling grapes, the company would sell the names of grapes instead. The company's global patents would guarantee it a future payment on every grape, peach, plum, and nectarine that Egyptian farmers toiling in the Western Desert might one day grow.[7] The government agreed to provide 20 percent of the farm's capital and granted it the twenty-year tax holiday enjoyed by large investments, but the government and Prince al-Walid were still looking for other private-sector partners willing to put up money for the project.

In the meantime the state was subsidizing urban property developers as well, selling public land cheaply and building the required expressways and Nile bridges in rapid time. The state was also involved directly, as a property developer. Down the road from Dreamland, adjacent to a U.S.-managed speculative development named Beverly Hills, the Radio and Televison Union, a commercial arm of the Ministry of Information, was building a 35-million-square-meter theme-park and filmmaking facility called Media Production City, billed as the world's biggest media complex outside Hollywood.[8] And the largest builder of Cairo's new neighborhoods, far bigger than the builders of Dreamland or Beverly Hills, was the Ministry of Defense. Military contractors were throwing up thousands of acres of apartments on the city's eastern perimeter to create new suburbs for the officer class.

If one's first reaction was amazement at the scale and speed of these developments, one soon began to wonder about the contradictions. The IMF and Ministry of the Economy spoke calmly of financial discipline and sustainable economic growth, but made no mention of the frenzied explosion of the capital city or the ecologically disastrous irrigation schemes in the desert.[9] The role of the state in subsidizing this speculative investment, and the networks linking speculators, bankers, and state officials, went unexamined. Officially, financial stabilization and structural adjustment were intended to generate an export boom, not a building boom. Egypt was to prosper by selling fruits and vegetables to Europe and the Gulf, not by paving over its fields to build ring roads. But real estate had now replaced agriculture as the country's third-largest non-oil investment sector, after manufacturing and tourism.[10]

The reforms that were supposed to open Egypt to trade with the global market had, in fact, the opposite effect. The country's openness index, which measures the value of exports and imports of goods and nonfactory services as a proportion of GDP, collapsed from 88 percent in 1985 to 47 percent in 1996/97. In the same period, Egypt's share of world exports also dropped by more than half.[11] The value of non-oil exports actually shrank in 1995/96, then shrank again in 1996/97, leaving the country dependent on petroleum products for 52 percent of export income. By the end of 1998 the situation was still worse, as the collapse of world petroleum prices briefly forced Egypt to halt its oil exports.[12] In 1998/99 Washington quietly set about rebuilding the OPEC oil cartel through secret negotiations with Iran, Saudi Arabia, and Venezuela in which it traded political concessions for their promises to cut production. The negotiations were a success, doubling the price of oil again within six months.[13] But this unpublicized state management of world trade was too slow to solve Egypt's new balance of payments crisis and the repeated shortages of foreign currency.

The most publicized element in Egypt's idyll of success, the stabilization of the value of its money, owed nothing to the power of the market but rather because the government was now better able to insulate the local currency against speculative exchanges of international finance. In other words the reforms depended not on freer trade and greater global integration, as in neoliberal dogma, but on reorganization of exchange markets. The protection of the currency relied upon the often-announced $18 billion of foreign reserves, a figure that alone came to symbolize the strength of the economy. The symbolism was so important that the government was unwilling actually to spend its reserves in defense of the currency. When exports fell even further and the trade balance worsened again in 1998/99, it resorted to a series of ingenious measures to impede the flow of imports and thus the exodus of hard currency, insulating the country further against the global market.[14]

Hidden Questions

How does one account for developments that seem so at odds with official representations? The conventional story was that by 1990 the Egyptian economy was in crisis, no longer able to support loss-making public industries, an overvalued currency, profligate government spending, an inflationary printing of money to cover the budget gap, and astronomical levels of foreign debt.[15] After fifteen years of foot-dragging and partial reforms, including agricultural price reforms, in 1990/91 the government was forced to adopt an IMF stabilization plan that allowed the currency to collapse against the dollar, decreased the government budget, tightened the supply of money, and cut back subsidies to public-sector enterprises, which the government reorganized into holding companies that were to privatize them or shut them down. These "prudent" fiscal policies were implemented more drastically than even the IMF had demanded, achieving a drop in the government deficit that the IMF called "virtually unparalleled in recent years."[16]

Some accounts admitted that the story was more complex than this simple tale of a prodigal state starting a new life of prudence. They may have added, for example, that among the most profligate of the government's expenditures was the purchase of military equipment, much of it supplied and subsidized by the United States—as part of Washington's own system of subsidies to U.S. military industries. An impending default on these military debts, causing an automatic suspension of U.S. aid, helped trigger the collapse in 1990. (Egypt had begun to default as early as 1983, but for several years the U.S. government illegally diverted its own funds to pay off Egypt's military loans.)[17] Some accounts may also have acknowledged that the crisis was brought on not just by a spendthrift state but by wider disruptions beyond its control, in particular the decline after 1985 in the price of oil (the largest source of government revenue); the halting of secret U.S. purchases of Egyptian weapons for Washington's covert war against Afghanistan (1979–89); and the decrease in workers' remittances, arms exports to Iraq, and other foreign income caused by the 1990/91 Gulf conflict.[18] The Iraq crisis enabled the United States and other creditors in Europe and the Gulf to write off almost half Egypt's external debt, cutting it from US$53 billion in 1988 to $28 billion. The saving on interest payments, amounting to $15.5 billion by 1996/97, accounted for all of the increase in currency reserves.[19] So the major contribution to Egypt's fiscal turnaround resulted from a political decision of Washington and its allies. It had nothing to do with the magic of neoliberalism.

Furthermore, an important part of government revenue in Egypt in the 1990s came not from taxing productive activities but from the rent derived from public resources. About one-third came from two state-owned enterprises, the Egyptian General Petroleum Corporation and the Suez Canal Authority. The revenues of these enterprises were earned in U.S. dollars, so the one-third devaluation of the Egyptian pound against the dollar increased their value by 50 percent. This increase contributed the bulk of the growth in government revenues in the stabilization period. Again, the fiscal magic was little connected with free-market principles, but owed more to the extensive ownership of resources by the state.

Beyond all this there was another, still more complex, story, one that contradicted the official accounts and was pushed aside into footnotes. The crisis of 1990/91 was not just a problem of public enterprises losing money or a profligate government overspending. It was also a problem of the so-called private sector and the chaos created by deregulated international flows of speculative finance. The financial reforms that followed were not so much an elimination of state support, as the official version of events portrayed things, but more a change in who received it. The "free market" program in Egypt was better seen as a multilayered political readjustment of rents, subsidies, and the control of resources. In the following pages I retrieve this story from the footnotes. The second half of the chapter then considers what its burial there can tell us about the larger questions these events pose: how should we understand the relationship between the expertise of economics and the object we call the economy? What combination of understandings and silences, forces and desires, makes possible the economy? Why do these forces at the same time render the making of the economy incomplete?

First, it was not in fact the case that public-sector enterprises were losing money. In 1989/90, on the eve of the reforms, 260 out of 314 nonfinancial state-owned enterprises were profitable and only 54 were suffering losses. While the latter lost E£300 million ($110 million), the profitable companies made after-tax profits of E£1.5 billion (about $550 million).[20] At the center of concern in 1990/ 91 was a crisis not of state-owned industry but of the financial sector, which brought the country's banking system close to collapse. Since 1974 the number of banks had increased from 7 to 98, as commercial banks sprang up to finance the imports and investments of the oil-boom years. The four large state-owned banks made loans mostly to public-sector enterprises. It was estimated that at least 30 percent of these loans were nonperforming.[21] But the state banks were also part-owners of the private-sector banks, enabling them to channel public funds toward a small group of wealthy and well-connected entrepreneurs.[22] These large private-sector borrowers were also in trouble.

By 1989, 26 percent of private and investment loans were in default, more than half of them belonging to just 3 percent of defaulters. Many of the big debtors were able to delay legal action and others fled the country to avoid the courts.[23] The largest default came in July 1991, when the London-based Bank of Credit and Commerce International collapsed. (The biggest bank ever to collapse, BCCI had been the leading global finance house for the funding of secret wars, helping the CIA launder payments for U.S. campaigns in the 1980s against Nicaragua and Afghanistan.) Depositors in BCCI's Egyptian subsidiary were protected by an informal insurance scheme among Egyptian banks, which had to contribute 0.5 percent of their deposits and share the cost of a E£1 billion interest-free loan to make up the missing funds.[24]

These difficulties reflected the problems of a state in which public interests, as we will see, were increasingly entwined with the projects of a well-connected group of financiers and entrepreneurs, whose actions it was unable to discipline.[25] As with the 1997–99 global financial crisis, however, the problem of public resources overflowing into private networks cannot be separated from the difficulties caused by global speculation, especially currency trading.[26] Following the U.S. abandonment of international currency controls in 1980, daily global foreign exchange turnover increased from $82.5 billion in 1980 to $270 billion in 1986 and $590 billion in 1989 (by 1995 it was to reach $1.23 trillion).[27] This explosive growth of private and institutional speculation in national currencies overwhelmed the attempts of governments to manage their currencies according to local needs.

In Egypt, global deregulation coincided with a sudden increase in private foreign currency transfers, as expatriate workers sent home earnings from the Gulf. More than one hundred unregulated money management firms were formed to transfer and invest such funds, five or six of them growing very large.[28] These Islamic investment companies (so called because they appealed to depositors by describing the dividend they paid as a profit share rather than an interest payment) invested successfully in currency speculation, later diversifying into local tourism, real estate, manufacturing, and commodity dealing, and paid returns that kept ahead of inflation. The public- and private-sector commercial banks, subject to high reserve requirements and low official interest rates (essential to the government financing of industry), could not compete and were increasingly starved of hard currency. The financial system was in crisis.

In 1988/89 the bankers finally persuaded the government to eliminate the investment companies. It passed a law that suspended their operations for up to a year, then closed down those it found insolvent (or in many cases made insolvent) and forced the remainder to reorganize as joint-stock companies and deposit their liquid assets in the banks. The measure protected the banks and their well-connected clients, but provoked a general financial depression from which neither the banks nor the national currency could recover.[29]

Neoliberal Myths

In response to the financial crisis, the centerpiece of the 1990/91 reforms was an effort to rescue the country's banks. After allowing the currency to collapse and cutting public investment projects, the government transferred to the banks funds worth 5.5 percent of GDP in the form of treasury bills.[30] To give an idea of the scale of this subsidy, in the United States during the same period the government paid for the rescue of the savings-and-loan industry which had collapsed following financial deregulation, transferring a sum that amounted to about 3 percent of GDP over ten years. The Egyptian payment was almost twice as large in relation to GDP, and occurred in a single year. Moreover, the government declared the banks' income from these funds to be tax free, a fiscal subsidy amounting to a further 10 percent of GDP by 1996/97. In 1998 the government attempted to end the subsidy by reintroducing the taxing of bank profits, but the bankers thwarted the implementation of the law.[31] The banks became highly profitable, enjoying rates of return on equity of 20 percent or more. All of these profits were accounted for by the income from the government rescue.[32]

A further support to the banking sector came when the government tightened the supply of money to raise interest rates, pushing them initially as high as 14 percent above international market levels. Nonmarket interest rates brought in a flood of speculative capital from abroad. This was quickly taken to indicate the success of neoliberal discipline and market orthodoxy. It was nothing of the sort. The money consisted of highly volatile investment funds chasing interest income, the attractiveness of which was due not to "market fundamentals" but state intervention. After two years interest rates were brought down and the miniboom passed.

In 1996/97 the government manufactured another miniboom, by announcing an aggressive program of privatization. It began to sell shares in state-owned enterprises on the Cairo stock market, which it had reorganized to exclude small brokers and eliminate taxes on profits.[33] By June 1997 the government's income from the privatization sales amounted to E£5.2 billion ($1.5 billion). It used 40 percent of this income to provide further support to the banking sector, by paying off bad debts. In May 1998 the IMF praised Egypt's "remarkable" privatization program, ranking it fourth in the world (after Hungary, Malaysia, and the Czech Republic) in terms of privatization income as a share of GDP.[34]

The sell-off fattened the banks and the government budget and fueled a short-lived stock-market boom. But its outcome was not a switch from state-run enterprise to a reborn private sector. The conventional distinction between a private and a public sector, used by the government and the IMF, was too simple to capture the range of political and economic relations involved.[35] Many of the largest government-owned enterprises, such as Arab Contractors, the country's largest construction firm, and Eastern Tobacco, the cigarette manufacturing monopoly, had their own "private-sector" subsidiaries or joint ventures, typically run by members of the same family managing the public-sector parent.[36] The state banks were part-owners of private-sector banks, as we saw, and of other nonstate enterprises. A large number of government ministers and other senior officials, together with their spouses, siblings, and offspring, were partners or principal investors in many of the largest so-called private-sector ventures.[37]

In addition, the reorganization of state enterprises into corporate entities, under the control of public holding companies, further complicated the distinction between public and private sector. By June 30, 1999, the government had sold shares in 124 of its 314 nonfinancial public enterprises. However, it fully divested only a handful. The holding companies remained the largest shareholder in many, and the state managers continued to control others though employee shareholder associations.[38] The press was full of stories of phony privatizations, such as the December 1997 sale of al-Nasr Casting, which in fact had been sold to the public-sector banks.[39] (A year later, state officials forced the chairman of the stock exchange to resign after he tried to improve its surveillance of company finances and share trading.)[40] The state holding companies also set up new private-sector subsidiaries, such as al-Ahram Cement, and began to bid for shares in other cement companies the government was "privatizing."[41] And many government ministries, with the support of public-sector banks, began to launch new profit-making ventures, typified by the vast Media Production City project of the Ministry of Information.

The IMF's confident report that Egypt ranked fourth in the world in privatization missed the complexity of these rearrangements and the multiple forms of ownership, interconnection, and power relationship involved. As David Stark argues in a study of Eastern Europe, by focusing on the enterprise as a unit and simply tallying the number and value of those moved from public to private ownership, orthodox accounts are unable to grasp the multiple methods of control, or the importance of the networks that combined them.[42] The blurred boundaries between "public" ownership and "private" had always offered ambiguities for state officials, enterprise managers, and other insiders to exploit to their own advantage. Structural adjustment offered opportunities for further combinations and new ambiguities. The economic reform was a complicated readjustment of the networks connecting and combining a variety of property assets, legal powers, information sources, and income flows.

The stock-market boom lasted less than eighteen months, with the EFG index of large capitalization companies reaching a peak in September 1997, then losing one-third of its value over the following twelve months.[43] As the stock market slid the government halted the sell-offs, suspending most privatizations after the summer of 1998 and stalling on an IMF demand to begin privatizing the financial sector. Instead, to stem the collapse of the market, the government used its financial institutions to invest public funds. Between December 1997 and October 1998, the large state-owned banks and insurance companies and the state pension fund pumped at least E£2 billion ($600 million) into the market, suffering large losses.[44] In the process the state reacquired shares in most of the companies it had recently claimed to be privatizing—further complicating the fairy tale of private capital replacing public ownership. The market recovered briefly in the winter of 1998/99, when the financial crises in East Asia, Brazil, and Russia made Egypt appear, thanks to its state-subsidized banking system, one of the few safe havens for international speculative funds, but after February 1999 the decline resumed. By the following summer the market was so flat that a single stock, the country's newly privatized mobile phone monopoly, MobiNil, was regularly accounting for over 50 percent of daily trading, and often up to 70 percent.[45]

Most of the remaining stock-market activity and privatization progress was confined to just one economic sector, construction. The Toshka irrigation scheme and other large government projects, together with the state-subsidized real-estate boom and tourism development, provided the only significant source of economic growth. Cement-makers, manufacturers of steel reinforcing bars, and contracting companies all prospered, with the contractors' profit on government projects said to average 30 to 40 percent of income. The demand for cement increased so rapidly that the world's three largest cement makers, Holderbank of Switzerland, the French-based Lafarge group, and Cemex of Mexico, scrambled to buy up Egypt's government-owned cement plants.[46] The construction boom had turned the country into an importer of cement, so these foreign investments in local cement production should be classified as a return to the unfashionable policies of import-substitution industrialization. They had nothing to do with the growth of export-oriented industry that the economic reformers had promised.[47]

Real-estate booms and stock-market swings failed to address the problem of the country's low levels of domestic investment. Gross domestic investment dropped from 28 percent of GDP in 1980 to 19 percent in 1998, compared to an average of lower- and middle-income countries of 25 percent.[48] Between 1990 and 1997, investment grew at only 2.7 percent a year, compared to 7.2 percent for all middle-income countries and 12.7 percent for those in East Asia.[49] In addition, by June 1996 the number of loss-making public enterprises had almost doubled since the start of the reforms, from fifty-four to one hundred, and accumulated losses had risen from E£2 billion to E£12 billion ($3.5 billion).[50] The government had redefined its finances to exclude public-sector companies from the fiscal accounts, however, so this worsening situation was hidden from view.[51] The reformers could continue to claim that they were replacing government deficits with a balanced budget.

Crony Capitalism

The reform program did not remove the state from the market or eliminate profligate public subsidies. Its main impact was to concentrate public funds into different and fewer hands. The state turned resources away from agriculture and industry, and ignored the underlying problems of training and employment. It now subsidized financiers instead of factories, cement kilns instead of bakeries, speculators instead of schools. Although the IMF showed no interest in examining the question, it was not hard to figure out who was benefiting from the new financial subsidies. The revitalized public-private commercial banks focused their tax-free lending on big loans to large operators. The minimum loan size was typically over E£1 million and required large collateral and good connections.[52] So the subsidized funds were channeled into the hands of a relatively small number of ever more powerful and prosperous financiers and entrepreneurs.

At the top were about two dozen business groups, such as Bahgat, Seoudi, Mohamed Mahmoud, Mansour, Arabian International, Osman, and Orascom. These family-owned enterprise networks typically began as construction companies or import/export agents, which had prospered after 1974 when the government allowed large private entrepreneurs to reemerge following the years of import restrictions and state monopolies. Many depended upon lucrative contracts to supply goods and services to the Egyptian military. Most expanded subsequently into tourism, real estate, food and beverages, and computer and Internet services, and in some cases the manufacturing of construction materials or, where tariff protection made it profitable, the local assembling of consumer goods such as electronics or cars. Several shared in ownership of the private-sector banks, which emerged in the same period. They enjoyed powerful monopolies or oligopolies, in particular as exclusive agents for the goods and services of Western-based transnationals. Nothing one reads in the documents of the IMF or USAID mentions the nature, history, or power of these groups, whose existence was hidden behind the bland formulations of "the private sector" and a revitalized "Egyptian economy."

The Seoudi Group, for example, had its origins in a local trading company set up in 1958 by Abdul Moniem Seoudi. In the mid-1970s, with the opening of the consumer economy, the company began to import foodstuffs, general merchandise, and Suzuki commercial vehicles, and used the new tax-free zones to manufacture and export acrylic yarns. The family was involved in establishing two of the new private-sector banks, Al-Mohandes and Watany. In the 1980s they expanded into agribusiness, producing factory chickens and eggs with U.S.-subsidized feed grains, and importing American pesticides, feed additives, and agricultural equipment. They also established their own construction company to build facilities for their expanding enterprises. By the 1990s they were assembling Suzuki vehicles and manufacturing car seats and radiators, were the sole importers of Nissan vehicles, and had become the exclusive agents for NCR computers.[53]

The Metwalli family took control of Arabian International Construction when the company was denationalized in 1987, and built it up as the local partner of transnational firms constructing power stations and other government projects. In the 1990s AIC acquired the local share of two of the largest government contracts, to pipe drinking water under the Suez Canal for the North Sinai Development Project and build the canal and pumping station for the Toshka scheme. The company's profits on such projects averaged 40 percent of turnover, and enabled AIC to become the largest private construction company in Egypt. The income was channeled into eight other family-owned companies, all of them, it was claimed, becoming larger than AIC itself, the largest of them a real-estate development company.[54]

The Mohamed Mahmoud Sons group traced its origins to 1895, when Mohamed Mahmoud inherited his father's shoe-making workshop, becoming a shoe retailer in the 1920s and by the 1950s the largest shoe manufacturer and exporter in the Middle East. Like other groups, they diversified in the mid-1970s into the wholesale import and distribution of consumer goods, and they became the country's largest manufacturer of corrugated cardboard boxes. In the 1980s they set up their own engineering and construction arm, and imported and later began to assemble aluminum windows and doors, household and office furniture, and Ukranian-made tractors and irrigation pipes. By the 1990s the group's thirteen companies included the MM chain of luxury fashion stores, carrying lines such as Yves Saint Laurent, Church's, and Fratelli Rossetti; financial interests in the Egyptian Gulf Bank and the Pharaonic Insurance Co.; the Datum Internet service provider; the sole Egyptian agency for Jaguar Cars; and showrooms selling motor vehicles from Rolls-Royce and Ferrari.[55]

The Mansour family were large cotton traders whose business was nationalized under President Gamal Abdel Nasser. In 1975, when private trading companies reemerged, Mansour began importing Chevrolet trucks from General Motors, and later Caterpillar earthmoving equipment and John Deere tractors. A decade later, as the local agents of General Motors, they began assembling Chevrolet and Isuzu commercial vehicles, and by 1993 controlled 60 percent of the country's commercial vehicle market, including contracts with the Egyptian military. In the 1990s they acquired the licenses to distribute Marlboro cigarettes and other consumer products, half the Egyptian McDonald's franchises, and interests in tourism construction and Internet technology.[56]

The Sawiris family worked abroad as contractors in Libya before President Anwar Sadat's reopening of the economy to private entrepreneurs. They returned to prosper as local agents of Hewlett-Packard and AT&T, building U.S.-funded communication networks for the Egyptian military. The profits (30 to 50 percent of turnover was normal, the family claimed) funded an expansion into civilian communications, construction, and tourism. By the 1990s their holding company, Orascom, controlled a dozen subsidiaries that included Egypt's largest or second-largest private construction, cement making, and natural gas supply companies, the country's largest tourism developments (funded in part by the World Bank), a military technology import business with offices close to the Pentagon outside Washington, DC, more than half the local market for Microsoft, Hewlett-Packard, and Lucent Technologies, 60 percent of the country's Internet service provision, and mobile telephone businesses in collaboration with France Telecom controlling a majority of the Egyptian market and taking over local mobile operators in Jordan, Syria, Pakistan, and a dozen countries of sub-Saharan Africa.[57]

The Bahgat group, the biggest producer of televisions in the Middle East with a dominant position in the Egyptian market, graduated in the 1990s from assembling Korean sets to making Philips and own-name brands. It was linked to senior military officers and used military-owned factories to build its products. The group's forty companies (with just three thousand employees) were also involved in assembling electrical appliances and computers, importing medical equipment and irrigation systems, wholesale and retail marketing, tourism development, and computer software and Internet service.[58] They were the builders of the Internet-wired Dreamland. Dr. Ahmed Bahgat, the family head, was reputed to be a front man for unpublicized profiteering by the presidential family, which may explain why the express roads out to Dreamland were built in such rapid time.

All these cases share certain features. Most large business groups were nurtured on government contracts, both civilian and military. Many of these contracts involved projects promoted and supported by USAID. Besides receiving state funds, they relied on close ties with private banks, which were often part of the same family networks. Most avoided the more public method of raising funds on the stock market. The exceptions were those groups that expanded faster than the banks or government could support. The Lakah family, for example, importers of timber and other construction materials since they arrived from Syria in the 1890s, claimed by 1999 to be the largest private business group in Egypt, in terms of paid-up capital share. Rami Lakah had diversified into importing medical equipment and setting up high-tech facilities for the government's new U.S.-supported "cost-recovery" hospitals for the affluent.[59] To fund further growth, in August 1999 Lakah had launched the stock market's largest-ever share offer, and in November became the first Egyptian enterprise to borrow on the international bond market. (Disaster, as we will see, was not far ahead.) A final feature shared by these groups was the relatively small number of jobs which their enterprises generated. With the exception of one or two garment manufacturers, the largest business groups had workforces of only two or three thousand. Most employed considerably fewer.

By the 1990s these enterprises were increasingly concentrating on supplying goods and services affordable to only a small fraction of the population. A "Value Meal" at McDonald's cost more than the day's pay of most workers. A family outing to Dreampark, the entertainment complex under construction at Dreamland, would consume a fortnight's average wages. A pair of children's shoes at MM's fashion stores might exceed the monthly pay of a schoolteacher. The Ahram Beverages Company, which produced soft drinks, bottled water, and beer, calculated its potential market (including expatriates and tourists) at just five to six million, in a country of more than sixty million.[60] This narrow market was the same part of the population that could afford, or could just imagine affording, the country's 1.3 million private cars—which is why local manufacturers concentrated on assembling Mercedes, BMWs, Jeep Cherokees, and other luxury models.[61] A company selling upmarket flower bouquets under the U.S. franchise Candy Boutique did its own market research and arrived at a narrower and perhaps more accurate assessment of the affluent: "Egypt has a population of 60 million, but only 20,000 can afford what we are selling."[62] Beyond this small group of state-subsidized superrich, modest affluence probably extended to no more than 5 percent of the population.[63]

What of the other 95 percent? Real wages in the public industrial sector dropped by 8 percent from 1990/91 to 1995/96. Other public-sector wages remained steady, it was claimed, but could be held up only because the salaries remained below a living wage.[64] A schoolteacher took home less than $2 a day. A sign of the times was the reappearance of soup kitchens in Cairo, which an article in the national press characteristically interpreted not as a mark of how harsh conditions had become, but as a welcome return to the kind of private benevolence among the wealthy not seen since the days of the monarchy.[65]

Household expenditure surveys showed a sharp decline in real per capita consumption between 1990/91 and 1995/96. The proportion of people below the poverty line increased from about 40 percent (urban and rural) to 45 percent in urban areas and over 50 percent in rural. There was no reliable guide to the changing share of consumption by the very wealthy, because the surveys failed to record most of their spending. If household expenditure surveys for 1991/92 are extrapolated to the national level, the figures show the population as a whole spent E£51 billion. Yet national accounts gave the total expenditure as E£100 billion. In other words, half the country's consumer spending was missing from the surveys (although this did not deter the World Bank and other agencies from referring to such figures as reasonable indicators of income distribution).[66] As in India, where a similar disparity was discovered following a decade of economic restructuring, the household surveys probably missed the sharply rising consumption by the very rich, who "downplay their extravagance when the survey people come calling" (or simply have the servants deal with them).[67] An analysis of the kind of expenditures missing from the Egyptian survey and the relative proportion of incomes that different groups spent on food supported the view that the figures underrepresented the concentration of wealth among the rich. Even when categorized quite broadly as those spending more than E£14,000 (about $4,000) a year, wealthy households in Egypt represented only 1.6 million people. One study estimated that this group, less than 3 percent of the population, accounted for half of all consumer spending.[68]

Economy as Illusion

The difficulty of knowing how much of the country's wealth was becoming concentrated in the hands of the rich was a symptom of a larger problem. The politics of economic reform was based upon the illusion that the economy existed as a space that could be surveyed and mapped, much as the Nile valley had been surveyed by Colonel Lyons a century before. It imagined the economy as a territory whose boundaries could be drawn and whose separate elements could be located, transcribed, enumerated, and reorganized. In 1941, when Simon Kuznets of the National Bureau of Economic Research in Cambridge, Massachusetts, first systematized a method for estimating the total size of a nation's income, he had warned that "a national total facilitates the ascription of independent significance to that vague entity called the national economy."[69] Although many economists since Kuznets might have agreed with his warning, the method of their work enabled this vague entity, the economy, to acquire its independence.[70] The numbers representing national income and output, consumption and savings, employment and productivity, deficits and debt, whatever their degree of reliability, were taken to refer to processes that in principle formed a finite and mappable object.

Some of the contradictions of this methodology are well known. The most frequently mentioned is the impossibility of measuring what is called the informal or parallel sector of the economy. In Egypt, the household or neighborhood-based production and distribution of small-scale goods and services, unregistered with the state and operating on the margins of its systems of revenue and regulation, represent a large but unknown proportion of the country's productive life.[71] These activities were traditionally excluded from calculations of GDP and other representations of the economy, although increasing efforts were made to include some estimate. To give one idea of their scale, in 1996 about three-quarters of the population of Greater Cairo was living in informal housing, covering two-thirds of the land area and accounting for 85 percent of its dwelling units.[72] Those living in informal housing were not necessarily employed in informal livelihoods, but the figures indicate the extent to which one sector, the construction and possession of urban housing, was conducted outside the regulation of the state. Estimates of the overall size of informal economic activities ranged from 20 to 35 percent of GDP, but these were guesses and implied a straightforward division between formal and informal that was too simplistic to capture the interconnections involved.[73] The economic reforms were aimed chiefly at formal economic activities. As Mahmoud `Abd al-Fadil points out, however, policies aimed at the formal sector may have had an opposite impact on the parallel sector, while transformations in the latter had a profound effect on the former.

Not all activities of the parallel sector were small-scale and local. Some played a large role in the country's international trade and finance, as the example of the hemp industry illustrates. In the 1980s, Egypt imported large quantities of processed hemp—cannabis resin—from the Beqa`a valley in central Lebanon, where civil war had stimulated export-oriented production. The value of Egypt's clandestine imports was estimated at two to four billion U.S. dollars. Even the lower of these figures exceeded all Egypt's income from nonpetroleum exports.[74] After the end of the civil war in 1990, Syria gradually eliminated Lebanese production.[75] This coincided with currency devaluation in Egypt, which raised import prices, and with declining personal incomes and a tough government campaign against drug importers—conviction for drug dealing now carried the death penalty. As Lebanese hashish became scarce and unaffordable, consumers responded by developing a taste for smoking *bango*, locally grown, milder, unprocessed cannabis (few regions in the world can produce hemp rich enough in resins to process into hashish).[76] Hemp production rapidly became a significant village industry, especially in southern Egypt and Sinai, facilitated by the ending of government crop controls.[77] Thus another import-substitution industry had sprung up, eliminating one of the country's largest demands for hard currency. None of this was captured in official representations of the Egyptian economy—although the IMF puzzled over an unexplained and unusually rapid decline in the circulation of dollars.[78]

Discussions of the problem of measuring informal and clandestine activities usually imply a contrast with the formal sector, which in comparison is assumed to be fixed and known. Yet with the formal sector too it is difficult to ascribe an "independent significance" to the economy. There can be legal activities whose extent and value is never made public, such as the extensive production, trade, and consumption organized by the Egyptian armed forces. As the U.S. government put it, military spending in Egypt was "not transparent," so none of this activity was accurately represented in national accounts or in the government budget. In 1989, government spending on the armed forces was estimated at E£4.7 billion, or about 20 percent of government outlays, a figure that excluded foreign military assistance from the United States ($1.3 billion) and Saudi Arabia, income from Egyptian arms exports, and possibly the army's civilian agriculture and manufacturing projects.[79] So one-fifth of government spending and perhaps 10 percent of GDP was unmeasured and unreported. In fact the entire government budget was misleading, for in the 1990s Toshka and other giant investment projects were financed without being accounted for in the official figures. The government reported a spending deficit of just 1.3 percent of GDP for 1998/99, but a year later quietly revised this figure to reflect "off-budget spending," which more than tripled the deficit to 4.3 percent of GDP.[80]

The problems of informal, clandestine, and unreported economic activities are so great that these alone would provide sufficient reason to question the idea that the economy is an object that can be mapped and measured. But these issues are not the most profound problem. The idea of the economy presents a larger difficulty. Even the most visible and regulated acts of economic exchange have effects that escape observation or measurement. In any economic transaction, the parties involved attempt to calculate, as best they can, what they will gain from the exchange and what it will cost them. The transaction will also affect others, however, either positively or negatively. These further costs and gains will not enter into the calculation, because those affected are not parties to the transaction. Since the size of the economy is measured as the aggregate of all individual transactions, the additional effects are excluded from the representation of the national economy. Economists call the excluded elements "externalities," and often give the example of pollution: the owners of a cement factory contract with a customer to supply so many tons of cement, and do not include in the price the cost of the air pollution the factory creates, because those living nearby who are harmed by the bad air are not parties to the exchange. In the language of neoclassical economics, externalities are an example of "market failure," situations where the price mechanism that governs exchanges fails to reflect the true costs involved, and therefore is unable to act as an efficient regulator of social action.[81]

By using examples such as pollution, and by labeling them as externalities or failures, the method and language of economics treats these uncounted costs as something residual. They represent an imperfection in the market, a lapse in its mechanisms, a secondary rather than essential aspect of its operation. The example of pollution inadvertently points to much larger externalities, however, such as the destructive impact of a general level of economic activity on the ecological balance. These represent not individual market failures but an inability of the principle of the market to account for complex effects whose value cannot be monetarized. But disregarding these wider issues, there is a more general problem with treating externalities as something exceptional. Since no transaction takes place in a vacuum, all acts of exchange produce externalities. Every decision to purchase an object or service involves all the costs that went into it that were excluded, or not properly recognized or compensated.

It is not surprising that an economic actor should want to acquire something without paying all the associated costs—without accounting for all the ways its production and consumption might affect others. Indeed, exchange would be impossible if people were made to account for every cost. A market economy requires conventions and powers that enable the completion of an exchange without satisfying such a standard. So when the calculation of the economy excludes not only much that is informal or clandestine, but also the "external" aspects that occur within what is considered formal and regulated, the exclusion is hardly secondary in significance. As Callon points out, a lot of work and expense goes into achieving these acts of exclusion.[82] Without them, in fact, the market would cease to function. For example, to sell the cement a factory produces, the management of the factory must prove they own the product. They must deny the claims of others who may demand some share, such as the kiln workers who produced the cement but may not have been fully compensated for the value contributed by their labor, or those who supplied the machinery or the raw materials, as well as those who demand compensation for the damage pollution has done to their health and other outsiders. By proving ownership, the managers exercise a form of exclusion, the power to deny the claims of others.

Elsewhere, I have examined the genealogy of one kind of ownership claim in Egypt, the private ownership of land. I traced the process by which a person called the "landowner" came to monopolize the rights to the produce of the land and exclude the entitlements that cultivators, the indigent, the ruling household in Cairo, and other claimants had previously enjoyed. Organizing these exclusions was a complex political project, requiring a variety of forms of violence, supervision, policing, military occupation, legal argument, imprisonment, and economic theory. As that example showed, property is not a simple arrangement nor a static one. In the twentieth century the cultivators managed to reestablish some of their claims, as did the government. Toward the end of the century, reasserting the prerogatives of private ownership required new rounds of violence, policing, and economic argument.

Thus the simple idea of "externality" rests upon the operation of complex and mobile forms of law, international convention, government, corporate power, and economics. These multiple arrangements make possible the economy. Property rights, tax rules, contract and criminal law, administrative regulation, and policing all contribute to fixing the difference between the formal and the informal, between the act of exchange and its externalities, between those with rights and those without, between measurable values and the unmeasurable. In economic theory many of these forms of regulation and enforcement are called institutions. A distinction is sometimes made between formal institutions, such as laws and administrative rules, and informal institutions, such as codes of conduct, implicit understandings, and norms of social action. Institutional economics understands these rules and norms as constraints that organize and set limits to human action.[83] Like the concept of externality, the term "constraint" characterizes these arrangements once again as secondary, as something outside the economic process itself. The economic act is by definition the expression of an individual choice, the fulfillment of a desire, just as the economy is the sum total of these economic choices and their fulfillment. The desire is the starting point of the economic, while institutions are understood as arrangements that limit the desire, restrict the ways in which needs can be satisfied, prevent others from disrupting their satisfaction, and reduce delinquency or misunderstanding. Constraint is the opposite of desire, an element of incompatibility, and can combine with it only as something external and subordinate. Yet these secondary, external, residual, arrangements at the same time are something prior. The rules, norms, and unwritten understandings must exist before the act of exchange, otherwise they could not regulate it.[84] They are also ubiquitous, dwelling surreptitiously within every economic act. So although economics must portray them as external, secondary, and residual, they are also the condition of possibility of the economic.

The constraints, understandings, and powers that frame the economic act, and the economy as a whole, and thus make the economy possible, simultaneously render it incomplete. They occur as that strange phenomenon, the constitutive outside.[85] They are an interior-exterior, something both marginal and central, simultaneously the condition of possibility of the economy and the condition of its impossibility. Callon describes what he calls the "dual nature" of these constraints or frames.[86] Their purpose is to exclude, to keep out of the picture all those claims, costs, interruptions, and misunderstandings that would make the act of exchange, and thus the economy itself, impossible to complete. To achieve this "enframing," the rules, procedures, institutions, and methods of enforcement are thought to have a special status.[87] Just as a frame seems distinct from the picture it enframes, and a rule is supposedly an abstraction in relation to the concrete actions it governs, the institutions that enframe the economy are imagined to have a different, and extraeconomic, nature. They are the arena of economic actions, as distinct from the actions themselves. In practice, however, this distinction is not a stable one. Each piece of the frame, each rule, procedure, and sanction involves potential exchanges of its own. To apply a rule, for example, one must negotiate its limits and exceptions, since no rule contains its own interpretation. These negotiations become part of the act of exchange they are supposed to regulate. To enforce a regulation involves all the expense and interactions of adjudication, resort to force, and monitoring. At every one of these points the "frame" opens up and reveals its dual nature. Instead of acting as a limit, containing the economic, it becomes a series of exchanges and connections that involve the act of exchange in a potentially limitless series of further interactions.[88] Thus the problem of fixing the economy is not a residual one of accounting for informal and clandestine activities, or turning externalities into internal costs. The problem is that the frame or border of the economy is not a line on a map, but a horizon that at every point opens up into other territories.

The Myth of the Market

There are several epistemological issues to resolve before we return to the question of the relationship between economics and the economy. First, the rules of the market are by no means the only kind of frame for economic transactions. Despite the importance given to laws of property and the principles of the price mechanism, it would be difficult to establish that the market is even the most significant arena of exchange. Many other forms of social practice structure the way transactions occur, often with the purpose of preventing them from leaking across into the market. One institution that has always offered alternative rules and powers to those of property and contract is the household or family. In

Egypt, as in many parts of the world, the new large-scale economic activities that flourished with free-market reforms operated through networks of family-held businesses. Here, the main economic institution was not the market or even the business enterprise, but a web of personal ties drawing together a series of businesses, often establishing connections within and across state institutions, the banking sector, the armed forces, or the local agencies of transnational corporations. These networks operate through relations of kinship or marriage and put to work all the powers of loyalty, affection, discipline, and compulsion on which such relations depend.

These powers, like so many other noncapitalist forces operating at the center of so-called capitalism, need constant attention. They are never entirely controlled by those who use them and can easily take their own course. Trouble can follow, for example, when the forces of affection or ties of matrimony break down. In 1995, the entire Egyptian banking and political system was shaken by the rupturing of one family network. The Ayuti family controlled, among other interests, one of Egypt's large private-sector financial houses, Nile Bank. `Isa al-Ayuti, the eighty-one-year-old chairman of the bank, had become estranged from his daughter `Aliya al-Ayuti, the bank's managing director, following her marriage to Mahmud `Azzam, a large contractor and a member of parliament. In December 1995, the father accused his daughter of making unsecured loans to her new husband, providing his construction company with almost E£80 million. A government investigation of the fraud later widened to include thirty-two bankers and entrepreneurs involved in E£1 billion in fraudulent deals, including a former minister of tourism, Tawfiq `Abdu Ima`il, who was chairman of Dakhiliya Bank and also an MP, and two other members of parliament.[89] This was one of a number of fraud cases in this period arising from the breakdown of family networks. What such incidents reveal is not that all family networks involve fraud. Rather, the sensational cases publicized in the media indicate the quieter, everyday work that must be done to maintain family networks, and the costs that can follow from their collapse.

Another well-known example of a large-scale nonmarket economic network is the transnational corporation—an institution whose history and power must be discussed in relation to a parallel mechanism for limiting the operation of the market, the nation-state. Of course we know from Marx that any capitalist enterprise is a means of employing nonmarket arrangements to produce goods or services for the market. While the owners of the enterprise sell its products on the market, those who are employed to produce the products are typically subject to multiple forms of discipline, surveillance, compulsion, and, in many cases, the threat or use of violence. The fact that the employment relation takes the outward form of a contract only thinly disguises the "dull compulsion of economic relations" (as Marx described it in volume one of *Capital*) that gives most employees—especially those outside the more privileged economic enclaves of the West—little room to bargain over the terms of their labor.[90]

The large corporation, however, develops nonmarket arrangements to a much further extent. It establishes extensive hierarchies and controls based on supervision, surveillance, rules, sanctions, and the manufacture of a corporate culture. It separates the management of economic processes from the old powers of ownership. And it organizes multiple transactions within the corporation itself, producing, distributing, and consuming goods and services among its various divisions and subsidiaries. Indeed the closely governed, nonmarket movement of goods and services within corporate hierarchies represents as much as one-third of international trade.[91]

By the time he drafted volume three of *Capital*, Marx was aware that the modern corporation represented a break with the principles of capitalism he had outlined in volume one. He described the joint-stock company as "the abolition of the capitalist mode of production within the capitalist mode of production itself."[92] For Marx this contradiction illustrated the crisis-ridden nature of capitalism and its tendency toward internal conflict and eventual collapse. But it could equally be taken to illuminate the centrality of nonmarket relations within the core of what is called capitalism. If economic textbooks continue to give temporal and epistemological priority to the rise of markets, with the joint-stock corporation seen only as a later and secondary outgrowth, the real history of capitalism is the other way around. The major institutions for organizing large-scale global trade in the seventeenth and eighteenth century were not markets but monopolistic colonizing corporations, such as the Dutch and English East India companies and the joint-stock companies that were given monopolies for the colonization of North America.[93]

Neoclassical economists like to trace the origin of their field to the formulation of the market principle in the classical work of Adam Smith. But Smith wrote *The Wealth of Nations* as an attack on the power of these colonizing corporations, and formulated the idea of individual exchange in "the market" as the program for an alternative. He devoted long sections of the book to discussing the world's first successful campaign against the corporate monopolies, the revolt of Britain's American colonies, and to examining the simultaneous crisis in the largest such monopoly, the East India Company. Writings such as *The Wealth of Nations* helped to construct the idea of "the self-regulating market" as a novel alternative to corporate power, and this and subsequent writings in political economy began to formulate the market's rules and principles. But the idea of "the market" was not the only response to the crisis of the colonizing corporation. In 1776, the year *The Wealth of Nations* appeared, two alternative methods of governing the wealth of nations were devised. The American colonists articulated an antimarket principle of economic organization, the nation-state; and the East India Company proposed a new system of colonial government, the Plan of Settlement, recasting arbitrary corporate power as a colonial "rule of property."[94] Within fifty years, moreover, the United States and Britain began to resort once more to the joint-stock corporation as an institution with which to organize nonmarket transactions. The unusual legal powers of incorporation were no longer restricted to ostensibly public projects, such as colonization, but were made available for any large economic purpose. At the same time, further projects of colonization were undertaken by Americans and Europeans using the new powers of the state itself. So the sovereignty of the market once again was limited by the powers of the corporation and the colonial monopoly.

The point of this historical detour is the following. By the twentieth century, the colonizing corporation had been replaced by directly ruled colonies on the one hand, and modern joint-stock companies on the other, the largest of which developed into transnational corporations far larger than most postcolonial states. By midcentury the system of colonies was giving way in most places to one of nation-states. Like the colony, the nation provided a nonmarket system for organizing economic exchange, especially for preventing free markets in labor and money. Since the science of economics had concentrated its efforts on framing the rules of the market, parallel fields of expertise emerged to help coordinate the forms of knowledge needed for the nonmarket institutions: for the corporation, law, accounting, and business studies; for the nation, statistical organizations and the field of macroeconomics, which as we have seen developed around the concept of "the economy" in the middle decades of the century. In addition, immigration laws, national banks or reserve systems, complex taxation and tariff systems, and extensive state planning and investment all helped to construct the late-twentieth-century national economy as anything but the mythical marketplace of neoliberal theory.

Neoliberalism as Violence

Both neo-Smithian orthodoxy and institutional sociology tend to expunge the constitutive role of violence in economic relations. For example, the notion of "framing" used to describe the operation of social institutions like the market, family, economy, and state is usually derived from the work of Erving Goffman, who made particular use of metaphors from the theater.[95] This choice of language and metaphor gives the impression of an essentially benign process, in which rules and roles operate by convention, and coercion has only a residual or reserve function. This reflects a tradition that sees rules and violence, law and coercion, as opposites. One is based upon reason, on the application of principles "unquestionably true in every country."[96] The other is an element of irrationality and disorder. However, this antinomy of law and violence is misleading, from a method of enframing that enables an abstract code or structure of rules to appear separate from the practices through which they are brought into being and reproduced. Acts of enframing are works of force as much as reason.

In the Egyptian economic reforms, the reports of the IMF and other bodies had nothing to say about the kinds of coercion necessary for their implementation. Yet it was obvious that alternative claims, visions, and agendas had to be

kept out of the picture, using various combinations of persuasion, threat, and violence. Indeed, the economic reforms were facilitated by a continuous narrowing
of already limited opportunities for dissent. The repressive apparatus of reform
included a parliament more than one hundred of whose members the courts declared fraudulently elected, but that proclaimed itself above the law in such matters; and in which the handful of opposition deputies were increasingly deprived
of any opportunity to question the government.[97] "Reform" also removed the
right of villages to select their own heads, of religious communities to choose
their own preachers, and of university faculties to elect their deans.[98] Neoliberalism also included a steady remilitarization of power, especially as control shifted
away from ministries, many of which were now run by technocrats, to provincial
governors, most of whom were still appointed from the high ranks of the military. It included the systematic use of torture against those detained in police stations and the offices of the State Security Intelligence, including electric shocks,
beatings, suspension by the wrists or ankles, and threats of death or sexual abuse
of the detainee or a female relative.[99] It included the imprisonment of tens of
thousands of political opponents, detained without court orders or judicial
process, under emergency powers in place for twenty years, in conditions described as cruel, inhuman, or degrading.[100] It included the silencing of professional associations, with the engineers' and lawyers' associations placed under
judicial sequestration in 1996, and the doctors', pharmacists', teachers', and sci-
entists' associations prevented from holding elections.[101] And it included the
repeated intimidation of human-rights workers and opposition journalists by
closures, court cases, and imprisonment.[102] In 1999 the regime consolidated these
new restrictions by passing a law on civic associations that dissolved all the country's licensed nongovernmental organizations and required them to apply for permission to re-form under new and more restrictive regulations, including a ban
on any activity the state considered political. Meanwhile, the United States and
other Western governments refused every appeal to speak out against the repressive policies of the Mubarak regime. Washington quietly dropped the "Democracy
Initiative" it had introduced in the early 1990s when political transformations in
Eastern Europe seemed to threaten the system of autocracy it had helped sustain

in the Middle East, and declared no serious concerns in Egypt beyond the survival of the regime and its neoliberal reforms.[103]

It is not uncommon, among the proponents as well as critics of the reforms, to admit that structural adjustment and the opening of markets may require massive political repressions. From a neoliberal perspective, repression is an unforeseen, unfortunate, intermittent, and probably temporary side effect of the shocks that accompany the expansion of the global market. From a more critical perspective, that of the Marxist tradition, violence is the ordinary tool that allows the penetration of capitalist relations into new territories. Force speeds up the development of capitalism, "like a hot-house," as Marx himself put it, in regions where changes in the relations of production have lagged behind the global history of capital.[104] For this reason, however, violence must be considered "a common contingency" rather than something *"logically* necessary."[105] It aids the logic of capital, but, as an element of randomness and unpredictability, or as a means of simply forcing the pace of history, it must be contingent or external to the logic of history itself.

In contrast, I would argue that violence is constitutive of both markets and monopolies, and that real economic history is much more contingent, messy, and brutal than depicted at the level of grand logics (of either the market or the mode of production). By homogenizing contemporary politics into ineluctable and universal logics of capitalist globalization, we attribute to reform programs, to the market, to capital, or to globalization a coherence, energy, and rationality that they could never otherwise claim. The continuous political struggles under way in places such as Egypt are not the consequences of a more global logic, but an active political process whose significance is repeatedly marginalized and overlooked in reproducing the simple narratives of globalization, whether for or against.

Unruly Dreams

At the start of this discussion I called the economy a fabrication, but that term should not be misunderstood. It does not mean that the economy is merely a work of imagination, or that the problem with the economy is that it is not real.

Such criticisms slide back into the language of real versus imaginary, original versus copy, an object world versus its representation. These distinctions are complicit in the project of making the economy and cannot be used to understand it. The politics of the late-nineteenth and twentieth centuries attempted to organize a world whose complexities were resolved into the simple dualities of real and representation, objects and ideas, nature and techno-science, land and the abstraction of law, the country and the map. The social sciences emerged in the same period to confirm and reproduce this binary world. The role of economics was to produce the economy, not as a work of imagination but as a practical project. The economy is an artifactual body—a fabrication, yes, but as solid as other fabricated objects, and at the same time as incomplete.

Thus economic discourse works very hard to help format and reproduce the exclusions that make the economy possible. This is why there are no particular farmers or villages in economic discourse on Egypt. It is the reason why the Sawiris family and Ahmed Bahgat, the Seoudi group and the Metwallis, are never encountered in the writings of the IMF. It is why nowhere in the reports of US-AID can one discover the role of government ministers, senior officials, and their families in the rent circuits of the so-called private sector. It is why the extensive importing, manufacturing, and consumption of goods by the Egyptian armed forces are left opaque in official statistics. Examining any one of these issues leads away from a closed economy, away from the map, away from what is transparent and calculable, into farming, households, family, state, power, and so on. The closure unravels.

Likewise, Egypt's vaunted economic reform—the mythology embroidered by the IMF and Washington—had also unraveled by the beginning of the new millennium. During 2000, the Cairo stock market collapsed, losing almost 50 percent of its value. By the end of that year share prices were lower than when the government first revived the exchange in 1995.[106] The real-estate boom had gone bust. Ahmed Bahgat, the builder of Dreamland, suffered a heart attack in July 2000 while on a trip to Washington, where he was part of an official delegation making an unsuccessful effort to encourage investments from large U.S. corporations. When news reached Cairo that he was in a hospital in Bethesda, Maryland, undergoing surgery to the aorta, shares in his company collapsed. Dreamland was effectively bankrupt. Beverly Hills and most of the other, smaller developments also came to a halt, as speculators discovered they had overbuilt and luxury property prices dropped by more than half.[107]

Public-sector entrepreneurs were also in the same hot water. The debts of the Radio and Television Union, the commercial arm of the Ministry of Information creating the media complex next door to Beverly Hills, reached E£3.8 billion, and the Ministry of Finance had to bail it out.[108] The Arab Contractors Co., the family-run, state-owned construction corporation building Media Production City and many other large projects, was facing financial crisis.[109] There was panic in the banks, which had overextended credit for real-estate projects. The chairman of the National Bank of Egypt, the public-sector bank with the largest investments in failed speculations, was removed.[110]

As a recession set in and the government began to fall far behind on domestic payments, other businesses whose prosperity came from contracts with the state began to fail. Rami Lakah, the thirty-nine-year-old entrepreneur who had developed the country's largest business group by building fee-paying government hospitals for the affluent—hailed in 1999 as the first Egyptian enterprise to borrow on the international bond market—within a year had fled the country. He returned only after the government and the banks agreed to reschedule his debts, which were reported to have reached E£1.5 billion.[111] As the government tried to slow the flow of funds, the supply of dollars dried up, affecting importers, including manufacturers who needed supplies from abroad. Toward the end of 2000 the government was forced to abandon efforts to peg the currency to the dollar, and the Egyptian pound lost 20 percent of its value. Almost the only economic activity that seemed to thrive was the use of mobile telephones. The country's million or so subscribers used their phones four times as many minutes per month per subscriber as the worldwide average. The E£5.6 billion that they spent talking on their telephones in 2000 exceeded the country's revenue that year from exports.[112]

Some actually blamed the money spent on mobile phone conversations for the country's recession. Others blamed it on the off-budget spending by the state.

The government had pushed ahead with what it called its "Pharaonic" development projects, concentrating its resources on the most ambitious of them, the Toshka irrigation scheme. Convinced, like the United States Agency for International Development, that Egypt's fundamental problems were defined by the limits of natural resources—not enough land, too many people—it pursued President Mubarak's dream of creating a second river Nile in the desert. Toshka was very much a twentieth-century idea. The century that opened with the construction of the first Aswan Dam ended with an even bigger project, not just to store up all the waters of the world's longest river but to divert them to build another.

Dreamland was an amusement park in the desert, a mirage under construction, a place of desire promised in television commercials and newspaper advertisements long before it was finished. Perhaps it would remain forever a mirage, an unfulfilled desire. It was one of many dreamlands. Toshka was the object of a ruler's desire, as he passed his seventieth birthday, to build something by which his rule would be remembered, a fairy tale to be fulfilled with the help of a billionaire prince and the bankrupt owner of Superior Seedless grapes. These dreamlands are the places of desire that global capitalism cannot contain.

Capitalism has no singular logic, no essence. It survives parasitically, like the malaria protist, drawing its energies from the chemistry of others, its force from other fields, its momentum from others' desires. The projects of economic reform in Egypt had to excite the desires that fueled the building of Dreamland and Toshka, yet capitalism could not discipline those desires. Such desires, such forces, such other logics, are presented as something exterior to capitalism. They appear as a noncapitalist excess that derails capitalism from its course. Yet this outside, these excesses, are at the same time vital to capitalism. They are a source of its energies, the condition of its success, the possibility of its power to reproduce. They are a heterogeneity that makes possible the logic of capital, and thus ensures both its powers and its failures.

2

Arg-e Jadid: A California Oasis in the Iranian Desert

Marina Forti
(Translated by Graeme Thomson)

A pleasant breeze rises from the lake across a freshly mown lawn; the only sounds are the gushing of an artificial fountain and the quiet voices of passersby. A well-paved sidewalk climbs a small knoll toward the restaurant, an odd-looking edifice in the shape of a cut-off cone from which, on a single floor, a curving wing extends with big windows sloped toward the lake. Entering by the circular vestibule you pass into the windowed room to see groups of families clustered around the tables, kids who adore French fries and pizza, teenagers hunched over their slices of cake and sodas: the atmosphere is one of informal elegance, the men in sports shirts, their Finnish cell phones lying next to the cutlery, the young women wearing short jackets and brightly coloured head scarves, pulled back slightly to reveal hair that is lovingly combed and faces discreetly made-up.

Outside in the cool of evening crickets sing amid the pine forests that surround the lake. If it wasn't for the dry desert wind you might forget you were in the Iranian uplands: this is Arg-e Jadid, on the state highway that runs southwest from the city of Kerman, capital of the province whose name it bears, down to the Sistan Baluchistan bordering on Afghanistan to the north with Pakistan to the east. A mere ten miles away is Bam, sadly famous as the site of the tragic 2003 earthquake that killed thirty thousand people. For hundreds of miles the view is one of rolling rock desert intermittently broken by the occasional natural oasis with its village and date plantations, a scattering of dilapidated caravanserai and modern gas stations set against an impressive horizon of snowcapped mountains.

Arg-e Jadid is itself thus an oasis, albeit an artificial one. *Arg* is the Farsi word for "citadel," *Jadid* is "new": an "instant citadel" that is startling especially for the way it contrasts with its desert environment. Arg-e Jadid is one of the "special economic zones" set up by Iran at the beginning of the 1990s to encourage foreign investment, including from the wealthy Iranian diaspora. Here the result was two sprawling auto assembly plants. Next to the industrial complex, however, planners also choose a tourist resort and "model town": private worlds so unexpected in the Islamic Republic of Iran that they command our detailed attention.

A Garden of Security

The surprises begin on landing: "Bam Airport—Private Terminal of Kerman Automotive Industries Company" says the lit-up sign on the building. Inside, the terminal is strikingly modern, spacious and functional, a lot different from what you would expect of a small airport in a run-down province. Exiting the terminal you take the highway, little traveled even on workdays, and drive southwest; after barely ten minutes of arid terrain, you turn off onto a side road and suddenly everything changes. To one side you see the ample forecourt of a hotel, an ochre-colored two-story building in front of which is an artificial fountain with its circular basin. Up ahead the road passes through an improbable triumphal arch; two private security men in marine-style uniforms raise their hands in smart salute. On the other side of the arch you enter a spacious boulevard lined with acacia and palm trees. A roundabout encircling a manicured garden leads to more palm-fringed avenues. Welcoming signs announce that you are in Arg-e Jadid, as do the car license plates embossed with the citadel's coat of arms, and here and there a lamppost bearing the same insignia, a stylized silhouette of a bird of paradise.

"Before, this was nothing but desert," says Mr. Fahmi, the director of Faradid Arg, the investment consultancy agency that also manages the sale of building land in this private citadel (he carries two business cards, the second revealing that he's also the manager of Arg-e Jadid Travel Co., with branches in Bam, Kerman, and Tehran). Construction work on the artificial oasis began in 1994 on a 5,000-acre site, half of which was occupied by the industrial compound and technicians' quarters, the other half by the residential zone. The private airport became fully operative in 1997; by 2006 Iran Air was running two flights a day to and from Tehran. "When the earthquake struck, our airport played an important role in the relief work," Fahmi notes. There are plans to extend the site eastward by another 10,000 acres.

On the right side of the boulevard are impressive villas. These well-spaced buildings of two or occasionally three floors with flower gardens are the VIP zone whose residents include the town's managers. Nearby are branches of all the country's major banks. (Are there enough clients for all these banks, I ask, and Fahmi tells me that Arg-e Jadid will soon have 50,000 inhabitants; for now there are only 3,000, but the banks, he says, mainly serve the industrial compound.) On a square landscaped with well-watered gardens is the auditorium which seats several hundred people. A somewhat boxlike light-stone building with an interior of polished floors, tinted mirrors with golden palm brocade, and leatherette seating, it was host to a film festival dedicated to Bam in 2004, after the quake.

The town center consists of two blocks that house supermarkets, offices (mainly tourist and real-estate agencies), a bakery that sells excellent bread; both these and the town's primary and lower secondary school (high school students are ferried to Bam by private bus) are just a short walk away. More gardens. You wonder where this oasis finds so much water. The answer is an undersoil rich in water from the snowcapped mountains on the horizon. Every village has its own warren of ancient *qanat*, tunnels dug in the rock that convey water from underground springs. Arg-e Jadid currently has three *qanat*, and for its future expansion is counting on a new dam being built in the mountains west of Bam.

Zoning here is rigorous: on one side is what is called the "resort" with its lake encircled by a path dotted with benches and an eight-kilometer cycleway, and among the trees a café-patisserie and the bizarre cone-shaped restaurant, the Phare. Then there's the *manège* and riding grounds; a recreational pavilion for children; a fast-food restaurant; an indoor sports center; and a swimming pool (which boys and girls must use at separate hours). In addition there is the public library and cultural center (offering computer and language courses), a small clinic, and a prayer room. A proper mosque is under construction, its minarets already visible; while on the edge of the citadel a huge cupola supported by concrete pillars is rising—the Palace of Intercultural Dialogue, a circular theater facility that will seat up to 2,500 people.

On the other side of the central block, meanwhile, are streets bordered with young saplings and rows of smaller, more closely bunched houses (this is the middle-class zone), yet each with its own little private garden, parking space, and spacious terrace. "Here in Arg-e Jadid we haven't had a single robbery or crime of any kind," says Fahmi with satisfaction. The town has its own private police and a system of CCTV cameras to monitor activity in the street: "Security is our first priority."

The town is based on a condominial system of ownership. The Arg-e Jadid company sells lots of building land to condominiums, which are responsible for the actual construction and must respect the company's standards, including those for seismic activity. That way, even though they are built in a similar style (with flat roofs and terraces) and use more or less the same materials (basically brick and stone, ideal for a desert climate) the houses are not completely identical.

Islamic Neoliberalism

Where does the money come from? Who financed this cute, New Urbanist suburb with its villas and artificial lake? Fahmi presses on the accelerator of his dark Avante (the Iranian name for the powerful Hyundai model he drives), leaving the houses under construction in a cloud of dust, and turns toward the gates of the industrial compound, the entrance sign of which reads "Economic Free Zone." Inside are rows of industrial warehouses: date packaging plants (the area's most renowned agricultural product) along with other food and car-parts factories, plus one that produces engine lubricant, two makers of wood furniture (the wood is brought in from the outside by truck), a fiberglass boat hull business, and a liquid propane depot for domestic use.

Here the roads are wide and half-deserted. No water is wasted on gardens; the only shrubbery to be seen are a few acacias in the parking lot next to what was once a Daewoo plant. Here we have the zone's real raison d'être, its two car-assembly plants. The first plant was opened in 1997 by Kerman Automotive Industries to assemble Daewoo cars. Production was brisk in the beginning with cars rolling off the assembly lines each year, exported to Syria. But in April 2002 Daewoo was acquired by General Motors. Because Iran was subject to a U.S. economic embargo, GM-controlled Daewoo was forced to abandon the Iranian market, leaving Kerman Industries to look for new partners. Today two plants assemble Hyundais and Volkswagens and are currently negotiating a deal with Skoda. The ultimate aim is to get production up to 400,000 vehicles a year for export to Iran's neighbors in the Gulf and the rest of the Middle East.

Assembly workers come from Bam and the surrounding villages, arriving by bus each morning and being ferried back home at the end of their shifts. "Before, unemployment in this region was officially twenty-four percent," Fahmi explains. "In five years we're expecting we'll have to bring in workers from elsewhere. We're even thinking about building dormitories."

Bordering the north side of the industrial compound is the Kerman–Bam railway line and the site where a new station is being built: when it's finished, raw materials and parts for the factories will arrive, and finished products transported by rail, but for the time being everything is moved in and out by truck. You might wonder why anyone would want to build an industrial compound here, far from commercial ports or major cities: Kerman, 120 miles away, has a population of less than half a million; the distance to Isfahan is around 540 miles, Tehran 750. The port of Bandar Abbas on the Persian Gulf is nearly 300 miles away and not connected to either Kerman or Bam by rail. The answer clearly has nothing to with rational logistics.

Instead you have to go back to the early 1990s, to the so-called time of reconstruction after the devastating Iran–Iraq war. The president at the time was Ali Akbar Hashemi Rafsanjani (reelected for a second mandate, he held office from

1989 to 1997). Though petroleum and natural gas were and still are the driving force of Iran's economy, Rafsanjani tried to stimulate trade in general and develop the internal consumer economy, promoting a more diversified manufacturing industry, into which he hoped to channel new private investment, in a strategy of economic liberalization. Though Rafsanjani was at Ayatollah Khomeini's side during the revolution and remains a pillar of the Islamic Republican establishment—a man who since leaving office has presided over the Expediency Council, one of Iran's most powerful state institutions—he is widely regarded as a "pragmatist," and his followers are considered "technocrats." Originally from Kerman province, the ex-president is also one of the richest men in Iran, scion of a wealthy family of pistachio producers, head of a financial empire that encompasses his brother's copper mines and various import-export businesses; through a network of foundations and dummy companies he also controls one of the major oil refineries and numerous other businesses, though he denies owning any of them.

In the early 1990s Rafsanjani launched neoliberal economic reforms that began to transform the country. An Institute for the Development of Kerman was established under Rafsanjani's son-in-law Hossein Marashi to mobilize private investment in productive projects: among these was a project for Sirjan (a town located to the south of the capital on the road to Bandar Abbas) and one for tourist development in the province. A key investor was an Islamic foundation called the Mol-Al Movahedin.

Known as *Bonyads*, these foundations, halfway houses between charities and religious trusts, are one of Islam's traditional economic institutions. In Iran those created after the 1979 Revolution, when the revolutionary government seized the vast fortunes of the Shah's *clientes* who had fled the country, now play a leading role in Iran's economy. The management of many nationalized banks and industries was handed over to charitable foundations, controlled by the most conservative elements of the clergy. The official mission of the revolutionary *Bonyads* was to administer funds and economic activities, provide welfare (to war veterans, widows and orphans, and so on), and guarantee the general redistribution of wealth. However, directly controlled as they are by the Supreme Guide, these revolutionary foundations became a source of income for the clerical establishment and in some cases a slush fund for paramilitary groups and "Islamic volunteers" recruited to repress students' and social movements. They have provided a route to social and economic advancement for the revolutionary elite; directors of state bodies, especially the revolutionary guard after their active military service, have gradually been "pensioned off" in the foundations. Through their network of employees, users of price-controlled supermarkets and credit cooperatives, and the widows and orphans who receive from them small pensions and other benefits, they also organize mass support for the clerical regime.

Over time the *Bonyads*, then, have become veritable empires with tax-exemption status not subject to the control of the Court of Accounts: neither public nor private, each employs hundreds of thousands of people and has interests that range from hotels, import-export, and manufacturing to supermarkets and credit institutes. In Kerman in 1991, for instance, the Mol-Al Movahedin foundation set up Mahan Air, now Iran's third biggest airline (96 percent owned by the foundation), which began operating in 1993 and since 2001 has been a member of IATA. And again it was Mol-Al Movahedin that in 1990 created Kerman Automotive Industries, taking advantage of a law which permits "unproductive" public land to be donated to development projects. The foundation then sent its managers to Seoul to cut a deal with Daewoo: first for the license to import and distribute its cars on the Iranian market, and second as part of a joint venture to assemble them on the new industrial site. Today the Arg-e Jadid Economic Free Zone houses over fifty companies (operating in the manufacturing, agriculture, tourist, and service sectors); apart from the car-assembly joint venture, they are all Iranian owned. Taken as a whole the Arg-e Jadid compound employs 3,200 people, a figure which rises to around 5,000 if you count jobs in the residential zone (including building sites), plus another 1,200 in Tehran in connected agencies and businesses. In 2005 the Arg-e Jadid Economic Free Zone declared a turnover of $200 million.

"We've created a development pole in a depressed region where there is terrible unemployment," says Hamid Masinani, vice president of the Arg-e Jadid Economic Free Zone's board of directors. But what about the idea of adding on a private town to the industrial zone? "We needed a residential complex that would be attractive enough to get the companies' managers and technicians to move to Arg-e Jadid with their families, rather than just work away from home. We also thought that the area had potential for tourism but that it lacked the necessary infrastructure. So we came up with the idea of a resort, a kind of Club Med in a quiet area with sports facilities and organized tours of the desert villages." Masinani insists: "It was all part of the same plan: to develop and bring jobs to the region. Young people here didn't have many options open to them. The only viable economic activity was drug trafficking." That is certainly true. Crossing Baluchistan and Kerman is one of the world's major opium routes, running from Afghanistan toward the Caucasus and then into Europe (or the clandestine ports of the Gulf of Oman). "It was a dangerous area, and the best way to make it safer was to inhabit and develop it. That's where the idea for Arg-e Jadid came from."

When I ask him "Why here?" Fahmi reels off a list of reasons: a large pool of manpower, abundance of land, water, proximity to Arg-e Bam, which brings in tourism (or did until the earthquake reduced it to rubble). "What we've done here," he goes on, "is to create both an industrial infrastructure and a place that will attract both residents and tourists or day-trippers. We've organized events, festivals, a horse-riding competition in the season of Nowruz [Iranian New Year]: we've even invented an annual date festival that combines promotion of local produce with a celebration of the place's historical roots." A case of the "invention of tradition" in the Iranian uplands, the date festival serves not only to improve the place but also creates a sense of community in what is a fairly recent residential enclave.

From Kish to Kitsch

Fountains of multicolored water explode on the screen, heralding a procession of images that includes the modern airport, the triumphal arch, smart businessmen, gleaming sedans, elegantly dressed women marshalling broods of ecstatic children by the lakeside, sumptuous interiors, before ending with a shot of fireworks bursting in the night sky. It is a somewhat hackneyed and unimaginative promo, but the message is still eloquent: come to Arg-e Jadid, where you can mix business with pleasure. The "new citadel" is pitched as a tourist resort, a second home for the province's wealthier inhabitants, with hotel and amusements to reel in the shoals of visitors who come here to visit the ancient citadel of Bam. "At first, visitors only came for a day from Kerman, since hospitality structures in Bam were fairly rudimentary," Fahmi explains as he shows me the hotel Arg-e Jadid's generous vestibule: the hotel, the only four-star establishment between here and Kerman, offers the kind of luxurious elegance normally found in the Arab Emirates: halls with artificial plants and leatherette sofas, tinted windows, gilded decor, clocks synchronized to the time zones of the world's major cities. Computers in the business center are linked to Arg-e Jadid's own broadband Internet server (visitors flying in from Tehran immediately notice that here there are none of the usual filters that limit Web access in Iran). There's also a fake-traditional bar whose clay-colored walls and desert furniture attempt to recreate the atmosphere of the old *chaikhaneh*, the teahouses.

Sale of building land in the private citadel was slow at first. But then came the earthquake, which wiped out the area's main tourist attraction, Arg-e Bam. In theory this should have been a mortal blow to the Arg-e Jadid project, at least its residential-tourist side, but the opposite happened. Only a few hours after the quake on December 26, 2003, rescue workers from all over the world began pouring into Bam. Then, once they had dug through the rubble, the big aid agencies moved in—the UN, the Red Cross, and the major international NGOs—to attend to the survivors. While tents and containers were brought in to house the victims, the foreign "humanitarian workers" went to Arg-e Jadid: it seemed nothing short of a miracle that only twenty minutes away from the disaster on a road almost untouched by the quake was a smart residential complex ready to be occupied. For months the hotel was "fully booked" (the badly cracked walls of one wing of the building were quickly patched up), and the bigger agencies rented entire villas to use as their foreign offices, while less well-endowed NGOs moved into the rows of bungalows near the industrial zone. They also provided work for the people of Bam and its surrounding villages, since there was a need for cleaning women, cooks, drivers, and guides. The "new citadel," which had been more or less spared by the quake, became a booming humanitarian suburb.

Every morning for more than a year, a procession of Land Rovers decked in aid agency symbols would exit through the enormous triumphal arch to go to wade in Bam's river of human misery, set up refugee camps, assist widows and orphans, and help out in the field hospitals. After a day's full immersion in dust and rubble, they would troop back to their villas and bungalows, as though entering another world. To unwind they could go down to the lake or sit in the café-patisserie, go for a bike ride or, toward evening, when even in the sweltering desert summers the air becomes breathable again, simply chill out on the terrace. The Amirza restaurant had its habitués, as did the café; the evening air was filled with the sounds of polyglot conversations; the bakery's ovens were never cool; and it was hard to get a table for dinner: Arg-e Jadid was happening.

The humanitarian aid agencies rented directly from the owners of Arg-e Jadid's houses and flats: professionals, functionaries, well-to-do families who had bought properties in the new enclave in the previous years. Launched as a tourist resort, the "new citadel" had instead attracted the area's middle classes who saw it more as a modern enclave, a safe place to live in a land of earthquakes and drug caravans. Like the Rashid family: he a chemist, she a housewife, and their two teenage children. When the Bam earthquake struck they had just moved into a handsome, detached two-story house in Arg-e Jadid's "middle-class" neighborhood. Buying the property had swallowed up all the family's financial resources, so after the quake they made the sacrifice of living for an entire year in a container they had installed in the garden, while renting both their large first-floor apartment and their small garden flat for the considerable sum of one thousand euros a month. Their sacrifice paid off and within a year they were able to cover the debts they had incurred in buying the house, thanks to the rent paid by the aid agencies. Though they remained in the area for just over a year, for Arg-e Jadid's homeowners the international aid workers' presence was like manna from heaven.

As the earthquake made the citadel even more desirable in the eyes of the zone's inhabitants, land sales have boomed. One person happy with her choice is Mrs. Amina Bayat: "It's a wonderful place, very safe, ideal if you have children: there's everything here from a playground to the swimming pool, there's lots for kids to do and it's all really handy." Her physician husband Farhad leaves by car every morning to go to his medical practice in a small town forty minutes drive down the dusty Zahedan-bound state highway. He's happy to return to his tranquil suburban enclave: "There's no place safer in Iran, you can leave your car open on the street and nobody will touch it. And then it's so spacious." Amina is an excellent patissiere, supplying two restaurants and preparing cakes on commission for private parties. "Here you can go and see friends even when it gets dark, or just go for a walk; the streets are completely safe." In certain seasons the cultural center organizes group excursions: "the keenest get a prize," Amina tells me in her enormous American-style kitchen, which opens onto a modern-style living room with its comfy sofas and blond wood furnishings—there's even a fireplace. Here, she explains, parents don't have to worry about letting their kids go out, both boys and girls: there's no danger "because there's always police around, sometimes on horseback." After an afternoon's riding or swimming or computer lessons teens can meet in the games room of the (mixed) sports center with its six pool tables, assorted arcade games, and a coffee shop, also too modern with polished wooden floors and pop music in the background. Toward evening groups of ladies or entire families go out for a stroll, perhaps to take some air in the woods: this is the citadel's initial nucleus, where the green is more lush, the ground opportunely undulant. A pavilion surrounded by picnic tables sits nestled in the green. There's a path running by a stream that cuts through the trees, or else the paved walkway, fringed with eucalyptus and palm trees, with its little gurgling canal that runs down the middle, like those found in the gardens of the Moghul princes of Central Asia.

Fahmi has no doubt about the template for Arg-e Jadid. "We were inspired by Kish." Kish is an Iranian island in the Persian Gulf which became famous in the 1960s when the Shah transformed it into a glamorous VIP enclave and luxury vacation resort. After a period of decline during the years of revolution and war, it picked up again in the 1990s, when going on holiday ceased to be considered a decadent bourgeois habit. (Indeed Rafsanjani's neoliberal economic reforms have given rise to a culture of rampant consumerism, of making and spending money.) For many Iranians today Kish has an almost mythical aura. With its silken sandy beaches (separate ones for men and women, though there's also a mixed beach exclusively for foreigners), grand hotels, and shopping centers selling the top international brands, it has become a "dream holiday" destination. Kish is a small island (approximately nine miles long and five miles wide) with a population of 16,000 and traces of ancient human settlement that testify to its onetime role as a trading center. It has brilliant multicolored seabeds and an international airport with flights that are always fully booked: the Iranian middle classes go there in part for the beach, but above all they go to shop. In Kish you can find everything, it's "like a little Dubai." In high season the shopping centers organize entertainments, including mini-lotteries with prizes for the day's lucky shoppers. ("If you're getting married or about to have your first child," a young woman from Tehran's smart set explained to me, "you have two choices: either you go to Dubai for your trousseau, otherwise Kish.")

If Dubai is an imaginary California on the Persian Gulf and Kish a miniature Dubai, then Arg-e Jadid sees itself as a budding Kish. With every passage, however, the model changes shape, the idea shrinks: even if also in this "new citadel" the developers have called in big-name architects like Rashid Khomarloo to give it the right tone. Khomarloo tells me that designing the restaurant was fun to do: "Normally with a project they set very precise limits on what you can do, but here I had almost complete carte blanche. Sure, there are the limits of the environment to contend with: the desert climate means it's impossible to use wood, even wood that's treated, because the heat damages everything, even the glue of the casings. So you're left with either bricks or stone. The other problem is the water. When I saw that awful lake with nothing that would give a sense of movement to the landscape, I immediately thought about putting the restaurant right in the middle: but the water is too brackish and the spray would have made maintenance difficult." Environmental constrictions aside, however, Khomarloo had complete freedom. "I could design more or less exactly what I dream of doing. It was fantastic." Dubai may have has its hotel in the shape of a sail but Arg-e Jadid is equally proud of its bizarre truncated cone and is planning a revolving restaurant tower for the future.

Kish may be the model but the real attraction of Arg-e Jadid lies in the idea of a secure, well-organized residential enclave where one can enjoy an urban lifestyle that even has a frisson of exclusivity about it, even in a somewhat backward, conservative province. The Californian burbs have landed in the Iranian desert, refracted through the prism of Dubai and Kish. Here the middle classes enjoy the amenities of the chic zones in big cities: they can practice sports, go for walks, take computer courses, go out with friends, take the children to the playground—without any of the traffic, risk, and general unpredictability of the city. Girls are safe to go out with their friends, female dress codes aren't overstrict, and there's a general climate of relaxed freedom, without things going too far or representing a challenge to the system in the same way as "westernized" city dwellers given similar freedoms.

The Bayats, both natives of the province, are glad to have left Kerman with its noise and pollution. They appreciate their new suburban lifestyle. They too have had "humanitarian" tenants and enjoyed even foreign friends. Even so, disenchantment has begun to set in. Dr. Bayat believes Arg-e Jadid cannot expand much further: "It's the limits of diplomacy: President Khatami was in favour of opening Iran to dialogue with the West, which drew European investment. But as for Ahmadinejad . . . we know he's not keen on opening doors, in fact, he would like to shut those that are already half-open. A new investment will take at least two years to come to fruition. Who knows what could happen in those two years, everything might change. The development of the economic zones depends directly on the government's foreign policy, and with the government we've got now I wouldn't get my hopes up too much." Dr. Bayat tells me about the competing business elites that conduct their affairs behind the façade of charities ("They exploit religion for business reasons"), but says it's just the way things work here, even the citadel is part of it. But now with the current ultraconservative presidency other business committees are gaining the upper hand, and there are rumors that the Free Economic Zone will be forced to curb its future plans.

Back in Tehran, Mr. Masinani denies that Arg-e Jadid is on the verge of crisis: "While it's true the project arose in the Rafsanjani epoch and political loyalties have since changed," he says, "we haven't been affected, partly because the decree instituting the Free Economic Zones has been ratified by both the Council of

Guardians and the Expediency Council. And then the government (of Ahmadi-nejad) has recently approved a decree for the development of depressed zones, which includes zones like Kerman." He's hopeful: he says, "business is good."

Sitting in his living room with its blond wooden furniture, Dr. Bayat shakes his head, saying that in his view the *system* (a synonym in Iran for the state) is becoming "Pasdaranized," referring to the *Sepah-e Pasdaran*, the Revolutionary Guard, a military body created after the 1979 revolution, which also played a key role in the Iran-Iraq war and is now responsible for the defense and control of the nation's borders (this is the institution that president Mahmoud Ahmadinejad and many of his men come from). Bayat believes the future is far from certain: "If the industrial compound is forced to close it would be a pity, because it provides work for many people. But the residential part could go on functioning perfectly well by itself: it's the best place to be if you live in this area."

Leaving the sheltered, virtual world of Arg-e Jadid, one joins again the southwest-bound highway. You pass the turnoff for the airport and the big roundabout outside Bam where at dawn dozens of men gather in the hope of being taken on as day laborers on some building site (with much rebuilding still to be done after the quake, construction is booming at the moment and people come here from the remotest villages in search of work). You get on the road to Kerman: two lanes of relentless traffic. A few miles on, the road is blocked with sandbags and concrete blocks diverting traffic. A line of waiting trucks stand parked at the roadside: this is the Mersad checkpoint, one of the narcotics squad's major tools in their fight against drug traffickers—a reminder that you're on one of the world's major heroin-smuggling routes. Once past the roadblock you find yourself back in the familiar uplands scenery of rocky hills, date plantations, and the snow-crested horizon: once again the desert has the upper hand.

3

Sand, Fear, and Money in Dubai

Mike Davis

"As your jet starts its descent, you are glued to your window. The scene below is astonishing: a twenty-four-square-mile archipelago of coral-colored islands in the shape of an almost-finished puzzle of the world. In the shallow green waters between continents, the sunken shapes of the Pyramids of Giza and the Roman Colosseum are clearly visible. In the distance, three other large island groups are configured as palms within crescents and planted with high-rise resorts, amusement parks, and a thousand mansions built on stilts over the water. The 'Palms' are connected by causeways to a Miami-like beachfront crammed with mega-hotels, apartment skyscrapers, and yachting marinas.

"As the plane slowly banks toward the desert mainland, you gasp at the even more improbable vision ahead. Out of a chrome forest of skyscrapers soars a new Tower of Babel. It is an impossible half-mile high: taller than the Empire State Building stacked on top of itself. You are still rubbing your eyes with wonderment as the plane lands and you are welcomed into an airport shopping emporium where seductive goods entice: Gucci bags, Cartier watches, and one-kilogram bars of solid gold. The hotel driver is waiting for you in a Rolls-Royce Silver Seraph. Friends had recommended the Armani Inn in the 170-story tower, or the seven-star hotel with an atrium so huge that the Statue of Liberty would fit inside it, and service so exclusive that the rooms come with personal butlers; but instead you have opted to fulfill a childhood fantasy. You always have wanted to play Captain Nemo in *Twenty Thousand Leagues Under the Sea*.

"Your jellyfish-shaped hotel, the Hydropolis, is, in fact, exactly sixty-six feet below the surface of the sea. Each of its 220 luxury suites has clear plexiglass walls that provide spectacular views of passing mermaids and of the famed 'underwater fireworks': a hallucinatory exhibition of 'water bubbles, swirled sand, and carefully deployed lighting.' Any initial anxiety about the safety of your sea-bottom resort is dispelled by the smiling concierge. The structure has a multilevel fail-safe security system which includes protection against terrorist submarines as well as missiles and aircraft.

"Although you have an important business meeting at Internet City with clients from Hyderabad and Taipei, you have arrived a day early to treat yourself to one of the famed adventures at the Restless Planet themepark. After a soothing night's sleep under the sea, you board a monorail for this Jurassic jungle. Your first encounter is with some peacefully grazing brontosaurs. Next you are attacked by a flock of velociraptors, the animatronic beasts—designed by experts from the British Natural History Museum—so flawlessly lifelike that you shriek in fear and delight. With your adrenaline pumped up by this close call, you round off the afternoon with some snowboarding on the local indoor snow mountain (outdoors, the temperature is 105 degrees). Nearby is the world's largest mall— the altar of the city's famed Shopping Festival, which attracts millions of frenetic consumers each January—but you postpone the temptation. Instead, you indulge in some expensive Thai fusion cuisine. The gorgeous Russian blonde at the restaurant bar stares at you with vampirish hunger, and you wonder whether the local sin is as extravagant as the shopping . . ."

Fantasy Levitated

Welcome to a strange paradise. But where are you? Is this a new Margaret Atwood novel, Philip K. Dick's unpublished sequel to *Blade Runner*, or Donald Trump on acid? No. It is the Persian Gulf city-state of Dubai in 2010. After Shanghai (current population 15 million), Dubai (current population 1.5 million) is the planet's biggest building site: an emerging dreamworld of conspicuous consumption and what the locals boast as "supreme lifestyles." Despite its blast-furnace climate (on typical 120-degree summer days, the swankier hotels refrigerate their swimming pools) and edge-of-the-war-zone location, Dubai confidently predicts that its enchanted forest of six hundred skyscrapers and malls will attract fifteen million overseas visitors a year by 2010, three times as many as New York City. Emirates Airlines has placed a staggering $37 billion order for new Boeings and Airbuses to fly these tourists in and out of Dubai's new global air hub, the vast Jebel Ali airport.[1] Indeed, thanks to a dying planet's terminal addiction to Arabian oil, this former fishing village and smugglers' cove proposes to become one of the world capitals of the twenty-first century. Favoring diamonds over rhinestones, Dubai has already surpassed that other desert arcade of capitalist desire, Las Vegas, both in sheer scale of spectacle and the profligate consumption of water and power.[2]

Dozens of outlandish megaprojects—including the artificial "island world" (where Rod Stewart has reportedly spent $33 million to buy "Britain"), the earth's tallest building (Burj Dubai, designed by Skidmore, Owings and Merrill), the underwater luxury hotel, the carnivorous dinosaurs, the domed ski resort, and the hypermall—are already under construction or about to leave the drawing board.[3] The seven-star hotel, the spinnaker-shaped Burj Al-Arab—looking much like the set of a James Bond film—is already world-famous for its $5,000-per-night rooms with one-hundred-mile views and an exclusive clientele of Arab royalty, English rock stars, and Russian billionaires. And the dinosaurs, according to the finance director of the Natural History Museum, "will have the full stamp of authority of the Museum in London, and will demonstrate that education and science can be fun"; and profitable, since the "only way into the dinosaur park will be through the shopping mall."[4]

The biggest project, Dubailand, represents a vertiginous new stage in fantasy environments. Literally a "themepark of themeparks," it will be more than twice the size of Disney World and employ 300,000 workers who, in turn, will entertain fifteen million visitors per year (each spending a minimum of $100 per day, not including accommodation). Like a surrealist encyclopedia, its forty-five major "world-class" projects include replicas of the Hanging Gardens of Babylon, the Taj Mahal, and the Pyramids,[5] as well as a snow mountain with ski lifts and polar bears, a center for extreme sports, a Nubian village, Eco-Tourism World, a vast Andalusian spa and wellness complex, golf courses, autodromes, race tracks, Fantasia, the largest zoo in the Middle East, several new five-star hotels, a modern art gallery, and the Mall of Arabia.[6]

Gigantism

Under the enlightened despotism of its emir and CEO, fifty-eight-year-old Sheikh Mohammed al-Maktoum, Dubai has become the new global icon of imagineered urbanism. Multibillionaire Sheikh Mo—as he is known to Dubai's expats—has a straightforward, if immodest, goal: "I want to be number one in the world."[7] Although he is an ardent collector of thoroughbreds (the world's largest stable) and super-yachts (the 525-foot-long *Project Platinum*, which has its own submarine and flight deck), his consuming passion is over-the-top, monumental architecture.[8] Indeed, he seems to have imprinted Scott and Venturi's bible of hyperreality, *Learning From Las Vegas,* in the same way that pious Muslims memorize the *Qur'an.* One of his proudest achievements, he often tells visitors, is to have introduced gated communities to Arabia, the land of nomads and tents.

Thanks to his boundless enthusiasm for concrete and steel, the coastal desert has become a huge circuitboard upon which the elite of transnational engineering firms and retail developers are invited to plug in high-tech clusters, entertainment zones, artificial islands, glass-domed "snow mountains," *Truman Show* suburbs, cities within cities—whatever is big enough to be seen from space and bursting with architectural steroids. The result is not a hybrid but an eerie chimera: a promiscuous coupling of all the cyclopean fantasies of Barnum, Eiffel, Disney, Spielberg, Jon Jerde, Steve Wynn, and Skidmore, Owings and Merrill. Although compared variously to Las Vegas, Manhattan, Orlando, Monaco, and Singapore, the sheikhdom is more like their collective summation and mythologization: a hallucinatory pastiche of the big, the bad, and the ugly.

The same phantasmagoric but generic Lego blocks, of course, can be found in dozens of aspiring cities these days (including Dubai's envious neighbors, the

wealthy oil oases of Doha and Bahrain),[9] but al-Maktoum has a distinctive and in-
violable criterion: everything must be "world class," by which he means number
one in the *Guinness Book of Records*. Thus Dubai is building the world's largest themepark, the biggest mall (and within it, the largest aquarium), the tallest building,
the largest international airport, the biggest artificial island, the first sunken hotel,
and so on. Although such architectural megalomania is eerily reminiscent of Albert Speer and his patron's vision of imperial Berlin, it is not irrational. Having
"learned from Las Vegas," al-Maktoum understands that if Dubai wants to become
the luxury-consumer paradise of the Middle East and South Asia (its officially defined "home market" of 1.6 billion people), it must ceaselessly strive for visual and
environmental excess. If, as Rowan Moore has suggested, immense, psychotic as-
semblages of fantasy kitsch inspire vertigo, then al-Maktoum wants us to swoon.[10]

Table 1a
World's Tallest Buildings

	Building	Location	Height in feet	Completion year
1.	Burj Dubai*	Dubai	2600+	2008
2.	Al Burj*	Dubai	2300	?
3.	Taipei 101	Taiwan	1667	2004
4.	Shanghai World Financial Centre*	China	1613	2008
5.	Fordham Spire*	Chicago	1550	2010
6.	Petronas Tower	Kuala Lumpur	1483	1998
7.	Sears Tower	Chicago	1451	1974
8.	Jin Mao	China	1381	1999
9.	Freedom Tower*	Manhattan	1362	2012
10.	Two International Finance Centre	Hong Kong	1362	2003
[...]				
13.	Emirates Tower One	Dubai	1140	1997
22.	Burj al-Arab Hotel	Dubai	1053	1999

Table 1b

World's Largest Shopping Malls

	Building	Location	Area in million sq. ft.	Completion year
1.	Dubai Mall*	Dubai	12.0	2008
2.	Mall of Arabia*	Dubai	10.0	2010
3.	Mall of China*	China	10.0	?
4.	Triple Five Mall*	China	10.0	?
5.	South China Mall	China	9.6	2005
6.	Oriental Plaza*	China	8.6	?
7.	Golden Resources	China	7.3	2004
8.	West Edmonton Mall	Canada	5.3	1981
9.	Panda Mall*	China	5.0	?
10.	Grandview Mall	China	4.5	2005

* planned / under construction

From a booster's viewpoint, the city's monstrous caricature of futurism is simply shrewd branding for the world market. As one developer told the *Financial Times*, "If there was no Burj Dubai, no Palm, no World, would anyone be speaking of Dubai today? You shouldn't look at projects as crazy stand-alones. It's part of building the brand."[11] And its owners love it when architects and urbanists, like George Katodrytis, anoint it as the cutting edge:

> Dubai is a prototype of the new post-global city, which creates appetites rather than solves problems. . . . If Rome was the "Eternal City" and New York's Manhattan the apotheosis of twentieth-century congested urbanism, then Dubai may be considered the emerging prototype for the 21st century: prosthetic and nomadic oases presented as isolated cities that extend out over the land and sea.[12]

In its exponential quest to conquer the architectural record books, moreover, Dubai has only one real rival: China—a country that now has 300,000 millionaires and is predicted to become the world's largest market for luxury goods (from Gucci to Mercedes) in a few years.[13] Starting from feudalism and peasant Maoism, respectively, both have arrived at the stage of hypercapitalism through what Trotsky called the "dialectic of uneven and combined development." As Baruch Knei-Paz writes in his admirable précis of Trotsky's thought:

> In appending new forms the backward society takes not their beginnings, nor the stages of their evolution, but the finished product itself. In fact it goes even further; it copies not the product as it exists in its countries of origin but its "ideal type," and it is able to do so for the very reason that it is in a position to append instead of going through the process of development. This explains why the new forms, in a backward society, appear more perfected than in an advanced society where they are approximations only to the "ideal" for having been arrived at piecemeal and within the framework of historical possibilities.[14]

In the cases of Dubai and China, all the arduous intermediate stages of commercial evolution have been telescoped or short-circuited to embrace the "perfected" synthesis of shopping, entertainment, and architectural spectacle on the most pharaonic scale.

As a sweepstake in national pride—Arabs versus Chinese—this frantic quest for hyperbole is not, of course, unprecedented; recall the famed competition between Britain and imperial Germany to build dreadnoughts in the early 1900s. But is it an economically sustainable strategy of development? The textbook answer is probably not. Architectural gigantism has always been a perverse symptom of economies in speculative overdrive, and each modern boom has left behind overweening skyscrapers, the Empire State Building or the former World Trade Center, as its tombstones. Cynics rightly point out that the hypertrophic real-estate markets in Dubai and urban China are the sinks for global excess profits—of oil and manufacturing exports, respectively—currently being pyramided by rich countries' inability to reduce oil consumption and, in the case of the United States, to balance current accounts. If past business cycles are any guide, the end could be nigh and very messy. Yet, like the king of the enigmatic floating island of Laputa in *Gulliver's Travels*, al-Maktoum believes that he has discovered the secret of eternal levitation.

The lodestone of Dubai, of course, is "peak oil" and each time you spend fifty dollars to fill your tank, you are helping to irrigate al-Maktoum's oasis. Fuel prices are currently inflated by industrial China's soaring demand as well as growing fears of war and terrorism in the global oil patch. According to the *Wall Street Journal*, "consumers will [have paid] *$1.2 trillion more* in 2004 and 2005 together for oil products than they did in 2003."[15] As in the 1970s, a huge and disruptive transfer of wealth is taking place between oil-consuming and oil-producing nations. Already visible on the horizon, moreover, is Hubbert's Peak, the tipping point when new petroleum reserves will no longer offset global demand, and thereafter oil prices will become truly stratospheric. In some utopian economic model, perhaps, this windfall would become an investment fund for shifting the global economy to renewable energy while reducing greenhouse gas output and raising the environmental efficiency of urban systems. In the real world of capitalism, however, it has become a subsidy for the apocalyptic luxuries that Dubai is coming to epitomize. ⚒

Miami of the Persian Gulf

According to his hagiographers, Dubai has arrived at its blessed state thanks largely to the entrepreneurial vision that al-Maktoum inherited from his father, Sheikh Rashid, who "committed himself and his resources to turning his emirate into a modern world-class entrepôt where free enterprise flourished."[16] In fact, Dubai's irresistible rise, like that of its parent, the United Arab Emirates, owes as much to a sequence of fortuitous geopolitical accidents. Dubai's chief regional advantage, paradoxically, has been its modest endowment, now rapidly being exhausted, of offshore oil. With a tiny hinterland lacking the geological wealth of Kuwait or Abu Dhabi, Dubai has escaped poverty by a Singaporean strategy of becoming the key commercial, financial, and recreational hub of the Gulf. It is a postmodern "city of nets"—as Brecht called "Mahagonny"—where the superprofits of the international oil trade are intercepted and then reinvested in Arabia's one truly inexhaustible natural resource: sand. (Indeed, megaprojects in Dubai are typically measured by volumes of sand moved: one billion cubic feet in the case of the "island world.") If the current megaproject blitzkrieg, exemplified by Dubailand, succeeds as planned, Dubai will derive all of its GDP from non-oil activities like tourism and finance by 2010.[17]

The platform for Dubai's extraordinary ambitions has been its long history as a haven for smugglers, gold dealers, and pirates. A late-Victorian treaty gave London control over Dubai's foreign affairs, keeping the Ottomans and their tax collectors out of the region, but otherwise allowing the al-Maktoum dynasty to exploit their ownership of the only natural deepwater port along four hundred miles of what was then known as the "Pirates' Coast." Pearl fishing and smuggling were the mainstays until oil wealth began to generate increased demand for Dubai's commercial savvy and port services. Up to 1956, when the first concrete building was constructed, the entire population lived in traditional *barastri* homes made from palm fronds, drawing water from communal wells and tethering their goats in the narrow streets.[18]

After the British withdrawal from East of Suez in 1968, Sheikh Rashid joined with the ruler of Abu Dhabi, Sheikh Zayed, in 1971 to create the United Arab Emirates, a feudal federation bound together by the common threat of the Marxists in Oman and, later, the Islamists in Iran. Abu Dhabi possessed the greater share of the UAE'S oil wealth (almost one-twelfth of the world's proven hydrocarbon reserves), but Dubai was the more logical port and commercial center. When the city's original deepwater "creek" proved too small to handle burgeoning trade, the UAE's leadership used some of their earnings from the first "oil shock" to help Dubai finance construction of the world's largest man-made port, completed in 1976.

Following Khomeini's revolution in 1979, Dubai also became the Persian Gulf's Miami, providing refuge to a large community of Iranian exiles, many of whom specialized in smuggling gold, untaxed cigarettes, and liquor to their puritanical homeland, and to India. More recently, Dubai, under the tolerant gaze of Tehran, has attracted large numbers of wealthy Iranians who use the city—more like Hong Kong than Miami—as a base for trade and binational lifestyles. They are estimated to control as much as 30 percent of Dubai's current real-estate development.[19] Building on such clandestine connections, Dubai in the 1980s and early 1990s became the Gulf's principal dirty-money laundry as well as a bolt-hole for some of the region's most notorious gangsters and terrorists. As the *Wall Street Journal* recently described the city's underside:

Its gold and diamond souks, houses of barter and informal cash-transfer storefronts have long formed an opaque business world based on connections and clan allegiances. Black-market operators, arms dealers, terrorist financiers and money launderers have taken advantage of the freewheeling environment, even if the vast bulk of business is legitimate.[20]

In early 2006 the U.S. Congress erupted in a furor over Dubai Port World's imminent takeover of the London-based Peninsular and Oriental Steam Navigation Company, which operates docks from New York to Miami. Despite support from the Bush Administration, Dubai was forced to withdraw from the deal after a firestorm of accusations on cable news programs and radio talk shows about the supposed dangers of ceding control of American commercial ports to a Middle Eastern government. Much of the controversy was unquestionably fueled by anti-Arab bigotry pure and simple (U.S. port operations are already largely under management of foreign-owned firms), but Dubai's "terrorist connection," an outgrowth of its role as the Switzerland of the Gulf, has been well documented.

Indeed, since 9/11 a huge investigative literature has explored Dubai's role as "the financial hub for Islamic militant groups," especially al-Qaeda and the Taliban: "all roads lead to Dubai when it comes to [terrorist] money," claims a former high-ranking U.S. Treasury official. Bin Laden reportedly transferred large sums through the government-owned Dubai Islamic Bank, while the Taliban used the city's unregulated gold markets to transform their opium taxes, paid in gold bullion, into laundered dollars.[21] In his bestselling *Ghost Wars*, Steve Coll claims that after the al-Qaeda car-bombings of the U.S. embassies in Nairobi and Dar es Salaam, a CIA scheme to target bin Laden with cruise missiles while he was falcon hunting in southern Afghanistan had to be aborted because he was in the company of unnamed Emirati royalty. Coll adds that the CIA "also suspected that C-130s flying out of Dubai carried weapons to the Taliban."[22]

In addition, al-Maktoum for almost a decade provided luxurious sanctuary for Bombay's Al Capone, the legendary gangster Dawood Ibrahim. His presence in the sheikhdom in the late 1980s was hardly low-key. "Dubai," writes Suketu Mehta, "suited Dawood; he re-created Bombay in lavish parties, flying in scores of the city's top film stars and cricketers as guests, and took a film starlet, Mandakini, as his mistress."[23] In early 1993, according to the Indian government, Dawood, working with Pakistani intelligence officials, used Dubai as a base for organizing the infamous "Black Friday" bombings in Bombay that killed 257 people.[24] Although India immediately requested Dubai to arrest Dawood, he was allowed to flee to Karachi, where he is still sheltered by the Pakistani government; his criminal organization, D-Company, meanwhile, has reportedly continued to be active in the sheikhdom.[25]

War Zone

Dubai now enjoys high marks from Washington as a partner in the War on Terror and, in particular, as a base for spying on Iran;[26] but it is probable that al-Maktoum, like the other Emirati rulers, still keeps a channel open to radical Islamists. If al-Qaeda so desired, for example, it could presumably turn the Burj Al-Arab and Dubai's other soaring landmarks into so many towering infernos. Yet so far Dubai is one of the few cities in the region to have entirely avoided terrorist bombings and attacks on Western tourists: eloquent testament, one might suppose, to the city-state's continuing role as a money laundry and upscale hideout, like Tangier in the 1940s or Macao in the 1960s. Dubai's burgeoning black market economy is its insurance policy against the car bombers and airplane hijackers.

In many complex and surprising ways, Dubai actually earns its living from fear. Its huge port complex at Jebel Ali, for example, has profited immeasurably from the trade generated by the U.S. invasion of Iraq, while terminal two at the Dubai airport, always crowded with Halliburton employees, private mercenaries, and American soldiers en route to Baghdad or Kabul, has been described as "the busiest commercial terminal in the world" for America's Middle East wars.[27] Post-9/11 developments have also shifted global investment patterns to Dubai's benefit. Thus after al-Qaeda's attacks on America, the Muslim oil states, traumatized by the angry Christians in Washington and lawsuits by WTC survivors, no longer considered the United States the safest harbor for their petrodollars. Panicky Saudis alone are estimated to have repatriated at least one-third of their trillion-dollar overseas portfolio. Although nerves are now calmer, Dubai has benefited enormously from the continuing inclination of the oil sheikhs to invest within, rather than outside, the region. As Edward Chancellor has emphasized, "unlike the last oil boom of the late 1970s, relatively little of the current Arab oil surplus has been directly invested in U.S. assets or even deposited in the international banking system. This time much of the oil money has remained at home, where a classic speculative mania is now being played out."[28]

In 2004, the Saudis (500,000 of whom are estimated to visit Dubai at least once a year) were believed to have plowed at least $7 billion into al-Maktoum's major properties. Saudis, together with investors from Abu Dhabi, Kuwait, Iran, and even emulous Qatar, bankroll the hubris of Dubailand (officially developed by Dubai's billionaire Galadari brothers) and other colossal fantasy projects.[29] Although economists stress the driving role of equity investment in the current Gulf boom, the region is also awash with cheap bank credit thanks to a 60 percent increase in the local deposit base and the slipstreaming of the U.S. Federal Reserve's easy money policies (the currencies of the Gulf emirates are all linked to the dollar).[30]

Much of this money, of course, dances to an old tune. "A majority of new Dubai properties," explains *Business Week*, "are being acquired for speculative purposes, with only small deposits put down. They are being flipped in the contemporary Miami manner."[31] But what is too often flipped, some economists predict, may ultimately flop. Will Dubai someday fall from the sky when this real-estate balloon bursts, or will peak oil keep this desert Laputa floating above the contradictions of the world economy? Al-Maktoum remains a mountain of self-confidence: "I would like to tell capitalists that Dubai does not need investors; investors need Dubai. And I tell you that the risk lies not in using your money, but in letting it pile up."[32]

Dubai's philosopher-king (one of the huge offshore island projects will actually spell out an epigram of his in Arabic script)[33] is well aware that fear is also the most dynamic component of the oil revenues that turn his sand dunes into malls and skyscrapers. Every time insurgents blow up a pipeline in the Niger Delta, a martyr drives his truck bomb into a Riyadh housing complex, or Washington and Tel Aviv rattle their sabers at Tehran, the price of oil (and thus Dubai's ultimate income) increases by some increment of anxiety in the all-important futures mar-

ket. The Gulf economies, in other words, are now capitalized not just on oil production, but also on the fear of its disruption. According to a recent survey of experts by *Business Week*, "the world paid the Persian Gulf oil states an extra $120
billion or so last year because of the premium in prices due to fear of unexpected
supply disruptions. Some cynics argue that oil producers welcome the fear of disruption because it boosts their revenues." "Fear," according to one of the senior
energy analysts that the magazine consulted, "is a gift to oil producers."[34]

But it is a gift that the oil rich would rather spend in a tranquil oasis surrounded by very high walls. With its sovereignty ultimately guaranteed by the
American nuclear supercarriers usually berthed at Jebel Ali, as well as by whatever secret protocols (negotiated during falcon hunting trips in Afghanistan?) govern the Emiratis' relationship to Islamic terrorism, Dubai is a paradise of personal
security, from the Swiss-style laws governing financial secrecy to the armies of
concierges, watchmen, and bodyguards who protect its sanctums of luxury.
Tourists are customarily ordered away by the security guards if they attempt to
sneak a peek at Burj Al-Arab on its private island. Hotel guests, of course, arrive
in Rolls-Royces.

Milton Friedman's Beach Club

Dubai, in other words, is a vast gated community, the ultimate Green Zone. But
even more than Singapore or Texas, it is also the apotheosis of the neoliberal values of contemporary capitalism: a society that might have been designed by the
economics department of the University of Chicago. Dubai, indeed, has achieved
what American reactionaries only dream of—an oasis of free enterprise without
income taxes, trade unions, or opposition parties (there are no elections). As be-
fits a paradise of consumption, its unofficial national holiday, as well as its global
logo, is the celebrated Shopping Festival, a monthlong extravaganza sponsored by
the city's twenty-five malls that begins on January 12 and attracts four million upscale shoppers, primarily from the Middle East and South Asia.[35]

Table 2

The Triumvirate

	"Public"	Private
Mohammed al Gergawi	Executive Council	Dubai Holdings
Mohammed Alabbar	Department of Economic Development	Emaar
Sultan Ahmed bin Sulayem	Jebel Ali Port	Nakheel

Feudal absolutism—the Maktoum dynasty owns the land area of Dubai—meanwhile has been spruced up as the last word in enlightened corporate administration, and the political sphere has been officially collapsed into the managerial. "People refer to our crown prince as the chief executive officer of Dubai. It's because, genuinely, he runs government as a private business for the sake of the private sector, not for the sake of the state," says Saeed al-Muntafiq, head of the Dubai Development and Investment Authority. Moreover, if the country is a single business, as al-Maktoum maintains, then "representative government" is beside the point: after all, General Electric and Exxon are not democracies and no one—except for raving socialists—expects either to be so.

The state, accordingly, is almost indistinguishable from private enterprise. Dubai's top managers—all commoners, hired meritocratically—simultaneously hold strategic government portfolios and manage a major Maktoum-controlled real-estate development company. "Government," indeed, is really an equities management team led by three top players who compete with one another to earn the highest returns for al-Maktoum (see table 2). "In such a system," writes William Wallis, "the concept of a conflict of interest is barely recognized."[36] Because the country has one ultimate landlord, and myriad streams of rent and lease payments all flow to a single beneficiary, Dubai is able to dispense with most of the sales, customs, and income taxes essential to governments elsewhere. The minimal tax burden, in turn, leverages the sale or lease of Dubai's golden sands. Oil-rich Abu Dhabi, meanwhile, subsidizes the residual state functions, including foreign relations and defense, entrusted to the Emirates' federal administration—itself a condominium of the interests of the ruling sheikhs and their relatives.

In a similar spirit, personal liberty in Dubai derives strictly from the business plan, not from a constitution, much less "inalienable rights." Al-Maktoum and his executives have to arbitrate between lineage-based power and Islamic law, on the one hand, and Western business culture and recreational decadence on the other. Their ingenious solution is a regime of what might be called "modular liberties" based on the rigorous spatial segregation of economic functions and ethnically circumscribed social classes. To understand how this works in practice, it is necessary briefly to survey Dubai's overall development strategy.

Although tourist development and its excesses generate most of the buzz about Dubai, the city-state has extraordinary ambitions to capture as much value-added as possible through a series of specialized free-trade zones and high-tech clusters. "One of the ways that this trading town along a creek has reformulated itself into a megalopolis," writes an ABC News commentator, "is by throwing in everything and the kitchen sink as incentives for companies to invest in and relocate to Dubai. There are free-trade zones where 100 percent foreign ownership is allowed, with no individual or corporate taxes or import/export duties whatsoever."[37] The original free-trade zone in the port district of Jebel Ali now has several thousand resident trading and industrial firms, and is the major base for American corporations selling to the Saudi and Gulf markets.[38]

Most future growth, however, is expected to be generated within an archipelago of specialized "clusters." The largest of these cities-within-the-city are Internet City, already the Arab world's principal information technology hub, with local subsidiaries of Dell, Hewlett-Packard, Microsoft, and others; Media City, home to the Al Arabiya satellite network and various international news organizations; and the Dubai International Financial Centre, whose DFIX al-Maktoum hopes will grow into the largest stock exchange between Europe and East Asia as foreign investors rush to tap the Gulf's vast reservoir of oil earnings. In addition to these mega-enclaves, each with tens of thousands of employees, Dubai also hosts or is planning to build a Humanitarian Aid City, as a base for disaster relief; a free-trade zone dedicated to the sale of used cars; a Dubai Metals and Commodities Centre; a Chess City headquartering the International Chess Association and designed as a vast chessboard with two "King" towers, each sixty-four stories high; and a $6-billion Healthcare Village, in collaboration with the Harvard Medical School, that will offer the wealthy classes of the Gulf region state-of-the-art American medical technology.[39]

Other cities in the region, of course, have free-trade zones and high-tech clusters, but only Dubai has allowed each enclave to operate under regulatory and legal bubble-domes tailored to the specific needs of foreign capital and expat professionals. "Carving out lucrative niches with their own special rules," claims the *Financial Times*, "has been at the heart of Dubai's development strategy."[40] Thus press censorship (flagrant in the rest of Dubai) is largely suspended inside Media City, while Internet access (regulated for content elsewhere) is unfettered inside Internet City. The UAE has permitted Dubai to set up "an entirely separate, Western-based commercial system for its financial district that would do business in dollars, and in English." Although not without ensuing controversy, Dubai even imported British financial regulators and retired judges to bolster confidence that DFIX plays by the same rules as Zurich, London, and New York.[41] Meanwhile, to promote the sell-off of Palm Jumeirah mansions and the private islands that make up the "island world," al-Maktoum in May 2002 announced a "freehold revolution," unique in the region, that allows foreigners to buy luxury property outright and not just as a ninety-nine-year lease.[42]

In addition to these enclaved regimes of greater media and business freedom, Dubai is also famously tolerant of Western vices, with the exception of recreational drugs. In contrast to Saudi Arabia or even Kuwait City, booze flows freely in the city's hotels and expat bars, and no one looks askance at halter tops or even string bikinis on the beach. Dubai—any of the hipper guidebooks will advise— is also the "Bangkok of the Middle East," with thousands of Russian, Armenian, Indian, and Iranian prostitutes controlled by various transnational gangs and mafias. The Russian girls at the bar are the glamorous façade of a sinister sex trade built on kidnapping, slavery, and sadistic violence. Al-Maktoum and his thoroughly modern regime, of course, disavow any collusion with this burgeoning red-light industry, although insiders know that the whores are essential to

keeping the five-star hotels full of European and Arab businessmen.[43] When expats extol Dubai's unique "openness," it is this freedom to carouse and debauch—
not to organize unions or publish critical opinions—that they are usually praising.

An Indentured, Invisible Majority

Dubai, together with its emirate neighbors, has achieved the state of the art in the
disenfranchisement of labor. In a country that only abolished slavery in 1963,
trade unions, most strikes, and all agitators are illegal, and 99 percent of the private-
sector workforce are immediately deportable noncitizens. Indeed, the deep thinkers
at the American Enterprise and Cato Institutes must salivate when they contem-
plate the system of classes and entitlements in Dubai.

At the top of the social pyramid, of course, are the al-Maktoums and their
cousins, who own every lucrative grain of sand in the sheikhdom. Next, the native 15 percent of the population (many of them originally Arab-speakers from
southern Iran) constitutes a leisure class whose uniform of privilege is the traditional white *dishdash*. Their obedience to the dynasty is rewarded by income
transfers, free education, subsidized homes, and government jobs. A step below
are the pampered mercenaries: more than 100,000 British expatriates (thousands
of other UK citizens own second homes or condos in Dubai), along with other
European, Lebanese, Iranian, and Indian managers and professionals, who take
full advantage of their air-conditioned affluence and two months of overseas
leave every summer. The Brits, led by David Beckham (who owns a beach) and
Rod Stewart (who owns an island), are probably the biggest cheerleaders for al-
Maktoum's paradise, and many of them luxuriate in a social world that recalls the
lost splendour of gin-and-tonics at Raffles and white mischief in Simla's bungalows. Dubai is expert at catering to colonial nostalgia.[44]

The city-state is also a miniature Raj in a more important and notorious aspect. The great mass of the population are South Asian contract laborers, legally
bound to a single employer and subject to totalitarian social controls. Dubai's luxury lifestyles are attended by vast numbers of Filipina, Sri Lankan, and Indian
maids, while the building boom (which employs one-quarter of the workforce) is
carried on the shoulders of an army of poorly paid Pakistanis and Indians, the

largest contingent from Kerala, working twelve-hour shifts, six and a half days a week, in the asphalt-melting desert heat.

Dubai, like its neighbours, flouts ILO labor regulations and refuses to adopt the international Migrant Workers Convention. Human Rights Watch in 2003 accused the Emirates of building prosperity on "forced labor." Indeed, as the *Independent* recently emphasized, "the labor market closely resembles the old indentured labor system brought to Dubai by its former colonial master, the British." "Like their impoverished forefathers," the London paper continued, "today's Asian workers are forced to sign themselves into virtual slavery for years when they arrive in the United Arab Emirates. Their rights disappear at the airport, where recruitment agents confiscate their passports and visas to control them."[45]

In addition to being superexploited, Dubai's helots—like the proletariat in Fritz Lang's *Metropolis*—are also expected to be generally invisible. The local press (the UAE ranks a dismal 137th on the global Press Freedom Index) is restrained from reporting on migrant workers, exploitative working conditions, and prostitution. Likewise, "Asian laborers are banned from the glitzy shopping malls, new golf courses, and smart restaurants."[46] Nor are the bleak work camps on the city's outskirts—where laborers are crowded six, eight, even twelve to a room, often without air-conditioning or functioning toilets—part of the official tourist image of a city of luxury, without poverty or slums.[47] In a recent visit, even the UAE minister of labor was reported to be shocked by the squalid, almost unbearable conditions in a remote work camp maintained by a large construction contractor. Yet when the laborers attempted to form a union to win back pay and improve living conditions, they were promptly arrested.[48]

Dubai's police may turn a blind eye to illicit diamond and gold imports, prostitution rings, and shady characters who buy twenty-five villas at a time in cash, but they are diligent in deporting Pakistani workers who complain about being cheated out of their wages by unscrupulous contractors, or jailing Filipina maids for "adultery" when they report being raped by their employers.[49] To avoid the simmering volcano of Shiite unrest that so worries Bahrain and Saudi Arabia, Dubai and its UAE neighbors have favored a non-Arab workforce drawn from western India, Pakistan, Sri Lanka, Bangladesh, Nepal, and the Philippines. But as Asian workers have become an increasingly restive majority, the UAE has reversed course and adopted a "cultural diversity policy"—"we have been asked not to recruit any more Asians," explained one contractor—to reinforce control over the workforce by diluting the existing national concentrations with more Arab workers.[50]

Discrimination against Asians, however, has failed to recruit enough Arabs willing to work at the lowly wages ($100 to $150 per month) paid to construction laborers to meet the insatiable demands of the exploding skyline and half-built megaprojects.[51] Indeed the building boom, with its appalling safety record and negligence of workers' most basic needs, has incubated Dubai's first labor rebellion. In 2004 alone, Human Rights Watch estimated that as many as 880 construction workers were killed on the job, with most of the fatal accidents unreported by employers or covered up by the government.[52] At the same time, the giant construction companies and their subcontractors have failed to guarantee minimum facilities for sanitation or adequate supplies of potable water at remote desert labor camps. Workers also have been exasperated by longer commutes to worksites, the petty tyranny (often with a racial or religious bias) of their supervisors, the spies and company guards in their camps, the debt-bondage of their labor contracts, and the government's failure to prosecute fly-by-night contractors who leave Dubai or declare bankruptcy without paying back wages.[53] As one embittered laborer from Kerala told the *New York Times*, "I wish the rich people would realize who is building these towers. I wish they could come and see how sad this life is."[54]

The first tremor of unrest came in fall 2004 when several thousand Asian workers courageously marched down the eight-lane Sheikh Zayed Highway toward the Ministry of Labour, only to be met by riot police and officials threatening mass deportations.[55] Smaller demonstrations and strikes, protesting unpaid wages or unsafe working conditions, continued through 2005, drawing inspiration from a large uprising of Bangladeshi workers in Kuwait during the spring. In September, an estimated seven thousand workers demonstrated for three hours, the largest protest in Dubai history. Then, on March 22, 2006, bullying security men ignited a riot at the vast Burj Dubai tower site.

Some 2,500 exhausted workers were waiting after the end of their shift for long-overdue buses to take them back to their dormitories in the desert, when the guards began to harass them. The enraged laborers, many of them Indian Muslims, overwhelmed and beat the guards, then attacked the construction headquarters: burning company cars, ransacking offices, destroying computers, and smashing files. The following morning, the army of laborers defied police to return to the site, where they refused to work until Dubai-based Al Naboodah Laing O'Rourke raised wages and improved working conditions. Thousands of construction workers at a new airport terminal also joined the wildcat strike. Although some minor concessions along with draconian threats forced most of the laborers back to work at the Burj Dubai and the airport, the underlying grievances continue to fester. In July, hundreds of laborers at the Arabian Ranches project on Emirates Road rioted to protest the chronic shortage of water for cooking and bathing at their camp. Other workers have held clandestine union meetings and reportedly threatened to picket hotels and malls.[56]

The unruly voice of labor echoes louder in the deserts of the UAE than it might elsewhere. At the end of the day, Dubai is capitalized just as much on cheap labor as it is on expensive oil, and the Maktoums, like their cousins in the other emirates, are exquisitely aware that they reign over a kingdom built on the backs of a South Asian workforce. So much has been invested in Dubai's image as an imperturbable paradise of capital that even small disturbances can have exaggerated impacts on investors' confidence. Dubai Inc. is thus currently considering a variety of responses to worker unrest, ranging from expulsions and mass arrests to some limited franchising of collective bargaining. But any tolerance of protest risks future demands not just for unions, but for citizenship, and thereby threatens the absolutist foundations of Maktoum rule. None of the shareholders in Dubai—whether the American navy, the Saudi billionaires, or the frolicking expats—want to see the emergence of a Solidarnosc in the desert.

Sheik al-Maktoum, who fancies himself the Gulf's prophet of modernization, likes to impress visitors with clever proverbs and heavy aphorisms. A favorite: "Anyone who does not attempt to change the future will stay a captive of the past."[57] Yet the future that he is building in Dubai—to the applause of billionaires and transnational corporations everywhere—looks like nothing so much as a nightmare of the past: Speer meets Disney on the shores of Araby.

Capital of Chaos: The New Kabul of Warlords and Infidels

Anthony Fontenot and Ajmal Maiwandi

The re-establishment of the rule of law in Afghanistan is essential to the peace process. Without reform of the institutions of justice . . . impunity for armed lawbreakers will persist, citizens will remain deprived of justice, and the confidence of international investors will remain low.[1]

Amid the ruined mud-brick buildings of a city that has been devastated by war and neglect, divided into sinister, heavily fortified, military compounds, and occupied by armed local and foreign mercenaries, stand randomly dispersed extravaganzas of glass-and-tile palaces: symbols of the plunder that currently provides the economic base for the "reborn" Kabul. One result of the so-called War on Terror in Afghanistan is that vast amounts of money are now pouring into luxury real estate. In return for military intelligence and armed cooperation, the U.S. military has "supplied weapons and cash to many warlords since 2001,"[2] with the result that power has been restored in the outlying provinces to a handful of armed despots who are willing to risk military affiliation with the "coalition" forces in Afghanistan in return for vast rewards. This cash, along with the

profits from the flourishing drug trade and various other sources, has been reinvested in Afghanistan's cities, spurring an unprecedented building frenzy. The
construction boom is mainly centered in Kabul, but it affects all major urban areas, including the historic center of Herat, which has witnessed the destruction of
many of its most notable buildings during this onrush of speculative construction. More importantly, in addition to cash paid in advance for cooperation, an
unspoken agreement now ensures that the Afghan authorities will overlook a
booming black economy. This arrangement has led to a boom in the illicit narcotics trade, which is controlled mainly by allies of the current government. As
Pierre-Arnaud Chouvy points out:

> several factors have favored the rapid restoration of opium production since the
> Taliban prohibition. Prior to 2004 at least, the United States largely condoned opi-
> ates production both in areas traditionally controlled by the Northern Alliance, for
> example in Badakhshan, and in areas held by local commanders whose support was
> deemed strategically necessary to fight the Taliban and Al-Qaeda.[3]

Afghanistan is the world's largest producer of opium (roughly 87 percent of
global production), and generates a local income of US$2 to 3 billion in 2005.[4]
This is more than half of the country's gross domestic product and nearly ten
times the estimated domestic revenue collected by the government for the same
year (US$333 million).[5] According to Human Rights Watch, "drug profits [for
2004] led to continuing insecurity in rural areas, and stifled reconstruction and development efforts, including efforts to improve rule of law."[6] The power relations
associated with the drug economy have an immense influence on the reality of
everyday life in the cities and provinces of Afghanistan.

Considering the ample resources that are available (a US$1.2-billion budget for
core development that prioritizes expenditure on basic infrastructure)[7] and, contrary to the international community's assumptions concerning the rebuilding of
Kabul, there has been very little progress in the reconstruction of the city. Except
for highway projects, which seem to have been implemented to facilitate military
operations rather than civilian traffic, and the millions being spent on the coalition forces' new facilities at Bagram (United States), Helmand (United Kingdom),

and Darluman (NATO), there is little evidence of internationally sponsored large-scale reconstruction of infrastructure taking place in Kabul. On the contrary, just as some observers predicted, the real impetus in construction comes from the private sector fueled by the opium trade. As they rush to take advantage of the current state of lawlessness and corruption in Kabul, warlords and drug traffickers are changing the face of the city.

Land as Power

Just as illegal transactions have become the hallmark of the new Afghan economy, the dubious or blatantly illegal acquisition of land has become a dominant real-estate practice in the capital. Tracts of land on the outskirts of Kabul are routinely confiscated by warlords and militia commanders and then sold off to the highest bidders. Since an exact survey of new construction in Kabul does not exist, it is difficult to calculate the number of buildings illegally constructed on these expropriated sites, but conservative estimates put the total number, including private homes, in the thousands.

Many areas of Kabul have experienced radical transformations over the last few years. In the centrally located district of Sherpur, for example, land belonging to the Ministry of Defense had been occupied since the 1950s by squatters who had streamed to Kabul from outlying villages. Their simple mud-brick dwellings had always been tolerated until 2003, a year following the establishment of the Transitional Administration, when the minister of defense suddenly ordered the mass demolition of the entire squatter community. Giving residents only one day's notice, the ministry bulldozed Sherpur, injuring several residents who resisted these actions. The cleared area was subsequently converted into a new residential district for powerful politicians, warlords, and businessmen. The land was divided and sold in large parcels, which in turn were further subdivided and resold at immense profit. A report by RAWA (Revolutionary Association of the Women of Afghanistan) alleged that in Sherpur "300 plots [amounting to] around 120 hectares (120,000 square meters) were distributed among senior governmental officials including ministers, deputy ministers, governors, commanders, generals, intelligence (KHAD) administrators, and businessmen."[8] The group who seized the land offered a few "land grants"—a common practice employed by the Afghan government—to civil servants and senior officials in order to dispel any potential resistance to the illegal acquisition and to serve as a decoy while it actually sold the majority of the plots at market rates. Several ministers in the Hamid Karzai interim government were implicated in the ensuing scandal when it was exposed that they had received free plots of land in Sherpur in return for expulsion of the poor residents.

It was only when the international news media reported on the takeover of Sherpur that the Karzai administration hesitantly referred the matter to the newly established Human Rights Commission in Afghanistan. The Special Rapporteur on Adequate Housing to the UN Commission on Human Rights, Miloon Kothari, concluded in a public interview: "essentially what we have found there is that ministers and people at the highest level are involved in occupying land and in demolishing the homes of poor people. . . . In fact a number of ministers, including the minister of defense, [are] directly involved in this kind of occupation and dispossession of poor people, some of whom have been there for 25 to 30 years." Kothari went on to warn that "there is a great climate of insecurity that is being created across the country, which is for reasons other than armed conflict; it's for reasons of occupation, it's for reasons of land speculation, it's for reasons of property conflict," and he predicted that "unless these issues are addressed at the judicial level, at all other levels, what we are seeing in Afghanistan today is that we are sowing the seeds for decades of conflict . . . due to a land and property and housing crisis."[9]

Kothari's forthright denunciation of land piracy enraged the perpetrators: that is to say, the powerful ministers, bureaucrats, and warlords who supposedly represent "democracy restored" in Afghanistan. They complained to UN Special Representative Lakhdar Barhimi, who punctually reprimanded Kothari for daring to criticize the land grab. But the abuses were too blatant to be easily swept under the rug, and eventually pressure from international human rights groups and the foreign media forced the Karzai regime to undertake a token remediation: the land pirates were formally required to pay the government the equivalent of 20 percent of the market value of the property wrested from the poor residents of Sherpur. Yet it is unclear if any reparation has actually been received, and for most poor Kabulis the Sherpur scandal continues to epitomize the reign of greed, corruption, and extravagance that has followed the expulsion of the Taliban and the advent of the pro-Western Karzai regime.

Despite their occasional criticisms of slum evictions, the international community in Kabul has become hopelessly entangled in the city's sinister real-estate economy. The demand for first-class accommodations and offices for the UN, the NGOs, foreign contractors, and major aid agencies generates much of the inflation in land values and, indeed, has spurred strategic land grabbing by high officials and warlords. The international entities (as our fieldwork in Sherpur and similar districts reveals) seek high levels of physical security as well as standards of First World luxury rarely available in the world's fifth-poorest country. The result of this quest has been the creation of informal colonial enclaves or "green zones," new fortified segregations of space that belie the noble mission statements of foreign agencies.

Foreign tenants spend a majority of time in the security of their homes and offices, so their properties are characterized by the ubiquitous and menacing presence of heavily armed guards. Within these compounds, luxury is defined by the presence of en suite bathrooms adjacent to each room, and by kitchens designed with plenty of storage space for food and supplies, so as to minimize the need to leave the house too frequently (as a local realtor explained to during a guided tour of the district). Some houses are even equipped with underground parking, offering secure and direct access to the house. These self-sufficient, inward-focused worlds are designed to maintain their subjects in isolation and security, and are offered at extravagant premiums. Rents approach US$15,000 per month, or approximately twenty times the average annual income in Afghanistan, according to the U.S. government.[10]

Following a coordination meeting at ACBAR (the Agency Coordinating Body for Afghan Relief) in 2002, members of the NGO community in Afghanistan sent an e-mail to Ashraf Ghani, the then director of the Afghanistan Aid Coordination Authority and later minister of finance. They complained that:

> Housing costs have escalated dramatically in the past few months, sometimes by twenty or thirty times and more. . . . A major cause of housing costs has been demand at the high end of the market triggered by demand from the UN, INGOs, international financial institutions, donors, and embassies. A trickle-down effect results as those evicted from high-end residences seek new accommodation further down the scale, leading to further evictions as landlords seek to profit from this uncontrolled market. NGOs are concerned that many of these evictions are illegal, and tenants, particularly the poor, have no practical legal recourse to protection. Some landlords are making fraudulent claims that high taxes are forcing them to raise rents. They are then insisting that tenants sign two leases in order to avoid these taxes (one for the tenant at a high rent and one presented to the government at a lower rent).[11]

The international community's complicity in rewarding the criminal land grabs by Afghan elites has become increasingly intolerable in the eyes of the poor— who constitute the majority of the population in Kabul. The realization that the international presence is increasingly helping the rich and powerful to consolidate their positions by exploiting and evicting the poor is creating new levels of resentment toward the foreign forces and local criminal elements who collectively control the city.[12]

To complicate matters further, many local power brokers feel that the confiscation of land is their "God-given right," a reward for fighting the holy war to repel the foreign invaders (by which they mean the former Soviet Union and the Pakistani-backed Taliban). The Karzai government continues to turn a blind eye to this incessant plunder, preferring to pamper the powerful (including members of the recently elected parliament) instead of bringing them to justice.

Architecture as Alchemy

In a permanent crisis marked by foreign political interference on one hand and internal political jockeying on the other, the fledgling government of Afghanistan is unable to hold its own civil servants accountable for their actions. This results in the further corruption of institutions, while at the same time producing ineffective bureaucracies for the control of urban growth and building practices. The inevitable consequence of this administrative stalemate is that private development continues to advance at an astonishingly rapid rate along the path of least resistance. Kabul has become the new architectural Babylon of Central Asia, notorious for its crude displays of wealth and blatant aesthetic of excess. A plethora of wildly decorated buildings sporting extravagant colors, patterns, textures, and materials are blossoming in the Afghan landscape. An Afghan thug aesthetic has emerged, marking the warlord palaces and commercial centers of the new city with bold, flashy, untrained, and stunning visual effects of glistening, outrageously colored glass and mirrored tiles.

As a result of the highly inflated construction costs, tangled bureaucracy, corrupt building bureaucracies, and land confiscations, only those with money and influence are able to build in Kabul. They wage an intentional architectural battle with one another as they engage in strange displays of conspicuous consumption. Extravagance and ornamentation determine both the design and execution of the new construction. As in many parts of the world dominated by chaos and the naked struggle for power, the eccentric Afghan aesthetic forged by businessmen, militia commanders, drug barons, and warlords represents the first signs of an emerging postwar order and pathology. From surreal, Disney-style scenic settings—for instance, featuring plastic deer grazing alongside white doves who tentatively sneak a sip of water from the lavishly decorated fountains—to intricately designed exterior façades plastered with multicolored tiles, the new architecture of Kabul is a collage of generic international products fused with kitsch samplings of Afghan vernacular architecture and textile patterns, all of which reflect the schizophrenic psyche of a war-torn society.

More than any other form of cultural production, the recent urban development in Kabul—and in Afghanistan at large—represents the emergence of a fractured identity. The individuals responsible for the design and construction of this new environment range from farmers, brick masons, drug barons, and warlords to local contractors and tradesmen. In this new version of the city they make, the *mohandis* (architect) is no longer consulted for technical or aesthetic services. On the contrary, designs for buildings are being imported into the country much like imitation Gucci handbags.

In Kabul, real-estate developers not only organize their own financing and determine the use of buildings by themselves; they also design and supervise the construction. In a collage-like process, they select images from various sources, mixing together unrelated architectural styles and construction methods. The assemblage is then discussed with the builder in order to customize and "morph" the fragments into what the developer considers to be a "coherent" building. As in a Photoshop collage, windows, doors, balconies, gardens, and water features are all copied and then reduced or enlarged to suit the site and the wishes of the designer. The internal organization of the building is usually left up to the builder, who extrapolates floor plans and structural requirements from the mosaic of various images. The design and construction process can take as little as six months. In commercial developments, the upper floors are often left incomplete, in order to allow for future expansion. This method ensures that the building remains in a perpetual state of incompletion, capable of absorbing prevailing tastes and fluctuating trends when construction resumes. As a whole, however, this complex of unfinished architectural collages only accentuates the ad hoc and chaotic aspects of the urban environment in Kabul.

"Warlord kitsch," as one might characterize Kabul's *nouveaux riches* architecture, is also fraught with contradiction. If the import of foreign typologies advances a process of globalization and Westernization, the inherent qualities of the imported architecture are simultaneously undermined as local builders attempt to conform to local customs and construction methods. For example, if certain foreign patterns of fenestration appear too "exposed" for the male-dominated Afghan society—making the private and interior world in which women are segregated vulnerable to the public gaze—a common solution is to replace the transparent glazing with mirrored glass, and then to draw heavy curtains across the opening. The importing of "foreign" architecture has become second nature. Along with certain intended architectural expressions come the by-products of its mutation, which together point to a lack of cohesion in the overall reconstruction process occurring in Afghan society as a whole.

Beyond questions of taste, the extravagant and brutal aesthetic that now dominates the new construction in Kabul raises critical questions about the ways in which architecture symbolizes power, wealth, and, most importantly, freedom from control and regulation. This architecture of impunity sets the stage for the drama of disillusionment now current among the general public, who are growing increasingly skeptical about the ability of the government and its agencies to regulate such powerful forces in the city. What is at stake ultimately is political sovereignty itself. An expanding illicit urbanism highlights the paralysis of the government and is understood by increasing numbers of ordinary citizens as an almost open invitation to act in the same vein. In a vicious cycle, this, in turn, exacerbates the impotence of corrupt and overloaded institutions. Afghanistan is sinking into a ruthless cycle of abuse and impotency as it struggles to conform to the West's double standards.

Military Strategy as Urban Planning

Alongside these phantasmagoric commercial and residential structures that Afghans build for themselves stand equally outrageous and aggressive fortified compounds built by foreigners. Overwhelming the public realm with bladed barbed wire, video cameras, floodlights, and elaborately designed walls of concrete, these well-guarded enclaves have become the hallmark of the NGO and military presence in the city. Located in the heart of Kabul, many compounds employ extreme defensive measures that have adverse effects many blocks beyond their own location. These include: the confiscation and razing of public spaces for the creation of "killing fields" (a term used by the security and military community to describe cleared areas where attacking enemies are left without cover), the closure of nearby streets to thwart car bombers, and the intimidation of members of the general population who stray too close to cleared areas. In addition, the reckless driving and strong-arm tactics practiced by heavily armed convoys that move from compound to compound has blurred the distinction between the ordinary residents of Kabul and "enemies of the state." Many Kabulis are left with the feeling that they are under constant attack in a city that has come to resemble a prison in which the guards live among the inmates. In fact, the collective actions of the international donor/NGO communities along with the International Security Assistance Force (ISAF) and the U.S. and NATO military forces all either deliberately or inadvertently contribute to the terrorization of the local population.

Their frustration and anger exploded into a riot on May 31, 2006, following a hit-and-run traffic accident involving a U.S. military convoy. Crashing into twelve cars in the space of five hundred meters, the careening convoy killed five people. Carlotta Gal reported for the *New York Times* that "the crash tapped into a latent resentment of the American military presence here, and violence radiated quickly through the city as rumors circulated that the crash might have been deliberate."[13] Fourteen people were killed in the ensuing riots (including a seven-year-old boy), and dozens of buildings were torched, among them international NGO offices that were intentionally targeted.

In a regression to Soviet-style tactics and policies that focused on conducting both military operations (destroying) and development programs (rebuilding), the international forces have created PRTs (Provincial Reconstruction Teams) that have the dubious task of simultaneously attacking while reconstructing the provinces. In a context where reconstruction is often indistinguishable from urban destruction, the occupying international forces have increasingly alienated the local population instead of "winning hearts and minds." In a recent interview, Ali Seraj, a businessman and a member of the Afghan royal family, contended that "the American military showed a careless attitude toward human life that was becoming a growing problem, whether it was the bombing of villages in counterinsurgency activities in southern Afghanistan or car accidents in the capital, and that this type of attitude has created a great deal of mistrust and hatred."[14] Yet Washington and the international community seem to pay little heed to the devastating effects of their military tactics.

They seem especially unaware of how their own actions thwart the civil society frameworks that the occupation forces officially seek to create. Yet this is painfully self-evident to pedestrians in Kabul, who are often confronted by armed guards who aggressively deter them from approaching so-called sensitive areas, streets, and buildings. Paradoxically, the U.S. government repeatedly reprimanded Saddam Hussein for locating his military installations in civilian areas, where they might avoid allied bombing. Yet the coalition forces in Kabul have used similar tactics, with the result that the civilian population has been repeatedly injured or killed.

In a 2004 suicide attack against the offices of DynCorp (President Karzai's private foreign bodyguards, subcontracted by the U.S. Department of Defense), nine people were killed and several bystanders were injured . Located in a heavily populated residential area, the company's compound was described as "highly visible, with M-16-carrying employees streaming from it to roam Kabul in armored cars. DynCorp guards, many of whom are former SWAT team officers, have become notorious for their rudeness—breaking reporters' cameras, bossing around dignitaries, and disrespecting the polite Afghan culture."[15] In response to growing unrest and public demonstrations against the effects caused by these urban usurpations, President Karzai finally demanded that international organizations dismantle their security barriers and return the streets and sidewalks to the public. Unfortunately, many of the culprits are military installations that are immune to this presidential decree, which is applicable only to international NGOs and aid agencies.

Perhaps the greatest fear raised by the occupation and militarization of Kabul is that the current patterns of infrastructural and urban development, will become permanent—i.e., the current strategies of exclusion will be institutionalized in ways that will have both symbolic and practical repercussions in the long term. Serving as a gateway into the country, Kabul houses the regional headquarters of many organizations associated with the reconstruction projects in Afghanistan. In a perverse turn, the reconstruction of Kabul is being done for the benefit of those rebuilding it. Projects blatantly disregard local priorities and needs, in favor of those of those who have come to "help." A prime example is the widening and repaving of the 2.8 kilometer–long road connecting Kabul airport to the U.S. Embassy. Estimated to cost US$16 million (U.S. taxpayer funded), the road project is widely seen as having been implemented only for the benefit and security of the U.S. diplomatic corps.

Kabul in addition has new shopping districts dominated by English signage on storefronts, beer and liquor advertisements, stores stocked with Western goods that are affordable and available only to Westerners. Circulation and access to these districts are controlled by countless military checkpoints, and large "no-go" zones are accessible only to the rich or foreign who move between them in luxury vehicles. These transformations force many Afghans to conclude that Kabul is an alien entity, built by and catering to "infidels" and local unbelievers. They view the city as a haven for those advancing ideologies alien to a poor Muslim nation, and imposing inappropriate cultural norms through the institutions and support of a local government more concerned with American public opinion than the welfare of its own people.

Reconstruction as Myth

One could argue that the hype associated with the reconstruction of Kabul has had more of an impact on Kabul than the physical process of reconstruction itself. The myth of Kabul's rebuilding has caused a mass influx of Afghans from the provinces and beyond. Attracted by the UN's repatriation policy and inspired by the international community's claims that Afghanistan is well on its way to stability and democracy, Afghans are arriving by the tens of thousands from Iran, Pakistan, and other countries.

According to UNHCR figures, an estimated 4.14 million Afghans have returned since 2002, highlighting fears that refugees are being returned prematurely into insecure areas that lack the necessary institutions to provide needed services. Simultaneously, and in an apparently unrelated move, the Pakistani government is forcibly closing refugee camps across the Afghani border, some of which have existed for over twenty years, on the pretext that they pose a security threat. Between 2003 and 2004, an estimated five hundred thousand to one million returnees arrived in Kabul alone. With minimal aid and a promise of work to assist them through the transition, millions of Afghans are being lured back by hype alone into what most responsible observers view as a precarious situation at best. They reach Kabul only to find themselves abandoned and left to their own devices. According to UNHCR spokesperson Jennifer Pagonis, "returning Afghans receive between US$4 and US$37 in travel grants—depending on the distance to their destination—and, regardless of age, US$12 to assist with short-term needs upon arrival in Afghanistan," the equivalent of two days' supply of food for a family of six (average family size).[16] As a result, makeshift container and tent settlements have emerged throughout the city. Instant ghettos have appeared in Chaman-e-Hazoori, Gozargah, Taimani, Khoshal Khan Mina, and countless other areas.

This epic migration into Kabul has drastically increased the burden on an already overpopulated and devastated city. It is estimated that of the 3.7 million people currently living in Kabul, 58 percent live in informal settlements with very limited, if any, services. With nearly 40 percent of its buildings destroyed in the factional fighting between 1992 and 1996, barely functioning sewage systems, and substandard streets and roads, Kabul is in desperate need of new urban infrastructure. In a surreal response to these shocking conditions, a faction within the Afghan government is pushing for the creation of a new satellite city on the fringes of Kabul. The planning of this development, which is intended to address the mass influx of people arriving in the city, has itself been compromised by facts on the ground: armed men shooting at survey teams, etc.

Although the rebuilding of Afghanistan should ideally include the construction of institutions, laws, and norms of social and economic welfare, all too often reconstruction is expressed purely in terms of physical rebuilding. In this context, what is being reconstructed in Afghanistan is the construction industry itself. Four main sectors are currently thriving: major military-related projects subcontracted to foreign companies (seen as safe in the current climate of distrust); small-scale governmental projects usually subcontracted to insiders, the relatives of officials, or other interested parties in exchange for hefty kickbacks; a mushrooming private sector, which uses both legitimate and dubious resources to fund larger-scale developments; and small-scale retail and residential developments.

To add to the already chaotic conflation of reconstruction with construction, UN agencies—which include the United Nations Office for Project Services (UNOPS, the only self-financing entity within the UN) and the International Organization for Migration (IOM)—have continued to administer postwar reconstruction projects, despite the fact that such activities fall outside their mandate. Considered both trustworthy and transparent, these organizations fund-raise directly in the donor countries and then establish frameworks to ensure that the distribution of funds is channeled exclusively through their own agency. In essence, they have created a monopoly over certain types of reconstruction funds that allow them to dictate conditions to the Afghan government. Local authorities that resist the agencies' conditions are threatened with the withdrawal of aid. These agencies, which are notorious for the scrappy jobs known in Kabul as "hit and run" affairs, often operate outside internationally accepted standards and sometimes draw as much as a 30 percent "overhead" on each project. An independent consulting economist, Mark Watson, summed up the current UN operation and its history in Afghanistan as follows:

> Until the transition government (2001) was formed, the UN was effectively in charge. The modus operandi of most UN agencies reflected their grueling experience . . . [and] most tried to minimize their exposure to government and were, and to some extent still are, deeply distrustful of its motives.

Watson goes on to say that "something of a power struggle has emerged. The government believes, with a good degree of justification, that it is competing for the same aid resources as the UN agencies." He also points out that certain UN operations "in a cash-strapped world, seem to see Afghanistan as a cash cow, to be taken for all it is worth. Overheads are on occasion excessive, and 'mission creep' seems to be the order of the day." Not only are these agencies skimming off the cream—the most lucrative projects—but they also often lack the technical expertise or experience to carry out the job. According to Watson, "One organization proposed a US$30 million schools building program, despite having no track record in large-scale building of schools." Most important, the UN determines how a large portion of aid that comes through its agencies is to be distributed, just as it also decides who is to carry out the work. Calling the shots in this fashion, the UN continuously alienates the Afghan government. According to Watson, "The government wants UN agencies to focus principally on humanitarian and not reconstruction activities, and to compete as a supplier of services. No more monopolies, and much greater transparency! This is highly desirable, but hardly popular among the agencies. Creating a new ethos is bound to also create resistance and resentment from some quarters."[17]

Although less lucrative than the multibillion-dollar reconstruction boondoggles in oil-rich Iraq, Afghanistan is still a Klondike for foreign companies who do not dare venture into the killing fields of the Iraqi insurgency. Kabul is the center of a web of intrigue as foreign multinationals exploit "reconstruction" in partnership with fly-by-night local construction outfits. As in Iraq, a large portion of investment quickly disappears into a black hole. Recently the U.S. Embassy in Kabul sent an alarming cable back to the State Department accusing the United States Agency for International Development (USAID) of incompetence in multimillion-dollar reconstruction projects. In 2002, USAID selected Berger, a private engineering firm, to lead the U.S. effort in rebuilding Afghanistan, granting the company a contract worth US$73 million to build schools and clinics. In an article titled "A Rebuilding Plan Full of Cracks," Joe Stephens and David B. Ottaway quoted an internal memo written by Patrick Fine, head of USAID's Afghanistan operation:

> The numbers of schools and clinics to be constructed were not determined through careful analysis, instead, they were based on back-of-the-envelope calculations outside USAID. . . . the schools and clinics program has been marked by a series of missteps and miscalculations that resulted in a flawed business model, inadequate supervision, and poor execution.[18]

As a result of this mismanagement, only 138 of the 1,000 schools and clinics scheduled for completion by the end of 2004 were handed over to the Afghan government by November 2005. Concerned individuals are astonished that this same company currently holds another US$665 million contract to build infrastructure, including dams, power plants, and roads.

The Karzai administration is no less culpable in sending out unrealistic messages to the international community about the potentials for urban growth in Afghanistan. His preposterous claims that Kabul would become the Dubai of Central Asia within a decade have only added to the confusion, demonstrating that his administration is out of touch with the realities on the ground. Influenced by World Bank and IMF, international advisors in the Ministry of Finance have pushed for Public-Private Partnerships in order to free the government of its obligation to provide services by subcontracting or, in certain instances, by selling off entire segments of state operations and assets to the private sector. For example, the local bus service, owned and operated by the state until 2004, was contracted out to the private operators, resulting in widespread cuts in lines and services. By encouraging the move toward privatization of state assets in such an unstable environment, the administration is gambling with Afghanistan's economic future on the basis of unrealistic and outdated models that have proven disastrous for many African and Latin American countries.

Although the U.S. invasion of Afghanistan in 2001 was accompanied by inflated promises about the reconstruction of Kabul, there are today no master plans to debate nor large-scale public initiatives to consider. Instead, there are fragmentary and independently pursued urban schemes—a hodgepodge of every scenario imaginable. Kabul is a city of fragments simultaneously held together and torn apart by an invisible web of interests that has been spun by groups as diverse as warlords, NGOs, government officials, and destitute widows with children. Occupying the blurry periphery of a vaguely articulated vision of the city's future, while attempting to survive in the absence of viable economic, security, health, and social frameworks, the citizens of Kabul fluctuate between euphoria and desperation. This manic-depressive succession of highs and lows in itself reflects the contradictory processes currently at work in the city. And it is in this maelstrom of default urbanity that the reconstruction of everyday life—an abnormal normality—unfolds.

Impunity as Democracy

In the chaotic political context of Afghanistan, it is difficult to assess who actually holds greater influence: the national government, the warlords, or the United States and the international forces. The unholy alliances that were initially forged between various ruling factions, the government, and the international forces in order to defeat the Taliban in 2001 continue to have profound repercussions on the postconflict environment, posing significant problems for the Afghani government and its international allies. Warlords, in particular, continue to play decisive roles in the current administration. While the Karzai government and U.S. forces attempt to gain legitimacy by invoking the rule of law, "warlords and their troops in many areas have been implicated in widespread rape of women and children, murder, illegal detention, forced displacement, human trafficking, and forced marriage."[19] As outlined in a report before the UN Commission on Human Rights, "local military and police forces, even in Kabul, have been involved in arbitrary arrests, kidnapping, extortion, torture, and extrajudicial killings of criminal suspects." The warlords' abuse of power, with the central government's complicity, is perhaps the single most dangerous threat to stability.

It is customary for American spokespeople to excuse and explain away the current situation in Afghanistan as the "growing pains" of a nascent democracy. Yet one has to wonder if democracy, in the form in which it is being dictated to Afghanistan, was not stillborn. While much of the local population has been pessimistic from the outset about the prospects for security and economic development, a now similar attitude is emerging amongst foreign aid works. A senior western diplomat in Kabul recently stated, "If we fail now we will have a narco-terror paradise and a population of 15 million people who will be even more miserably off than they are now, and a lot angrier to boot . . . [and Afghanistan] will be *a small chunk of hell on earth* in the middle of Asia."[20]

When President Karzai was interviewed by a local television station prior to the parliamentary elections in 2006, he was asked why the government was allowing people with criminal backgrounds to stand as candidates instead of bringing them to justice. His reply, which shocked the Afghan population, was that if the public considered certain candidates to be war criminals or drug traffickers, they should simply vote for someone else. Karzai's extraordinary nonchalance made clear the assumption that has been tacitly held by the government since the fall of the Taliban, i.e., if the transition from anarchy to democracy is to succeed, then justice for those responsible for past and, in instances, continuing crimes would have to be set aside. For many Afghans, this automatic amnesty for all anti-Taliban leaders, no matter how heinous their past crimes or current criminal activities, seriously undermines any possibility of forging a democracy and reduces the democratic process to a hollow drama. Recently, the Afghan Human Rights Commission conducted a nationwide consultation with the Afghan people to survey their views concerning transitional justice in general and the prosecution of past and current violators of human rights in particular. Their report, "A Call for Justice," concluded that: "[a] vast majority of people . . . have a deeply eroded trust in public authorities due to the absence of justice and protection of their rights, and they desire deeply that their suffering be recognized . . . to date, this past has not been confronted."[21] When asked what impact the prosecution of war criminals would have on Afghanistan, 76 percent of the people surveyed believed that it would "increase stability and bring security." (Quite tellingly, 41 percent of those surveyed believed that the international community supported war criminals.)

If the state of Kabul is a cipher of the current political realities in Afghanistan, then there is little reason to be encouraged. The stalled political process and the discernible growth in support for the insurgency only justify the fears of many Kabulis that the country will again collapse into chaos. Consequently, the hapless American, Canadian, and British contingents in Afghanistan are now being reinforced by even more troops who will have to take on the daunting task of patrolling the most dangerous stretches of Afghanistan. This, in turn, only exacerbates the default urbanism of Afghanistan's capital. Suspended within a web of larger political and military relations, Kabul cannot extricate itself from this vicious circle and so continues to bear the stigmata of the so-called international War on Terror.

Delirious Beijing:
Euphoria and Despair
in the Olympic Metropolis

Anne-Marie Broudehoux

On July 13, 2001 the International Olympic Committee announced that Beijing had won the bid to host the 2008 summer Olympic Games. From that moment, the city began an ambitious overhaul that is profoundly transforming both its physical landscape and international image. As a symbol of China's world stature, Beijing promised the best Olympics ever. As the ambitious plan was carried out, it soon became clear that the 2008 games would be the most lavish ever staged, with investments of almost $40 billion: three times what Athens spent, and more than all the summer games since 1984 combined.

While other cities have monumentalized the Olympics, Beijing's megaprojects are unprecedented. After winning the bid, Beijing commissioned a series of iconic Olympic projects whose common denominators are size, ostentation, name-brand design, and cost. Beijing's Olympic transformation comes in the midst of an extraordinary building boom that is transforming China's landscape at a velocity perhaps unequaled in human history. Experts estimate that in Beijing alone, one billion square feet of offices, shops, and apartments will be added to the skyline by 2008—the equivalent of three Manhattans—totaling $160-billion worth of construction.[1] China's spectacular urban revolution now consumes one-half of the world's annual production of concrete and one-third of its steel output, pushing up world prices to the point that long-closed iron-ore mines throughout the world are now being reopened.[2]

Beijing's Olympic makeover, although larger in scale, recalls earlier bursts of intensive construction that periodically transformed its landscape throughout the twentieth century in response to major shifts in ideology. In the late 1950s, for example, Mao commissioned a series of Soviet-inspired monuments to mark the rise of a new socialist nation, while in the late 1980s, Mayor Chen Xitong tried to reassert the capital's distinctive Chinese character by imposing a neotraditional design code.[3] The new round of conspicuous construction initiated by president Jiang Zemin in sight of the Olympics underscores China's claims to great power status. It celebrates China's public emergence as an authoritarian nation fully committed to capitalism.

This latest cycle of creative destruction epitomizes a new China, where the monotonous equality of socialism has been replaced by the spectacular inequalities of capitalism. The delirious grandeur of Beijing's Olympic makeover climaxes a generation of breakneck marketization and uneven development, accompanied by increased sociospatial polarization, rampant land speculation, the proliferation of public-private partnerships, the popularity of gated communities, and the spectacularization of the urban landscape. For many, Beijing has become a paradise of opportunity, creativity, and lifestyle. But for those who are bypassed by this fast-paced modernization, the city represents a place of betrayed promises, injustice, and despair.

The Great Transformation

The staging of the Olympics itself, of course, is the primary competition, as each new host attempts to create monuments and spectacles more dazzling than those of its predecessors. Beijing has followed other aspiring world cities in exploiting the emblematic power of avant-garde architecture as cultural capital.[4] Drawing upon cutting-edge designs bearing the signature of global architectural celebrities, the city hopes to reform its world image, capturing the semiotic advantage over rival destinations through the branding of its urban skyline.[5]

The first *grand projet* with the Olympic deadline in mind and involving an international design competition was the National Theater.[6] Conceived by President Zemin as a monument to his leadership, the Theater competition was won by French airport designer Paul Andreu, despite popular protest against its futuristic eggshell design, the choice of a foreign architect, and its site next to Tiananmen Square, the symbolic heart of the nation. Critics also pointed that its $350-million price tag is ten times what the state spends yearly on poverty alleviation.

Undeterred by this controversy, Beijing announced a new series of competitions for the design of the main Olympic venues. Superstar Swiss architects Jacques Herzog and Pierre de Meuron were selected to design the National Stadium, the centerpiece Olympic project. Dubbed the "bird's nest" by locals, the stadium is being fabricated from fifty thousand tons of steel rods intertwined into a huge basketlike structure. Designed to become one of the most visible icons of contemporary China, the most striking feature of this $400-billion structure is its ability to stand without a single vertical pillar being used.[7]

Another spectacular Olympic venue is the National Swim Center, designed by PTW Architects of Australia. The building's deceptively simple steel box structure will be coated with an innovative, lightweight transparent Teflon membrane, assembled in irregular cushions, which play on the geometry of water bubbles. This envelope has been designed to act as a support upon which light and images can be projected to create a visual and sensory experience that can be shared by millions of television viewers worldwide. At a mere $100 million, this 50,000-square-meter "Watercube" will be one of the Games' cheapest venues.

A fourth Olympic project is the Beijing Wukesong Cultural and Sport Center, designed by Burckhardt and Partners from Switzerland. Described as a basketball arena that is also a hotel, a shopping mall, and a 10-story-high television screen with a $543-million price tag, the project is pure spectacle. Its four facades, made of giant LED screens, will be used for the live broadcast of events taking place inside or elsewhere in the city, as well as for advertising.

Another important Olympic project underway is the International Airport's third terminal, designed by Sir Norman Foster. This $1.9-billion modern gateway to Beijing will double the capacity of the capital airport and represents the second makeover of the airport since 1999, when a second terminal was built. Shaped as a kilometer-long dragon, it will be the largest building in the world. An army of 35,000 construction workers, working in three shifts, twenty-four hours a day, seven days a week, will ensure that it is ready for the opening of the Games.

A last and highly controversial Olympic project is the new headquarters of CCTV, China's central television network, designed by Dutch architect Rem Koolhaas. This $600-million gravity-defying trapezoidal loop, housing the party's main propaganda machine, promises to be one of the world's most technically complex buildings.[8] Apart from these projects and other venues built and upgraded for the Games, the city has also budgeted $7 billion to build new expressways, expand light rail and subway tracks, and improve urban streets and parks.

The Price of Olympic Fame

One cannot help but wonder how the Chinese government could afford such a lavish Olympic potlatch in a country where the national per capita annual income barely reaches the $1,000 mark.[9] The bulk of Beijing's Olympic funds will come from the sale of sponsorship and broadcasting rights for the Games. Since the Olympics represent a unique opportunity for companies around the world to gain visibility, especially within the exploding Chinese market, the competition for official partnership is fierce, and Beijing's Olympic income is projected to be the largest in history.[10]

The private sector is integrally involved in the construction of these Olympic venues, mostly through a build-operate-transfer system, in which private investors responsible for overseeing construction become operators for a thirty-year contract period.[11] In other words, despite being partly funded by the public sector, most Olympic facilities will be privatized and commercialized after the Games. These projects have therefore been built with their post-Olympic functions in mind. The National Swim Center, for example, was designed as an entertainment palace, complete with wave pool, artificial beach, fitness club, skating rink, cinema, restaurants, and shops. The Beijing Countryside Horse Racetrack will be turned into a golf course, while the Olympic village will be converted into a commercial residential area, with privatized facilities including an entertainment center, a convention center, and an international school. Other venues will be turned into professional sports stadiums, private health clubs, and leisure spaces for the wealthy.[12]

Most people, however, are unaware that the Olympic facilities that are being built on the ashes of their old neighborhoods will not be accessible to the general public, but will be for the exclusive benefit of China's emerging elite. The use of public-private partnerships, moreover, does not necessarily guarantee the economic success of the Games, whose most lasting legacy may still be tax increases, inflation, soaring rents, and an enormous debt that could undermine future welfare investments. As in previous Olympic cities, the benefits from public investments in the Games will likely be enjoyed by private entrepreneurs, while Olympic costs, both social and financial, will be borne by those at the bottom of the economic ladder.[13]

Part of what makes Beijing's Olympic construction truly extraordinary is that, despite its spectacular price tag, the construction cost of most Olympic projects was deceptively low, compared to what it would have been elsewhere. One of the conditions that made it possible for Beijing to afford building more than a dozen brand-name landmarks for the Olympics was its exploitation of a vast, pliant, and disposable labor force. Construction costs in China are notoriously low thanks to China's vast army of migrant workers (an estimated 94 million), who enjoy few rights in the city and are easily exploited by greedy contractors. Paid an average of $4.87 a day, they work seven days a week and live in makeshift barracks on the construction site. It is not uncommon to hear of workers who are owed over a year's worth of back wages, or have been injured and received no compensation.[14] China's construction boom has left a tangle of debts among developers, contractors, and subcontractors that often results in workers not getting a paycheck. The Chinese government has estimated unpaid migrant wages for 2003 alone at an extraordinary $12.1 billion.[15]

The Olympic boom has only made conditions worse for many workers, and violence against superiors, destruction of property, and mass protests by migrant workers are becoming increasingly common.[16] Suicides by jumping off high-rise buildings are becoming so prevalent among unpaid construction workers that a Mandarin expression, *tiao lou xiu* (literally, jumping off buildings to show), now denominates these desperate attempts to draw attention to their plight.

Another reason why Beijing could afford to splurge on such extravagant Olympic projects is that most of the land on which they are built was acquired well below market value, thanks to the state's ability to confiscate land in the name of the public interest. The Geneva-based Centre on Housing Rights and Eviction estimates that by 2004, 300,000 citizens had been uprooted and saw their homes demolished to make way for Olympic facilities and infrastructure projects in Beijing.[17]

Both the exploitation of migrant workers and the mass eviction of residents are facilitated by China's paradoxical status as a market economy led by an authoritarian state. Local party and government officials use their power to exploit provisions in the Chinese legislation that allow land confiscation, and then make a fortune leasing this land to private developers.[18] Residents are given a month's notice to leave and are offered compensation at a fraction of their property's value. People, of course, often resist eviction, but in the face of coercion, even violence, have no choice but to comply. Demolition companies hired by developers to clear the land prior to redevelopment routinely hire eviction squads to force "stubborn nails" or recalcitrant residents to leave. Some of their tactics include disconnecting utilities or deliberately damaging parts of a house so as to render it uninhabitable.

Every day groups of angry residents gather to petition the government over the demolition of their homes, and thousands have filed lawsuits against unfair evictions. But China's current legal system subordinates the interests of displaced residents to those of the rich and powerful. Lawsuits are rarely heard in court, and protesters are routinely intimidated into dropping charges, by being detained, harassed, or put under police surveillance. In addition, several lawyers protecting the rights of evicted residents have been arrested and charged with bogus allegations such as stealing state secrets.[19]

Residents who resist are also sometimes physically threatened and beaten by demolition squads. In one case, thugs conducted a night raid on a house in Beijing, tied up the family, and demolished their home, leaving their possessions buried in the ruins.[20] Such intimidation discourages residents from speaking to the media or complaining to authorities. Amnesty International's annual report for 2004 highlights the prevalence of such abuses—a human-rights embarrassment for the Chinese authorities.[21] In addition to the trauma of being ruthlessly uprooted from their homes, displaced Beijingers face increased costs of living due to their relocation far away from former schools, jobs, and services. Property prices around the Olympic Park have also risen dramatically, making it less affordable for people to live near the city center.

The sense of dislocation and social upheaval caused by widespread demolitions and the psychological impact of living in constant fear of eviction is taking its toll on Beijingers, especially older residents. The loss of beloved homes and communities is compounded by the distress of being powerless and disenfranchised. Indeed, the problem has reached such extent that several people have committed suicide in public to protest their eviction.[22] A famous case is the story of the Ye brothers. On October 1, 2003, China's National Day, Ye Guoqiang tried to kill himself by jumping off a bridge in the historic Forbidden City in front of hundreds of onlookers to protest the forced demolition of his family's home and restaurant and the unfair compensation received. Ye Guoqiang survived the jump but received a two-year prison sentence for "disturbing the social order." His brother, Ye Guozhu, was also briefly jailed and their eighty-year-old father was allegedly roughed up by the local police.[23] Having lost their home and their livelihood, the family squatted in a pedestrian underpass, working with a lawyer to obtain rightful compensation for their loss. While Ye Guozhu continued to organize local residents to fight unfair evictions, his family was constantly harassed by the police, who tried to persuade Ye to drop the case. In August 2004, after applying for permission to hold a mass protest against forced evictions in the capital, Ye Guozhu was jailed for four years, having been found guilty of "picking quarrels and stirring up trouble."[24]

The Great Divide

Social polarization has become an explosive issue in twenty-first-century China, constantly exacerbated by relentless urban redevelopment.[25] While liberalization has proved highly efficient in generating wealth, the benefits have not been shared equally, and the gap between rich and poor, urban and rural is constantly widening.[26] Economic growth has been accompanied by inflation and rising prices, and lower standards of living for the very poor. In many instances, new wealth is generated at the direct expense of the poor, as local governments evict residents and sell off the land for private development projects.[27]

Once egalitarian, China has now become one of the world's most unequal societies: the divide between rich and poor, in fact, is now greater than before the 1949 revolution, and the poverty rate is now higher in China's cities than in the countryside.[28] In June 2005, the Chinese leadership announced that poverty levels in China had risen for the first time since 1978, and that the richest 10 percent of the population now controlled 45 percent of the country's wealth, while the poorest tenth held little more than 1 percent.[29] The Chinese Academy of Social Sciences estimates that at least 10,000 businesspeople in China have net assets that exceed $10 million.[30]

One of Beijing's most famous *nouveaux riches* is Zhang Yuchen, a Communist Party member and former senior official at Beijing's municipal construction bureau, turned real-estate developer. Zhang made his fortune in the 1990s building China's first luxury ranch-style homes in a Beijing suburb. In 2001, having secured rights to a parcel of wheat fields in suburban Beijing, Zhang built a $50-million copy of the famous Château Maisons-Laffitte, designed by François Mansart in 1650. Château Zhang-Laffitte is now a five-star hotel surrounded by exclusive homes that share its manicured sculpture garden, equestrian trails, and golf course. A deep moat and a spiked iron fence circle the perimeter of the castle and bar access to all but authorized workers and guests.

The eight hundred residents of Yangge Village, who used to farm the land and to grow wheat collectively until local leaders sold the parcel to Zhang, have lost their livelihood and must now buy their grain, vegetables, and meat at the local market. Local leaders had promised to use the sale of the property to fund local companies, shares of which would be distributed to all who had farmed the land. But the promise was never honored. Instead, Zhang's company currently gives the village's elderly a $45 monthly stipend, while the young can apply for jobs maintaining the grounds and waterways of the estate, or crushing grapes from its vineyard, for a mere $2 a day.[31] Anger is mounting among the disgruntled peasants who continue their tireless campaign for fair compensation. (In China as a whole, the government itself admits that at least 40 million farmers have lost land to urban-industrial or infrastructural development.)[32]

Social tension across China is compounded by growing awareness that wealth is too often linked to corruption. A recent study of China's twenty thousand richest people found that only 5 percent had made it on their own merit, and that more than 90 percent had connections to senior government or Party officials.[33] Increasingly protests by have-nots escalate into full-fledged riots, even local insurrections. A famous example took place in 2005 in Anhui province, where a student was savagely beaten by private bodyguards after his bicycle crashed into a wealthy businessman's car. A vehement crowd of ten thousand filled the streets, and outraged residents torched police cars, threw stones at antiriot troops, and looted a nearby supermarket.[34]

As similar clashes between rich and poor become more common, China's new economic elite is seeking refuge in American-style gated communities. Initially built for foreign expatriates, who, for fear of ideological contamination, were not allowed to live in the same housing compounds as Chinese nationals, these segregated residential districts are now getting increasingly popular with China's new rich, especially on the outskirts of Beijing.

When regulations requiring the separation of foreign and local residents were relaxed and sale restrictions were lifted in 2003, domestic buyers flocked into the previously foreign housing market for its high-quality, single detached homes with full property rights.[35] The gated compounds offered the possibility of a prestigious and opulent first-world lifestyle, including swimming pools, fitness centers, tennis courts, bowling alleys, cinemas, and other privatized neighborhood services such as restaurants, business centers, and apartment cleaning services. Another key attraction for Beijing's local elite with cosmopolitan aspirations is the concentration of other world-class facilities: international hospitals, shopping malls and superstores, as well as the international school.

But, more than anything, what such communities offer to white-collar retirees and successful young professionals is a comfortable distance from the "other China" that is increasingly perceived as backward, hostile, and dangerous. Just like their counterparts in the capitalist world, Beijing's nouveaux riches seek to escape the capital's downtown pollution, noise, high density, and visible social polarization. They are also attracted by the perceived security afforded by gated communities, guarded by video surveillance and patrolling security agents. In some residences, security cards are required for entering the compound, the building, the elevator, and the apartment.

These fortified havens for the rich and connected allow their residents to emulate the lifestyle of the global bourgeoisie and to partake in an imagined cosmopolitanism. Bearing exotic names such as Orange County, French Riviera, or La Firenza, these imported dreamscapes are often designed by foreign architects, in a nostalgia-tinged neotraditional urbanism. The popularity enjoyed by gated communities also reflects their residents' desire to escape the local reality and to isolate themselves to enjoy their newfound wealth.[36] While entirely dependent on the labor of migrant workers, China's rising economic elite is constantly trying to limit their presence by creating new segregated social worlds. The price of such properties effectively excludes all but the very rich: homes at Orange County sell for about $975 per square meter, while the average per capita disposable income in Beijing is only $1,447 a year.[37]

Although they are daily confronted with China's enduring poverty as they commute through the urban fringes in their air-conditioned cars and exclusive shuttle buses, the emerging bourgeoisie is oblivious to the plight of their poorer counterparts. Its sense of social solidarity has been replaced by a jealous desire to protect its newly acquired wealth and a total absence of class guilt.[38] Yet despite blatant inequality, discussion of class is uncommon in contemporary China. The official declaration that class struggle was no longer relevant for China after the Cultural Revolution has hindered the creation of a public discourse on economic inequality and prevented social exclusion from becoming a focus of analysis or politics. In fact, China's rapid economic growth had a perverse effect on democratization: it has reduced pressure on the ruling elite to liberalize and seek political reforms. Reluctant to part with power, now easily convertible into wealth and privilege, they would rather enjoy the status quo.[39]

A Social Time Bomb

But disparities are becoming harder to ignore as farmers whose land is confiscated to build exclusive residential projects increasingly take their complaints to the street.[40] Chinese authorities are visibly worried about the potentially explosive consequences of unruly development. Disputes over land have led to violent clashes, and public anger over confiscations and evictions increasingly raises questions about national stability.[41] The Chinese Construction Ministry recently admitted having received three times as many complaints in the first quarter of 2004 as in the same period the previous year: by the end of June, 4,000 groups and more than 18,600 individuals throughout China had lodged petitions over allegedly illicit land transfers.[42]

All over China, public expressions of discontent are increasingly heard from the millions who have lost homes, jobs, health care, and pensions. According to government reports, 3.76 million Chinese in 2004 were involved in 74,000 "mass incidents," or an average of 203 a day, a tenfold increase over a decade earlier.[43] While tensions over the widening income gap, falling social services, nepotism, corruption, and self-serving alliances between party leaders and businessmen have increased, land-related disputes remain the chief engine of social disturbances in contemporary China.[44] Demonstrations have become near-daily occurrences in the countryside, as farmers protest loss of land to development as well as excessive taxation.

The centrality of land equity issues is hardly accidental. Land redistribution was one of the core tenets of the 1949 Revolution, and much new wealth and corruption arises from real-estate development and speculation.[45] Property that was once seized from rich landlords and redistributed to the poor is now being taken from the poor and passed on to developers and enterprising local governments. For many, these transactions represent a breach in a social contract that has linked China's masses and the Communist Party since 1949. Anger stems not just from the loss of livelihood and residence but especially from the violation of a fundamental citizenship right. This deep feeling of injustice is likely to erode much of the popular allegiance that the Party still retains among the underprivileged.

Containing Chaos

Chinese officials are acutely aware that growing social unrest can undermine economic development, threaten national stability and, ultimately, weaken the party's grip on power. A November 2004 editorial published by China's official news agency tacitly suggests that the nation is at a social "crossroads" that could lead to a "golden age of development" or a "contradictions-stricken age of chaos."[46] Such surprisingly candid admissions testify to the important changes that took place in China's leadership in September 2004, as Hu Jintao gained full power following Jiang Zemin's resignation as head of the Chinese military.

Presented as populist, pragmatic, and transparent, Hu's government immediately initiated a series of measures to address mounting tensions and appease social discontent. Among other things, the state publicly vowed to slow land confiscations, reduce demolitions, and ordered a freeze on the conversion of agricultural land to industrial use.[47] The Chinese parliament also announced its plan to abolish the country's long-standing agricultural taxes, putting an end to a levy that had burdened China's farmers for 2,600 years. To demonstrate its concern over growing inequalities, and to focus public attention on its poverty-alleviation programs, the Chinese leadership also embarked on a "harmonious society" propaganda campaign that emphasized awareness of the country's widening income gap.[48] Upon close examination, however, these highly publicized initiatives and rhetorical statements proved to be no more than symbolic gestures meant to dissipate anger and alleviate resentment. They did nothing to address fundamental problems faced by China's poor, and, without proper political reforms, they are unlikely to be implemented by increasingly predatory local governments now accustomed to turn their unchecked power to their own advantages.

Similarly, to muffle public criticism of the state's Olympic program and appease mounting popular anxieties about the use of public funds to build vanity projects in the nation's capital, Hu's government called for a complete reassessment of Olympic preparations, after it was revealed that Athens had exceeded its Olympic budget by 30 percent. Several venues were scaled down and their construction deadlines were pushed back a year. But once again, most changes were symbolic and appeared to be motivated more by a desire to assuage tensions than by a true commitment to financial austerity. None of the modifications dramatically affected the projects.[49] Cost-cutting measures were accompanied by a change in the Olympic rhetoric as authorities began to talk about a "frugal and prudent" games, and sought to revive popular enthusiasm for the Olympics by recasting the event as "the people's games."[50]

In its attempt to divert attention away from the nation's most pressing problems, the Hu government increasingly uses the Olympics as a propaganda tool to promote national cohesion and rally an increasingly divided people around a grand patriotic endeavor.[51] The spectacular preparations surrounding the 2008 Olympic Games also serve as an instrument of pacification by mystifying Chinese citizens through a grandiose spectacle celebrating China's rise as a world power.[52]

Such instrumental use of the Games could prove to be a double-edged sword. As the Olympics grow near, the state is obviously wary that different interest groups may use the international media presence generated by the Games as a platform to make their plights heard. Authorities know that violent demonstrations could pose a serious threat to the operation of the Games, as was the case in Mexico City in 1968, and in Seoul in 1988, when students took advantage of the Olympics to lead major protests shortly before the Games.[53] While an incident-free Olympics could cause a shift in worldwide opinion in favor of China, any violence associated with the Games would generate negative media coverage and compromise the state's costly image construction efforts.

In the face of such eventuality, simple diversion tactics and symbolic pacification may prove insufficient to control public protests, while violent repression on the part of the state would compromise the carefully orchestrated event.[54] The Chinese government will thus have to resort to more devious ways to suppress dissent. Recent repression against outspoken journalists, cyberdissidents, critical writers, liberal intellectuals, labor activists, and socially engaged lawyers has instilled a climate of fear throughout China, which seeks to intimidate potential protesters and encourage self-policing. Hu Jintao's deceptive public image as a people-centered, benevolent leader may prove to conceal a more sinister ruler, intent not on addressing China's endemic problems but on maintaining the new bourgeoisie's grip on power.

Conclusion: Evil Beijing

The Olympic Games will play a watershed role in transforming postsocialist Beijing, both physically and politically. They act as a developmental engine, legitimating large-scale urban transformations and giving the government a license to reprioritize the urban agenda. Preparations for the Olympics have already exacerbated the inequalities arising from China's rapid transition to capitalism. The national image of prosperity that is being constructed for the Games is built on the backs of the poor, who are doubly taxed, first by the diversion of public funds for monumental projects, and then by their direct exploitation as workers or evictees. Those who will pay for the Games through self-sacrifice and underfunded social services will not be the ones who reap the benefits. What the masses can expect to gain from the Games are more evictions, tax increases, inflation, restricted civil liberties, and shrunken welfare programs.[55]

As the Olympic deadline approaches, a new, dazzling city emerges from behind the cranes and construction fences. For some, it is a city of endless possibilities, offering the promise of a bright future. The spectacular rise of this new metropolis has succeeded in diverting public attention from the human tragedies that take place in its shadow. In despair, those marginalized by Beijing's transformation have also turned to the spectacle as a way to attract attention to their plight— by holding public protests, jumping off buildings, or through self-immolation. But their dramatic displays of misery and grief look like pathetic sideshows in the face of Olympic grandeur.

For the most critical, this new delirious Beijing is a city of competing egos, of selfish opportunism, and of betrayed promises. It is a city without urbanity, where megalomaniacal architectural objects are built on the ashes of an organic urban fabric. This new metropolis mirrors the society that builds and inhabits it: an increasingly individualist society that willfully sacrifices a more cohesive one, where a predatory elite of private entrepreneurs, technocrats, and party members preys on a disenfranchised and vulnerable populace. A city glittering on the surface but hollow at the core: a truly evil paradise.

"Palm Springs": Imagineering California in Hong Kong

Laura Ruggeri

Palm Springs, of course, is a famous, star-studded resort town in the desert 110 miles east of Los Angeles. But it is also the name of an upscale gated community near Yuen Long in Hong Kong. An imagined—or, rather, *imagineered*—California lifestyle has become a distinctive trope of the emergent culture of conspicuous consumption in contemporary China, and decoding the meaning of "Palm Springs" can teach us much about the dynamics of postrevolutionary social inequality as well as about the processes of urban mythmaking in general.

The Return of the Walled City

Social inequality in Hong Kong is obvious and spatial segregation is an old story. The British, for example, chose to live on the Peak, distancing themselves as far as possible from ordinary Chinese and the diseases that plagued lower-elevation, less salubrious areas. Their imposing residencies were closely policed and access to Peak Road was granted only to servants and Chinese notables. Walled villages were also a common feature of precolonial Hong Kong and, to a minor extent, of the colonial city as well. A few of these villages can still be seen in the New Territories, now converted into museums and tourist attractions. Walls both reflect and maintain hierarchical human relationships; they divide the sacred from the profane, the civilized from the barbaric (e.g., the Great Wall), and safety from danger. But whereas the residents of traditional walled villages belonged to a clan and shared common ancestors, the inhabitants of the new gated communities share only the dream of living in a safe and socially homogeneous environment, preferably in an imaginary part of California.

Gated subdivisions are a recent strategy of status in Hong Kong. Formerly, the closer one approached the (spatial) top and center, the greater one's social status; inversely, power and prestige diminished as one moved toward the periphery. This obsession with the "center" led to an extraordinary concentration of density in what is improperly described as the "business district." The gated suburb challenges this traditional fetish of centrality as well as the preference for verticality, which means the top floors are always the most prestigious and desirable.

Developers, of course, benefit greatly from the recent suburbanization of wealth. Profits are highest when otherwise unattractive lots at the edge of city, usually of low market value, are transformed into prestigious enclaves. The old advantages of proximity are replaced by the new cult of isolation, and the negative characteristics of a dreary, hard-to-reach location are alchemized into the advantages of "security" and "open space." Indeed, gated communities can be conjured into existence almost anywhere, independent of context or history. Often the immediate neighbors of the new affluence are old squatters' settlements, impoverished rural surroundings, landfills, and wastelands. In part, this is the perverse result of modern zoning, which has dictated low-rise or medium-density construction in the New Territories, thus encouraging developers to think of alternative strategies of profit maximization to the traditional thirty-story tower blocks. Elite, themepark communities provide an alluring solution.

Gates not only protect leisure amenities such as golf courses, swimming pools, and tennis courts, but also economic and social status as they provide points of coherence around which the residents can organize social experience into meaningful patterns. Property developers are able to construct new landscapes of power, dreamscapes for visual consumption, using designer reconstructions of spatially remote objects and lifestyles: the Spanish villa, the Roman column, the clubhouse, etc. The use of American or European elements in order

to sell all types of commodities is a very common practice in China; they are cod-
ified as something conferring high status.

Gated communities, fashioned after their American counterparts, have become a standardized product, like cars or television sets, offered in a finite range
of models. The same developer, Sun Hung Kai Properties, has developed an almost identical enclave just a mile away from Palm Springs, and called it Royal
Palms. Sun Hung Kai is also involved in similar projects across the Chinese border and in the Philippines.

The advertising material I have examined shows a conscious appropriation of
the idea of community by the developer. The concept of community has been
commodified, marketed whole-cloth and in standardized units, like any other
consumer product. However, these are not communities in the sociological
sense, because rather than constructing rich networks of relationships, residents
tend to isolate themselves in their homes.

New, exclusive enclaves such as Palm Springs are underwritten by an explicit
marketing text, a strategy of "place advertisement" that is accentuated by postmodern architectural "imagineering" that defines a commodity laden with mythical content. Images and texts are inseparable from the commodity system in
which residential developments such as Palm Springs exist. In Palm Springs, both
the direct advertising message and the motifs of landscape form are received and
retransmitted as cultural signals by those who live there. A dreamscape is conjured up by the means of space compression—one can experience California, the
epicenter of global image and fantasy, without leaving home. Palm Springs becomes the base camp for an adventure of the imagination, an imagination that often feeds on films and TV programs.

Representational techniques rely on certain visual codes to construct the subjects' experience. My argument is that the way residents of Palm Springs perceive
and organize perceptions of their living environment presupposes familiarity
with a cinematic culture that extends across a larger landscape of technologies,
media influences, and social relationships. The developers of Palm Springs made
a conscious attempt to translate this cinematic imagery into 3-D form. California,
a place that enjoys an almost mythical status among Hong Kong residents, is pre-

sented as the site of a wholesome life, upward social mobility, unfettered consumerism, and traditional family values. The appeal of Palm Springs relies on cultural codes that are by and large produced elsewhere, imported into Hong Kong,
and here naturalized. Prospective, individual buyers are interpellated as East-
meets-West pastiche subjects; they respond to an ideology that mixes Orientalist
cliches (supposedly anchoring the experience to a familiar locale) with Hollywood narratives of the American Dream.

A gated, themed compound like Palm Springs, moreover, can be understood
as a type of "cultural interface." In Lev Manovich's interpretation, interfaces are
cultural objects that we can understand because they are built on the language
and metaphors of things we are already familiar with.[1] As interface, Palm Springs
is more than a simple location. It is a shrine to its message, and in order to succeed
it must be bounded and isolated from the ordinary landscape. Unlike American
gated communities, where security is often regarded as a chief concern by residents, in Hong Kong the fence and the gate serve to separate the inside from the
outside, rather than keep the "undesirables" out. Gates heighten the sense of spatial distinction. By establishing the simulation of an ideal, separated environment
within, they protect its economic and symbolic value. Living behind gates, protected by armed security guards, constitutes a prestige factor, separating the truly
rich from the merely well-off. Palm Springs ushers in the new (cosmetic) style of
"real imitation life," the Californian lifestyle, which can be imported like any
other commodity.

Saturday Night and Sunday Morning

My friends the Chans have invited me to their barbecue party. From a bus stop located in front of the Star Ferry Terminal in Central, I catch the shuttle bus that
will take me to their home at Palm Springs, in the New Territories. The journey
takes approximately forty-five minutes, during which we pass Kwai Chung freight
container station, several car demolition sites, industrial estates, illegal dumping
sites, and an endless row of girlie bars. When we finally arrive at the gate of Palm
Springs, two men in uniform ask the passengers to produce a proof of identity.
As I do not carry any identification document, I am requested to wait inside the

guard post, while they inform the Chans of my arrival. When Mr. Chan finally comes to my aid, he greets me by saying, "Welcome to Palm Springs. Did you really think you could travel to California without a passport?"

We drive through a maze of identical avenues and streets, all named after Californian towns. He turns down Santa Monica Avenue, then turns again on Sacramento followed by Napa. After covering most of California in less than five minutes, we finally reach Orchid Path, off Monterey Avenue, where the Chans live. Eva is waiting for us in front of their white and pink, three-story house. Saturday night barbecue is a collective ritual; smoke fills the air as hundreds of Palm Springs residents grill pork ribs, king prawns, and cuttlefish in their back gardens.

Before the customary mah-jongg game, Mr. Chan invites me to climb up to the rooftop, from where he says I can enjoy a "spectacular view." The roof is partly occupied by a small prefab shed where their Filipino maid sleeps with neither light nor air conditioning—thousands of foreign domestic workers in Hong Kong live in similar hovels. Mr. Chan wants to show me the view that stretches across the Chinese border, which is only a few miles away from Palm Springs. We gaze upon the edge of what has become the largest industrial concentration in the world, the Pearl River Delta. The sky is incredibly bright, but the moon plays little part in it. Here the night is turned into day by the neon signs of Shenzhen, whose skyscrapers rival those of Hong Kong. When I decide to leave, it is past midnight, already too late to catch the last shuttle bus. Luckily the Chans invite me to spend the night in their daughter's room.

Sunday morning at Palm Springs produces some surprises. My suggestion to go for *yám cha* (Cantonese expression for *dim sum*) is received with stupor. My hosts hastily explain that there are no *dim sum* restaurants in Palm Springs, and that those outside are not worth the effort. We have breakfast in the garden: cereals, croissants, and French baguettes served with butter and jam. It is my first continental breakfast since I moved to Hong Kong, and I am not particularly happy to trade delicious shrimp dumplings for frozen baguettes. But one would be wrong to assume that the Chans have gone out of their way to make me feel at home. Their neighbors, who have no western guest, are enjoying the same type of breakfast in the adjacent garden. Only a very old man (the grandfather?)

is served a bowl of *congee* and what looks like chicken liver. I suppose the American lifestyle fails to capture the imagination of the elderly.

Later, we watch Mr. Chan play tennis and stroll through the community theme-park, where Disney characters are surrounded by mock Greek columns and neo-classical pavilions. Everybody seems to be wearing Ralph Lauren polo shirts, khaki shorts, and immaculate white trainers: "smart casual," they call it here. The settlement is guarded by armed Gurkhas, recruited among the thousands laid off by the British army in 1997. By a strange irony, some of their present employers are likely to be the same "illegal immigrants," now wealthy homeowners, they once tried to prevent from entering the colony. On leaving Palm Springs I have to check out at the guard post.

An hour later I am walking in Wanchai. The contrast couldn't be more striking: I jostle in the crowd, among the wavering fumes of diesel and cooking oil, weaving between and among bodies, and brushing against different textures. This is an electric city, whose "smellscapes" and "soundscapes" are as exciting, rich, and varied as its skyline. Coping with the city, its sultry heat, the jumbled mix of pungent aromas—a veritable "olfactory geography"—and the combination of noises generated by numerous human activities, my body comes to life, roused by the resistance which it experiences. A gigantic billboard displays pictures of a busy street market, a Chinese junk, two rickshaws, and Pei's Bank of China; the caption reads "The city owes its liveliness to the movements of life that unfold in the streets. Hong Kong. City of Life." This is the (fast-disappearing) city promoted by the tourist board, an orientalist cliché. Roland Barthes once observed that it is the peculiar mixture of bells, rickshaws, and opium dens that constitute "China" for a European. Myths die hard, especially when they are reappropriated for marketing purposes. The Chans have traded this orientalist cliché for another cliché, the "American Dream."

Selling California

The Chans moved to Palm Springs in 1991, when major construction works were still under way. They said they felt almost like pioneers. According to the photos they showed me, the development was a far cry from the computer-simulated images that had captured their imagination six months earlier. Construction rubble still surrounded their semidetached, three-bedroom house, and the newly planted palm trees looked unhealthy and unpromising. Orchid Path had not yet been paved. They had moved with their teenage daughter and a Filipina domestic from their small flat in urbane North Point to what was still regarded by most people as a borderland, neither picturesque nor healthy. Local farmers had already realized that they could make a better living by renting their plots to car demolishers or by turning them into dumping sites or container parks. Moreover the location was only a stone's throw away from the People's Republic, surrounded by barracks and (then) British soldiers. Many people would scarcely consider the move a sound decision, but the Chans (whom a sociologist would describe as "upwardly mobile middle class") had been lured by an irresistible fantasy.

The Chans, like many residents of Palm Springs, were not born in Hong Kong, and their dreamworld reflects many of the classical anxieties of immigrants. Indeed the hinging of class status upon house type, tenure, and location is particularly pronounced in immigrant cultures with significant quotients of social mobility. In a fluid, immigrant society that lacks visible and established class or caste structures, other markers are introduced to delineate the social order and communicate its meaning. Thus in Palm Springs, both the direct advertising message (as in the glossy brochures that the Chans showed me) and the motifs of the landscape transmit powerful cultural signals.

Sun Hung Kai Properties promoted Palm Springs (a 286,740-square-meter development, whose 374 units are arranged as terraced and semidetached three-story houses) the way most developers do in Hong Kong, by advertising on TV, newspapers, popular magazines, and on large billboards placed in central Hong Kong. The Chans then went to look at the models, computer simulations, and videos that were being shown in an upmarket shopping mall. There they were treated to a variety show hosted by a well-known TV personality, who repeatedly hinted at the fact that some Canton Pop stars were planning to move to Palm Springs "as it had been rumored." They, then, enjoyed some complimentary refreshments, and took part in a drawing for a holiday in the "real" California. According to them, it was an "exciting experience, a bit like being in a TV show." From the beginning they were made to feel part of a dreamworld, were welcomed with large smiles, shook hands with celebrities, and were dazed by the glitz and glitter.

They also read a brochure that boasted: "We bring to Hong Kong the look, feel and beauty of southern California. You can hear gentle laughter as you walk along the streets and sense the warmth of your neighborhood as it welcomes you with open arms. Palm Springs has been designed with quality of life in mind. That's why the atmosphere here will enchant you. There are palm-lined streets and picturesque scenery. You'll also marvel at the dancing fountains, colorful flowers, nostalgic lampposts, and street sculptures. All of it created to give you a sense of well-being and happiness."

A dreamscape is conjured up by the means of space compression: one can experience California without leaving home. Names such as Palm Springs conjure the memory of alternative geographies, making the lived experience of the urban increasingly vicarious, screened through simulacra, those exact copies for which the original has been lost. In fact, as Edward Soja points out, California itself has come to resemble "a gigantic agglomeration of themeparks, a lifespace comprised of Disneyworlds. It is a realm divided into showcases of global village cultures and mimetic American landscapes, filled with whimsy and pastiche."[2]

The reference to "nostalgic lampposts and street sculptures," ubiquitous in shopping malls, again, reinscribes the urban in a purely aesthetic form. The picture at the bottom of the text shows a red phone booth and looks rather idiosyncratic even in this context. The British icon may be suggesting that Palm Springs residents are British passport holders—much coveted in those days and a prestige symbol in certain social circles—or it may simply quote the colonial past as a decorative element, infused with nostalgia.

Further on the brochure recites: "Unlike communities anywhere else in Hong Kong, Palm Springs presents a total concept in living. This includes community activities and celebrations that bring everyone together to share happy moments and events. We have brought back the real meaning of neighborhood. . . . Feel the burdens of the day melt away as you go from your work mood to playtime.

Enjoy yourself in the refreshing and relaxing atmosphere of the Clubhouse, where your heart and soul are reborn. It is all a clear reflection of the true easygoing Californian lifestyle." The language used is both lyrical and evocative. Ways of living are objectified as "lifestyle" and the Californian lifestyle is made myth. Palm Springs is presented as not only "merely a place to live"—that is, to reside— but also the stage upon which one may practice the "art of living" while following the proposed script: "Loosen your necktie, toss aside the suit and the Rolex, and see just how wonderful life is."

As the rigidities of established social distinction become increasingly hard to sustain in eras of rapid social and physical mobility, new forms of distinction are continually being elaborated. The gated community is also described as a world apart, a holiday resort to which one can retreat every day. Vacation is therefore not a break with home life but an integral part of it. Palm Springs is depicted as a sophisticated club where one can enjoy a "total way of life." In Hong Kong, where leisure activities are seen as ways of accumulating or losing distinction, being a member of a golf or tennis club immediately bespeaks one's socioeconomic status.

One Happy Family

Another brochure is organized as a photo album: "a collection of the most exciting, memorable moments" of the "happiness and harmony" supposedly enjoyed by Palm Springs residents. Its declared aim is to offer "an unforgettable picture of the real California lifestyle." Buying a house in Palm Springs, it claims, enables anyone to become a welcome member of what is portrayed as a happy extended family, and thus escape the anonymity and isolation that supposedly characterize urban life. The idea of the "community as extended family" could be particularly appealing to many Hong Kong citizens who look at the traditional Chinese extended family with a sense of nostalgia. Due to migration, diaspora, and family planning, large families have become a thing of the past.

The album portrays parents playing with their children in the swimming pool, and children in a drawing class sketching images of the dream homes in which they live. In fact, there has been little research on children growing up in gated communities. Are their childhoods truly as idyllic as represented? Gated communities produce new and stronger forms of ideological control and social engineering. This is a particular concern for children who have not themselves chosen such totalizing controls and have a right to grow up in a public community. The eradication of difference within such enclaves may also breed intolerance and homogeneity. I suspect, together with Kim Dovey, that they might "produce and reproduce a generation stunted in their abilities to deal with a diverse and problematic world."[3]

A section of this same brochure cum photo album is devoted to traditional Chinese celebrations such as the Mid-Autumn Festival, during which Palm Springs hosts a variety show and singing performances. Under the full moon, parents and their children carry lanterns and stroll along the enclave's avenues. Another photo shows a Halloween party: "Every child looks cute and creative in his special costume." The juxtaposition of the two holidays seems to suggest that Palm Springs residents respect and uphold their Chinese traditions, but are nonetheless open to Western influences.

The promotional material presents the image of an island to which one can return every day, an escape from the city and its deteriorating environment where one can encounter an exclusive world of pleasure among peers. To convey the message that Palm Springs is a healthy and green environment, many pictures show community members involved in tree planting, natural-food-products sales, and recycling activities. The photo album is sprinkled with words like "village," "community," and "cozy" to suggest a friendliness and a manageable scale that is allegedly missing outside: "Under the radiance of sunshine, swaying palms, and lush greenery, friends call out and greet you warmly. We have created a truly harmonious neighborhood."

Both isolation and distance from the city are presented as solutions to the problem of achieving a better lifestyle. The city is demonized to the same degree that the enclave is utopianized. Structurally and semiotically, moreover, the gated community has similarities to the themepark and shopping mall. All establish a simulation of an ideal environment and enforce totalizing codes of behavior in order to construct such ideal imagery and to protect it as economic and symbolic value.

Palm Springs is also depicted as a paradise for car owners. Despite the forty-five-minute drive to the city center, the development is advertised as "close to the city." "Driving enthusiasts will love to take the car out for a spin. With the wind in your hair and the sun in your face, the trip to work will seem all too short." In fact, Palm Springs is not served by public buses or trains, and car ownership is a virtual requirement for residence in a city with notorious pollution and massive traffic jams.

Residents are well advised to cherish individuality in their automobiles since they are forbidden by ornate covenants and restrictions from altering or customizing their residences. In Palm Springs—like in most of its American counterparts—all homeowners belong to a residents' association that rigorously enforces obedience to uniformity of appearance and lifestyle. "No owner," reads the rules, "shall make alteration to the structure, installation, or fixtures of their unit, nor alter the facade or external appearance. No owner shall erect or affix any signs, advertisements, shades, or other protections or structures whatsoever extending outside their unit. No owner shall keep any dog, cat, live poultry, birds, or animals in their unit if the same has been the cause of complaint by another owner. No owner shall affix or install his own private aerial outside their unit. Facilities can only be used by residents and by no more than one of their bona fide visitors."

Security in Palm Springs is impressive but not broadcast with the same emphasis as you would expect in a comparable U.S. enclave. The brochures that I have examined seem to deliberately downplay the "armed-response" dimension of a gated lifestyle: only discreetly displaying on the very last pages a few small photos of Gurkha guards standing next to their Alsatians or driving four-wheel-drive SUVs. If Americans flock to gated enclaves because they are terrified by crime and its impact on property values, Hong Kong residents seem more interested in the promise of a socially homogenous, friendly, and fashionable neighborhood. Indeed some of my informants complained that the cost of maintaining private twenty-four-hour surveillance was too high, especially given nearby military and police barracks. However, they also feel that "times have changed" and that "Hong Kong has become much less safe than previously." In spite of the fact that reported crime rates have not substantially increased, their environment fosters a perception of increased peril. As Mike Davis has argued, "Fear proves itself: the social perception of threat becomes a function of the security mobilization, not crime rates."[4]

Conclusion

Palm Springs achieves coherence by drawing on a widely shared myth, California. Heterogeneous elements ultimately conflate: one can walk past mock Greek columns and a giant Mickey Mouse, signs printed in Art Deco typefaces, palm trees next to a neoclassical pavilion, British phone boxes and Chinese lanterns. In a way, this is typically Hong Kong. As the anthropologist Gordon Mathews (himself born in the former Crown Colony) astutely observes: "The Hongkongese had to invent their identity, neither Chinese nor British, they had no choice but going lifestyle shopping in the global cultural supermarket."[5] Indeed, in Hong Kong it is no longer possible to distinguish what is local and what is not.

Or perhaps it is more accurate to say that it is the transnational that is authentically local. Hong Kong constitutes one of the world's most heterogenous cultural environments: its citizens experts in the transnational idioms of fashion, sports, music, clothing, cuisine, and travel. Imported gated lifestyles are both an expression of Hong Kong's constitutive trendiness and a paradoxical attempt to transcend the anxieties of cosmopolitanism. Palm Springs, like other theme-parks, lies at the threshold between the chaotic, often conflicting forces of the everyday and the almost tongue-in-cheek simulation of an orderly world. Since the myth enshrined is supposed to be beyond the influence of history, the landscape appears to be frozen in some vague period, 1950s and 1960s America as nostalgically recreated in internationally popular TV serials such as *Happy Days* and movies like *American Graffiti*. The gated community offers Hong Kong's and China's nervous new elites a socially sanctioned passport to a never-never land that calls itself California.

Johannesburg:
Of Gold and Gangsters

Patrick Bond

What's in a Name?

Johannesburg is the setting for the film *Tsotsi*, meaning "gangster." Based on a 1960 novel by Athol Fugard, it won the 2006 Oscar for best foreign-language film. Against the background of a pollution-choked Soweto neighborhood, director Gavin Hood updates Fugard's tale into a dark vision of post-apartheid South Africa. Like a JoBurg version of *Boys in the Hood* or *City of God*, *Tsotsi* pulsates with the beat of *kwaito* (raplike local music) and the sounds of *tsotsi-taal* (a mixed language favored by young toughs). It reaches middle-class audiences through its portrayal of a wealthy black professional family, repeatedly robbed despite high-tech security protecting their home in a formerly white suburb, while a Sotho-speaking Afrikaner (the only white in the film) leads the police investigation. The plot is neither impossible nor typical in today's Johannesburg, but it is also largely a distraction from the film's core message: how important it is for ambitious youth to escape the tragedy of the townships at any cost.

Tsotsi's Soweto is characterized by tiny tin shacks on dirt roads; informal pubs run with iron fists by "shebeen queens"; dice-gambling entertainment; car batteries serving as electricity sources—for those who haven't hooked up illegally; communal taps with long queues providing a few gallons of water for women to carry home; homeless children surviving in stacked concrete piping; unemployed young adults without hope; crime-ridden trains; domestic strife and wife beatings; endemic disease; pervasive, often gratuitous violence.

Despite its pretense to gritty uncensored realism, *Tsotsi* in fact reproduces Soweto as seen through the stereotypes and fears of Johannesburg's elites: a state of mind numb to worsening class and durable racial inequality, and dismissive of a resilient culture of social movement activism. The film makes little effort to show how "subsistence crime" is rooted in neoliberal economics. Yet as social critic Percy Ngonyama emphasizes:

> The horrific living conditions in the squatter camps—brought about by government's strict fiscal policies—are a major cause of the high crime rate. And given South Africa's well-documented tumultuous past, the crime is accompanied by senseless violence. The movie also accurately illustrates the growing inequalities between the new black elite—very out of touch with reality—in plush suburbs, who drive around in their luxurious German vehicles, and the hungry masses in the shacks who are struggling to make ends meet.[1]

If Johannesburg is one of the world's crime capitals, it is largely because of the reproduction of one of the world's highest ratios of urban inequality.[2] Since it won municipal and national power in the mid-1990s, the African National Congress (ANC) has rapidly moved away from the far-reaching reforms promised in its *Reconstruction and Development Programme* (1994). A preemptive neoliberalism rather than incremental socialism has shaped government policies, resulting in worsening urban poverty and a growing township housing crisis. Even on the symbolic level, the ANC has commercialized the image of JoBurg as Africa's capital of glitz and conspicuous consumption, rather than as a laboratory of social justice.

The city's very name, honoring Johannes Rissik, surveyor of the stolen land where gold was discovered in 1886, is an apartheid hangover. A genuine liberation movement—or even self-conscious black nationalism—would have relabeled the city "iGoli" ("city of gold" in isi-Zulu), perhaps, or "Soweto," or even the more hip version "Jozi." Instead, in 2001, elite opinion concluded that "JoBurg" was "an opportunity to revitalize the image of the city," whose official name would go unchanged. As Mayor Amos Masondo put it, "The new logo seeks to galvanize citizens of Johannesburg behind a common vision of building a world-class African city: young, ambitious, and successful. . . . We have learned valuable lessons from cities like Singapore and New York that a brand is one of the most important assets of a city. . . . It's about value, prestige, and emotional attachment."[3] South Africa's largest metropolis, responsible for 16 percent of the country's economy, Johannesburg is the only African "world-class city" typically included in such lists.[4]

The city fathers' desperate attempt to brand Joburg as a neoliberal economic utopia soon merged with Gauteng Province's inanely branded "Blue IQ" investment-incentive gimmickry that favors foreign investors and local wealthy entrepreneurs at the expense of the citizenry. The Afrikaner-controlled construction sector—the heart of the city's growth coalition—won two key victories in the mid-2000s that have established the template for Johannesburg's neoliberal future. On one hand, the city will host the 2010 soccer World Cup (with vast stadium refurbishment costs) and, on the other, it will construct a $3-billion "Gautrain" fast service connecting the newly renovated international airport to the new Sandton financial district and then Pretoria and central Johannesburg. The new transit system—with fares out of the reach of most working people—omits links to Soweto and other black townships. The entire design reeks of apartheid-era planning principles.[5]

Meanwhile Johannesburg has been restructured by a vast but uneven wave of property speculation. From 1997 to 2004 real-estate prices in South Africa rose 200 percent (two and a half times more rapidly even than in the bubble-ridden United States), and as a result, "the banks' high level of property exposure is a source of vulnerability," warned the International Monetary Fund in 2005.[6] Casinos and shopping malls were the mainstays of this boom: at a rate in Johannesburg alone that sometimes exceeded the entire national low-income housing budget. The city appears unable to break from its inherited built environment, because of the speculative character of South African capital accumulation, or its rulers' neoliberal dogmas.

Tragically, the ANC has come to epitomize the politics of unequal growth.

Beginning in 1994, South Africa's traditionally racist and pollution-intensive companies began to open the doors to a new black elite, offering almost overnight wealth to a number of former activists, political prisoners, and trade-union leaders. To be sure, the onset of free-market economic policies based on an export-orientation fetish preceded Nelson Mandela's ANC government by a few years. But a small clique of "new guard" ANC officials today work closely with the left-over "old guard" bureaucrats whose commitment to racial apartheid is conveniently forgotten but who prosper just as nicely while building class apartheid. Together, the ruling party and its newfound Afrikaner co-conspirators:

- allowed vast sums of rich white people's loot to escape through relaxing already porous exchange controls in 1995;
- let the largest firms (Anglo American, DeBeers, South African Breweries, Old Mutual, Didata) relocate their financial headquarters to London from 1998 to 2000, in the process evacuating profits and dividend flows forever;
- cut primary corporate tax rates from 48 percent in 1994 to 30 percent five years later—achieving a level that is fifth lowest when compared to more than two dozen OECD countries—in search of new fixed-capital investment that never materialized;
- watched helplessly or indifferently as business fired a fifth of all formal-sector workers;
- allowed industries like clothing, footwear, and appliances to collapse under international competition; and
- privatized or corporatized once-formidable public assets, including Johannesburg's municipal suppliers of water (to the Paris firm Suez) and electricity (to the U.S. firm AES).

Johannesburg Top-Down

If attracting international capitalists and Northern Hemisphere tourists to JoBurg is one of the government's highest priorities, what do foreign visitors actually see when they fly into the city? More than likely, their first view is the thick brown cloud of pollution that enshrouds the city during the April–November dry season. Despite Johannesburg's 1,500-meter altitude and frequent brisk winds, temperature inversions and the lack of rain keep the smog in place. The pollution has multiple sources: the east-west factory strip south of the city; the giant eight-chimneyed power plant astride the airport; gold-mine dumps straddling the industrial land, ceaselessly blowing sand and dust into Soweto and other black townships; periodic bush fires; and universal dependence upon coal, paraffin, and fuel wood for cooking and heating in impoverished shack settlements.

Across South Africa, the drive toward electricity commercialization and privatization since 2000 has forced several million low-income households off the grid; the poor then resort to cheaper but much dirtier forms of energy. This helps to explain the reemergence of tuberculosis and other respiratory illnesses (not to mention periodic waterborne disease epidemics) now rampant in the townships. In any event, unregulated industrial coal consumption would foul the air: South Africa's energy-intensive economy, centered around mines and smelters, is responsible for the emission of twenty times more carbon dioxide per unit of per capita GDP than even the United States.[7]

Meanwhile, the visitor looking out from her plane window will soon see glass and steel towers breaking through the pollution. Johannesburg has two major conglomerations of skyscrapers, in the Central Business District (CBD) and the northeasterly edge city known as Sandton. The CBD was originally constructed during the 1890's gold rush, and then rebuilt many times, ultimately to become Africa's most intimidating concrete canyon. From the mid-1980s, black South Africans were finally allowed into the center without their passbooks, which had long regulated internal apartheid migration to satisfy the fluctuating employment demands of white-owned mines and factories.[8] From the early 1990s, as township "hawkers" (sidewalk sales operations) edged out shop-based commerce and as wars between rival "kombi-taxi" gangs littered the CBD with dozens of dead riders, virtually all Johannesburg's white-run corporations fearfully fled the desegregating inner city. Mid-1970s office blocks—such as the Carlton Center, Africa's tallest building at fifty floors—were soon valued at 10 percent of their replacement cost, thanks to mass white capitalist disinvestment and bank redlining. Even the provincial parliament in the center of the CBD is surrounded by desolate empty buildings whose ground-floor retail shops are the only income source; too many well-organized rent strikes drove landlords to empty the residential upper floors. Elevators, electric wiring, water boilers, and pipe systems are in any case rotten beyond repair. Ongoing "crime and grime" characterizes the downtown, in spite of a new camera surveillance system—operating in a few safety zones near residual corporate offices—that Foucault would have recognized.

The edge city of Sandton, twenty-four kilometers to the northeast, is the chief beneficiary (in addition to London and "EsCapeTown") of the CBD's abrupt decline. In the 1990s billions of rands were drained from the country's urgent priorities to support a gold rush of investment in Sandton's office parks, conspicuous consumption, and discordant postmodern architecture. Sandton Square was quickly surrounded by skyscrapers, banks (including a brand-new Citibank tower), boutiques for the ubiquitous nouveaux riches, five-star hotels, a garish convention center, Africa's biggest stock exchange, and other displays of brazen economic power.

Meanwhile moneyed suburbanites cower behind three-meter-high walls topped with razor wire—now a renowned South African export—to keep out the *tsotsis*. Johannesburg's cutting-edge high-tech surveillance systems are staffed by poverty-level black security-sector workers, who go on strike for higher wages every few years, to the panic of the petite bourgeoisie. Expensive car-tracking systems identify heart-of-darkness "NoGoZones" like Alexandra township three miles east of Sandton; if drivers dare venture to Alex, satellite alarm beams are automatically activated and rescue teams are mobilized.

The township slums stretch to the horizon and house the majority of Gauteng Province's ten million inhabitants.[9] Because of catastrophic government policies based on World Bank advice in mid-1994, shortly after Mandela was elected president, Johannesburg's new formal residential areas for low-income black residents are actually further away from job opportunities and are worse served with community amenities, schools, and clinics than even apartheid-era ghettoes. The new houses—often termed "Unos" (after Fiat's tiniest car), or "smarties" (a candy equivalent to U.S. M&Ms), or even "kennels"—are generally half the size of apartheid's old forty-square-meter "matchbox" shanties and represent the limitations of building with the government's stingy $2,500-per-unit housing grants. Postapartheid housing policy, although originally administered by Communist leader Joe Slovo, has slavishly followed the prescriptions of the World Bank. Johannesburg, in particular, quickly adopted a long-term metropolitan growth strategy (Vision 2030) that sacrificed historical movement goals, like subsidized utilities and decent shelter for the poor, in order to concentrate the budget on the Bank's goal of making JoBurg a "a world-class business location."

As the Vision 2030 plan itself conceded, "Post-apartheid developments have often exacerbated the apartheid city form," which forces much longer and more expensive commutes than should be necessary, as well as far greater spending on bulk infrastructure.[10] De facto class apartheid has supplanted—indeed in many cases, exacerbated—legalized racial apartheid, and because housing policy is driven by developers and banks, working-class and poor Africans will continue to be pushed further into the periphery. They will live in smaller houses than during apartheid, located even further from jobs and community amenities, characterized by ongoing disconnections of water and electricity, with lower-quality state services ranging from rare rubbish collection to dirt roads and inadequate sewage and storm-water drainage.[11]

The Neoliberal Drought

In South Africa, entitlement to water remains a fundamental, existential dividing line: on one hand, the pleasing bright green quilt of well-watered English-style gardens and thick alien trees that shade traditionally white—now slightly desegregated—suburbs; on the other, the dusty, often toxic deserts of the townships and new slums. The runaway-train-like growth of the urban region will only exacerbate the contradictions between those who spend weekends soaking in their private pools and those who can barely afford drinking water for their children.

Thanks to migration, the annual growth of Johannesburg's population has been 4.2 percent (with job creation of less than 3 percent). By 2015, Johannesburg and four surrounding cities will host an estimated 14.6 million urban residents; the young metropolis will be the twelfth largest in the world. When gold was discovered in 1886, thousands of fortune hunters and proletarians were drawn inland immediately. Johannesburg soon became the planet's largest city with no substantial natural water source. Seventy-five kilometers to the south, the Vaal River is pumped uphill to Johannesburg, but by the 1980s it became apparent that the source would be insufficient for the next century.

Apartheid-era engineers and World Bank project officers tried to solve the looming shortages with a dam-and-tunnel scheme that draws water several hundred kilometers from across a mountain range atop the small and perpetually impoverished nation of Lesotho. The Lesotho Highlands Water Project—Africa's largest infrastructure project—is now less than half finished but has already become one of the world's highest-profile corruption cases, displaced tens of thousands of Basotho peasants, inundated sacred land, and threatened endangered species from minnows to vultures.

The bill for this ongoing attack on people and nature is being disproportionately paid by the urban poor. Johannesburg water prices went up by 35 percent during the late 1990s, but township residents in the lowest consumption tier pay 55 percent more because of the cost of the Lesotho dams, for which the old P.W. Botha regime needed surreptitious funding during the mid-1980s due to apartheid-era financial sanctions. The World Bank set up a secret London account to facilitate matters, overriding objections from the liberation movement. When the ANC subsequently accepted the dams, that entailed rejecting grassroots demands from Alexandra, Soweto, and Lesotho that overconsumptive water users in the mines, factories, and mansions be made more responsible for paying the bills, for conserving water so as to prevent future dam construction, and for repairing ubiquitous leaks in the apartheid-era township infrastructure, where half of Soweto's water is lost. But bankers were anxious to continue financing, and construction companies ready to keep building, the multibillion-dollar dams. The World Bank's Inspection Panel refused a full investigation of township residents' complaints in 1998.

Privatization is also changing the nature of water and sanitation services delivery. A clear relationship between urban water commodification and ecohealth dangers is evident in Soweto, where Suez began installing prepaid meters in mid-2003. Suez inherited a dysfunctional system in low-income areas, especially the

shack settlements, which are home to nearly a third of the city's 3.2 million residents: 65 percent use communal standpipes and 20 percent receive small amounts
from water tankers (the other 15 percent have outdoor yard taps). For sanitation,
52 percent have dug pit latrines themselves, 45 percent rely on chemical toilets, 2
percent have communal flush toilets, and 1 percent use ablution blocks. Needless
to say, these conditions are both particularly harmful to women and children, and
breed disease at a time when Johannesburg's HIV rate has soared above 25 percent and cholera and diarrhea epidemics are still spreading.

Instead of expanding supply to these unserved areas, Suez's response to
poverty was to implement massive water disconnections (which should be
deemed unconstitutional). At peak in early 2002, just before community resistance became an effective countervailing force, Johannesburg officials were disconnecting more than 20,000 impoverished households per month from power
and water.[12] Eco-blowback was inevitable, as water minister Ronnie Kasrils, admitted to parliament in 2001: "Unacceptable sanitation services resulting in se-
vere water pollution, especially bacteriological pollution, is a grave concern in
Gauteng."[13] By 2001, Suez began installing pit latrines, a new "shallow sewage"
system, and prepaid water meters, and spent $2.5 million constructing 6,500 la-
trines between 2003 and 2005. Shallow sewage is attractive to the company because maintenance costs are transferred to so-called condominium residential
users, where a very small water flush and slight gravity mean that the pipes must
be manually unclogged every three months (or more frequently) by the residents
themselves.[14]

Johannesburg managers balked at offering a genuine free lifeline supply and
rising block tariff that might redistribute water from rich to poor, and simultaneously incentivize conservation. During the late 1990s, Johannesburg also became
liable for Lesotho dam repayments, resulting in a spectacular 69 percent increase
from 1996 to 1999 in the nominal cost of water purchased from the Rand Water
Board. Johannesburg's water prices became more regressive than during apartheid (i.e., with a flatter slope in the block tariff). Finally, a free basic lifeline was
conceded in 2001, amounting to 6,000 liters of water each month for each
household. That policy came from the December 2000 municipal elections—held

in the wake of rising protest and alienation, as well as the cholera epidemic—and was meant to fulfill this promise: "The ANC-led local government will provide all residents with a free basic amount of water, electricity, and other municipal services so as to help the poor. Those who use more than the basic amounts, will pay for the extra they use."

Johannesburg undermined this progressive mandate, however, by adopting a relatively steep-rising convex tariff curve, in contrast to a concave curve starting with a larger lifeline block, which would have better served the interests of lower-income residents. The marginal tariff for industrial/commercial users of water, while higher than residential, actually declines after large-volume consumption is reached. Behind the sabotage of the water promise was Suez, which had an incentive to avoid giving poor people water for free.

Meanwhile, the city was pleading cash shortage as an excuse to begin selling off its assets in the late 1990s. Capital drought was genuine insofar as the national Department of Finance had reduced the country's central-local operating grant system by 85 percent (after inflation) from 1991 to 1999, leaving Johannesburg with only $4 million in 1999.[15] When the finance department granted Johannesburg $83 million in 2000, it came with extremely tight strings attached, as central government insisted upon the rapid implementation of the city's corporatization strategy, known as Igoli 2002.

As Johannesburg desegregated, the capital market institutions turned off their loan funds for municipal capital bonds, preferring to send financial resources into the stock market, suburban shopping centers, and office buildings.[16] Finally, wealthy households and corporations did not pay their fair share of the city tax bill. For decades, white taxpayers received an enormous subsidy from black township residents. Township workers labored in factories and offices, and township consumers bought goods in shops that were located in white-controlled municipalities. Those factories, offices, and shops paid taxes to Johannesburg, while township administrations such as Soweto and Alexandra relied mainly on beer-hall revenues and, during the 1980s, some central government funding. During the mid-1990s, the Sandton Ratepayers Federation and Liberty Life insurance company, a major Sandton property investor, challenged redistributive rates that would subsidize Sowetans. Although the wealthy white residents lost their case in the highest courts in 1997, the effect was to intimidate Johannesburg politicians at a crucial moment. Moreover, fiscal stress at the time of Igoli 2002 led to a dramatic decline in capital spending from $200 billion in 1997 to $50 million in 1999.

Yet there was still scope for substantial redistribution, given the enormous wealth base in South Africa's main city. Instead, Johannesburg imposed the Igoli 2002 privatization program over objections of the SA Municipal Workers Union (whose 20,000 workers went out on strike in 1999) and periodic community protests. This earned the Johannesburg Council a celebratory—if highly misleading—"success story" box in the World Bank's *World Development Report 2004*. According to a front-page *New York Times* story in May 2003, Suez officials "acknowledged that in communities like these, billing people for water has been like squeezing water from a stone. . . . Orange Farm women, who live by doing other people's laundry, said they barely had enough money to pay for food and school fees. Many of them already have prepaid electricity meters in their homes, and they say their families end up in the dark for several days each month."[17]

Resistance

In the mid-1980s, Johannesburg hosted the largest contingent of what was possibly the world's most impressive urban social movement, the South African township "civics."[18] But the SA National Civic Organization suffered systematic demobilization of their ranks by the ruling party during the mid-1990s.[19] Hence an independent network of community groups arose in several Johannesburg townships beginning with the formation of the Soweto Electricity Crisis Committee in early 2000.[20] Led by former ANC councillor and Soweto regional leader Trevor Ngwane, the group took what was already a popular township survival tactic—illicitly reconnecting power once it was disconnected by state officials due to nonpayment (13 percent of Gauteng's connections in 2001 were illegal)—and added a socialist, self-empowered ideological orientation.[21]

Within a few months, the Anti-Privatization Forum (APF) was formed to unite nearly two dozen community groups across Gauteng, sponsoring periodic mass marches of workers and residents. One of the key activists from Orange

Farm township, Bricks Mokolo, quotes the popular APF graffiti slogan: "destroy the meters and enjoy the water. The government promised us that water is a basic right. But now they are telling us our rights are for sale."[22] Regular arrests in Orange Farm, the Phiri suburb of Soweto, and other sites have not intimidated activists from organizing against prepaid meters. A major court battle to declare the devices unconstitutional is also imminent, catalyzed by the APF, facilitated by an invaluable radical NGO (the Freedom of Expression Institute), and backed by one of the country's top lawyers.

APF activists are highly regarded around the world for liberating electricity and water from expensive (and unreliable) meters and advocating (and partially winning) access to free basic lifeline electricity and water.[23] Although the APF remains split in part on ideological lines (with classical socialist/autonomist and social movement/political party rifts), the sense of unity against ubiquitous neoliberalism, paranoid ruling-party nationalism, and worsening state repression has been maintained. Across South Africa in 2005 alone, some 5,800 protests—a large proportion based upon urban grievances—were recorded by the police, who deemed 13 percent of these "illegal."

Aside from managing left-ideological conflict, at least five durable organizational problems face APF activists: raising resources (the movement is supported in part by small membership dues but also by left international institutions such as War on Want and the Rosa Luxemburg Foundation); avoiding the one-off "IMF riot" style of urban uprising (very common in areas where the police and ruling party quickly snuff resistance); distinguishing themselves from the co-opted and corporatist sections of civil society; stemming the sorts of urban movement ebbs and flows that win immediate victories yet then quickly lose momentum; and turning their consistent anti-neoliberal activist work into a substantive *political* program for social change.

There is another challenge, however, which is much more daunting: to take interlocking and overlapping struggles across South Africa and forge them into what appears as the next logical step: construction of a broader movement of social forces in Johannesburg and other cities not only unified with organized labor, but also actively demanding decommodified, destratified public services.

None of the small-scale modes of resistance will immediately overturn the Johannesburg ruling elite, nor will minor electoral campaigns by APF affiliates do more than gain a council seat here or there (as in the 2006 municipal elections). The *tsotsis* running South Africa's largest municipality will continue to impose new deprivations upon poor and especially black people, women, and the environment. Yet profound contradictions bubble to the surface regularly, reminding the citizenry of the costs of a neoliberal dystopia. So far, no matter their weaknesses, Johannesburg's broadly defined independent left groups appear the only set of forces with the creativity, militancy, and political vision to curtail the worst excesses of this evil paradise, until an opportune moment arises for a more powerful assault and breakthrough.

"Nueva Managua": The Disembedded City

Dennis Rodgers

The "Palimpsest" City

The expression *"Managua es Nicaragua"*—"Managua is Nicaragua"—is commonly heard by all visitors to the city, and there is some truth to the selfish claim.[1] The metropolis contains almost one-quarter of the country's 5.5 million people, and over 40 percent of its urban population.[2] It dominates the country both economically and politically, and is a primary symbolic national reference point. This was not always the case historically, as Managua was little more than a sleepy provincial town when it was chosen as a compromise capital for Nicaragua in 1851 over the then more important but constantly feuding cities of León and Grenada. But Managua eventually grew into a thriving metropolis of some 500,000 inhabitants, and by the mid-1960s had developed a reputation as a playground for the wealthy as well as a regional magnet for tourism. On December 23, 1972, however, the city was devastated by an earthquake that killed 20,000 people, destroyed 75 percent of the city's housing and 90 percent of its commercial capacity—including the bustling city center—and left 300,000 people homeless.[3] Although international aid poured into Nicaragua, most of it was pocketed by the ruling Somoza dictatorship, and little reconstruction actually took place, thereby leaving Managua but a shadow of its former self.[4]

The overthrow of the Somoza dictatorship in 1979 by the Sandinista revolution—partly abetted by the regime's negligent urban policies—saw ambitious plans for the self-help construction of low-cost basic housing.[5] Although some pilot projects were successfully carried out, the subsequent war against the U.S.-backed Contras drained state resources and prevented any large-scale reconstruction effort, and Managua redeveloped in an anarchic fashion. As David Wall describes,

> the destroyed central part of Managua was not rebuilt and . . . was virtually abandoned. Only a few buildings survived the earthquake, and the central core took on a post-apocalyptic look. . . . The rebuilding effort that did take place following the 1972 earthquake created new residential areas east-southeast of the city center. . . . This gives the city the appearance of a deformed octopus. The tentacles of the octopus reach out along major transport arteries away from the old centre, but the octopus's body is riddled with gaping holes.[6]

The general disorderliness of the city was further compounded by the slow deterioration of the surviving urban infrastructure and the emergence of spontaneous squatter settlements, including some in the ruins of the old city center. The change of regime in 1990, when the Sandinistas unexpectedly lost elections, made little difference to Managua's haphazard urban development, and as a 2001 guidebook put it, the contemporary city has "no center, no skyline, and no logic."[7] Not surprisingly it is widely known as "*la ciudad caótica.*" Another way of considering it, however, is as a "postmodern" metropolis, "a 'palimpsest' of past forms superimposed upon each other, and a 'collage' of current uses."[8] The squatter settlements in the ruins of the old city center are an obvious example of such a process, but the notion also applies more generally. The businesses and services that used to be in the city center have reemerged in a decentralized manner, creating a fragmented metropolis of semiautonomous districts connected by a byzantine transport network. Perhaps most paradigmatically, the population of Managua adapted to the post-earthquake shape of the city by mapping old reference points onto the new cityscape, with addresses in the city often designated in relation to extinct urban features.

Although the city remained a sea of poor slums and dilapidated neighbor-hoods until the mid-1990s, new upscale developments emerged in the wake of the change of regime. The return of wealthy Nicaraguans who had fled the rev-olution led to "determined efforts by the 'Miami boys' (as they are called) . . . to recreate their cherished Miami social and cultural 'scene.'"[9] Neon-lit bars and dance clubs began to appear, and expensive cars again cruised the streets. Inter-national franchises like Subway, Pizza Hut, the Hard Rock Cafe, and McDonald's displaced more humble local eateries. The return of McDonald's was particularly symbolic: the first branch had opened in Managua in 1975 but lost its franchise shortly after the revolution. It was reopened by "Ronald McDonald" and Vice-President Enrique Bolonos, who thanked the gringo megachain for helping Nicaragua "take off its loincloth."[10]

The transformation of Managua accelerated during the late 1990s, and new and expensive bars, restaurants, nightclubs, luxury hotels, and exclusive super-markets emerged in different points of the city, as did two North American–style shopping malls, the Plaza Inter and Metrocentro malls. Both of these boast multi-screen cinemas, food courts, and shops selling a variety of imported consumer items: Benetton and Liz Claiborne clothes, Sony electronic goods, original CDs and DVDs, and Victorinox Swiss army knives. They cater exclusively to the (rela-tively few) tourists that come to Nicaragua and the neoliberal elite.[11] Although numerically small in size, this group constitutes a significant concentration of economic power, as is well reflected by the luxurious new condominiums and walled compounds they live in, whose often cheery pastel colors and fanciful ar-chitecture contrast strikingly with the monochrome and dilapidated housing of the city's numerous slums. Two gated-community developments in the southeast of the city, purposeful imitations of U.S. suburbia surrounded by tight security perimeters and guard towers, add a further edge to Managua's socioeconomic disparity.

Nueva Managua

Although these recent transformations can be located within the historical expe-rience of Managua as a "palimpsest" city, they are arguably associated with a qualitatively new kind of urbanism. In contrast to the city's past pattern of disorganized development, the late 1990s and early 2000s witnessed a much more purposeful and wide-ranging interventions in favor of the urban elite. The goal was not simply to superimpose a new urban form over past layers, but to actively reshape the overall fabric of the city through an explicit separation of certain urban spaces from the metropolis as a whole.

My first intimation of this process came about anecdotally, through the starkly contrasting juxtaposition of two conversations I had with affluent Nicaraguans in the planes taking me from Miami to Managua in 1996 and 2002. In 1996, when I told my travel companion that I was planning to spend a year in Nicaragua, he launched into a tirade on how impossible Managua was to live in: it was much too dangerous, there were incredible amounts of crime and violence, you got held up all the time at traffic lights, the roads were so bad that you always risked breaking down and being attacked, there was nowhere to eat, drink, or dance safely in the city, and finally he had been in Miami to buy a house in order to move there with his family as soon as possible. My subsequent stay in Nicaragua showed that my travel companion was not wrong about the chronic insecurity of life in Managua: police statistics record crime levels more than tripling between 1990 and 2000.[12]

Seven years later, however, I had a conversation of an entirely different tenor. My new travel companion enthused about how completely the city had changed over the past few years: thanks to President Arnoldo Alemán, it was now safe and livable, with nice restaurants, bars, and hotels. In bizarre symmetry to my conversation six years previously, my seatmate boasted that he was moving back to Managua after eight years in Miami. It quickly became apparent on my return after almost five years of absence that the city had indeed changed dramatically. The rather decrepit and extremely basic Augusto Sandino International Airport had been replaced by the brand-new and surreally modernist Managua International Airport. Driving into Managua from the airport, I was dumbfounded by the proliferation of luxurious new buildings, as well as the number of monumental architectural features built since my last stay.

A variety of factors can be invoked to explain this unlikely transformation of Managua—insofar as the country's dramatic macroeconomic predicament had not changed since the 1990s—but as intimated by my travel companion to Nicaragua in 2002, Arnoldo Alemán clearly played a pivotal role. He was elected mayor of the city in 1990, and came to power with a definite urban project for Managua, one that focused principally on making the city a more comfortable place for the urban elite. This initially translated into a series of ostentatious public works to "beautify" the city, among them a large roundabout with a big fountain that when lit up seemed to spout water of different colors, the massive Catedral Metropolitana de la Purísima Concepción de María, and the reconstruction of the *malecón*, or waterfront, alongside Lake Managua, which had fallen into disuse after the 1972 earthquake. Other initiatives included regular campaigns to clear traffic intersections of street children and peddlers, painting over revolutionary murals, and razing several informal settlements in the city center ruins. None of these initiatives were terribly effective or uncontroversial. The roundabout fountain wasn't working most of the time, people grumbled about the cathedral's avant-garde architecture, the *malecón* continued to be unused, and campaigns against street children, revolutionary murals, and squatters were both sporadic and unpopular.

Alemán was financially constrained as mayor, partly because he belonged to the opposition Liberal party. When he was elected to the presidency of Nicaragua in 1996, however, he suddenly found himself able to mobilize greater resources, and his campaign to transform Managua took off. Alemán personally oversaw, for example, the building of new government offices in the old city center including a new presidential palace (financed by Taiwanese aid) with bulletproof windows and a fountain whose jets of water mark the time of computerized musical melodies.[13] Similarly, Managua's International Airport was completely overhauled in 2000–01 with US$33.4 million of central funding from the Office of the Presidency.[14] The national government furthermore indirectly stimulated new construction by providing (illegal) tax breaks to companies wanting to erect new buildings. The Pellas Group, for example, spent US$20 million on a fourteen-story, ultramodern tower for which they obtained a US$2.5-million tax exoneration.[15] Comparable tax breaks were also reportedly given to the Taiwanese and Salvadoran commercial groups that built the Plaza Inter and Metrocentro malls.

Alemán's "beautification" efforts have focused principally on locations directly impinging on the lives of the urban elite, such as the government offices where many are employed, or the International Airport which many use to travel back and forth to Miami. The renovation of the latter most prominently included the construction of a luxurious duty-free shop stocked almost exclusively with imported items that are clearly beyond the reach of the vast majority of Nicaraguans, and most of the new check-in desks that were built supposedly in order to relieve passenger congestion are used to cater to business and first-class passengers. Together with the exclusive bars, restaurants, and malls emerging in Managua, it can be argued that an elite archipelago of locations and services was emerging in Managua by the late 1990s. This was however not enough in itself to make the city attractive for the urban elite, given the high levels of crime and insecurity that continue to characterize postrevolutionary urban Nicaragua into the present,[16] and the successful apotheosis of Alemán's project of a *"Nueva Managua"*—a "New Managua"—required two further developments, namely the proliferation of private security and the improvement of Managua's transport infrastructure.

The Privatization of Security

The development of the private security industry in Nicaragua has coincided with rising levels of crime and insecurity, as well as the institutional erosion of the competence of the National Police. Since regime change in 1990, the police force has undergone a reduction both in size and budget, to the extent that by 1999 it had only limited patrolling capacity in urban areas, and was completely absent in 21 percent of the country's 146 municipalities.[17] Conversely, while there was just one registered private security firm in 1990, there were fourteen in 1996,[18] and fifty-six in 2003.[19] Similarly, while there were 7,664 police officers in Nicaragua in 2003,[20] there were 9,017 registered private security guards,[21] although the real number was probably higher considering that 29,414 firearm permits were delivered to private security firms in 2000.[22] To a certain extent, the proliferation of private security is a functional response to the declining ability of the police to respond to crime, but it is also an integral aspect of the so-called fortified enclave model of urban segregation.[23]

As Teresa Caldeira explains in her classic study of São Paulo, the fearful withdrawal from the general space of the city by the affluent into gated communities and closed condominiums—which she collectively terms "fortified enclaves"—is inevitably accompanied by a need to ensure the exclusion from these spaces of anyone perceived or stereotyped as potential criminals. Since fortified enclaves cannot depend on public security agencies to enforce their exclusion, security becomes a private matter.[24] Florence Babb argues that the same logic applies in Managua, where "the wealthy . . . shield themselves as much as possible from crime and other social problems, constructing higher walls and better security systems for their homes and hiring armed guards to patrol their neighborhoods. In doing so, they create segregated enclaves that, in Managua as elsewhere in Latin America, alter the character of public space and public life and enforce rules of inclusion and exclusion . . . [with] the streets of Managua . . . left to those who cannot afford to retreat to enclaves."[25]

Babb is both right and wrong in her observations. There is no doubt that high walls and armed guards have proliferated in Managua during the past decade and a half. At the same time, such security tends to occur in relation to individual residences rather than whole neighborhoods. The few affluent neighborhoods that exist in Managua—such as Las Condes, Los Robles, or Altos de Santo Domingo, for example—are not the fortified enclaves that Babb describes, but rather concentrations of individually fortified dwellings. The relatively small size of the urban elite in Managua makes self-sustained gated communities economically unviable. In a large city like São Paulo, residents hardly ever need to leave their compounds which contain a variety of shops, businesses, schools, and entertainment centers. In Managua, by contrast, the elite is too small to support such an enclosed economy. Indeed, it can be argued that the small size of the Managua elite means that the luxury bars, restaurants, and supermarkets that cater to them in the city almost inevitably need to be able to offer their services to the whole group, and not just a small, captured subset.

In face of these constraints the urban elite in Managua has not retreated from public space in the same way as Caldeira describes as having occurred in São Paulo. They must continue to regularly leave their highly fortified individual homes to work and play in the new government offices, business edifices, bars, restaurants, and shopping malls scattered around Managua. Private security is therefore critical, as it allows the members of the urban elite to live their lives within a limited number of heavily protected locations, which the private provision of security de facto converts from public to private spaces. As Doña Yolanda, an inhabitant of *barrio* Luis Fanor Hernández, the poor urban neighborhood where I have been carrying out fieldwork since 1996, succinctly described: "all those nice shops and malls are not for the poor. The guards don't let you in if you don't look rich."[26]

But private security is only half the story of the new spatial segregation in Managua. As my travel companion to Nicaragua in 1996 bemoaned, the deplorable condition of city roads, with their potholes and lack of adequate surfacing, as well as the constant risk of carjacking at traffic lights and busy intersections, made traveling between different locations a constant gamble for the urban elites during the early and mid-1990s. Although they could protect their homes, offices, and bars by hiring private security guards, there was little they could do to avoid potentially dangerous encounters when commuting between home and work. Despite the rise of exclusive locations protected by private security, these continued to be located within an endemically dangerous and insecure Managua, and short of moving about in armed, radio-connected convoys—as UN vehicles sometimes did in the mid-1990s—this meant that the urban elite were forced to engage with the violence of the wider city whether they wanted to or not. Under such conditions, it is perhaps not surprising that from 1998 onward, alongside his efforts to "beautify" the city, Alemán explicitly set out to reform Managua's transport network.

Roads, Roundabouts, and Road Deaths

Alemán began his presidential overhaul of the city's transport network by sponsoring a large-scale program to fill in potholes, resurface and widen Managua's major arteries, as well as financing the building of a bypass road in the southwest of the city, and replacing (generally out-of-order) traffic lights with roundabouts. The official objectives were to speed up traffic and reduce congestion, but the proliferation of roundabouts was clearly intended to reduce the risk of carjacking (since cars do not have to stop), while the primary purpose of the bypass was obviously to connect two of the more affluent areas of the city in a way that allowed drivers to avoid a part of Managua reputed for its high levels of crime. Alemán also launched the construction of a system of well-lit high-speed roads throughout the city. When this new network of roads is mapped, a pattern very clearly emerges suggesting a rather selective building or rebuilding. Starting from the airport in the northeast and moving toward the southwest, the new road network spins a sparse web connecting the airport to the presidential palace and government ministries to the luxury hotels to the malls to the nightlife spots to the affluent neighborhoods of the city. The bypass mentioned above, for example, connects two of the principal affluent neighborhoods in Managua, Los Chiles— where Alemán has his family residence—and the rich neighborhood of Las Colinas, making intra-elite socializing easier.

Simultaneously the government has neglected the maintenance of those parts of the road network—around the Mercado Oriental or in the northwestern quadrant, for example[27]—that do not serve elite commuters. This selective pattern of infrastructure investment has resisted the moderate attempts of Sandinista Mayor Herty Lewites—who unexpectedly defeated Alemán's handpicked successor, Roberto Cedeño, in 2000—to introduce a more equitable program of urban development. When Lewites proposed spending $6 million on general improvements to Managua's 1,157 kilometers of streets and roads, President Alemán refused to provide any assistance, although the national government eagerly funded improvements to the highway between Managua and Granada, which increasingly serves elite families commuting to walled homes and estates in the bucolic countryside.[28] A similar logic undoubtedly underlies Alemán's willingness to finance thirteen massive roundabouts in Managua, while Lewites has gained little support for a plan to add 259 traffic lights to the paltry 78 that currently exist.[29]

These transformations go beyond simply allowing members of the elite to move safely within the city. As Fiona Wilson remarks in a stimulating article on the political economy of transport, roads are not just "neutral lines . . . going from . . . point *a* to point *b*" but "stretched-out places where intersecting social relations cluster and adhere."[30] How this intersection occurs in Nueva Managua is highlighted when the new road network is viewed from the perspective of the poor. As Doña Yolanda makes clear, it is not just the homes, offices, and leisure locations of the urban elites that the poor are excluded from, but also the spaces of connection between these places: that is to say, the roads and roundabouts themselves:

> Everything that Alemán has done, he's done for the rich. It's all big, luxurious, American-style. You go and see the Purísima roundabout, it's huge! The Jean Paul Genie roundabout is massive as well. So is the Güegüense roundabout, and the Metrocentro one. You've also seen how they're improving the Road to Masaya, no? It now has six traffic lanes, three in each direction. But the thing is that we're not living in the US here, we're living in poor little Nicaragua, where almost everybody is poor. They say that there are thousands of new cars on the roads now, but whose cars are they? Can the poor afford Cherokees and pickups? Of course not! None of these new roads and buildings are for us poor folk; they're only for the rich and their big cars. What have they brought us? Nothing! The buses that the poor use still go on the old, broken roads full of potholes . . . I tell you, . . . the roads are not for the poor. It's impossible to go anywhere now with all those big cars cruising around so fast. Have you tried crossing those roads? It's impossible, especially at those roundabouts where you don't know where the cars might come from! Before the traffic was slower, and there was less of it, but now . . . You know Doña Aurelia, three houses down, no? Her son was killed a few months ago, just trying to cross the road. The car didn't even stop, it just hit him and went right on. . . . It's like they were saying to us that the roads are not ours but theirs. . . . It's as if they've ripped out the parts of the city they want and we're no longer allowed to use them.

Doña Yolanda's observations about the increased number of vehicles in Managua are supported by official statistics. Certainly, there was a 54 percent rise in the number of vehicles in Nicaragua between 1998 and 2002, compared to an 11 percent decline between 1995 and 1998, and over 60 percent of all vehicles in

Nicaragua are concentrated in the capital city.[31] Similarly, her intimation that the new roads are leading to a greater number of road deaths is also borne out by official statistics, which according to Police Commissioner Carlos Bendaña recorded a significant rise in traffic deaths in Managua during 1998–2000, coinciding with the major changes to the city's transport network.[32] Pedestrians were the largest single group of traffic victims (over 40 percent of all deaths), with many fatalities at the Güegüense and Metrocentro roundabouts mentioned by Doña Yolanda as well as two of the new high-speed arteries.[33] In 2004 there were just two official pedestrian crossings in the whole of Managua, only a few pedestrian overpasses, and only a few residential streets with sidewalks.[34]

From this perspective, Managua's new network of roads and roundabouts represents the foundation of a new form of urban segregation: what might be termed a "fortified network" rather than the "fortified enclaves" described by Caldeira in São Paulo. The development of a strategic set of well-maintained, well-lit, and fast-moving roads that link the different places of work, life, and entertainment of the city elite has allowed them to construct viable modes of living amid a wider context of insecurity that does not necessitate their withdrawal into private, self-sufficient "safe havens." Although both fortified network and fortified enclaves constitute modes of separation from the wider city fabric that seclude those within them from the rest of the city, they are crucially different insofar as a fortified network is by its very nature constituted through processes of securatized interconnection rather than protective isolation.

"Disembedding" the City: The Revolt of the Elites?

As Alan Smart remarks, "all cities attempt to govern their constituent spaces and those who live there, although to variable extents."[35] The question is how they do so and for what purpose. It is increasingly being recognized that the governance of cities is becoming more concerned with the management of space rather than the disciplining of offenders.[36] The classic example of this new form of spatial governance is the fortified enclave that Caldeira and others have observed around the world, which produces order by creating spaces that exclude offensive behavior. There are many parallels between the fortified-enclave model of urban development and some of the transformations that Managua has undergone during the past decade and a half. But it can also be argued that "New Managua" presents a number of novel elements. Fortified enclaves are disconnected "off-worlds" that are the antithesis of urban public space, constituting a withdrawal from the fabric of the city, leading to its fragmentation.[37] The new spatial order in Managua, however, has been established not so much through an insular withdrawal from the city, but rather through the constitution of a fortified network that extends throughout the metropolis. Rather than fragmenting into an archipelago of self-sustaining and isolated islands of wealth within a wider sea of poverty, urban space has undergone a process whereby a whole layer of the metropolis has been disconnected from the fabric of the city, arguably giving rise to an unprecedented urban morphology.

The process can perhaps best be described as a form of "disembedding." I borrow this term from Anthony Giddens, who uses it to describe how social, cultural, and economic relations can become detached from their localized contexts as a result of modernity and globalization.[38] The notion of "embeddedness" can be said to have territorial dimensions, particularly in relation to "the extent to which an actor is "anchored" in particular territories or places."[39] Cities are primary sites of territorial embeddedness, fundamentally shaping the way that social actors within them live their lives. The "palimpsest" urban history of Managua exemplifies this process well, with new urban forms adopting, reinterpreting, and being shaped by past ones. The recent spatial transformation of Managua has arguably led to the emergence of a new urban social form that no longer relates to its wider context, however, and can therefore be labeled "disembedded." The fortified network of the urban elite excludes others from specific locations, but also from the roads and intersections in the city that connect these locations. In doing so, it actively encroaches on the public space of the city in a much more extensive way than do fortified enclaves, "ripping out"—to use Doña Yolanda's expression—large swathes of the metropolis for the sole use of the urban elite, thereby creating a "disembedded city."

As Teresa Caldeira points out, the dynamics of urban spatial organization are perhaps most meaningfully considered in terms of "how social groups relate to each other in the space of the city."[40] Such a perspective focuses our attention squarely on the underlying nature of urban governance—for whom and by whom is it being carried out? The transformation of Managua during the past decade and a half has specifically favored the neoliberal elite, with public resources mobilized to accommodate their needs and desires irrespective of the rest of the city. As Doña Isabel poignantly put it in an interview in 2002, "for the rich, everything's different, life has got easier, it's like their city now . . . you could say that for the rich it's as if there were a *nueva Managua*." For the poor, the new metropolitan features have meant an increasing circumscription of urban space. Because those benefiting from the transformation of the metropolis are often also those effectuating the changes—Alemán and most of the Nicaraguan political class emanate from the "elite"—the disembedding of Managua can plausibly be said to represent an instance of what Christopher Lasch has called "the revolt of the elites."[41] Following a decade of popular revolutionary rule, followed by an anomic and spontaneous "revolt of the masses" in the form of rampant crime and delinquency, the Nicaraguan urban elite—increasingly transnational in nature and interest, and therefore no longer concerned with either Nicaragua or the general impoverished mass of population as objects of economic exploitation[42]— have decided to go their own way, not so much by withdrawing from the city, but instead by partitioning it. In doing so, however, they actively "betray"—to continue the analogy with Lasch—the social contract of the city that implicitly comes by virtue of being embedded in a common urban space constituted through a plurality of people, and produce "worlds of inequality, alienation, and injustice."[43]

Becoming Bourgeois: (Postsocialist) Utopias of Isolation and Civilization

Judit Bodnár

"We have finally become European in what we offer and the way we live. We can live now like real bourgeois," is how an upscale Budapest real-estate developer sums up proudly the philosophy of his business and changes in his country. Notwithstanding the problematic identification of Europeanness as a virtue and its equation with bourgeois existence, he may be right—partly.

In Budapest, one learns from urbanist scholarship, average life expectancy in District 2 is "on the level of Belgium, while in District 10 it approximates that of Syria."[1] Setting aside such analogies, in plain numbers there is a six-year difference in average life expectancy between the two parts of the city. In the number of welfare recipients, the difference is threefold,[2] which correlates inversely with average real estate prices and the average income of households in the two districts.[3] "Budapest is splitting into two parts," concludes sociologist János Ladányi when observing the increase of socioeconomic residential segregation in postsocialist Budapest.[4] "Parts of the city inhabited by higher-status social groups look more and more like similar areas in western Europe. By sharp contrast, other parts, inhabited by the losers of postcommunist transition, tend to resemble parts of cities of the Third World."[5]

It is this spatial and class split that is the theme of this essay: its simultaneous nonrecognition and exploitation in bourgeois utopias of isolation. This is a story of the invisible foundations of embourgeoisement and the uneven production of urban space in postsocialist Budapest, but which in no way should read as unique to either postsocialism or Budapest.

Neo-Hapsburg Kitsch

The concurrent surfacing of two worlds in Budapest is an expression of the increasing social polarization that is a general feature of the contemporary urban condition. Similar tropes of urban duality juxtaposing the First and the Third Worlds in a new synchronicity of sorts are often applied to today's globalizing cities.[6] The reference to the West and Europe in the context of Budapest, however, is more than a simple marker of development. State socialism put a twist on the fundamental fissure in modernity, which casts some areas as modern and others in need of "development," some as *being* modern, others in the perpetual state of *becoming* so. State socialism and its oppressive and restrictive institutions conflated systemic economic and social difference with a cultural European triumphalism and a sense of inferiority in peripheral, formerly colonized, regions.[7] The West, Europe, civilization, modernity, modernization, moral superiority, and goodness have long occupied a tightly intertwined semantic space in Hungarian political rhetoric and identity construction, as in other noncore regions of the world.[8] It has been the achievement of bourgeois hegemony that even elements that had been invented by other social classes in earlier periods became subsumed and effectively promoted under the heading of bourgeois culture.[9] "Bourgeois," as a partial representation of the class content of modernity and capitalism, has not lost its historical dimension with the passing of time but has turned into a polysemic term at the core of the rhetoric of modernization, civilization, and progress.

The Hungarian public, which from the nineteenth century had cast its envious eyes on the Western monuments of progress and civilization, was convinced that state socialism forcefully disrupted the realization of its collective aspiration to modernize and "catch up" with the West. When our developer pronounces that "we finally can live like real bourgeois," he resumes the dream of embourgeoisement that had been disrupted by the Communist takeover.[10] What he means is that private agents are now setting things "right": renovating old buildings, increasing affluence, and helping an administratively unrestricted consumer culture to blossom: that is, they are suddenly assuming the responsibility of deferred maintenance that had accumulated during the landlordism of the socialist state. Krisztina Fehérváry vividly describes the outburst of home-improving energies, the construction of comfortable villas, luxury kitchens and bathrooms in the early years of postsocialism. She convincingly argues that this is the old catching-up frenzy of east Europeans, now portrayed as normalcy after the brief intermezzo of state socialism.[11]

The term "bourgeois" assumes a bundle of meanings both in scholarly and lay discourse. My analysis is concerned with the contemporary rhetoric of "bourgeois" as it relates to urban space and social change. However, since social criticism cannot do without the more historical and theoretical aspects of class analysis, I dip occasionally into the vast literature on class.[12] In Hungary, "bourgeois" (*polgári*) as an adjective in everyday parlance does not have much to do with the propertied bourgeoisie; rather, it is used as the incarnation of objects, lifestyles, manners, and arrangements that have been proven solid, efficient, and good. Its natural home is the bourgeois household with its interior dominated by traditional taste and propriety.[13] This set of meanings did not change much with the coming and going of socialism. Paradoxically, the term only gained a more positive connotation under state socialism as a combined effect of modernization, cheap mass production, and the ideological attack on the "bourgeoisie," which effectively made anything "bourgeois" an element of a desirable past and a constant source of nostalgia. A newly added component to this "positive" connotation is the economic grounding of the category, the reappearance of propertied bourgeoisie and the rentier.

The institutional agents of urban transformation and its interpreters have their own understanding of the material culture, the interior and exterior of this new bourgeois lifestyle, which they are slowly learning, shaping, and exploiting. The architect editor of *Beautiful Houses*, the home magazine with the largest readership, starts with a disclaimer: "we do not know how the wealthy live; even we are not allowed to see it." Architects who design for bourgeois clients share this insistence on the secrecy that surrounds wealth, underscoring that it belongs to the very definition of privilege. After they overcome their due reservations about "revealing secrets," these interpreters nevertheless delineate what constitutes a proper bourgeois home these days, and explain how residential architecture and homemaking have changed in the last two decades. They agree that recent embourgeoisement has coincided with an explosion in the size of the dwelling; in fact, all remark that houses are way too big for the needs of families and for the standards of the country. This should not come as a surprise. Size is the most obvious marker of status after location. Anyone who matters builds in the green areas of the Buda side of the Danube. The more isolated and less visible the house, the more precious it is. Dead-end streets and plots with narrow street frontage and broad interior property lines are the most highly valued sites. The floor plan of the presocialist bourgeois apartment and house has been revived, but it is now swaddled in modern luxury.

> The living room, the kitchen and the study, everyone in a bourgeois family likes them to open from the dining room or the hall. One does not need to reinvent the wheel, what is good was already invented at the end of the nineteenth century. They are called bourgeois homes. Every client is happy to see the architect draw similar plans.[14]

The basic floor plan, however, has integrated a few modern additions. Traditional separate kitchens are replaced by "American" kitchens that are incorporated in the living area; bathrooms have multiplied and are constructed for a semipublic display.[15] "From the garage that leads into the belly of the hill, one takes the indoor elevator to the underground living space. The service level in between accommodates the center of the digital "smart house," the server room along with the sauna, the laundry room, and the leisure bloc," reads the description of an average item in the home magazine.[16] Built-in electrical appliances, such as central vacuum cleaners, entertainment electronics, cameras, and fully automated security systems that are connected to the police station and can be activated through wireless Internet connection have become standard features of bourgeois home construction.[17] Swimming pools, especially outdoor ones whose maintenance requires ample resources in the Hungarian climate, are perceived as signs of senseless and truly conspicuous consumption. The editor of *Beautiful Houses,* however, doesn't disguise the new inequality represented by such lifestyles: "It is not in the poor neighborhoods such as the Dzsumbuj [a semiofficial slum of Budapest] or some housing estates infamous for their electricity cuts that the greatest stealing of energy is taking place, but in quarters where the path to the garage or the swimming pool is heated. It is there that people connect to someone else's electricity or to public sources."[18] Sumptuous gardens have also become a must for proper homes; the residential landscape has been taken over by "alien evergreen vegetation," laments this acute observer of bourgeois lifestyles, who still has not quite recovered from the shock of learning that his son's twenty-something-year-old friend just spent $50,000 on her new kitchen. He does not hide his aesthetic contempt for the new bourgeoisie: "the most kitschy buildings are erected by families in trade."[19]

This disdain for the new residential kitsch is widely shared in professional circles. The chief architect of Budapest also notes the "unimaginably low quality of the houses built by the new elite, only a fragment of which are designed by architects."[20] Architects are eager to emphasize not only the bad taste of their clients, but also their hopeless lifestyles: "the entrepreneur-bourgeois gets home at 10 PM, and does not even sit down to watch TV. The TV set that is installed in the wall of the bedroom is tilted in such a way so that one can see it from the bed. This is the only luxury he enjoys."[21] The "early to bed, early to rise" work-oriented values of the early modern European bourgeoisie[22] is neither a conscious ideological choice nor a morally motivated habit on the part of the new bourgeoisie, but a necessity rooted in the fragility of Hungarian semi-peripheral capitalism.

The globalization of material culture and taste is partly responsible for the success of the Hungarian middle classes' efforts to "catch up" with the West. The paraphernalia of bourgeois existence and material culture still emanate symbolically from the West, even if manufactured in the East; the same globally recognized brands of home furnishing and equipment are ubiquitous in the country as elsewhere in trendsetting Europe. Such brands are relatively more expensive in Hungary, where the purchasing power of the middle classes is not great enough to create a competitive downward pressure on prices. Keeping up with the European bourgeoisie and its material culture is increasingly possible yet requires proportionately more effort, hence the comparative misery of the semi-peripheral middle classes.

New Enclosures

Although much of this domestic embourgeoisement is invisible to the mere visitor or tourist, the parallel transformations of public space are sometimes jarring. Defensive architecture, fences, landscaping, and intensified market-driven class-based residential segregation have all contributed to the increased segmentation of the environment. The most striking monuments to the interaction of the new bourgeoisie with the postsocialist landscape are the car-based suburbs and a new genre of housing called residential parks. Low-income housing construction practically stopped in the 1990s—from an already reduced level the 1980s—and the little that has been built since then takes the form of private family housing in the suburbs and developer-initiated residential parks in both *urbs* and suburbs. Residential parks are the Hungarian vernacularization of gated communities or CIDs (common interest developments): that is, privately planned, developed, owned, and managed comprehensive housing units that emphasize their separation from the environment either by gating or through less imposing physical and social barriers. Gated communities or residential parks are spaces of global neoliberalism par excellence.[23] The proliferation of private enclosures, of course, is part of a worldwide urban restructuring, whose features include the growth of social inequalities, the intensification of social polarization, and the fragmentation of cities. Such enclosures are privatized reactions to the perceived vulnerability and fear of the middle classes generated by the increasing number of cracks in the social body, the waning of the idea of social integration, and the loosening of the post–World War II social contract between the classes.

Although the public image of the gated community is that of an island of affluence amid the squalor of the city,[24] the new, suburban residential park is not radically different in aspiration and class content from its urban fortified counterpart. Both are manifestations of the collective dream of isolation that has emerged amid the turbulence of modernity, in which the increasing fragility of social prestige and class position is compensated for by the spatial separation of classes. From its eighteenth-century origins, suburbia was an enactment of the bourgeois utopia of family life, community, neighborliness, leisure, and well-being.[25] Yet, as Fishman emphasizes, "this 'utopia' was always at most a partial paradise."[26] The genuine desire to escape the alienation of the modern world into a better familial and collective life and a more "natural" environment was based on exclusion: the exclusion of work from the household, industry from nature, women from the danger of the public eye, but most importantly the lower classes from the bourgeoisie.

David Harvey takes the argument further: exclusion is almost always at the very core of such utopias.[27] Their simultaneously exclusionary and authoritarian characters explain why such developments inevitably become "degenerate utopias."[28] Although the exclusionary element is present in every utopia, it has come to define the very genre of the gated community in both urban and suburban spaces. Evan McKenzie traces the history of gated communities and common-interest developments back to Ebenezer Howard's garden city, which gave the intellectual impetus to suburbanization. The adaptation of the garden city ideal to the American context, concludes McKenzie, resulted essentially in its privatization in the form of CIDs.[29] The suburban utopia degenerated into "privatopias," expanding both the exclusionary and authoritarian elements of the initial design, severely curtailing individual freedom, and replacing community with class homogeneity and a highly restrictive private regime of rules and covenants designed to secure property values.

In Hungary, in all fairness, these forms of escape are limited by the more compact character of the European city and the relative lack of municipal resources for any large-scale restructuring. The bourgeoisie's reluctance to secede *completely* from relatively generous urban services such as mass transit, health care, schools, libraries, crime protection, and so on also puts a break on exit options. Instead, there is a more complex pattern of a "patchwork quilt of islands of relative affluence"[30] combined with the ethnicization of small sections of neighborhoods, a general tendency for increased social segregation on a larger scale (the district and beyond), and the growing social gap between the Right and the Left Bank, that is, Buda and Pest. The architect-editor of *Beautiful Houses* notes: "the wealthy go to the Buda side, the middle class builds in Pest. It is almost impossible to find a house that is worth presenting on the Pest side. The architects [the presentable ones] themselves live also on the Buda side."[31]

In Budapest, where previously one could hardly find large contiguous areas of class homogeneity that would extend beyond a few blocks,[32] the spatial representation of social differences is now becoming surprisingly simple. In fact enhanced segregation may be one of the truest manifestations—socially more important than the new interiors—of the fulfillment of the interrupted bourgeois aspirations of the Hungarian middle classes. Similar observations made Partha Chatterjee ask the title question of his essay "Are Indian Cities Finally Becoming Bourgeois?"[33] A neoliberal urban regime is in the process of achieving what the postindependence city could not: the formation of more homogeneous bourgeois neighborhoods and the spatial segregation of classes in Calcutta. The withdrawal of the middle classes from politics in general and urban politics in particular, their exit from some forms of parts of the public sphere, combined with their greater services, transportation, environment, and health regulation, and the shifting of government preferences away from aiding the poor toward pacifying the elite have all contributed to the restructuring of Indian cities,[34] and are very similar to models of urban restructuring elsewhere. What makes Chatterjee's Calcutta and today's Budapest different from many other places is precisely the the catch-up nature of their utopias; the sense they are "finally becoming bourgeois," and the resultant pride, however modest, attached to this achievement.

Slaves of the New Bourgeoisie

There is a noticeable silence in public discourse about the material foundations of this modest achievement. Bourgeois homes are not constructed in a strictly bourgeois law-abiding manner. A local sociologist who has worked on "the informal economy" for decades states: "What you have in the construction business, either skilled or unskilled labor, is basically undocumented and immigrant labor." Both the day laborers and long-term employees come predominantly from Romania and Ukraine; they belong to the "diasporic labor force," that is, ethnic Hungarians from neighboring countries who, according to general rules of informality work for lower wages and with fewer benefits and protections. In fact, they are willing to work under steadily worsening conditions. According to semiofficial estimates, wage increases in the informal sector have stayed significantly below those of the minimum wage in the last ten years. While the wages of formal labor have grown five to six times, the average undocumented wage has only doubled.[35] (This informalization and transnationalization of the construction industry, of course, is not a local phenomenon. By 2004 in the United States Latino immigrants held almost 20 percent of all construction jobs, and 40 percent of new jobs in that industry. They made up nearly half of all drywallers and plasterers, 35 percent of all roofers, and a third of hazardous materials removal workers.[36])

The bourgeois home also operates using rarely acknowledged informal labor. The editor of *Beautiful Homes* relates the following story:

> The other day a pipe broke downstairs and the plumber came—my wife and brother happened to be there at the neighbor's. The water was pouring from the pipe and everyone was discussing where the broken pipe might originate. A middle-aged woman was ironing in the living room. As they were still debating the whereabouts of the pipes, she intervened authoritatively: That pipe cannot originate there. They exclaim: What? How does she know? She explains that she used to be an engineer in Romania. Works as a housekeeper in Budapest now. . . . Today al-

most all work around the house is done by Hungarians from Romania. Transylvanian Hungarians. The housekeepers, maids, gardeners, care workers—they are all from Transylvania. . . . Everyone has a housekeeper in this building. None live-in.[37]

It is no surprise that older citizens greet the return of informal labor with a vague sense of déjà vu. Bourgeois households have historically relied on similar patterns of uneven development and drawn their labor force from the hinterland. In the interwar period the sources of comparatively cheap and obedient domestic labor were similar: domestic workers were recruited predominantly from the countryside and the Hungarian diasporas.[38] The comparative economic disadvantage of rural Hungary still exists, residents of the Hungarian countryside cannot compete very effectively with a cross-border migrant work force. The desire for privacy in the home, which associates trustworthiness with employees' communication skills, creates a demand via transnational labor-contracting networks for ethnic Hungarians from the diaspora. The linguistic affinity between employer and employee in Budapest households contrasts with the language gap between employers and servants in larger, more wealthy countries.[39]

Domestic workers are a taken-for-granted, rarely theorized element of bourgeois life. The bourgeois home was from the outset construed as a "haven protected from the world of competition and materialism, from politics and the public."[40] Its privacy and disdain for materialism also long protected it from class analysis. Its laborers, who work in the private spheres, perform unproductive and not consistently physically demanding labor, and are paid partly in kind, can easily fall through the cracks of traditional analytical categories.[41] Conversely, while the definition of bourgeois may include elements of ownership, authority, and market relations to varying degrees, falling on either the Weberian or Marxist side of class analysis, control over the labor of others is usually conceived as restricted to the sphere of production and the public realm.[42]

But what academic analyses tend to ignore is often foregrounded in the popular literature on new and restored lifestyles. Magazine descriptions of bourgeois homes, for example, painstakingly list rooms and describes the layout emphasizing that the number and genre of specific rooms are key signifiers of affluence.

The bourgeois home consists of a dining room, bedrooms, salon, boudoir, kitchen, bathroom, study, and children's room. The number of rooms can vary, and some of the rooms can even be left out, but there is one particular room that distinguishes a truly bourgeois household from a lower-class one: the maid's room.[43] In cultural analysis, then, the existence of a maid thus constitutes the very definition of bourgeois private space.

Historians have yet to catch up with this return to a supposedly superseded household order. While most social historians readily admit that "servants had been of utmost importance for nineteenth-century middle-class families,"[44] and their "work made it possible for the middle-class mother to give sufficient time to family life, transmitting 'cultural capital' to the next generation,"[45] they place them among the elements of bourgeois culture that have been lost in the modernization that followed. In his examination of the bourgeois household, Kocka, along with many others, elaborates on how gender relations have changed in recent decades as a logical extension of core bourgeois principles, but conspicuously he doesn't comment on the material foundations of women's liberation. It is true in general that since the First World War the number of servants in middle-class households has steadily declined and that the social content of the category of the servant has changed—the servant class has vanished insofar as its extreme subjection and consequently its "reliability and dependency" radically diminished—but broadly understood, domestic workers have not disappeared. There is plenty of evidence suggesting that with the general commodification of care work, they have in fact multiplied, and that predominantly female domestic and day-care workers are increasingly plugged into patterns of global labor migration.[46] Married and unmarried women from the global South and European postsocialist countries have been recruited to service an exploding demand for domestic labor in the United States, Canada, the European Union, Hong Kong, and the Middle East.[47] In a more politicized reading, women's labor force participation and growing autonomization in the advanced world stand on the back of immigrant nannies and maids.[48]

There should no longer be any illusion that the glory and civilization of the bourgeoisie, or even women's liberation in its Western sense, can be separated from the undocumented migration and labor of their unnamed servants. Paradise can turn evil, or simply sour, precisely from the hubris that accompanies the implementation of utopian projects and fails to acknowledge their material foundations, boundedness, and exclusionary tendencies.

10

"Extreme Makeover": Medellín in the New Millennium

Forrest Hylton

Only that historian will have the gift of fanning the spark of hope in the past who is firmly convinced that *even the dead* will not be safe from the enemy if he wins. And this enemy has not ceased to be victorious.

—Walter Benjamin, *Theses on the Philosophy of History*

Before and After

In 2005 Colombian television launched a local version of the U.S. television program *Extreme Makeover*, in which contestants submit to the surgeon's knife in order to radically alter their appearances.[1] The program's popularity was wickedly emblematic, especially in the country's second city, Medellín. The former citadel of Pablo Escobar and the Medellín "cartel," it was the homicide capital of the world for nearly a decade after 1986, and its carnage was truly industrial in scale.[2] Noting that 50 percent of all deaths were violent in 1989, one local economic historian called the city "the world capital of crime," and in 1991 the homicide rate peaked at 381 per 100,000. Between 1990 and 2002, an estimated 55,000 people—mostly young men between 18 and 34—were murdered in Medellín.[3]

With the resurgence of powerful right-wing narco-paramilitary forces on the one hand—linked to the army, police, intelligence, business elites, and politicians—and a progressive municipal government on the other, Medellín has recently undergone a series of drastic cosmetic operations. Even for cocaine capitalism the velocity of change has been startling: in 2005, at 32.5 per 100,000, Medellín's murder rate was lower than that of Baltimore (42), Washington, DC (45), Detroit (42), and other homicide capitals of the United States. For the first time in memory, homicide in Medellín had been reduced by a factor of six; New York City's much-touted crime statistics seem underwhelming in comparison.

Like New York, Medellín is a media-saturated, image-conscious city dominated by advertising, public relations, and advanced forms of commodity fetishism. Thus *paisas*—people from Antioquia, the northwestern region of which Medellín is the capital—have celebrated lowered crime and homicide rates not only for what they mean in terms of everyday life, but also for changing perceptions of the city—the better to sell it to outsiders and themselves. Mayor Sergio Fajardo, for example, considered the city's major fashion-textile convention an opportunity for *paisas* to "project" the image of a "vibrant city, which is once again taking its place as a business hub and tourist destination."[4] In an updated ideology of regional-racial exceptionalism dating from the late nineteenth century, middle- and working-class civic boosters, ranging from extreme right to center-left, boast that Medellín is improving at breakneck speed; the emphasis on progress and positive change is relentless.

Indeed, since 2002 apartment towers, luxury hotels, supermarkets, and shopping centers—all of which generate demand for private security and surveillance—have been sprouting from the ground at a breathtaking rate. The country's largest conglomerates and over seventy foreign enterprises now locate their Colombian headquarters in Medellín: Phillip Morris, Kimberly Clark, Levi Strauss, Renault, Toyota, and Mitsubishi, for example. A new, 60,000-square-meter international convention center, opened in 2005, and over a dozen international conventions are now held annually.[5] In addition to a thriving fashion industry second only to São Paulo's and a booming medical research sector (a Latin American leader in organ transplants as well as AIDS and cancer research) there is a world-class museum-park complex in the city center, housing the works of renowned painter, and native son, Fernando Botero, and featuring his sculptures in an open-air setting.

Symptomatically, the museum zone was formerly dominated by a red-light district on the north side and an open-air market for indigent drug addicts on the west. In the late 1990s, publicly sanctioned private security forces "cleansed" the area (*lo limpiaron*): displacing, murdering, disappearing, and threatening its "disposable" inhabitants—drug sellers, addicts, prostitutes, street kids, petty thieves, called *desechables*—to make it safe for urban redevelopment. After 2000, a city-wide "pacification" campaign was then waged by newer groups of right-wing narco-paramilitaries working closely with elements in the police, army, and intelligence services, supported by businessmen, politicians in both parties (Liberal and Conservative), as well as the Catholic Church. "Pacification," which received strong institutional backing, is the condition of possibility for the much-touted improvements in tourism, investment, and security. It has affected the very shape of the city's space.

The democracy that Medellín's neoliberal plastic surgery allows is a "weak" or "thin" citizenship, based largely on North Atlantic models of consumerism and electoral politics. The dream of a radical democratic citizenship focused on substantive civil, political, and social rights has, for now at least, been defeated. But volcanic social forces still rumble in the subsoil of the new boom, and in the capsule history that follows I examine the violent vectors of Medellín's past—the cocaine cartels, youth gangs, armed left insurgencies, and right-wing paramilitaries—with full understanding that in Colombia what is past is seldom really past.[6]

Disputing Territory, 1985–2002

> European feudalism was mainly gangsterism that had become society itself.
> —Barrington Moore Jr., *Origins of Dictatorship and Democracy*

People fleeing political violence and economic crisis in the countryside streamed into the city by the tens of thousands each year from the 1950s through the 1970s. Scores of "instant" neighborhoods sprouted up the steep green hillside slopes to the east and west of the Medellín River, especially in the northern Aburrá Valley (1,500 meters). By the mid–twentieth century, the city center had skyscrapers, cinemas and theaters, wide avenues, parks and monuments, schools and universities, commercial boulevards for pedestrians, as well as a train and trolley system. In 1947, *Life* magazine tagged it a "capitalist paradise." Its climate, hovering at twenty-four degrees Celsius, made it "the city of eternal spring," and because of its expanding textile industry, it was also called the "Manchester of Colombia."[7]

The central contradiction in oligarchic, industrial capitalist development was two-sided: the state did not rule its urban frontiers, the continued expansion of which its agrarian policies guaranteed, while industry did not create enough jobs to employ more than a minority of the new proletariat. Job creation stagnated beginning in the mid-1960s, and while occasionally the army and police were sent in to demolish illegal squatter settlements, the two major political parties trucked their clients to the polls on voting day, or fought for control of Juntas de Acción Comunal—neighborhood committees established under President Alberto Lleras Camargo (1958–62), to which meager state resources were funneled in order to establish a minimal clientelist base. Lleras Camargo was the architect of the bipartisan National Front (1958–74) accords. His urban policies set the mold through the 1970s.

While the new neighborhoods—hand-built from concrete brick, wood, cement, and *bareque*—organized, petitioned, and mobilized to obtain public services in the 1970s, there were fewer factory jobs with each passing generation.

Though the distribution of educational opportunities become slightly more equitable nationwide through the public university system in the 1970s, it remained abysmal in comparative terms, and led to the emergence of a new middle-class faction with higher education but without secure employment.[8] With the appearance of urban guerrillas and right-wing death squads, repression of community-labor-student protest deepened, and the broad urban left fragmented. Where worker, student, and insurgent projects had tended toward convergence in the late 1970s, each followed a separate course in the early 1980s.

This occurred, moreover, in the context of a shift away from manufacturing for the national market toward a neoliberal, extractive export-enclave economy based on gold, bananas, petroleum, emeralds, cocaine. Industrial manufacturing had generated enormous expectations for improvements in education, housing, health care, and working conditions, as people fought for political, social, and civil rights. Following the crisis of protected industry and coffee export agriculture in the 1970s and 1980s, however, hopes for social mobility were dashed.[9]

With a weak state, a ruling class in disarray, and increasingly mobilized urban communities of the new proletariat, pretenders to sovereignty emerged from left and right. By 1985 the Colombian census registered a count of 69 percent urban dwellers, up from 31 percent in 1938, and rural guerrillas—a permanent feature of the political landscape after the 1950s—turned their attention to the cities.[10] Working in "peace camps" negotiated with the Conservative administration of Belisario Betancur in 1985, Colombia's urban, media-savvy insurgents, M-19, and the Maoist EPL trained young men for urban warfare.[11]

When peace negotiations among three insurgent groups—FARC, M-19, and the EPL—broke down in 1985, the longstanding rural conflict accelerated sharply, as paramilitaries, fortified with funds from cocaine entrepreneurs and encouraged by the failure of negotiations, undertook the physical elimination of the political opposition of alleged supporters of the FARC, by far the strongest military force on the left. Together with the Colombian Communist Party, the FARC founded a broad left party, the Unión Patriótica (UP), which served as a clearinghouse for urban radicals of all ideological stripes. In Antioquia as elsewhere, students, professors, and professionals, as well as trade unionists and peasant activists associated with the UP, were subject to selective assassination. The broad urban left of the UP collapsed in the face of sustained right-wing terror.[12]

At the same time, young men in working- and lower-middle-class neighborhoods formed gangs involved in extortion, drug dealing, auto theft, armed robbery, contract murder, bus hijackings, jewel heists, and bank robbery. Following the demise of M-19 after the Palace of Justice disaster in November 1985, and in the midst of a recession engineered by monetary devaluation in 1986–87, "peace camp" veterans organized themselves into gangs in the northeastern *comunas*.[13] In the same district, but lower down the slopes, fifteen males from the lower-middle-class Prisco family did the same.

Some gangs—the Priscos, but also the Ramada in Bello and Quika's crew in Castilla—became integrated into the networks that revolved around Pablo Escobar and his Medellín Cartel. Gangs had existed since the 1960s, but before Escobar their activities had never impinged directly on everyday life. Now they put a brake on processes of community self-organization, imposing a new reign of murder and intimidation. Would the political process be broadened to include popular neighborhood civic participation in making and implementing decisions? Would civil, social, and political rights—for housing, health care, education, and better employment—be conquered by the majority? Or would gangsterism take over, reducing citizenship to consumerism for those with disposable income, and equal rights to poverty, grief, and fear for the rest?

Beginning in the mid-1980s, under the leadership of left community activists and former guerrilla insurgents, young men formed independent "popular militias" (*milicias populares*) to root out gangs and crime in their neighborhoods through force of arms. Squatters in the northeastern *comuna* (ward) organized self-defense militias spontaneously as early as 1985: the "Masked Ones" (*Los Capuchos*), composed of peace camp veterans and former M-19 militants, appeared in 1985–86. Near the territory controlled by the Masked Ones, the first militia group—MP/PP—made its appearance.

Militias were dedicated, at least in theory, to community empowerment and uplift, and their activities included night patrols, resolution of domestic and neighborly disputes, as well as neighborhood improvement projects such as cleanup, paving, painting, sports, and recreation. Responding to the deterioration of personal and collective security, militia growth was rapid and overwhelming in 1988–89. Commanders received popular support and enjoyed political legitimacy during initial phase of growth through 1991.[14]

The first left militias were independent, but the rural insurgencies were quick to exert their influence, with the ELN in the northeast and the FARC in the west.[15] When the state either ignored militias or looked favorably on them in the 1980s, militias defeated small and medium-sized gangs, only to give rise to more violent, professional gangs with closer ties to narcotrafficking, and, ipso facto, elements within state security agencies. Like Escobar's war against the government, war with militias served as a laboratory for gang mutation toward concentration, centralization, and fusion with the most authoritarian elements of the state.

Under siege, militias reproduced the same authoritarian state and gangster practices against which they had organized themselves. Ultimately, the armed urban left failed due not only to astonishing levels of state repression and growing gangster terrorism, but also because it lacked political strategy, substituted revolutionary rhetoric for political education and community organizing, and relied on armed young men.[16] In retrospect, former governor Gilberto Echeverry's fear of a communist takeover of the city, expressed in a letter to Liberal President César Gaviria, seems comically exaggerated—especially in light of global shifts then unfolding—but the spread of microsovereignties, exercised in the name of "the people," was real.[17]

Unlike militias, by employing gang youth en masse, Escobar shook the foundations of the state and contributed enormously to the specialization and professionalization of gangs; perhaps his most enduring legacy.[18] In 1989, Liberal President Virgilio Barco declared war on the cartel leader after Escobar, fearing extradition to the United States, killed Luis Carlos Galán, a center-left politician who was certain to have been the Liberal Party presidential candidate in 1990. Barco ordered a special Search Bloc (*Bloque de Búsqueda*) composed of elite police units from outside the city—natives were considered unreliable—to hunt for

Escobar. Escobar, in turn, hired an army from the northeastern and northwestern *comunas* in his war against the army and the police, the judiciary and politicians.

Hundreds from the *Bloque de Búsqueda* were killed, while massacres of impoverished youths soared. The price for a dead police officer in December 1989 was 500,000 pesos ($250), and by 1991 it had gone as high as 1,500,000 pesos ($750).[19] Escobar's minions set off 150 car bombs in 1990, while some five hundred policemen were assassinated in Medellín in 1990–91. Following the negotiation of Escobar's imprisonment under President Gaviria in July 1991, the Colombian military, police, and intelligence agencies led an "unprecedented wave of repression against *comuna* dwellers": twenty to forty young men were found dead each weekend.[20] By 1992, Escobar, who fled the prison he constructed and staffed with guards of his choice, was at war with the government again; for the second consecutive year, there were more than 6,000 homicides in Medellín.

President Gaviria engineered the neoliberal reconstruction of economy and society, but came under relentless pressure from Washington to extradite Escobar. To force Escobar to surrender, the DEA, the CIA, DAS, CTI, the Cali cartel, and, crucially, Escobar's former allies and associates in the Medellín Cartel formed an alliance publicly known as *Los Pepes* ("Those Persecuted by Pablo Escobar"). From January to December 1993, Carlos Castaño, a narco-paramilitary chieftain who started out in the early 1980s as an employee of Escobar's in the Magdalena Medio Valley, led the campaign against his former boss, using hit squads composed of gang youths from Medellín. He went after gangs and traffickers that remained loyal to Escobar, as well as their family members, but also his primordial enemies: "communist subversives."[21] The homicide rate stayed high, at 311 per 100,000.

Through *Los Pepes*, links between repressive organs of the state, narco-paramilitaries, and neighborhood gangs were strengthened. Carlos Castaño, "Don Berna," rose from hired gun to become head of security for one of Escobar's lieutenants, coordinated hit squads against Escobar before founding *La Terraza* in the mid-1990s. This "gang of gangs" was based in Manrique, one of the northeastern *comuna*'s toughest neighborhoods. *La Terraza* controlled a substantial portion of organized crime: bank robbery, contract killing, jewel heists, auto theft, armed robbery, extortion, loan-sharking, gambling, prostitution, and retail drug sales. Through Don Berna, *La Terraza* also coordinated cocaine exports through Urabá, building on the connection established with Carlos Castaño in the days of *Los Pepes*.

Not everyone lost in the lottery of gang warfare: for survivors, it provided a path to upward mobility and territorial clout. In 1992, a "peace process" between the government and independent militias led to the signing of the Media Luna Accords in 1994 and the demobilization of some eight hundred militia members. A security cooperative (COOSERCOM) founded by Metroseguridad, a municipal security entity, incorporated the ex-militia leaders as heads of security in the neighborhoods they had run as insurgent commanders.[22] The government's goal was to get citizens to take responsibility for their own security—in other words, to do the state's job, but within its purview. Militias tied to the FARC and the ELN in riposte formed the Popular Militia Bloc (BPM) and sought to occupy demobilized territory. BPM militias killed between 100 and 300 of the COOSERCOM ex-militia members by 1996, at which point COOSERCOM was dissolved because of allegations of widespread human-rights abuses.

Surviving gang leaders meanwhile regrouped in right-wing paramilitary groups, financed by private enterprise, operating with "the support and legal sanction of the State" under Liberal President Ernesto Samper and then-governor of Antioquia, Álvaro Uribe (1995–97).[23] In Antioquia and Córdoba, they were largely co-extensive with ACCU paramilitaries.[24] Following Escobar's death in late 1993 and Fidel Castaño's "disappearance" in 1994, Carlos Castaño became the chief of ACCU paramilitary forces in the lowlands and savannahs of Córdoba and Urabá. With massacres mushrooming nationwide on his orders, in 1998, Castaño took the war to Medellín. Allied with *La Terraza*, and led by "Doble Cero"—another veteran of *Los Pepes*—Castano's paramilitaries had few competitors. With Doble Cero and Bloque Metro making offers local gang leaders could not refuse, under Don Berna, Bloque Cacique Nutibara also prospered. The two groups, BM and BCN, conquered 70 percent of the city by 2002. Gangs that tried to hold out paid tribute or disappeared altogether.

Tragedy and Farce, 2002–2006

> When you play the fiddle at the top of the state, what else is to be expected but that those down below dance?
> —Karl Marx, *Eighteenth Brumaire of Louis Bonaparte*

Surviving militia redoubts in the northeast and central-west districts were stormed during a series of spectacular military operations in 2002 and 2003. Right-wing paramilitaries moved in behind the troops to take over the conquered territories, and by the end of 2002 Don Berna had assumed control of the city's underworld: 8,000 youth grouped into perhaps 200 gangs.[25] With the help of the state security agencies, he mopped up the last of the hold-out militias as well as the rival Bloque Metro. Official homicide and violent crime rates fell dramatically in the aftermath of Berna's victory, even if disturbing numbers of clandestine graveyards appeared in some neighborhoods (part of the cost, Don Berna would later explain, of creating the "necessary climate so that investment returns, particularly foreign, which is fundamental if we do not want to be left behind by the engine of globalization").[26] Berna was thus the first *capo* since Escobar to have unified organized crime within the city, and in November 2003 he became the first narco-paramilitary to officially demobilize.

Unofficially, he continued to manage extortion, intelligence gathering, contract killing, auto theft, bank robbery, gambling, drug sales, money laundering, and private security. He also had a hand in construction, transport, wholesale and retail, finance, real-estate development, and cable television. In the 2004 elections, thirty of his candidates won posts as heads of neighborhood associations (Juntas de Acción Comunal). They ran through an NGO called Corporación Democracia, led by Giovanni Marín, alias Comandante R, a butcher turned ideologue who later ran for Congress. According to Marín, "My conscience is clear. People should know that we collaborated in pacifying the city; that we handed over a city in peace."[27] By 2005, close to 4,000 demobilized right-wing paramilitaries had flocked to the city because of the generous benefits offered by the municipal government; an estimated 6,000 more were to follow by the end of 2007.

Superficially, the contrast between Don Berna's modus operandi and the mayor's office could hardly be sharper. Because of its ambitious public works, support for "peace" with the paramilitaries, and lack of corruption, Mayor Fajardo enjoys even greater popularity (est. 90 percent) than right-wing President Uribe (est. 70 percent). Since personal enrichment and the distribution of clientelist largesse are not among his goals as mayor, contracts are not doled out to friends, relatives, and retainers; accounting processes are relatively transparent, budgeting participatory. In this as in other respects, Fajardo—voted Colombia's "sexiest man alive" for several consecutive years—is unlike any mayor Medellín has had.

In hillside neighborhoods where the state has been absent, Fajardo has invested in education. The centerpiece of the administration is a program called "Medellín, the most educated," which envisions the construction of six parks with public libraries in poor areas like the northeastern and central-western *comunas*, to go along with ten new schools that will serve 20,000 students, at a total cost of US$1.6 billion. For the first time, city government is establishing a nonrepressive presence in *comunas* disputed by gangs, militias, and narco-paramilitaries until Don Berna's counterinsurgent triumph and demobilization.

Yet the school to be built in Las Independencias, in the central-west, looks like a barracks or a prison: composed of six two-story blocs joined by stairs, long black metal bars separate large glass windows on the front of each bloc, the first story of which is made from grey and white brick, the second from varying shades of green stone that suggest camouflage. The library in Santo Domingo, in the northeast, looks like a military research installation. This is the architecture pacification has enabled, with security functions built into design. It is worth asking what their impact on surrounding land values will be, and whether they will open the door to gentrification.

Meanwhile, Don Berna's trajectory from hired gun to mafia don, and from urban *latifundista* to "pacifier" of Medellín, epitomizes the refeudalization of power in Colombia's neoliberal export economy, underwritten by cocaine export production under paramilitary control. This fusion of politics, property, and organized crime, reflected in the paramilitary grip over security for capital investment, including but not limited to the cocaine export business, links the city's bad old days to its good new ones, and largely determines the present and future shape of the built environment.

But the city is part of a larger development process. Since 1990, Antioquia has pronounced itself "the best corner of America" for large-scale capital investment in mining, transport infrastructure, megaprojects like dams and canals, hardwood logging, and banana and African palm plantations. At long last, regional elites may achieve their desire, first expressed during the coffee export boom a more than century ago, to integrate their highland capital with the lowlands of the Caribbean and Pacific littorals.[28]

The contradictory unity of progressive municipal politics and private, narco-paramilitary power takes on its fullest significance, however, against the backdrop of U.S.-dominated free-trade projects in the hemisphere tied to large-scale, U.S.-funded counterinsurgent projects like Plan Colombia. After three generations of cocaine-fueled urban warfare, Medellín is now positioned to become the leading edge of economic integration with the United States by linking the coffee axis of the Andean interior to the Pacific and Atlantic coasts. Even if that dream—a variation on El Dorado—does not materialize, it is clear that the region's ruling class has shrewdly used narco-paramilitaries to re-secure investment, property rights, and neoliberal economic development.

Channeled into privatized consumption and leisure, the pursuit of individual freedom is no longer tied to the dreams of human liberation or social transformation that animated earlier struggles. The individual has been severed from collective solidarity, individual security divorced from social protections. As in most of Latin America, "state- and elite-orchestrated preventive and punitive terror was key to ushering in neoliberalism."[29] Terror was also the core of "pacification" after 2000, effecting reforms needed for Medellín's makeover into a paradise for tourists and investors. This is civilization as barbarism. As the exhumation of mass graves attests, even the dead are not safe.

11

The Most Unjust Country in the World

Emir Sader

Brazil presents a very contradictory image to the outside world. The seductive face of Brazil is represented by its music, soap operas, football, innovative cities like Curitiba, and, of course, the delirious aphrodisia of Carnaval. However, Brazil is also the daily violence of its cities and the misery of its countryside. It has the world's highest national ratio of socioeconomic inequality and remains wracked by violence—including the massacres of children and indigenous peoples—as well as by the record destruction of nature.

The real Brazil, in other words, remains foreign to the image of a country "blessed by God," according to the famous song of Gilberto Gil, one of the most important contemporary Brazilian composers and the present minister of culture. It is also very different from the country of its national anthem, which both idolizes and condemns Brazil as "eternally lying in the splendid cradle." And if the writer Stefan Zweig was correct when he described Brazil as the "country of the future," it may not be the future that he had in mind.

A Paradise of Latifundias

One of the greatest paradoxes of Brazil—an immense country of 8.5 million square kilometers, the fourth largest in land area on earth—is the centrality of landlessness as a political and social problem. In the abstract, the problem should hardly exist: owing to its excellent terrain, soil, and climate, Brazil has a vast cultivable area. If the agricultural potentials of other giant countries such as China, the United States, Canada, and Russia are limited by their very large areas of desert, mountains, or permanently frozen areas, Brazil has clearly enough arable soil to fully supply the needs of its current urban and rural populations. However, Brazil's entire history is built upon the mismanagement and betrayal of its potential agricultural wealth. Indeed the agrarian problem is at the very root of Brazil being the most unjust country in the world, with the most extreme maldistribution of income and land ownership.

Consider the macropicture: Brazil has 850 million hectares of land, including lakes, rivers, and mountains, of which 650 million are considered to be occupied. But what does "occupied" mean? Occupied in terms of production? No. Modern Brazil is characterized by the prevalence of noneconomic landuse and ownership: they are the property of someone who legalized them in some way, or they are simply in the hands of squatters. The remaining 200 million hectares are public land, belonging to the federal, state, and municipal governments, and most are in Amazonia, in completely uninhabited regions. There are also 95 million hectares belonging to indigenous peoples, less than half of which have been mapped.

As it has never carried out serious agrarian reform, Brazil has extreme levels of concentration of land ownership, including some of the largest latifundia in world history. Thus the twenty-seven largest properties in Brazil are about the same size as the United Kingdom, and the three hundred largest properties are as large, in aggregate, as Sweden. At the other end of the scale, 1,338,000 properties of less than ten hectares, accounting for 31.6 percent of the total number of properties, take up just 1.8 percent of the total area of Brazil.

Neoliberal theoreticians and apostles of the so-called "green revolution," of course, argue there is no longer any economic necessity or historical justification for agrarian reform. Capitalism in the countryside has already carried out all the technical reforms to make large-scale production efficient and profitable. Booming export markets for Brazilian soya and citrus products, they argue, demonstrate the success of large-scale agribusiness. Agrarian reform in a Mexican or

Russian sense would only undermine the dynamism of the agricultural sector and lead to economic retrogression. These apologetics, however predictable, simply skirt the gigantic social contradictions rooted in Brazil's extraordinary history of land ownership.

The Legacy of "Late" Slavery

Brazil was the largest-scale example since the Roman Empire of a slave-owning society. The extermination of indigenous peoples, of whom there were 2 million when the Portuguese invaded Brazil, was followed by the importation of millions of African workers, the first generation of the Brazilian working class, the productive base of successive export cycles that the colonizers imposed on Brazil: those of sugar, coffee, and rubber. The Portuguese administered the colony of Brazil as a royal property but acted with a brutal profit-making logic. Portuguese colonization differed in some important respects from the Spanish colonial model: while a university was set up in the Dominican Republic as early as the sixteenth century, Brazil had to wait until the twentieth century. The fundamental mechanisms of plunder and primitive accumulation, however, were similar.

The real divergence in historical trajectories began with the Napoleonic invasions at the beginning of the nineteenth century. While Spain gloriously resisted, and the pictures of Velásquez immortalize this; the Portuguese crown fled Lisbon for Brazil, whose ports it quickly opened up to "friendly countries." What seemed to be the embrace of liberal idelogy was, in fact, neocolonial dependence upon Great Britain, its main customer and creditor.

The survival of slavery in Brazil, moreover, was directly linked to the arrival of the royal court in Rio de Janeiro. Independence, in the Brazilian case, was a pact among the elite, in which the end of colonization did not mean the establishment of a republic but rather the switch to a monarchy, in which succession to the throne took place through placing the crown on the head of the son of the Portuguese monarch. The farce was even clearer as the son of the king, crowned as Pedro I, proclaimed independence with a shout—"Independence or death!,"—without it being clear exactly what he was fighting against, as he had actually received the crown from the hands of his father. And, to make matters worse, his father addressed him with words that were highly offensive to the Brazilian people: "My son, place the crown on your head, before some adventurer does so." The "adventurers" were the Brazilian people; and the coronation was the preemption of a real liberation led by a Brazilian Bolívar or San Martin.

The principal victims of this elite pact with monarchy were Afro-Brazilians, and slavery was officially abolished only in 1888, almost seven decades after independence. This "delay" had far-reaching legacies in the concentration of land ownership and the dispossession of former slaves. The crown, worried about rebellions of black workers, attempted to introduce new legislation that would restrict access to land, thereby guaranteeing the availability of labor, as the slaves would remain on the farms, now working as "free" wage earners.

The monarchy passed the crucial Lei de Terras (Land Law) in 1850, which defined the structure of land distribution in Brazil. Only those who had legalized their properties in the notaries' offices, paying a sum to the crown, could be considered proprietors. The law automatically discriminated against the poor and prevented free slaves from becoming proprietors since they lacked money to pay taxes. Meanwhile, the large landholders forged deeds—they put the phony documents in their drawers, where cricket excrement gave them the appearance of ancient papers—and thus these lands were fraudently legalized and were known as *griladas* lands and their occupiers as *grileiros*: *grilo* being the Portuguese term for "cricket."

Thus, through fraud in the shadow of slavery, the large latifundists became allpowerful in rural society. Those who had received land from the crown regularized their properties, thereby transforming them into private property. And the black people, once slavery had finished, were fixed as the poor, whether they stayed in the country or moved to the towns, where they became part of the miserable, stigmatized masses. Even when labor became "free," with the end of slavery, racial peonage continued. Thus, the problem of slavery was transformed into the problem of land ownership and has been the very foundation of social injustice in Brazil.

Radical Injustice

Brazil is the most unjust country in the world, with the worst distribution of wealth, and the roots of this radical inequality lie in the agrarian problem. As measured by the Gini index (a ratio of income and/or wealth concentration), Brazil is the country with the second-highest concentration of land in the world, second only to Paraguay, with an index of 0.94 (the nearer to 1, the higher the concentration). (As the majority of the large landowners in Paraguay are Brazilians, it can also be said that this, by extension, is also a projection of the Brazilian phenomenon.) More than 2.4 million properties (57.6 percent) occupy 6 percent of the area (27 million hectares) while less than 70,000 properties (1.7 percent) occupy an area of more than 183 million hectares or 43 percent of the national total. Likewise, 3 million small landholders who own less than 10 hectares account for 53 percent of the total population of farmers but own only 3 percent of all the land. Conversely, 50,000 large landholders account for just 0.8 percent of total proprietors but own 44 percent of all the agricultural land in Brazil.

Of these large properties, only 30 percent are classified as productive, contradicting the belief that says that large-scale ownership ensures modern productivity. The small properties, moreover, generate the greatest number of jobs in the countryside. Small properties produce more than 14.4 million jobs, that is, 87 percent of the total, while large properties account for only 2.5 percent (420,000) of jobs. More than 50 percent of the establishments with more than 200 hectares employ no contracted workers, also contradicting the idea that large properties mean more jobs.

Another fiction propagated by neoliberal discourse is that latifundia ensure mechanization and economies of scale: yet official data show that, in Brazil, 64 percent of the productive employment of tractors occurs in small production units and just 8 percent in the large units. Fertilizers are a special problem as just 38 percent of properties are able to afford their use, with the rest dependent upon the (diminishing) natural fertility of the soil. However more than half of the establishments—and 90 percent of smaller properties—use insecticides, weed killers, and other agrotoxins. Thus "the most spectacular result of the modernization" of agriculture has been the gradual poisoning of the land. The financing of agriculture is also extremely unequal, with relatively small streams of credit available—five times less than in the United states—and concentrated in the huge agribusiness units: less than 10 percent of properties receive more than 20 percent of loans. Yet in spite of the lack of land, technology, and credit, the smaller units produce the larger output of agricultural products and generate more income.

The Agrarian Problem in Neoliberalism

Thus the real role of the large-scale rural property—contrary to neoliberal theory—has not been to provide a dynamic axis of export production, let alone an engine of employment generation, but rather to ensure a reserve of owner-ship and social hegemony for the dominant elites, based on the misallocation of land and productivity. Brazil, to its shame, has never carried out an agricultural reform, has never democratized social relations in the countryside, and has never provided access to land to those who wish to work it and produce the food the na-tion needs. Brazil imports food while millions of workers remain landless. Mil-lions of these workers migrate to the cities, increasing urban overcrowding. In a country of 170 million people, the majority of whom are concentrated in seven metropolitan regions, the lack of agrarian reform prevents any dynamic expan-sion of the internal market led by the working-class demand. In brief, there is a vicious circle: more mouths to feed in the cities than in the countryside, which is full of unproductive land and a concentration of property by large companies, many of them from outside Brazil, which produce for exportation.

The neoliberal model of development may represent itself as the last word in globalized modernity, but in Brazil it preserves, indeed exacerbates, the worst el-ements of the past. Since the early 1990s small producers have been driven to the wall, as large properties, over 2,000 hectares, have increased their total acreage from 120 million to 150 million hectares. Conversely, more than 92,000 small pro-ducers (those with less than 100 hectares) have lost their farms, and almost 2,000,000 rural wage earners have lost their jobs. During the last decade and a half of ruthless neoliberal policies, moreover, both total cultivated area and total farm production have decreased.

This reduction in home-market agriculture, with the resulting rise in unemployment, the increasingly precarious labor relations, and the growing concentration of income has gone hand in hand with increased specialization on a handful of export crops, especially soy, corn, sugar, and citrus. Despite its almost unique capacity to meet its own food needs, Brazil has dramatically increased the imports of foodstuffs such as dairy products, beans, and fruit, which it can grow perfectly well at home.

This perverse decline of home production for the sake of export profits corresponds to the control that foreign multinationals now exercise over Brazil's food supply and agrarian landuse. The ever-increasing concentration of land ownership and production is functional to neoliberal policy because it favors export and foreign trade over internal consumption and rural democracy. The present trends, even under the populist presidency of Lula, is toward even larger production units and centralized ownership that will further destroy family-based agriculture and push more poor rural people into the cities and *favelas*.

The present social crisis, concentrated in the large conurbations, has its origins in the countryside, in Brazil's persistent agrarian problem. Nothing summarizes Brazil's contradictions more piquantly than the fact that in a great urban and industrialized country, after a decade and a half of "modernizing neoliberal reforms" and a famous "green revolution," and despite a vast extent of rich, cultivatable land, the most important and powerful national social protest movement is the MST, the Landless Rural Workers' Movement.

Bunkering in Paradise (or, Do Oldsters Dream of Electric Golf Carts?)

Marco d'Eramo

Translated by Graeme Thomson

Minnesota: The Mall That Swallowed America

Rising from a landscape as flat as a pool table and with temperatures hovering barely above zero, the Twin Cities of Minneapolis and St. Paul seem unlikely tourist destinations in January. Yet even in the bleak winter months they attract more than 100,000 visitors a day, 3 million per month, from as far away as Korea and Japan. The irresistible magnet isn't the charm of St. Paul's older neighborhoods or the bustling high-tech energy of Minneapolis, but rather the cult appeal of a consumer paradise in the suburb of Bloomington, not far from the international airport.

From a distance, the Mall of America (MoA) is a massive gray concrete slab surrounded by vast parking lots, easily mistaken for a large auto plant or oversized state prison. In fact it is the original *ubermall*: an unsurpassed epitome of the age of bourgeois consumption that began in the mid-nineteenth century with Benjamin's Parisian arcades and Zola's Bon Marche. Although no longer the largest U.S. mall (the title is currently shared by monstrosities in Schaumberg, a suburb of Chicago, and in King of Prussia, a suburb of Philadelphia), it retains the aura of having pioneered (in 1992) a new threshold of commodity fetishism and public spectacle. Even if the *Wall Street Journal* now dismisses it as a "dinosaur," its millions of loyal shoppers understand, at least instinctively, that MoA is the compendium and pardigm of all malls, the monumental herald of the Age of Edge Cities and Exurbs.[1] Like the Chrysler Building or the original Anaheim Disneyland, its charisma is not diminished by later knockoffs with larger commercial surface areas.

Even for supermall-sated Americans, MoA remains an overwhelming experience. Anchored by four huge department stores, it offers shoppers the choice of 525 shops and boutiques, as well as a fourteen-screen multiplex, eighteen full-service restaurants, and twenty-seven fast-food stands. The pièce d'résistance, under a vast glass roof, is a seven-acre central space that includes an aquarium, Dinosaur Walk Museum, a huge Lego playpark, and roller-coaster rides. Until 2005, the huge atrium was known as Snoopy Park, celebrating the cartoon creations of St. Paul native Charles Schulz. But Peanuts' *peluches* have now been sold for peanuts in a corporate turnover of logos and brands.

MoA, of course, is quintessentially suburban, meaning far from the old city center (otherwise where would its developers have found so much cheap land for car parks?) and heavily securitized. Americans, of course, are constantly bludgeoned by the media to fear traditional urban spaces. Indeed the specter of inner-city gangs (which is to say, of racial difference) helps drive the construction of larger and larger self-contained spaces for middle-class consumption and recreation. Since the riotous days of the late 1960s, Americans have come to accept malls as tranquil oases where they can enjoy evening family strolls, and wives can windowshop in safety. (Not by chance does the name "mall" derive from the tree-lined avenue running from Buckingham Palace along the northern edge of St. James's Park, where from the late seventeenth century affluent Londoners could take a walk or ride their horses.)

Everything about the mall is designed to tranquilize. The lifts all have glass walls to prevent "elevator rape," one of American culture's mythical topoi. Parking areas in malls have higher ceilings than usual and are lit during the daytime as a security measure against another great metropolitan legend—the car-park assault. The mall's private police, who can often be seen patrolling the corridors on horseback, work in tandem via radio with the local police precinct, while CCTV cameras check that the teenage mallrats do no more than they're supposed to, which is spend every last dime they have in their pockets (each visitor spends an average of $68).[2] Mike Davis coined the useful expression "Panopticon Mall"[3] to describe this institution, where the consumer is continually visible (and controllable), whether in the changing room or the bathroom, in line with the model of perpetual exposure to surveillance that Jeremy Bentham imagined for his nineteenth-century Panopticon prison, famously discussed by Michel Foucault in *Discipline and Punish*.

However, as we shall see in the case of private cities, the "securitarian obsession" (a French coinage that conveys the idea well) is just one of the factors that have contributed to the irresistible success of the mall as metaphor for modern life. The main reason for the mall's success is that unlike shopping centers of old that fulfilled only one of the city center's traditional functions—commerce—it aims to take care of them all: a place for entertainment (cinema, theater), for socializing (restaurants, bars, nightclubs), and for strolling (along the covered and heated boulevards). The bigger malls usually contain one or two large hotels. There are even people who go for an early morning jog along the boulevards before the shops open. The mall functions as both avenue and town square.

What we see here is a process that has frequently recurred during the course of modernity: a spontaneous preexisting configuration is dismantled or destroyed only to then be reconstructed artificially when the lack of what has been erased or swept away is sufficiently felt. During the 1800s rivers that traversed cities were filled in because they had become repositories for toxic waste and all manner of nauseating gunk. But then to restore an idealized semblance of nature,[4] landscape architects created artificial rivers and lakes in city parks such as Central Park, Bois du Boulogne, and Hyde Park: perhaps the most spectacular is Paris's Buttes-Chaumont, which in 1860 was nothing more than a garbage dump but within three years had been transformed by Baron Georges Eugène Haussmann's landscape architects "into a kind of romantic Switzerland, complete with ridges, woods, a 100-foot waterfall, river, lakes, a gorge spanned by a bridge and rocks."[5]

A similar logic of destruction and reconstitution is evident in the redevelopment of certain American suburbs. Real-estate developers level immense tracts of land, which are then overlaid with an enormous gridiron of single-family houses and straight roads intersecting at right angles: flat terrain and right angles are essential factors in mass production, keeping construction costs down.[6] But when the same suburbs undergo gentrification, the landscape is artificially reshaped by introducing hillocks and excavating hollows, while the monotony of the grid is relieved by curves, bumps, dips, and bends. In the realtors' jargon it becomes a question of bringing in "amenities," carrying out a "landscape upgrade" (by for example planting shrubs, the same ones that were systematically removed when development began) or better, creating a "softscape."[7] Typically, this nature regained is to original nature what a golf-course fairway is to a prairie.

The procedure is much the same in the case of malls: the functions of avenue, square, and city center are recreated once real streets, squares, and town centers have been devitalized. The process of emptying the street as "part of the public sphere" reached its conclusion in the twentieth century, though it had already commenced in the nineteenth century when the village thoroughfare was supplanted by the city avenue or boulevard. "The village road," writes Franco Moretti, "was certainly a thousand times poorer in stimuli than the city street. On the other hand, however—and this is the point—the near totality of life occurred in the road. The city has certainly given full value to the street as a channel of communication . . . but it has drastically and irreparably devalued it as a place of social experience. . . . The great novelty of urban life, in fact, does not consist in having thrown the people into the street, but in having raked them up and shut them into offices and houses. It does not consist in having intensified the public dimension, but in having invented the private one."[8]

The street, emptied of event and activity, subsequently became a space of signs. Only the oldest among us can fully recall the communal life that once claimed the neighborhood street as its outdoor living room. Until the 1950s in a city like Rome, whose population was about 2 million at the time, families on a summer evening would take tables and chairs down from their second- or third-story apartments to dine on the sidewalks with their neighbors. These days, of course, such a ritual would be impossible, not only on account of the automobiles and scooters claiming a monopoly of the street to themselves, but also because mentalities have changed. It is no longer deemed "proper" to expose the familial dimension of our lives—the intimacy of the kitchen table or parlor—to public scrutiny, although it has become completely normal to eat in the *déhors* of a restaurant.

Likewise children on the streets of European cities a half-century ago, like the urchins in Dickens's or Dumas's novels, formed play gangs and created worlds of their own, free of adult convention, with their own codes and precious secrets. But today, it is rare to see children playing alone on the street without an adult present, and not just because of traffic or concerns for safety. (The quest to regain this ideal of carefree childishness helped propel millions of Americans into suburbs after the end of World War II. Suburbia, as Lewis Mumford cannily noted, "was not merely a child-centered environment. It was based on a childish view of the world.")[9]

This desocialization or privatization of the street—the conversion of sidewalk communities into "lonely crowds"—has long been a tendency of urban capitalism. Even in early Victorian times, social life was already moving inside shops, offices, restaurants, and hotels. What blossomed in its place on the boulevards was the lyricism of the passerby, of Baudelaire's *Tableaux Parisens*:[10] the attractive stranger we will never have the chance to love; the eyes that meet ours for one brief moment before disappearing forever out of view; the hand we never brushed; fleeting glimpses of impossible happiness. The urban boulevard became the stage for a solitary intimacy, where each person followed the thread of his or her own experience.[11]

The street remained public only in exceptional cases: assembly became seen as a form of demonstration, a subversive act since in terms of its daily life the street had now become a zone of transit linking one private space with another. The street was now the setting for disreputable professions, from itinerant immigrant hawkers to beggars, drug dealers, and prostitutes who not by chance were known as "streetwalkers." Social street life is now a thing of the past revived only nostalgically and artificially in weekend markets and swapmeets, from Union Square to rue Mouffetard, where shoppers get a delicious anachronistic frisson from the quaintly disheveled sidewalk stalls, especially if the merchandise on offer happens to be Amish or organic fruit and vegetables. In the streets and squares of the modern city, communication via commodities has rushed in to fill the void left by the departure of social activity. People communicate with one another by means of signs that advertise a new fragrance or dress or item of jewelry. The main activity (aside from driving) is what the French, in a wonderful expression, call *lèche-vitrine*, "window-licking."

What makes this emptying of the public street even more radical is that many human pleasures can now only be sampled as commodities and therefore tend to isolate the consumer in the private sphere. At one time, for instance, to listen to music one had to go the square to hear the town band or to a concert hall for an orchestral recital, while to see a film or play required going to the cinema or theater. Today, in contrast, we are exiled into a domestic solitude where we communicate only through our possessions: the computer we use to surf the Web, the DVD player on which we watch the films we have bought, or the CD player that lets us hear a recording of a Mozart concerto we have purchased.[12] To see two dueling gladiators the ancient Romans had to go to the Colosseum; today you can buy a ringside seat at the Tyson-Holyfield bout on pay-TV. Everything is geared toward the transformation of services into commodities, use into consumption.

In the two-hundred-year process that has emptied the street and swollen to the extreme the sphere of possession, modern man has experienced a complete inversion of his own "ground state." For people of the preindustrial era the ground state of solitude was silence: the hieratic immobility of peasant farmers who could sit for hours leaning on their staffs without saying a word; modern man's ground state, in contrast, is a wall of deafening background noise, an unending soundtrack that populates his solitude. Each of us, moreover, is perpetually immersed in an environment of multi-tasking: listening to music as we write, checking our e-mail while on the phone, playing video games while searching for a title for an article, watching the news while fixing dinner. In the public spaces the preindustrial city dweller was bombarded with smells, noises, and bodies—a sensation one might experience today in the most densely populated Indian cities; whereas we traverse the public sphere cocooned in our car's air-conditioned silence, hermetically sealed off in the pristine digital enclosure of the iPod universe, or on the mobile phone, isolated from direct contact with our surroundings. This has resulted in a growing phobia of involuntary physical contact. A situational zoning of the body has been imposed: the only type of contact admitted between two people being sexual interaction, beyond which reigns an ideal of complete isolation accompanied by fear of contagion and horror of odors. These phobias have reshaped our use of space, just as the privatization of space reinforces our fear of intimacy with strangers.

The ultimate tendency has been to reduce the variegated arena of social relations to the single dimension of capitalist market relations: to corral the entire public sphere within the realm of private commercial transaction. The multidimensional variety of human relationships must be compressed into the single dimension of buying and selling. One of the most significant examples of this process of shrinkage is the contraction of the concept of freedom, perceived less and less in political terms. Free will is boiled down to the equivalent of the intense concentration of selecting from a restaurant menu, while individuality is defined by our sum total purchases.

It's precisely within this conflation between the human and commodity spheres that the mall effects its own particular revolution, reintroducing the square and the street but in completely inverted form. If these were formerly public spaces in which private ambits such as shops and stalls were installed, in the mall public activities like going for a walk now take place in a private environment. Unlike traditional department stores and supermarkets, which simply extended the idea of the humble shop, malls like MoA enclose public activities within a private ecosystem. The public is subsumed by the private. In this sense the mall represents *the invention of the private square*, an expression which might seem a contradiction in terms since the square by definition has always been synonymous with the public and the politicial: the forum or agora was at once a public place of market and a political arena: a center not only of mercantile but also human exchange, the place where the polis or res publica was constituted.

To fully understand the abyss that lies between the mall and the traditional town square, one has only to recall that at a certain hour the mall closes, while the idea of a square "closing" would seem a nonsense. The mall has an "owner," a situation unthinkable in the case of a square: the mall is a square equipped with locks and sophisticated alarm systems. A terrain for complicit encounters in the food court or shop-queue flirtations, the mall is where all forms of socialization are subsumed within the universe of commodities. The mall is therefore reassuring, though not so much for reasons of security as for the fact that it brings human relations into the familiar orbit of consumption, permitting us to "go out" while giving us the feeling of "being at home."

Like so many contemporary suburban homes whose street facade is simply an ugly and massive garage, the exterior of MoA is irredeemably ugly for the simple reason that no one cares: the outside public environment has been devalued to a service area of parking and traffic. MoA is like Disneyworld turned inside out: whereas the latter is a giant themepark with shops, the former is a giant shop containing a themepark.

It remains to be seen how long this beatitude provided by the mall and its dialectic of inversion will last, or how completely a society of erstwhile citizens can be reduced to the solipsistic solitude of consumption. Superficially alternative strategies to the enclosed supermall are the malling of historic urban districts or the creation of neotraditional town centers with make-believe auras of historicity. The increasing privatization of middle-class life in the suburbs creates a nostalgic longing for the legend of the city and urban space. But what the market actually offers exurbanites in the form of so-called lifestyle centers are denatured urbanity and carefully programmed, ersatz versions of the crowd.

A lifestyle center is basically an open-air mall with fountains and benches, which is to say a reconstruction of an old town center, a pedestrianized zone or an "open-air venue—like a cute little village."[13] The idea is to simulate the feel of the old center: "The lifestyle center evolves the model of the shopping mall by combining the fictitious qualities of the downtown shopping district with the control mechanism of the shopping mall. It is still a carefully crafted shopping environment, but with the outdoor charm its target shopping audience have found in vacation destinations such as New York City's Soho shopping district, though devoid of the Eurotrash."[14]

An exemplary instance is Victoria Gardens in Rancho Cucamonga, an hour's drive from Los Angeles, whose construction Kate Jacobs describes.[15] One of the objectives of lifestyle centers, Jacobs writes is "an approximation of the good life. And the good life largely resides in memory. That's why Victoria Gardens is built on an old-fashioned urban grid complete with traffic on narrow streets and genuine parking meters." Jacobs is "impressed by the care that has been taken to craft proper streetscapes," with fountains, street trees, gently modern streetlamps, occasional grassy squares, and the use of different architectural styles and materials. The developers studied and photographed Californian downtowns going back to 1854 to look for details that would enhance Victoria Gardens' *authenticity*. The architects were asked to build houses in different period styles, thus reconstructing the historical stratification of the town centers. Some houses were even given a slightly ramshackle, lived-in look, while signs advertising old long-forgotten brands were installed at street corners: "We call them the whispers of history," said one developer. Here the aim is to create with regard to time what a *faux semblant* is to space: a false memory.

One should be careful though not to get entangled in old debates about authenticity: the Heideggerian cliché of America as the chosen land of the inauthentic and of the *Geistlosigkeit*—to use Rilke's expression—that transforms objects into "pseudo-things." Firstly, because the old "authentically medieval" downtowns of continental Europe (Liege, Lille—the list is endless), have by now transformed their own centers into lifestyle centers with more or less identical pedestrianized zones, which in the evening, after the shops close, become as deserted and lifeless as U.S. shopping districts; and secondly, because false memories, as cases of recovered memory amply demonstrate, may be as painful and intensely felt as real ones.

The lifestyle center's real problem, like the enclosed mall's, is to find a solution to an impossible equation: how to have *a city without the city*. The pedestrianized walkways of lifestyle centers conflict with the need for parking as close as possible to shops; their *faux downtown* aspect makes it impossible to build those unavoidable enormous car parks. More generally, what is wanted is a combination of low suburban density and the abundant services typical of cities. Two irreconcilable utopias: "What they [the people in Paris] have is a very small amount of space *that is theirs*, and a lot of public amenities. What we have is a huge amount of space *that is ours and that we control*, and very little in public amenities," as one U.S. planner bluntly puts it.[16]

If the city is, in Robert Park's famous definition, "a mosaic of little worlds which touch but do not interpenetrate," that "encourages the fascinating but dangerous experiment of living at the same time, in several different, contiguous, but otherwise widely separated, worlds" and introduces "an element of chance and adventure which . . . gives it, for young and fresh nerves, a peculiar attractiveness,"[17] then it's clear that neither mall nor lifestyle center have the right cards to play the excitement or dangerous fascination game. You don't meet the unknown much in a closed environment, and lifestyle centers are only apparently open spaces: their private (and closed) character is evident from, for instance, the fact that some of them don't allow visitors to take photographs. There's little chance of excitement or adventure in a place where everything's kept so tightly under control. Like Achilles chasing, but never quite reaching, the tortoise, malls and lifestyle centers seek an impossible compromise between the utopia of private ownership and control and the thrill of city life. To attain the great capitalist dream of subsuming the public sphere within the private sector, malls and lifestyle centers are merely half-measures. Arizona offers a considerably more radical solution.

Arizona: Senile Utopias

Fifteen miles northwest of Phoenix one of our era's greatest (and most snubbed) social experiments has just entered its fortieth year. Aerial photographs show what looks like a Paul Klee canvas set against a dusty ochre desert backdrop, a mixed groundplan in which the developers have superimposed a structure of concentric circular rows of replicant houses, arranged around strategically placed green areas and two lakelets. This is Sun City, the prototype model for hundreds of similar agglomerations scattered throughout the United States. If the Mall of America is a mastodon among shopping centers, Sun City is a superheavyweight among private towns, or "planned communities" as they are more commonly known. Despite its high surrounding wall, Sun City, with its 38,309 inhabitants (2000 census), eighteen commercial centers, forty-three banks, seven recreational centers, twenty-five churches, three libraries, and two hospitals, represents something different from the idea of the gated community that has lodged itself in our imagination—from the enclaves of fear in the Los Angeles of Mike Davis to the fortified condos in the Saõ Paulo of Teresa Caldeira.[18]

Undoubtedly panic about rising crime rates is and has been one of the main reasons for the boom in common-interest housing developments (CID), of which planned communities constitute the most rapidly expanding sector (the other two forms of CID are condos and cooperatives). (There were some 10,000 CIDs in the United States in 1970; by 2002 there were 230,000 with an estimated 46 million residents!) Yet as with the malls, security is merely one of the factors behind the CIDs' extraordinary success, and perhaps not the most important since actual gated communities account for only one-fifth of the total.[19] Indeed an agglomeration such as Sun City is conceptually the opposite of securitized condos like the skyscrapers of the Morumbi complex in São Paulo or the enclosed enclaves of L.A.'s Rolling Hills or Chicago's Landmark Village. An enclave is exactly that: a fortified private isle in the middle of a public urban ocean. For this reason the gated urban community is merely an extension of the classic condominium so widespread in European cities. From this perspective, the urban enclave adds nothing new to the traditional urban landscape; it simply exasperates its private characteristics: just as luxury condos have a doorman to control who goes in and out, so too do urban enclaves have gates patrolled by teams of guards.

A private city, by contrast, is not simply a private isle carved out of a public universe but a private environment that incorporates and regulates its own public dimension. Far from being a private secession from the public sphere, it has its very own government which regulates all public activity. If the Greek word *polis* is the origin of "politics" as a category, the "private town" represents the privatization of the political. Its parliament is the homeowners association, just as the condominial assembly governs the life of a condominium. Its legislative body is composed of a "voluminous set of deed restrictions, rules, and regulations— sometimes known as equitable servitudes or 'covenants, conditions, and restrictions' (colloquially, CC&Rs)—and augmented by corporate bylaws."[20] The government taxes the town's inhabitants through condominial quotas, income which it uses to manage the infrastructure—sewage, roads, and paving—and "public" services such as libraries, the fire brigade, and private (and often voluntary) police force. As in the ancient Greek polis, but unlike the modern public state in which exile is no longer contemplated as a form of punishment, a citizen who doesn't bow to the (often oppressive) CC&Rs can be forced to sell their dwelling and banished from the planned community.

The private town thus constitutes a much more radical conceptual revolution than the mall. Its utopian aspect gives Evan McKenzie's term "Privatopia" a more cohesive and alarming meaning than he no doubt intended when he coined it in 1994. An America in which all local governments were replaced by private towns "would represent nothing less than the realization of Nozick's just society,"[21] which is to say the ultraminimal state theorized in 1974 by antistate thinker Robert Nozick, whose "publicoclast" fury is such that he regards income redistribution as "a violation of people's rights" and believes "taxation of earnings from labor is on a par with forced labor."[22] Sun City, far from being simply a blockhouse beseiged by the criminal underclasses, considers itself the realization of a utopia.

Like most utopias, the private city tends toward totalitarian rule. Its hawk-eyed panoptic control mechanisms recall the Jesuit communities of sixteenth-century Paraguay, which had elevated streets to enable the holy fathers to look through the Indios's windows to see what they were up to in their private lives. The list of CC&Rs is as bizarre as it is long. One can be forbidden from painting one's shutters blue, erecting a flagstaff on the lawn, or from keeping pets. One fifty-one-year-old woman (and grandmother) once received legal notice for having violated the code of her homeowners association "by kissing and doing bad things" in her parked car (she admitted only to having kissed a friend goodnight and filed suit against the association). At Leisure World (Arizona), the sheriff's posse reported members of the homeowners association for "having sex in the swimming pool."[23]

But the private town is totalitarian in an even more fundamental aspect: within its walls constitutional rights count for nothing. Just as in my home there is no "freedom of the press" and the only newspapers that come in are those I wish to read, so too in private towns the First Amendment of the U.S. Constitution has no weight, a famous case being that of the newsletter *Leisure World News*, which fell into disfavor with the Arizona town's board of directors, who stopped its circulation.[24] Faced with such tyrannies, one wonders why planned communities have been so amazingly successful, as the following table demonstrates:

Increase in CIDs Units by Type since 1970[25]

Type of Association	1970	%	1980	%	1990	%	1998	%
Condominium	85,000	(12.1)	2,541,000	(69.9)	4,847,921	(41.6)	5,078,756	(31.0)
Cooperative	351,000	(50.0)	482,000	(13.3)	824,000	(6.9)	748,840	(4.6)
Planned community	265,000	(37.8)	613,000	(16.8)	5,967,000	(51.3)	10,562,964	(64.4)
Total units	701,000	(100)	3,636,000	(100)	11,638,921	(100)	16,390,560	(100)
CID units as percentage of total U.S. housing units		<1.0%		4.1%		11.4%		14.6%

In 1970 the most widespread form of CID was the cooperative, followed by the planned communities, with condominiums a distant third. Between 1970 and 1980, however, condos grew most rapidly (a thirtyfold increase), while planned communities surpassed cooperatives. In the following decade, planned communities grew explosively (an almost tenfold increase); then between 1990 and 1998, growth in cooperatives and condos slowed, while planned communities continued their boom (177 percent), if at a slower rate than the previous decade. The opposing trend lines of cooperatives and planned communities geometrically shows the victory of the privatist ideal over its "socialist" counterpart.

Yet if social control is so all-pervasive and intrusive, and personal freedom is reduced to the point where you can't even repaint your shutters to your own taste, what on earth could have propelled this massive exodus toward private towns? First of all, anyone who buys into a private town presumably knows full well what they're getting into. According to "rational choice" theory, they have weighed the respective pleasures and obligations, and decided that the CC&Rs were a price worth paying for their quotient of happiness. Indeed, it is the very totality of control and the absence of individuality that may be most reassuring to many buyers. As one resident of a private city complained about their former (public) neighborhood: "It was the lack of control. . . . You could not maintain the environment you thought you had moved into." The irresistible magnet that attracts people to planned communities is their complete predictability.

But there is another, more sinister dimension to the CC&Rs that regulate planned communities: they also provide security and homogeneity to whites fleeing from cities of color. Not long ago, an acquaintance of mine went to visit her parents, who live in a gated community in California. On the way to the door she said hello to a Mexican gardener. When he failed to respond, she persisted in small talk. He ran away. "Are you crazy?" her mother said. "Here, if a Mexican speaks to a resident, he's out."

The ideal of utopian order seems inextricably linked to socioeconomic and racial homogeneity: diversity is associated with disorder and anxiety. It is no accident that the CID boom coincided with the age of Reagan: just as Proposition 13 (the famous California antitax initiative) represented "a revolt of the rich against the poor," so too CIDs have been characterized (by Robert Reich) as "the secession of the successful."[26] Indeed they have proven to be extraordinary experiments in resegregation: according to the 2000 census only 195 African Americans lived in Sun City (population 38,309) and a bare 41 in its Southern California counterpart, Leisure World (population 16,507).

The most astonishing use of covenants, however, is to restrict community membership to a single age group.

Some date back to the 1920s, when various labor, fraternal and religious organizations acquired relatively inexpensive property in Florida with the intent of creating a supportive living environment for their retiring members. Moosehaven, for example, was established in 1922 by the Loyal Order of Moose. . . . Other sponsored communities in Florida were created for benevolent purposes until a series of catastrophes, culminating with the stock market crash of 1929, brought their development to a standstill. The post–World War II period represented a new era of retirement community development, as private builders in Florida and other parts of the United States recognized the potential for marketing homes to a growing population of older Americans.[27]

Private towns designed exclusively for the elderly, however, are something entirely new.

When, on New Year's Day 1960, developer and Mob associate Del Webb inaugurated Sun City in Arizona—the world's first private town reserved for over-55s—he probably had little inkling that he was launching a social revolution. Two years later, however, he was on the cover of *Time* magazine, and rival developers had opened another "gated adult community," Leisure World in Seal Beach, California (additional Leisure World franchises would eventually appear in Arizona and Maryland). Webb soon followed with another Sun City in California and a third in Florida, then in 1972 he opened Sun City West just a few miles from the original. Demand for Arizona sunshine, however, remained so high that Sun City Grand eventually followed in 1996: a total population of more than 100,000 seniors in the three side-by-side Webb communities.

Undoubtedly climatic and economic factors have played a large part in the success of Webb's Sun Cities and their various imitators: a warm, dry climate that does wonders for arthritis and rheumatism, year-round sunshine, reasonably priced land that makes for affordable housing (in 2003 the average price for a house in Sun City stood at around $118,000, which is by no means expensive), and a favorable fiscal regime. But these reasons alone are insufficient to explain why so many elderly people are opting for self-segregation. Throughout human history, none of the world's civilizations could have imagined that the old should be confined separately. Only four years prior to Sun City's inauguration, Lewis Mumford wrote: "The worst possible attitude toward old age is to regard the aged as a segregated group, who are to be removed at a fixed point in their life . . .

from their normal interests and responsibilities."[28] No one could have imagine that within a few years the elderly *would aspire to segregate themselves* from the rest of society.

To Europeans not yet used to the idea of retirement communities, the notion that the elderly wish to live *alone* among themselves is something of a shock. And the European media continues to wear an expression of astonishment when dealing with the phenomenon, as can be seen from a recent report in *Die Zeit*, or a documentary commissioned by the Franco-German channel Arte.[29] In the United States, by contrast, they have become such a widespread phenomenon that, after a brief flurry of attention which petered out in the late 1970s, they are no longer considered an object worth reflecting on. The literature on the matter is less copious than one might imagine, and many of the books now look decidedly dated, listing the pros and cons of gated retirement communities, but for the most part unquestioning in the way they regard the desire for self-segregation itself as completely natural.[30] Indeed Americans now take such aspirations for granted, and numerous acquaintances whose parents live in adult retirement communities will boast about how comfortable and practical they are and all the advantages they offer. And candidates for the U.S. Senate can no longer allow themselves the luxury of making ironic quips about these "old" towns, as John McCain did in 1986: when addressing a college audience he "made a number of references to 'Seizure World,' with pauses for laughter. . . . He also joked that in the last state election 97 percent of the voters living at Leisure World cast ballots, adding, 'The other 3 percent were in intensive care.'"[31]

While the affection of grandparents for their grandchildren may be a topos of global sentimentalism, at Sun City minors are regarded as something of a nuisance: they can stay there for a maximum of thirty days per year and, if possible, only during school vacations. Children are permitted to use the swimming pool only on Sunday mornings between the hours of ten and twelve. The age-restriction clause admits no exceptions: at Leisure World (Arizona) for instance, a 42-year-old physician "had a nervous breakdown and became incapable of working or taking care of himself, so his parents had brought him into their home." Except there was the problem of the age regulation: no 42-year-old was allowed to live in

Leisure World. "If the parents wished to continue to care for their broken son, they had to move," and "they were going. They were leaving their home. They understood the association would enforce its rules if it had to."[32] On the other hand, youth are present to work for and wait upon the elderly, as bank clerks, shopping-center assistants, waiters, bathing attendants, gardeners, and caddies. Within the senile city, young people have the status of immigrant workers, *gastarbeite*. Youth is synonymous with social subalternity.

Young people (and Mexicans) work so that oldsters can devote themselves to the true religion of the retirement community—golf. For no private town is without its golf courses: at Sun City there are eleven. And golf is a "must" that must be paid for separately. Golf is in fact often cited as one of the main reasons for moving to a private town: golf as an idea of luxury and salubrious loafing, and as a sign of belonging to Thorstein Veblen's leisure class. In these sun-drenched deserts the golf courses happily guzzle torrents of water with shocking wastefulness: the intensity of the green provides an immediate chromatic measure of rank, with a yellowed and threadbare fairway marking out a town as irredeemably second-rate. Here we have a senescence that innocently allows itself one last blow-out: "After me the drought" would be the motto of these new sunvisored Louis XVs buzzing around in their golf carts, which were once electric, only now an enterprising Sun City dealer is offering new gasoline-fueled carts that can reach speeds of 35 mph, the last word in oldstermobile chic (with a corresponding climb in the number of accidents).

The golf courses ensure that, among the different typologies of private towns, those for the elderly fall under the category of lifestyle communities; and here our circle closes, for as we have seen, the last word in urban planning is the lifestyle center. Thus the privatization of the public square is doubly linked to that of the city *tout court* and indeed of the political arena. In 1999 Leisure World, California, became the first private retirement community that voted to incorporate as a city, with the name Laguna Woods: that is to say it was the first private town for the elderly to become a fully constitutional political subject. In this sense Sun City (and all its epigones) represents a double utopia: the proprietarian utopia of the private town on one hand; the self-segregating utopia of the retirement community on the other—a threefold order of wealth, race, and age. A utopia of clean streets free of the clamor of cackling kids, where it never rains. Not surprisingly then does its name refer to one of the great works of utopian thought in the western philosophical canon, Tommaso Campanella's *La città del sole*, translated into English as *City of the Sun*, although it should be *Sun City*, inhabited as it is by "solar" beings. Except the prophetic Campanella forgot to explain that they also played golf.

Careless People:
It's the *Real Housewives of Orange County*'s World; The Rest of Us Just Live in It

Rebecca Schoenkopf

It's a mean place, Orange County.

Its zip codes dominate the list of the nation's fifty most expensive places, and interested billionaires should make note that one Corona del Mar pied-à-terre (thirty thousand square feet) is currently listed at $75 million. (Someone usefully calculated that you could buy the Mighty Ducks of Anaheim, our local hockey franchise, or 20 million Starbucks mocha grandes for that much money.) In the meantime, the OC hoi polloi have to earn more than $125,000 per year to afford the mortgage on a median-value home, and a slave eking out the county's median household income of $63,000 cannot even afford to buy a one-bedroom condo of seven hundred square feet (that probably smells ferociously of beer and pee), because the monthly mortgage would exceed her take-home pay.

Yet somehow poor people—lots of them—manage to crowd into the dying stucco tenements and squalid converted garages that make Santa Ana the nation's largest suburban slum. Indeed Santa Ana was recently named the hardest city in the country in which to make ends meet, and that was when the nation's cities still included New Orleans. In the land of luxury lifestyles, one-third of OC's school kids are growing up in poverty. Yet when the lone Democratic supervisor proposed insuring the county's twenty thousand poorest kids—with an outlay of just $1.7 million that would have been matched with $2.1 million in counterpoint federal funds—local politicians screamed this was "socialism" and we'd be creating "an entitlement."

In the OC we take our rugged conservatism straight up, with no chaser of Bushite "compassion." It's the kind of place where the noisiest speakers believe taxes are fascist—except when they're going to oil subsidies (it's our fault, they explain, that after the disastrous 1969 oil spill in Santa Barbara that ExxonMobil had to drill so far offshore)—and the softness of our country stems from its promise of universal public education. It's the kind of place where a Republican assemblyman with a pro-environment voting record of *16 percent* is derided as a Republican In Name Only for his green and shifty ways. Meanwhile our beaches are shut down half of the year because our oceans are literally swimming in shit, and above that shit-filled sea are mansions and more mansions, five thousand to twenty thousand square feet scrubbed by Spanish-speaking immigrants, who since they're not really seen don't really exist.

Hollywood Discovers the OC

For years Orange County's fleshpots were Southern California's best-kept secret. Instead our white-flight burbs had a reputation since the early 1960s for reactionary extremism of the John Birch Society variety. We were the butt of liberal derision every time one of our homegrown crazy congressmen, like the late bigamist John Schmitz or "B-1" Bob Dornan, launched their mad rants. But of course I never believed that "outdated" view. Orange County isn't as conservative as all that, I insisted to myself, with ten years of magical thinking (since I first came down here to write for the *OC Weekly*) instead of Joan Didion's prescribed *one*. "There is art, and quiet liberalism, and Mexican protesters in a conga/picket line whenever the skinheads want to put on a white-power show," I hummed to myself like a mantra.

Then one day LA's media moguls finally discovered that the hick county to the south was actually a landscape of sumptuous sin and sultanic corruption, and there was a whole new OC image that I also didn't believe for a second. There's the primetime soap *The O.C.*, with its vacuous rich kids; the MTV reality show *Laguna Beach*, whose vacuous rich kids could have used a few of *The O.C.*'s screenwriters to bridge their streams of nothingness into listenable thoughts—and whose gaucheries are only exceeded by MTV's even more hideous brats planning their debutante balls in *My Super Sweet 16*; there was a movie, *Orange County*, with Jack Black, about which I remember nothing. And former NBA superstar Dennis Rodman created his own dramas every night of the week in his home—much visited by the police—in Newport Beach. Rodman, in between wearing a wedding dress and a nine-day marriage to the pneumatic starlet Carmen Electra, liked to throw really loud parties.

Where were the rest of us in the nation's perception? The millionaire hedonists, their bimbo wives, and spoiled children who constitute the illusion of the OC, I thought, existed *somewhere*, but they were not what Orange County truly meant. There were three million people here, and a lot of us live in landlocked, dingy Anaheim and Santa Ana, not in pastel manses on the coast. A lot of us were even of color—or at least brunette—instead of entitled blond society misses with pillowy lips, at play in the lush fields of South Coast Plaza. There were poor people, and middle-class people, who had as little to do with the charity dos and parties in jewelry stores that constituted our new national image as the rich had to do with the day laborers at Home Depot or the shoppers at Target.

Of this, I was sure.

Epiphany

It was like one of those safes falling on your head from a third-story window, a cartoon moment of consciousness flattening, tweeting bluebirds, and epiphany. And it happened as my small son and I sat glued to the merry adventures of Kim, Jo, Lauri, Vicki, and Jeana in the seven magnificent episodes of Bravo's newest and most marvelous reality show, *The Real Housewives of Orange County*.

"Perception is reality," Bree said on *Desperate Housewives*—The Real Housewives' ur-text—clearly providing her answer to the Kantian Question, "What are the powers and capacities constitutive of the human subject for apprehending the Real?"

Perception. Image. Get used to it. Those of us who live here may think the world's view of Orange County pertains only to that small segment pictured in the party pages of OC's decadent-riche lifestyle bible *Riviera*, but they are the ones who are real; the rest of us are Schrödinger's Cat, in a tertiary position between existing and not. Without the world's eyeballs, the rest of us simply aren't. And are. Sort of. I'm not sure; it's best to find a college kid to explain it to you.

The Real Housewives and Dick Cheney Are Very Bad People

So now, a few years into the nation's love affair with OC's greedy and tanned young idiots, who are our newest spokesmodels? The *Real Housewives* introduce us to our group of mostly middle-aged mothers who go against the OC trophy demographic: only three of the five are blond.

There is Kimberly, the outgoing long-blond-extensions-maned transplant who—even while making sure we knew she had self-awareness and was above all that silliness—dived right into the bleach and grossly inflated implants of her new home. There is Jo, the early-twenties, brunette (Latina, even!) party-girl fiancée of Hummer-driving Slade—think *DH*'s Gabrielle *sans* the calculation and if she ever smiled or was kind—and who always has a martini in her well-manicured hand. There is Lauri, the statuesque divorcee who most closely hews to OC's beauty standard of tall and Barbie-blonde, but because of her marital status and comparative poverty has been cast out of paradise. There is also Vicki, for whom Lauri works selling insurance, and who is self-made, a terrible control freak, and always looks as though she smells something bad. And there is Jeana, a plump former Playmate who sells real estate to her neighbors and gives homespun advice in a flat, affectless voice. There are various husbands. There is misbegotten spawn.

And there is the hive, its own organism, where they all (except Lauri) live: the rarefied hills of Coto de Caza. The hills that used to host John Wayne's hunting parties have been fenced in and become the *ne plus ultra* Orange County—an actual gated town! But unlike the swarmlike developments marching across the rest of South County, the manses of Coto's fifteen thousand acres were actually developed gracefully, nestled into folds in the hills so nothing mars the ridges or the sky. Most of the mansions actually have breathing room—an acre here, an acre there—instead of million-dollar homes built within inches of their lot lines and inches of each other. These are *proper* mansions, nothing Mc- or chintzy about them. And behind its gates, Coto even still has an orange grove. For all I know, it's the last of the lot. Coto's a pretty sweet place to live, if you like marble and beige, children driving brand-new Mercedes, and living among people who according to local legend gave Senator John Kerry a stunning *2 percent* of their vote. If that's your thing, you'd like Coto a lot.

And if you, like I, like to watch rich people behaving badly—and is there any other explanation for the popularity of Donald Trump?—you'll like Coto just as much. And you, like I, will realize that these people *are* the true Orange County, just as J.R. was the soul of Dallas, Kurt Cobain really was Seattle, and Wyoming, home to Dick Cheney, really is made for bigots. Did you know Cheney, as Wyoming's lone congressman, voted against making Martin Luther King Jr.'s birthday a national holiday, and against sanctions for apartheid? Oh well, never mind.

Here You May Watch Me Watch TV

EPISODE ONE

Jeana's children are monsters! Jeana's husband is a monster! Jeana (our plump real-estate agent) is no great shakes herself. Jeana's daughter Kara whines soulfully when her older brother Shane gets a brand-new car and she has to drive his hand-me-down convertible Mercedes. (Shades of almost Third World inequality between spoiled siblings.) Shane grunts angrily when Kara gets cold hard cash for making the volleyball team. Kara demands a new car. Kara gets a new car. Meanwhile, Shane gets drafted by the Oakland A's in, like, the one-thousandth round, and dad Matt Keough, who used to play for the A's and still works in the organization, calls home to find out how the draft went. Father and son share a monosyllabic conversation. "I think he's proud of you," Jeana says noncommittally, flatly and without affect, after the phone call. "He thought you were going to do a lot worse."

Kimberly (our outgoing transplant) makes fun of how everyone in OC has breast implants. But Kimberly likes her breast implants. We call this "cognitive dissonance," but it may be theological.

Slade wants twenty-four-year-old party-girl fiancée Jo to stay home and be a housewife. The camera lingers as she sits on the kitchen counter, staring at the phone, wondering what the fuck she's going to do with her day. Likely answer? Drink herself blind. Vicki (self-made insurance lady) is a bitch, and Lauri (the broke-ass divorcée who suffers under her) is a victim.

EPISODE TWO

Jeana's son Shane goes off to kill some little bunnies for the neighbors, who are tired of replacing their impatiens. He has an arsenal at his disposal, but it's a lot of Elmer Fudd for nothing. No rabbits were harmed in the making of this series.

Kim goes to buy a new car. "*I* don't care about my car," she says, not at all shallow like her neighbors, "but in *this* area . . ." But oh, as the car salesman is showing her all the great places to stow your kids in the SUV, he lets fly with "grandchild," as in, "Here would be a great place to put your grandchild, Methuselah." Everything stops for the smallest of most perfect beats. Kim does not buy the car.

Slade, who is a freak, does tai chi in his underwear and what appears to be an ice mask to reduce puffiness before showing us his power outfits for his big meeting. He yammers on about needing to appear wealthy so the dude he's meeting will know he's capable of . . . what? Being wealthy? Then he climbs into a Hummer, and I laugh and retch.

But then he meets with the guy, and the guy is so unbelievably rude, I thought it was a put-up job. I mean, no one acts that way. Not even Trump-times-ten acts that way. The guy is seriously, seriously damaged—and wait till you meet his wife, who puts cubic zirconia on the pink rims of her monster truck! The wife is really pretty awesome. Lauri notes, about being rich, "I really miss those things. *I'm* the maid now." The observant viewer will note the Mizrahi bedding from Target, which I saw on my shopping sojourn just today. It's cute—giant orange blossoms, splashy and colorful—but again, if Lauri still had her status, she would only shop at Target for the maid's bedding. Which, of course, I guess she did.

ASSHOLES, ETC.

Vicki's son Michael is an asshole. Jeana's son Shane is an asshole. But let me elaborate. Shane and his little brother Colton, who is thirteen, are in Mexico with their family, and they go to some dirt-racing track. Colton stalls his dune-buggy thingie a bunch of times—because he is thirteen—before he gets it right. He then beats Shane's time on the track. Shane's only possible response is to keep making fun of him for stalling. "It's my first time driving a stick, Shane," Colton says sensibly. "Come on, give me a little credit!" Shane grunts angrily, and like an asshole, "The first time *I* drove a stick, it was a *Ferrari*." Good comeback, Shane. Lauri's daughter Ashley is an asshole, but that doesn't come till episode four, and I'm tired of recapping the episodes, and so I will stop.

Except for this: Lauri's son Josh actually seems like a sweet kid, so he spends most of the season in juvie. (In that case, it seemed like the teacher he scuffled with was the asshole, but it was off-camera, so it can't really exist. In any case— go juvenile justice system!—they kept him doped up in juvenile hall to make sure he didn't have a mental illness *for over a month* before they sentenced him to an additional month because he'd been caught with pot in the past. So when he calls home, all lonely and fucked-up and locked away while big sister Ashley is having a party, she hears his voice and instantly hangs up on him with the same guilty manner you hang up if a woman answers when you call her boyfriend. *That was my little brother calling from juvenile hall,* she tells her friend very noncommittally and tra-la-la. *Should I have talked to him, do you suppose?*)

Barbarian (Me) at the Gates

Writing a story much like this one for my most excellent employer, the beloved and reviled *Village Voice* franchise, the *OC Weekly*, I drove through the gates of Coto de Caza to meet with the *Real Housewives*. There were all there, except for Jeana, who was out of town seeing her asshole son, who's off playing ball at an Arizona community college. If they were desperate, they were also nice, ladylike, funny, and outgoing, as well as far prettier than their television personas. Kim had looked manly on the telly; in person her features were softer and sexy. Lauri had looked plastic, the light and video catching awkwardly on what seemed to be less than organic features; at the table at the Coto country club, she was gorgeous. Vicki still looked like a rabbit, but I probably would have found her less rabbity if I had actually liked her as a person.

Vicki was a trial. She instructed the others not to answer questions about themselves she'd deemed too personal and tried to micromanage everything from what photos we would be using to how much Kim should talk. Outgoing Kim was saying something outgoing—perhaps it was when I'd complimented her for dancing and flirting with Little People and people in wheelchairs (I thought that was nice!) and she'd responded, "I am very much an equal opportunist!" So naturally Vicki sniped, "Oh, it's The Kim Show again." Kim thanked her genuinely for reining her in, said she was well aware that she often needed it, and apologized sweetly for monopolizing (she wasn't, really) the conversation. She begged to hear what Vicki had to say.

"Nothing, really," Vicki answered. "I don't really have a piece to say." Not only was Vicki schoolmarming Kim, she was treating me as if I were her eighteen-year-old daughter—the daughter that she wished would quit her job rather than miss a family weekend at their second home (they have *four*) at The River. To her husband's credit, he firmly (for him) explained that quitting your job for a weekend's play was not a good life lesson for a teenager.

My sources also tell me that, after I left, Vicki demanded of the Bravo publicist, who was in attendance with the series producer as we all had coffee and fruit, that Bravo pay for a $150 flower arrangement Vicki had bought for her coffee table in anticipation of a visit from *Access Hollywood*. As a person who makes a good, decent middle-class living—a living that, if the *Real Housewives* were making it, they would probably declare bankruptcy—I would like to say that I frequently buy myself flowers because it makes my house look nice. And I have never, once, demanded someone else pay for it. But maybe that's how you get four homes.

A Literary Interlude, Citing Fitzgerald

The very rich are different from you and me, Ernest Hemingway said, "appropriating" the thought, almost to the word, from F. Scott Fitzgerald. (Fitzgerald had said, "Let me tell you about the rich. They are different from you and me," which, you will notice, is almost just exactly the same!) But Fitzgerald had whole books of thought on the subject, while Hemingway mostly wrote about fish. Fitzgerald's most famous novel, *The Great Gatsby*, has probably even been read by some of the dimwitted spawn of the *Real Housewives of Orange County*. But I wonder what they made of this:

> They were careless people, Tom and Daisy—they smashed up things and creatures and then retreated back into their money or their vast carelessness, or whatever it was that kept them together, and let other people clean up the mess they had made.

Can you raise a son to wealth *and* compassion? Surrounded by Hummers encrusted in gold, can you enter the kingdom of heaven? And can you raise a rock star to treat women well? I've been trying to figure these things out for my own sweet son (who is honestly, terribly sweet), who has expensive tastes, loves caviar, and longs and aches for golden bling. And while he knows better than to whine around me, he's been known to do so in more fertile fields. Someday he may even drive a Hummer, if only to give his poor mother a stroke. I've been making suggestions to him lately: maybe you could be a chef or an artist, I tell him, and then you can hang out with rich people who admire you and treat you to these fine things, without actually getting your hands dirty yourself . . .

A mother does hope.

On Subjectivity

And here is my reality: I try never to interview anyone, because when they are nice people, and I like them, I feel I must soften my impressions, treat them kindly, present them in a warm and amberish light, moderating and adulterating their reality for the world. At our group roundtable, I am open to the possibility that the perception is *not* reality, that someone got a villain edit in the series. After all, if a camera crew were shadowing me, it would show me yelling at my son, ignoring my son, snapping at my son, and watching television for many hours each night as I lie in bed and fart, and it would be both true and untrue.

It would not show me *boiling hot dogs* for dinner, as some of the Real Housewives are wont to do (perhaps it's a Midwestern thing?), but then none of us is perfect. Most of the women are fun, nice, and pretty, though they fall into the categories of either ditzy or ballbusters. They're warm! And their manners, almost to the man, are the best manners of all: they try to make people feel at home.

So their worlds are really, really small, I start to tell myself. Not everyone likes to dance in conga/protest lines at white-power shows, or even to discuss politics or world events at all. Some people like to play tennis and buy their children brand-new cars! And that's . . . fuck, that's really not okay.

Those kids are little Hitlers. Is it the fault of their mothers? Yes. They play them off each other, they reward shrill whining by kowtowing to it, they work all the livelong day to give their children "the best" of everything—diamond shopping here is a bonding experience, like fathers and sons hunting among the Maori—while their rude, lazy children spit with contempt right in their faces. They have not raised their children to be citizens, but in the true Orange County ethos: they are entitled to anything they want.

But while we love to watch bad parenting—a la *Nanny 911* and *Anna Nicole*—and worse people, softened reality swoops down again. My own son has not yet reached the age where boys become dicks. Perhaps he will spit with contempt at me. Perhaps he will grow up to be an Orange County boy—his life's goal so far *is* of owning a mansion, one in a gated town, perhaps, with his name inscribed on it in solid gold. Maybe somebody with a good kid should know she's lucky, and not ascribe his goodness to her fabulous self, because maybe she will have another one, and that one will happen to be bad, and she certainly won't want people pointing any fingers. Still, my son has excellent manners because I *taught them* to him, something the *Real Housewives* kind of forgot.

"Hell Is Other People": Ted Turner's Two Million Acres

Jon Wiener

Ted Turner is America's largest landowner, with two million acres, mostly in Montana and New Mexico. His vast holdings are virtually uninhabited; they are pristine lands where 40,000 bison roam, along with elk, mule deer, and other native western range animals. Turner, of course, is the self-made man who started CNN and other cable channels, and eventually sold Turner Broadcasting Systems to Time Warner in 1996 for $9 billion. In 2005 *Forbes* ranked him number 133 on its list of the 400 richest Americans, and estimated his personal wealth at $2 billion. That's half of what it was in 2001, before the Time-Warner merger with AOL deeply damaged the new company.[1]

Turner bills himself as an "ecologically sensitive" environmentalist, and says his acquisitions are part of a project to protect the land and restore native and endangered species.[2] He's spent millions on ecological projects. But Turner's ecological empire has its dark side. To bring native trout to the stream running through his favorite Montana ranch, Turner is poisoning all the fish upriver—77 miles upriver—and has also poisoned the lake where the fish come from, which happens to be in a wilderness area. Turner is developing 1,000 gas wells in his New Mexico wilderness. He protects elk on his New Mexico ranches, but also sponsors an annual elk hunt where he charges each hunter $13,000 for a week of shooting. In every case, he combines ecological self-righteousness with a shrewd ability to exploit nature for profit.

Sprawling Montana ranches are a favorite of rich people these days: online real-estate listings include 317 acres on the Yellowstone River near Bozeman for sale for $15 million, 30,000 acres in the heart of Montana with an asking price of $12 million, and a 17,000-acre spread near the Idaho border available right now for $25 million—that one includes a house featured in *Architectural Digest*.[3] Tom Brokaw, Harrison Ford, and David Letterman own ranches in Montana.

But no one comes close to Ted Turner's lust for dirt. He started buying range land on a large scale in the early nineties and has never stopped: in 2004–5 alone, he purchased more than 300,000 acres in Kansas, Nebraska, and South Dakota. In Montana he owns four sprawling ranches, including the famed Flying D Ranch, 113,000 acres in the gorgeous area just outside the northern boundary of Yellowstone National Park. Ten other ranches bear the Turner brand in Colorado, New Mexico, and other states, and he has purchased vast *estancias* in Patagonia, the austral Montana. His combined acreage, according to Ken Auletta in the *New Yorker*, is roughly equivalent to the combined land area of Delaware and Rhode Island.[4]

His crown jewels include 250,000 acres of the Nebraska sandhills and 40,000 acres of Oklahoma tall-grass prairie. But his New Mexico ranches are the biggest and most spectacular. The vast Vermejo Park Ranch consists of 580,000 acres in the mountains at the Colorado border; its ponderosa pine forests provide habitat for bobcats, pronghorn, and bear, and even cougar, as well as 180 different species of birds. His Armendaris Ranch in south-central New Mexico has 360,000 acres of pristine Chihuahuan desert grassland as well as the entire Fra Cristobal mountain range. Its wildlife includes a reintroduced population of desert bighorn sheep, which are managed by the Turner Endangered Species Fund, plus pronghorn, desert mule deer, and cougar. It is also the site of the extraordinary Armendaris bat cave, which has the fifth-largest bat population in North America.

Turner is protecting the bats, but his real passion is bison—the buffalo on the nickel. He has gotten rid of the cattle and sheep on most of his land—introduced by gringos in the last 150 years—and restored the native bison to thirteen of the fourteen ranches. He started buying bison in the 1970s and now owns more bison than anyone else in the world. This passion won support from 400 traditional Indian leaders, whom he invited to his Flying D Ranch in 2002 to pray, feast on bison, and honor him with an Indian name. The Indian leaders, according to the *Bozeman Daily Chronicle*, "came from Guatemala to Greenland and from all Montana tribes for the 25th annual gathering of the Traditional Circle of Indian Elders and Youth." The *Chronicle* reported that "Joe Medicine Crow, an 87-year-old Crow elder from Lodge Grass, gave Turner the name of his great-grandfather, Buffalo Bull Chief," and that Turner appeared at the ceremony wearing a headdress and "was danced around the circle to traditional drumming."[5]

But Turner's "buffalo commons" is not just about ecological restoration: the giant ungulates are also part of his bottom line. He is probably the biggest purveyor of bison burgers in the world. To popularize bison meat, he started a restaurant chain he named after himself—Ted's Montana Grill—which now sells bison burgers at forty-one locations in fourteen states, along with bison steaks, bison prime rib, and bison pot roast.[6] At his ranch he serves bison osso buco. (Jane Fonda, his former wife, has a recipe for bison osso buco online.)[7]

Turner grew up in the South, in Savannah and Chattanooga, but in the 1980s decided he really belonged in the wide-open spaces of the West. When Ken Auletta interviewed him for a *New Yorker* profile in 2001, Turner sang him the old Roy Rogers theme song: "where the West commences, gaze at the moon till I lose my senses. . . . Don't fence me in." "I'm happiest when I'm on a horse on my ranch," he told Auletta.[8]

His turn to the West coincided with his embrace of environmental activism. In 1998 he issued his "Ten Voluntary Initiatives," which start with "I PROMISE TO CARE FOR PLANET EARTH AND ALL LIVING THINGS THEREON" (caps his). The list includes "I PROMISE TO USE MY BEST EFFORTS TO HELP SAVE WHAT IS LEFT OF OUR NATURAL WORLD IN ITS UNDISTURBED STATE AND TO RESTORE DEGRADED AREAS."[9]

To accomplish these noble goals, he started the Turner Endangered Species Fund, which, according to its Web site, "is dedicated to conserving biodiversity by

ensuring the persistence of imperiled species and their habitats." The fund's efforts "focus on carnivores, grasslands, plant-pollinator complexes, and species
that historically ranged onto properties owned by R.E. Turner" (that's Ted). The
Turner Endangered Species Fund is not a $1-billion operation like his UN Foun-
dation; its annual budget is only $400,000 (2004 figures)—some of which comes
from federal and state grants. You might think a man worth $2 billion would not
need federal grants for his Endangered Species Fund, but the foundation's 2004
report lists four federal grants totaling $85,000 for projects such as "Black-tailed
prairie dog restoration at Vermejo."[10]

Restoring native species sounds like a wonderful idea, but playing God can bring
problems: for example, the case of Cherry Creek, which runs through Turner's
107,000-acre Flying D Ranch south of Bozeman. The creek is a favorite fishing spot
for locals because of its abundant rainbow and brook trout. But those trout are not
native; they were introduced several decades ago. Turner, however, insisted that
the trout in his stream must be a native species, the westslope cutthroat trout.

Replacing the rainbow and brook trout with the westslope cutthroat trout required killing all the fish in the 75 miles of stream above Turner's ranch, as well
as all the fish in Cherry Lake, where the stream originates. In 2003 Turner paid
the Montana Department of Fish, Wildlife, and Parks almost half a million dollars to pour poison into Cherry Lake and Cherry Creek. The lake that was poisoned is in the Gallatin Wilderness Area. According to the *Bozeman Daily Chronicle*,
"The Forest Service gave permission to use a motorboat on Cherry Lake to churn
the poison."[11]

The locals didn't like Turner's plan and tried to stop him. They sought a federal injunction to block the plan on the grounds that pouring poison into the lake
and the river was an illegal act of pollution under the federal Clean Water Act.
That seems like a strong argument, but the state, unsurprisingly, sided with
Turner, as did the federal district court.[12] But it turns out that the westslope cutthroat trout is not native to Cherry Creek. According to Jack Hitt, writing for
Outside magazine, "no fish is native to the creek," because it's isolated by a foun-
tainhead lake at the top and a waterfall at the bottom. Nor is the westslope cutthroat trout an endangered species—the U.S. Fish and Wildlife Service concluded

that "abundant, stable, and reproducing populations remain well distributed throughout its historic range."[13]

Of course poisoning a lake and a stream kills more than fish—even the state department of fish conceded that the poison would kill insects and amphibians. But that wouldn't be so bad; "they will come back quickly," officials promised. Bill Fairhurst, spokesman for the Public Lands Association, had a different view: he told *Outside* magazine, "They are not killing fish, they are killing an entire ecosystem."[14]

The last report on the project—August 2005—said the poisoning had been going on for three years "but the job is far from complete," according to Pat Clancy, the Montana Department of Fish, Wildlife, and Parks biologist in charge of the program. At that point the lake and twenty miles of stream had been doused with deadly antimycin and rotenone, but springs and small bogs still harbored small fish. Other trout survived around downstream beaver dams. One former mayor who has sued to stop the project says Turner "will never be able to remove all the fish." On the other hand, Clancy, the man in charge of the poisoning, claims: "We could possibly be done with treatments by 2008 or 2009."[15]

Ted Turner poisons trout—and he also shoots elk. The annual elk hunt at his Vermejo Park Ranch is a big operation. "One of the last truly wild sounds heard in the Rocky Mountains today is the spine-tingling bugle of the bull elk," the hunt's Web site declares; "Vermejo's annual elk hunts are known far and wide as truly incomparable, featuring magnificent animals and delivering outstanding hunter success." It's not easy being an elk hunter these days: "it is increasingly more difficult to find opportunities to hunt mature trophy-class animals in a fair chase environment." But for those who join one of Turner's eight annual hunts, "Hunter success has been over 90 percent for years," and 95 percent of the antlers "harvested" are "6x6 or larger." Turner holds one archery hunt and seven rifle hunts each fall, and those who sign up are promised "exactly what the seasoned hunter is seeking: numerous mature animals, low hunter density, expansive habitat, spectacular scenery, and excellent accommodations."[16] The Turner ranch also offers hunters the opportunity to kill pronghorn, bison, turkey, and mule deer.

A week of elk hunting costs $13,000 ($9,000 if you share a guide), which includes room and board, license, guide, vehicle, and state sales tax, but does not include "liquor charges, gift shop, or gratuities."[17] One "satisfied hunter" told the *Bozeman Daily Chronicle* that he "shot a six-point bull on the Turner ranch, after three years on a waiting list, paying $10,500 for the privilege and hunting for five days." He said he was from New Jersey. As for the elk, "When you stalk them, that's the fun of it," he said. "They're all beautiful, these animals."[18]

The elk hunt isn't the only moneymaking enterprise at Turner's Vermejo ranch. The place, according to the *New York Post*, is "rich with billions of dollars in coal and methane reserves." And since natural gas prices have more than quadrupled in the last few years, Turner's New Mexico land is potentially worth more than his media holdings ever were. So in 2004 he signed a deal with El Paso Natural Gas to develop more than 1,000 wells in his wilderness. To help assure the future of natural gas, two of Turner's charitable foundations fund the Energy Future Coalition, which is lobbying Congress to mandate more smog-reducing vehicles—such as city buses that run on natural gas.[19]

When it comes to his neighbors in Montana, Turner's motto seems to be "Hell is other people." He's taken extraordinary and expensive measures to keep his neighbors away from his land, especially his favorite Montana ranch, the Flying D southwest of Bozeman. The *High Country News* explained that "Montana commoners will no longer be able to hunt, fish, or hike on state lands nestled deep within the private kingdom of media mogul Ted Turner," because Turner "offered the state a deal it couldn't refuse": he proposed to trade more than 12,000 acres somewhere else for the 6,000 acres of public land inside his Flying D.[20] The public land the state was losing included several prize fishing streams beloved by locals. They challenged the deal in court, but the local judge ruled for Ted: the land he was offering would go into trust for public schools, increasing the value of school trust lands by $217,000 and generating $6,577 in additional funds for Montana's public schools.[21]

Turner has also been sued by other neighbors in Montana for blocking access to their own ranch, which is off a road that goes through his Flying D ranch. Somebody put up a locked gate on the road. The manager for Turner's western ranches was quoted telling the local newspaper that "he had no comment" on the gate. This being Montana, the neighbors cut the locks and forced their way through the gate and down the road to their ranch. They claim they've used that road for decades without any problem from Turner's predecessors at the Flying D Ranch. Court records, according to the Bozeman newspaper, show that the ranch owned by Turner's unhappy neighbors "has been in the family since 1942, when it was purchased from the original homesteader."[22]

But it's not that Ted wants to keep everybody off his land, only local cowpokes. Corporate leaders and captains of industry are invited to his Vermejo Park Ranch in New Mexico, which offers "a unique setting to address contemporary business challenges." The ranch promises to combine "professional retreat services" with "first-class wildlife-viewing opportunities." For those uncertain about the possibilities, Turner's Web site explains that "many of the best decisions and ideas are generated away from the formality of the primary workplace," and that the ranch's "comfortable meeting space, gracious dining room, and acres of unsurpassed beauty set the stage for dynamic, productive interactions, quiet reflection, and relaxing recreation . . . a truly extraordinary conference experience." Turner has room for 50 corporate execs on the ranch's 580,000 acres.[23]

What will happen to Turner's two million acres? You might think a liberal, public-spirited citizen who has donated hundreds of millions to worthy causes like the UN might give some of his land to the public, to the National Park Service, where it could be protected and enjoyed by ordinary people for generations. But that's not his plan. "Turner says the land eventually will go into a trust and the Turner Family Foundation, headed by his five children," according to *Forbes* magazine. "They'll have some flexibility to sell parcels if needed."[24]

It's hard to escape the conclusion that Turner's utopia is a land without people (except for a few corporate execs on retreat, a few elk hunters, and a few Indians for a few days.) Sometimes, however, Turner's passion for uninhabited places leads him to see beauty in places others don't. In July 2005 he announced he would visit the DMZ between North and South Korea. The heavily fortified no-man's land, he said, was a haven for rare and endangered species. Even though it's only two miles wide, 80 species of fish thrive in DMZ rivers, including at least 10 found nowhere else on earth. In the DMZ, according to the *Atlanta Journal*

Constitution, "Hundreds of kinds of birds, including the endangered white-naped and red-necked cranes, fly . . . above leopards and Asiatic black bears and maybe tigers." Turner argues that we need to "plan now to protect the DMZ's ecosystem rather than risking its economic development in the event of Korean unification." Wildlife flourishes there because "few humans have ventured into the DMZ in the last half century."[25] If hell is other people, then the Korean DMZ must be heaven. That's something only Ted Turner would see.

People Like Hicks:
The Supreme Court Announces the
Antiurban City

Don Mitchell

Kevin Hicks only wanted to visit his girlfriend and bring diapers to his daughter. What he got instead was a thorough shellacking by the U.S. Supreme Court.[1]

Hicks's girlfriend and his children (along with his mother and aunt) lived in Richmond, Virginia's Whitcomb Court housing project. Kevin Hicks did not. In order to visit his family, he obviously had to use streets and sidewalks that ran alongside and into the housing project. Along his route, he passed a boundary, one that had been marked since late 1997 with signs that declared "NO TRESPASSING—PRIVATE PROPERTY." That year the Richmond city council passed an ordinance deeding all the streets "in and around" Richmond's public-housing projects to the Richmond Redevelopment and Housing Authority (RRHA). The ordinance required the RRHA to post no-trespassing signs and to close the streets to "public use and travel"; it also declared that while now private property (owned by a semipublic agency) the streets were to remain "public for the purposes of law enforcement."[2]

As it turns out, the RRHA did not close the streets to "public use and travel."

It erected no barriers or gates; and it allowed vehicle and pedestrian through-traffic. Indeed, as one RRHA official testified in court, "[i]t has never been our intent to deny anyone from using the sidewalks and streets for their intended purpose," and therefore the streets in Richmond housing projects "remained open to joggers, drive-though traffic, pedestrian 'walk-through' traffic, and all public use and travel."[3]

A Legitimate Business or Social Purpose

Instead, the RRHA sought to protect its new private property rights over the formally public streets by enforcing a "trespass-barment" rule. This rule said that any person found on the property of the RRHA (including the now-private streets and sidewalks) who did not have a "legitimate business or social purpose" (as determined by housing authority employees or city police) could be asked to leave. They could also be served with a verbal or written "barment" that declared that if they ever set foot on RRHA property again, for any reason whatsoever, they would be arrested for trespassing. Such barments were for life and the RRHA created no formal means of appeal.

The City of Richmond and the RRHA made clear their reasons for privatizing the streets and developing the trespass-barment policy. The streets around some of the public-housing projects had become what they called "open-air drug markets," and they were seeking to deter the drug trade by making it next to impossible to loiter in public space. The grounds of the projects, like many in the United States,[4] were already subject to trespass-barment policies, but the RRHA felt they were ineffective "because the sidewalks and streets of RRHA projects remained public property" and "intruders could avoid arrest and prosecution by simply stepping onto an adjacent street or sidewalk."[5] The manager of Whitcomb Court therefore sought to have the streets in and near public-housing projects privatized so they could be subject to the same rule. The city obliged.

Kevin Hicks was arrested twice in 1998 for trespassing—that is for simply being on the formerly public streets or sidewalks of Whitcomb Court. In court for the second of these arrests, Hicks was served with a trespass-barment notice, banning him for life from the streets, sidewalks, and grounds in and near Richmond's public-housing projects. This is odd, for in order to be arrested the *first* time for trespassing, Hicks must *already* have been served with such a notice. Perhaps this first notice was issued verbally, but we will never know since the circumstances of these two arrests are lost to the record. Based on testimony in related cases, however, it is likely that Hicks was never formally banned from the streets; rather he was simply arrested at the whim of a city police officer who decided Hicks should not have been where he was. The Richmond police, and employees of the RRHA, had adopted a policy of arrest on the basis of no reason at all: in the first year of privatization, arbitrary trespass arrest, often before a barment was issued, was common.[6]

Whatever the case may be, the written notice served after the second arrest was both unambiguous and implacable: Kevin Hicks was banished from a significant number of streets in the city, for life. He could not be on these streets for any reason, no matter how "legitimate." If his family wished to use these streets and sidewalks to visit him, that was okay. But if he wanted to visit his family, he could only do so at the risk of arrest and incarceration. And that was exactly what happened one day in January 1999, when Hicks tried to bring diapers to his kid. Although he knew he was banned, he entered the private property anyway. Perhaps Hicks was "my number-one candidate for hardheadedness," as his sentencing judge told him;[7] just as likely he cared about his kids, longed to see his girlfriend, and simply could not abide by his arbitrary, almost surreal banishment. For it was *arbitrary*: there is no evidence anywhere in the record that Kevin Hicks was involved in the drug trade, was himself a drug user, or was otherwise a target of the stated reasons for the privatization of the streets and the creation of trespass-barment rules. And *surreal*: his only "crime" had ever been to have used the streets and sidewalks of the city as he had always used them—both before and after their privatization.

People Like Hicks

Hicks's clean record seemingly made his case perfect one for testing the constitutionality of the street privatization and barment rules. Of course, Hicks's attorneys' main goal was to keep Hicks out of jail. They therefore appealed his conviction on as many grounds as possible. They asserted that the trial was held in the wrong court and before a biased judge; but that appeal went nowhere. They then argued that the Commonwealth of Virginia's trespass statute itself was overly broad and ambiguous, but appeals on these grounds did not go very far either. Finally, they appealed on First Amendment grounds, arguing that the trespass-barment policy potentially "chilled" political speech and assembly: that it might have the effect of closing off the streets for some people who might want to use them for political speech. In fact, the RRHA had adopted an *unwritten* policy that said that anyone who wished to hand out leaflets, solicit petition signatures, or otherwise engage in political activity on its grounds, (including the privatized streets) had to obtain the permission of the housing project manager.

On appeal, Hicks sought to show that the streets and sidewalks in and around Whitcomb Court were what is called a "traditional public forum."[8] The Supreme Court has defined traditional public forums as those public space—streets, sidewalks, and parks are their paradigmatic examples—where "from time immemorial" people have gathered to debate public questions, contest the power of the state, and so forth. In such spaces, the state cannot ban political speech; it can only regulate its time, place, and manner in order to assure the "general comfort and order."[9] Hicks sought to argue that the streets of Whitcomb Court remained a public forum, despite their privatization, and thus the mere threat of barment would likely deter people from engaging in political activity. That is to say, his argument was not that *his* rights to political speech were abridged—he was delivering diapers, after all—but rather that the trespass-barment rules were possibly acting as a form of prior restraint, discouraging others from entering the space for political reasons. As prior restraint, the trespass-barment laws were also having the corollary effect of assuring that no case of First Amendment violation would come before the court simply because people would be too afraid to risk arrest in the first place. Trespass-barment silenced speech and conveniently kept the contestation of those rules, on those grounds, out of the court.

A three-member panel of the Virginia Court of Appeals weighed these arguments. The majority ruled, however, that the streets and sidewalks of Whitcomb Court were *not* a public forum: they were private property, as the deed transfer showed. Indeed, the two judges ruled that the state's "interference" with Kevin Hicks's "intimate associations" with his family—that is, his third conviction for trespassing—was "reasonable, limited, and justified" because he had in the past been convicted of "crimes," leaving aside that the very reason for those convictions was *because* the streets had been privatized and he had been arbitrarily banned![10]

The dissenting judge in the appeal took a rather different view. He noted that the streets were not physically closed, that they remained open to vehicle and pedestrian through traffic, that they continued to function like other streets in the city, and that they therefore remained, despite the deed transfer, a "traditional public forum." The City of Richmond and RRHA thus "infringed on Hicks's right to move freely and be present in a "traditional public forum.""[11] Indeed, this judge asserted, Hicks's conviction was unjust on the most basic grounds of fairness: "[T]o be barred from Whitcomb Court one does not have to be guilty of a crime in Whitcomb Court or to have done anything wrong, but rather, one simply has to fail to fit within the category of people who RRHA has deemed entitled to be on the streets and sidewalks in the public housing development." The city is required, this judge averred, to make its streets safe, but it may not do so in a way that "unduly restricts or criminalizes innocent or protected behavior."[12] That is to say, the privatization, coupled with the trespass-barment rules, allowed the state and its agents to outlaw whole *classes* of people—people *like* Kevin Hicks—even if they had done no wrong, simply because others might.

The next step of the appeal was to the full Virginia Court of Appeals, which narrowly agreed with the dissenting judge from the panel. "The City of Richmond," the majority of the full court declared, "is not permitted to transform the public streets and sidewalks of Whitcomb Court into private, non-public property simply by passing an ordinance declaring them closed, conveying them to another governmental entity, the RRHA, and placing signs along the streets."[13] After further analysis, the appeals court declared both the trespass-barment policies *and* the very deed transfer itself to be unconstitutional and reversed Hick's conviction, not because Hicks was not trespassing, but because of the high social costs of the rules that led to his conviction, rules that "infringe upon a citizen's

First and Fourteenth Amendment rights to lawfully be present in a public place."[14]

Next the case went to the Virginia Supreme Court, which decided it would rule only on the "narrow issue" of whether the trespass-barment policies were overbroad and therefore might "chill" free speech and vacated the lower court's finding that the streets and sidewalks remained a "traditional public forum." It left aside the question of whether people have a right to be in public space together with the question of whether the government can privatize the public forum by fiat, and instead only ruled on the degree of power a representative of the government *acting as landlord* can exercise in publicly accessible property. The Virginia Supreme Court found that the manager of Whitcomb Court had indeed overstepped her authority—the unwritten rule requiring permission for political activity was too broad and vague, and on those grounds (and those grounds alone) the Virginia Supreme Court invalidated the trespass-barment policy and reversed Hicks's conviction. In doing so it might have preserved a small, highly regulated space for political rights, but it simultaneously erased what could be called urban rights, and particularly, the right (for Kevin Hicks and everyone else) simply *to be present* in public space—an erasure that would be enthusiastically endorsed and expanded by the U.S. Supreme Court.

Strollers, Loiterers, Drug Dealers, Roller Skaters, Bird Watchers, Soccer Players, and Others

When the case was heard by the U.S. Supreme Court, parties on both sides—those supporting Richmond's right to privatize public space and the RRHA's right to arbitrarily ban whomever it wanted to from that privatized property, and those who supported Hicks's right to be present in public space and to visit his family in the Whitcomb Court apartments—sought to convince the Court of the momentous issues at stake. For friends of the RRHA the rights of landlords (including governments-as-landlords) were at stake. Throwing out Hicks's conviction, they argued, would hamstring not only the RRHA's ability to control the grounds of its public-housing projects, but state universities' abilities to keep intruders out of dormitories; the federal government's ability to keep people off restricted parts of military bases; and even the Supreme Court's ability to keep spectators out of justices' offices and conference rooms.[15] Those sympathetic to Kevin Hicks, however, asserted the importance of the public forum for free speech; the basic right to be present in public space; and the rights of tenants who, because of these rules, found themselves unable to invite those they wanted as their guests.[16] The Richmond Tenants Organization, for example, filed a forceful brief asserting that the privatization of the streets and the implementation of trespass-barment deeply undermined tenants' rights to freely associate with whom they choose.

Weighing the arguments from both sides, the Supreme Court came down, unanimously, on the side of the RRHA. Hicks's conviction for trespass was upheld, and the Virginia Supreme Court's invalidation of the trespass-barment procedures was reversed. Antonin Scalia delivered the opinion of the Court. He argued that the only question the U.S. Supreme Court could entertain was "whether the claimed overbreadth in the RRHA policy is sufficiently 'substantial' to produce facial invalidity."[17] Scalia began by summarizing the Virginia Supreme Court's findings:

> The Virginia Supreme Court found that the RRHA policy . . . allowed the manager of Whitcomb Court to exercise "unfettered discretion" in determining who may use the RRHA's property. Specifically, the court faulted an "unwritten" rule that persons wishing to hand out flyers on the sidewalks of Whitcomb Court need to obtain [the manager's] permission.[18]

But, Scalia continued, "Hicks, of course, was not arrested for leafleting or demonstrating without permission. He violated RRHA's *written* rule that persons who receive a barment notice may not return to RRHA property."[19] And it was this written policy—the one that says that people without a legitimate business or social purpose could be served with a notice barring them forever from the property—that was at stake, according to Scalia. And here "Hicks has failed to demonstrate that this notice would ever be given to anyone engaged in constitutionally protected speech." Moreover, even if a barred person was arrested for returning to

Whitcomb Court to engage in protected speech, according to Scalia, that would "not violate the First Amendment" since the arrest would be for conduct—trespassing—not speech.[20]

Crucially, in making this argument, Scalia went out of his way to broaden his own decision and give it an importance that stretched far beyond the precincts of public-housing projects:

> *Most importantly*, both the notice-barment rule and the "legitimate business and social purpose rule" apply to *all* persons who enter the streets of Whitcomb Court, not just those seeking to engage in expression. The rules apply to strollers, loiterers, drug dealers, roller skaters, bird watchers, soccer players, and others not engaged in constitutionally protected activity—a group that would seemingly far outnumber First Amendment speakers.[21]

This verdict set an extraordinary precedent. By focusing on only a very narrow question—whether Hicks was engaged in constitutionally protected activity, and by finding that even if he was it would not matter since it was his conduct (trespassing) that was at stake, and by refusing to consider the reasons behind that trespassing (the wholesale privatization of public property as a means to criminalize the otherwise legal behavior of a suspect class of people)—Scalia and the unanimous Court endorsed a world in which public property can be made "private" merely by a deed transfer between two public agencies and *all* non–constitutionally protected activity (from drug dealing and bird watching to soccer playing and loitering) can simply be banned, and people engaged in such activity can be barred, arbitrarily, capriciously, and forever, from many city streets.

Indeed, the decision in *Hicks* makes it clear that the state does not just have the *power* to restrict all nonprotected activity (meeting friends, skateboarding down the street, delivering diapers to a girlfriend and baby), but a *compelling interest* in doing so. Government now can, and sometimes must, act with the full rights and arbitrariness of a landlord, though with the lonely exception that unlike most mall owners (for example), it might be required to permit leafleting and carefully regulated demonstrations on its property. The U.S. Supreme Court had laid down, on the narrowest of grounds, a most stunningly broad decision. The decision in *Hicks* announces a thoroughly *antiurban* legal regime, one that places no value on constructing spaces simply to be present—to be visible as a member of the urban public—the crucial precondition for what Henri Lefebvre called the "right to the city."[22]

While Hicks may have had little choice but to stake his appeal on First Amendment grounds—it might have been possible for him to stay out of jail if he could show that the law that snared him might have a chilling effect on political activity, even though he was not engaged in such activity himself—it turns out that this line of appeal ironically provided the pretext the Supreme Court needed to attenuate, rather than expand, rights in and to public space. The First Amendment may have been seen as something of a Trojan Horse by Hicks's attorneys. Yet what it contained was not a means to keep Hicks out of jail and together with his family, but instead a force allied instead with those who seek to reinforce order at the expense of liberty, security at the expense of freedom, and the rights of property owners, including the state, at the expense of the rights of the people who want to be in and use public space. A more wide-ranging defeat of Kevin Hicks— and of all who understand cities to be primarily a space of *access* and *association*— cannot be imagined.

A Right the Rich Have Long Had

But that is not how the *New York Times* saw the issue. In a short editorial on the case, the *Times* asserted that "The ruling gives the poor a right the rich have long had: to keep loiterers, and potential criminals, out of their homes."[23] In fact, "the poor"—the tenants of Richmond public housing joined by tenants from around the country—had specifically asked the Supreme Court to overturn Hicks's conviction and to declare the privatization of the streets and the trespass-barment rules to be unconstitutional. And, of course, the law at stake had nothing to so with keeping loiterers and criminals out of *homes*, or even out of common areas of public housing projects. However, it did—as the *Times* intuited—establish a legal basis for a geographical norm that many people find appealing—an antiurban norm in which street life is not just demonized, but actively banished.

In fact, in this sense the Supreme Court seems to have struck, and found a way to codify, a growing common sense about how city-space should be regulated and controlled. And not just in the United States either. Since 1999, Britain, for example, has made something of a fetish of banishing people from city centers, housing estates, and other swaths of public land. Britain's "anti-social behavior orders" (ASBOs) work something like a restraining order: a court determines that an individual is culpable for persisting in proscribed, threatening, or dangerous behavior that disrupts the peace and comfort, and sometimes threatens the safety, of neighbors, and orders the individual to desist from certain activities, or, at the most extreme, to be barred from specific locations.

A 2003 revision to the ASBO laws allows police (including parapolice "community support officers") to order "'persons in a group' to disperse if they think any member of the public might be 'intimidated, harassed, alarmed, or distressed.'"[24] In summer 2005, however, a judge in England overturned this provision. At issue were two fourteen-year-old boys who had spent an afternoon leafing through DVDs and CDs in two record shops in the Richmond area of London. As they left the second store, a uniformed community support officer handed the boys a leaflet with a map of the Richmond Green area marked as a "Designated Dispersal Area." The leaflet read: "Should you be required to leave this area by a Police Officer or a Community Support Officer, you must do so immediately. Failure to comply may render you liable to arrest, which could be punishable by three months' imprisonment and/or a fine up to £2,500."[25] Some 400 municipalities have adopted such dispersal orders, which they use freely against teens.[26] Striking a blow against the Kafkaesque intent of such orders, the judge in the case declared: "all of us have the right to walk the streets without interference from police constables or community support officers unless they possess common law or statutory powers to stop us."[27] The current ASBO law, the judge declared, did not grant such statutory power.

The British government responded first with an appeal, and then in January 2006 with new proposals for broad revisions and expansions of the ASBO law. Discouragingly, polls have found that 4 percent of the British population opposes the widespread use of ASBOs (including dispersal and banishment orders). As the *Economist* reports, ASBOs that target "perpetrators as young as ten years old

[who] can be banned from entering an area, wearing particular clothing, or even speaking certain words," are often handed out "on the slenderest of evidence (including hearsay)."[28] In a case that is far from unusual (except for the fact that a judge repealed the order), for example, a Nottingham beggar was banned from entering the city center for two years because he stood in front of a police officer and said, "Guess you do not want a *Big Issue*."[29]

While much in Britain's ASBO craze suggests a real distrust of democratic city life (ASBOs handed out to youth for merely occupying public space and thereby making others uncomfortable; beggars banned from city streets by fiat), the American case remains slightly different. For in *Hicks* the Court not only found a certain enthusiasm for banishment as an appropriate response to urban queasiness; but even more, it rather heartily endorsed the wholesale privatization of public space as the means to effect such banishment. In Britain, banishment remains a function of public authorities; in the United States it can now be more easily accomplished by a simple deed transfer that puts the power of exclusion in the hands of unaccountable public and semipublic authorities. *Trespass* laws—and private entities' legal right to exclude all those they do not like, and to exclude them for any or no reason at all—are the means by which authorities arbitrarily allocate the right merely to be present in urban public space. As an anonymous note in the *Harvard Law Review* put it, by failing to "address the underlying question of the streets' public forum status" the Supreme Court has enabled "local governments to continue curtailing constitutional rights in the guise of 'privatization.'"[30] And since the Court made no effort to distinguish a redevelopment and housing authority from other government agencies, or even other quasi-governmental landholding agencies, it is hard to see how this decision will not be used, for example, to transfer city land to a ballpark district or a urban renewal agency, which could then declare the property private and ban all manner of hitherto legal activities on it, even though it appears to remain fully open to the public. *Hicks* has not given to "the *poor* a right the rich have long had"; it has given such a right to *privatized* agencies that are free from a good deal of democratic accountability, and who can now more fully operate not in the interests of "the poor" (who remain opposed to the trespass-barment procedures in Richmond) but the urban elite who seek to make over their city as a more comfortable playground.

Kevin Hicks only wanted to bring diapers to his child and visit with his family. But in doing so, unfortunately, he provided the Supreme Court with the occasion it needed to massively restrict the rights of *all of us* to be on city streets. For what it has made clear is not only that the privatization of public space is a compelling good, but also that while citizens might have some rather restricted rights to political activity in public space, they have *no* right to simply hang out in the city. At minimum, we must always have a "legitimate business or social purpose"; and even then, if the owners of the (formerly public) streets we wish to traverse on our way to our business—delivering diapers, socializing with family—do not like us, then it is just too bad: we have no a priori right to be on the streets at all. Not only did the Supreme Court trounce on the rights of Kevin Hicks; it took our rights away as well: welcome to the antiurban city in its ultimate neoliberal glory.

Hubrispace:
Personal Museums and the
Architectures of Self-Deification

Joe Day

The British novelist J.G. Ballard might have dreamt the Mori. Like the postindustrial megalith of Ballard's 1975 *Highrise*, the Mori Tower dwarfs its surroundings
and alters its inhabitants' perceptions in subtle but inescapable ways. Both towers
presume and reinforce a direct correlation between altitude and affluence. Ballard's *Highrise* opens retrospectively, with the protagonist, a middle-tier resident,
dining on the Alsatian lapdog of the tower's architect. Soon we learn that the
apartment block of the title was designed to index wealth, power, and sexual allure by floor level, an arrangement that drives the lowly to scale and defile the upper tiers, and those above to barricade against and then co-opt their inferiors.
When an offspring of the lowest floors sullies a rooftop jacuzzi, a top-floor cabal
hurls the woman suspected of allowing the child on the roof to her death. Chaos
ensues, as promised on the book jacket, to eclipse *The Towering Inferno*.[1]

An azure-blue, elliptical extrusion pulled from a pristine Tokyo suburb, the
fifty-four-story Mori Tower looms over its neighbors like a sinister corporate

beacon. As in *Highrise*, most of the Mori Tower is a condo development, except for the top two levels, which house the Mori Museum and Viewing Deck.[2] The museum on the 53rd floor includes 21,500 square feet of "white box" gallery space, which is a grand exhibition venue at any altitude, but a stupefying expanse in a neighborhood where a 500-square-foot studio runs well over a million dollars. Much of the time, the Mori Museum curates neither art, as it has no permanent inventory,[3] nor culture, but the promise of pure vacancy. Whatever the museum's current offerings, the Mori's popular 360-degree Viewing Deck surveys all of Tokyo, giving constant pride of place to its founders Minori and Yoshiko Mori's real-estate empire, the actual heart of their collection.

From its perch on the crowning floors of a premier property in the world's most expensive city, the Mori distills the current message of the single-patron museum to its essence: would that our Present could be your Future. It is in certain respects a generous vision, inviting all visitors to speculate, in both senses of the term, on Tokyo's future evolution. Here, self-aggrandizement hovers very close to civic goodwill, but with both sentiments magnified, generalized, and abstracted to a point of benign neutrality. The Mori turns an all-seeing eye on a world to which, apparently, we often forget to aspire.[4]

More and more individuals are celebrating their lives and interests through edification, and with good reason. "Personal museums" perform a civic alchemy: they allow those of means to host the city on their own terms, and to share the experience of their largesse without forfeiting control over the context, agenda, and credit for their "gift." In return, personal museums and their benefactors can depend on a certain public enthusiasm, even, and sometimes especially, when their missions and manifestations seem completely misguided. And better to have one's name associated in perpetuity with a building, even a really bad one, than with corporate exploitation or malfeasance. As Joan Didion wrote of the original Getty Museum in Malibu, "In the end the Getty stands above the Pacific as one of those odd monuments, a palpable contract between the very rich and the people who distrust them least."[5]

In their architecture, personal museums often prioritize space and site over collection. Many, though not all, aspire to shock and awe their visitors as Versailles does, through an endless, geometric unfolding of indoor/outdoor possibility, with garden follies for scale, rather than following the example of the Louvre in its massive but neutral galleries, anchored by masterpieces. Their emphasis on locale rather than content has made personal museums the butt of much art-world ridicule, but has also left them the breeding ground for a lot of innovative design, especially since minimalism obscured or erased most boundaries between site, art, and building. Even in the staid Midwest, this dynamic has fostered radical, not to say decadent, explorations of form along the lines of Peter Eisenman's 1987 Wexner Center at Ohio State and Zaha Hadid's recent Rosenthal Center for Contemporary Art in Cincinnati—neither design constrained by a stellar collection.

Personal museums often manage to be both absurd *and* highly effective institutions. While they register the intraclass pecking order of extreme wealth that many of its ranks would prefer to keep veiled, and though they tend to parody rather than monumentalize their namesakes, both of these tendencies distract from how often personal museums succeed as instruments of privatized diplomacy: the Rockefellers used their dominant patronage of MoMA to mediate between the "cultured" classes of the United States and Europe for fifty years; the Guggenheim successfully bound post–World War II abstract painting and sculpture to a singular mythology of an earlier avant-garde; the Whitney continues to bridge the divergent sensibilities of urban and rural America (at least in the toney pages of *Town and Country*). When they have an agenda beyond the reification of their patron, personal museums often carry out—and carry on—their missions much more emphatically than do other beneficiaries like schools or charities.

While personal museums were pioneered in Europe, and their future is most evident in Asia, their twentieth-century escalation was led by the United States. Often founded as eccentric gifts to laborers (the Ford, Mercer, and Barnes Museums, for example), personal museums in the United States quickly devolved into ornamental tax shelters, both minor and vast. The single-benefactor "architectures of hubris" that proliferate in Los Angeles, anchored by both Getty campuses, illustrate both the megalomania and myopia that tend to drive these collections and their containment, but only hint at their current variety in the western United States. New York's array of personal museums operate on a more rarefied plane, but pursue the same ends as they define successive waves of contemporary art and contend for global reach.[6]

In a particularly American irony, we will see wealth made in the *fleeing* of cities—fortunes built on suburban expansion and its appetite for fuel, transportation, housing, and services—redeployed in urban fantasies that border on private, central-city utopias. These monuments grew out of an Enlightenment ambition to not only persist in memory, but to promulgate from beyond the grave. Intrepid heirs, both familial and institutional, ensure such legacies. As a senior Getty curator now stands trial in Italy for buying looted antiquities,[7] the directors of other single-benefactor museums chase the world's most bankable architects—and the collections of others—to extend their franchises.

Club Medici: Origins

Surprisingly, neither vanity nor guilt drove the earliest personal museums. The first private collections worthy of the name had little to do with underscoring the status of their owners and were often exclusive to the point of complete secrecy. The emphasis at the Mori on spectatorship and vision is likely the only direct link between it—and contemporary personal museums more generally—and their historical precursors. However, the orchestration of vision in earlier personal museums was intended not to entertain or condition a broader public, but to suit the interests and feed the passions of their owners. In contrast to the Mori Museum's monumental and vast purview over empty space, the earliest personal museums offered intimate tableaux, chockablock with relics and images. This is especially true of the "cabinets of curiosity" or *Wunderkammer* that were first assembled by European noblemen on the eve of the Renaissance, often strictly for their own private enjoyment.

More furniture than buildings, the *wunderkammer* took many forms, burgeoning in scale from intricately compartmentalized desks, appointed with drawers and vitrines for myriad texts and mementos, which were common in Eastern Europe, to the *studiolos* of Italian dukes and cardinals, in which deeply coffered palace interiors were installed with formatted paintings and statuary representing religious and secular subjects, often in fantastic communion. As Eileen Hooper-

Greenhill has observed, spaces such as the shrinelike *Kunstschrank* of Gustavus
Adolphus, completed in 1631, served the dual role of organizing "material knowledge" into its first protoscientific manifestations, while at the same time conferring on their owners a quasi-sacred (and in a Baconian sense, literally omniscient)
legitimacy.[8] Although almost all the early *wunderkammer* were objects within
larger architectural settings, Peter the Great imagined his as a massive building in
its own right, a neoclassical colossus anchored at its center by a surgical theater
under an dome to rival St. Peter's in Rome.[9]

The culmination of these early private collections was the Medici Palace,
an intergenerational personal museum that for the first time posed an entire
residence—but importantly, not the actual seat of royalty—as a space of exhibition, display, and patronage. As Hooper-Greenhill notes: "The space and its artic-
ulations were used to position the family and to construct the position merchant/
prince/patron. The structure, although based on feudal characteristics, was new
in that the "prince" was not a hereditary ruler, and he therefore had to use his per-
suasive power, symbol, and propaganda to establish his position of authority. . . .
Older practices included the amassing of bullion and medieval cosmology; newer
practices included a new view of the past, mercantilism, and a new way of co-
opting the gaze."[10]

Cosimo and then Lorenzo Medici's emphasis on aesthetic quality and competition between artists, rather than sentimental associations or the geographical diversity of the objects displayed, would revolutionize the production of art in
Florence. Though secular patronage was already well-established throughout
northern Europe, especially among the Dutch, the Medicis' commissions to major artists were the first major challenges to the cultural hegemony of the
Catholic church in Italy and to the Papal monopoly in Rome.

Equal parts fortress and ideal villa, the Medici Palace also brokers between the
sensibilities of the Renaissance and those of many modern collectors. In organization, many later museums including MoMA have followed the blank, austere,
and tripartite composition of the Medici Palace exterior, its variable sequence of
salons on each floor for exhibition, and its terraced internal organization around
a central courtyard. More broadly, the Medici led to the common equation of the

museum with all styles, and perhaps all things, Italian: witness the Roman literal-
ism of Getty Villa, the corporate travertine of the nearby Hammer Museum,
even the ill-starred neo-Venetian "lollipop" arches of the Gallery of Modern Art
at 2 Columbus Circle.[11][X]

Adopting Michel Foucault's epistemic historical model, Hooper-Greenhill
cites the micromuseological *wunderkammer* and the Medici Palace as two coun-
terexamples to what would quickly become the dominant Enlightenment em-
bodiment of the museum: the Louvre. Though the Louvre too could be assessed
as a personal museum to the extent that it held the French royals' own treasure,
it has come to be seen as the state museum par excellence, especially after its conversion to a national gallery organized by military campaigns to showcase the
spoils of Napoleon's conquests. While no doubt contributing to his imperial
legacy and perhaps to a national sense of his immortality, the Louvre had the
broader effect of equating state power and cultural magnanimity, a role national
museums have aspired to ever since. Since the late 1700s, personal museums have
developed, and occasionally flourished, in clear subordination and counterpoint
to the many museums of state established during the same period.

Everyman, His Castle

> We have no Egyptian mummies here, nor any relics of the Battle of
> Waterloo, nor do we have any curios from Pompeii, for everything
> we have is strictly American.
> —Henry Ford[12]

Personal museums—and private collecting in general—usually echo and distill
the preoccupations of their times. The scientific discoveries of the nineteenth
century, and the industrial and cultural upheavals of the early twentieth, all drove
a resurgence in individual collecting and curation, as did the massive shift in economic power from Europe to the United States in those years. In contrast to earlier aristocratic examples, personal museums in the United States were often
founded by "self-made" men. While the great collections of Europe were com-
piled over generations and only gradually and belatedly opened to any public
viewing, in the United States it would become the rule rather than the exception

that a single figure amasses a great fortune, spends much of it on Old World plunder, and then frets over how the spoils will be displayed for posterity. ▽

This cliché, however true it would ring through the twentieth century, does not fully account for a rash of early American museums that amassed eccentric, trade-based, and often native artifacts. The Philadelphia museums of Charles Willson Peale (completed in 1821) and Dr. Thomas Dent Mütter (founded in 1863) are perhaps the two most ambitious private attempts to use museology to showcase nineteenth-century science. Peale's museum offered the first taxonometric display of American species as a museum of natural history; the Mütter still stands as the ultimate collection of medical oddities and instruments ever assembled. Both took the form of exhibitions that outgrew their lodgings a few times over before being housed in independent structures. The Peale collection was finally purchased and dispersed by P.T. Barnum in 1854—a profound affront to many scholars who still argue that Peale's museum was the first and last stand to be made against the sensationalization of nature in circus funhouses.[13] As a condition of Dr. Mütter's $30,000 endowment of his collection, the College of Physicians was required to build the facilities that the Mütter still occupies at their campus.[14]

For roughly the same amount—in fact, precisely $38,944.99, spent between 1913 and 1916—Henry Mercer was able to house a vast trove of post-Revolutionary tools and products of early industry in his all-concrete, six-story museum in Doylesville, PA.[15] Limiting his collection to instruments and goods produced before 1820, Henry Mercer created a cornucopia of early American handiwork in order to illustrate his thesis that the great inventions of his time found their inspiration in the modest, makeshift innovations of the previous century. Henry Ford would cite the Mercer as the only museum he was even vaguely curious about (though not enough for a visit) before embarking on his own museum and park of Americana in Detroit in 1929. Greenfield Village and the nearby Ford Museum act as dual venues for Ford's preservation of American historical sites—President Lincoln's log cabin and Ford's family home are given equal billing—and the vehicles that might have transited between them. As the historic structures are consolidated within easy walking distance of one another, and all the planes,

trains, and automobiles are on blocks, the campus has an unexpected, concentrated stillness profoundly at odds with both the peripatetic Ford and the explosive sprawl of his Motor City. ✗

The Peale, the Mütter, the Mercer, and the Ford museums all gave stirring testament to nineteenth-century America's ingenuity, curiosity, and natural grandeur.
Still two more Pennsylvania fortunes, those of Henry Clay Frick and Albert C.
Barnes, underwrote two very different American rediscoveries of Europe. Often
caricatured as the ultimate robber baron of the antebellum period, Henry Frick
made his fortune in Pittsburgh overseeing the Carnegie steelworks. In 1898, he
famously erected an eleven-foot-high barbed-wire fence and mustered a private
army of three hundred Pinkerton men to fight the unionization of the plant,
thereafter nicknamed "Fort Frick."[16] Later in life (in fact after surviving an attempt on his life in which he was shot in the head and neck, then subdued his as-
sailant by hand), he created an edifice the opposite of Fort Frick in almost every
sense, though no less fortified. At a time when such sums rivaled the federal
budget, Frick spent $5 million on his Fifth Avenue, New York City, estate in 1913,
and bequeathed another $15 million for its running and upkeep when he died six
years later.[17]

Though a relatively small collection, the Frick's assembly of portraits by
Velázquez, Rembrandt, and Vermeer, among many others, is unparalleled in any
private or national collection in the world. J. Paul Getty's estate, at the height of
the Getty Center's buying power in the early 1990s, would have struggled to finance one or two of the Old Master portraits that Frick snapped up at the turn of
the century. For that matter, in their location, grandeur, and elegance, the Frick
mansion and gardens shame almost any conceivable exercise in contemporary
conspicuous consumption.

The Barnes Collection, by contrast, is astounding not for its blue-chip holdings
(though some of its impressionist canvases by Degas and Monet would already
have been sought after in the 1920s), but for its prescient accumulation of modern masterworks by Picasso, Matisse, Braque, and many other Cubist luminaries,
often purchased off the easel by Barnes on his annual European tour. As remark-

able as the collection was Barnes's mission for exhibiting it to "the working man," so that he might appreciate the congruencies between modern and African tribal art. To this end, Barnes installed the paintings in specific combinations, salon-style—tiled closely up the walls—and interspersed with his extensive collection of tribal masks and statuary. In his bequest, Barnes required that the work only be seen as he had displayed it, and (though this would be successfully disputed by his executors) only in his home gallery by appointment.[18]

In this last respect, involving conflicts between heirs, executors, and surrounding community interests, the Barnes Collection has proven a depressingly leading-edge institution. Alfred Barnes left his collection and the house it resides in to a small, historically African American college. Over the last ten years, trustees representing variously his family, the college, and major Philadelphia art patrons have come to blows over a plan to relocate the collection downtown to a site currently used to house youth offenders. The forced urbanization of the Barnes, if it comes to pass, will reprise a tested civic formula substituting spaces of exhibition for prohibition: one of the first British personal museums, the Tate Collection, was erected on the site of the former Millbank Prison in 1897,[19] and, closer to home, the abandoned Eastern State Penitentiary in Philadelphia was recently opened as a site for installation art.

The Plutocrat as Artist

> Museums could bear the inscription: Entry for art lovers only. But there clearly is no need for such a sign, it all goes without saying. The game makes the *illusio*, sustaining itself through the informed player's investment in the game. The player, mindful of the games meaning and having been created for the game because he was created by it, plays the game and by playing it assures its existence.
> —Pierre Bourdieu[20]

Among early American personal museums, the Frick and the Barnes lead more clearly into the present simply because they focused on art, which became almost the exclusive theme of single-benefactor museums for most of the twentieth century.[21] However, the roles of collector and artist would undergo profound alterations over that period, leading not just to many more personal museums, but to a spectrum of institutions commemorating distinct personalities, whether benefactor, artist, or both. Personal museums now run a gamut from those founded by a "mere" and perhaps absentee collector, to those shaped by a heavily involved patron, through collaborative spaces commissioned by enlightened amateurs (often other artists or architects), out to monographic institutions devoted to exhibiting a singular talent.

Probably the least contentious of these are the last: monographic museums based on the work of single artists. With first the Rodin Gardens and then the Musée Picasso, the French government recognized how centrally their national legacy was bound up in the legacies of specific artists, and set to preserving and propounding their work. In this, they often supported or extended a nineteenth-century French tradition in which an artist's home-turned-studio-turned-museum, as in the symbolist painter Gustav Moreau's townhouse in an outer arrondissement of Paris (which became a mandatory Surrealist pilgrimage), and Monet's Gardens at Giverny.

The most recent and extreme shoring of French cultural patrimony in this mode came unexpectedly. The Rodin Pavilion opened recently in a corporate atrium in Seoul, South Korea, to showcase just one sculptural series by the artist, *The Burghers of Calais*. The Pavilion was commissioned by Samsung, a Korean chaebol, and designed by American A&E giant KohnPedersonFox. KPF's foray into signature architecture for art led to a Frank Gehryesque swoop rendered in laminated, translucent glass, held aloft by a custom space-frame of point supports. At a cost of over $1,000 per square foot, the Rodin Pavilion is the most expensive investment in the display of a single work of art ever made, to suit a sculpture that the French government could reproduce ad infinitum if they so chose—and thus render almost valueless—from molds the artist bequeathed to the state.

Through the twentieth century, innumerable museums were established in honor of major artists, often in their historically preserved workspaces, such as the Casa Azul of Frida Kahlo, Salvador Dalí's palace, and Isamu Naguchi's studio in Long Island City. Many new monographic museums reside in structures designed or designated in the artist's memory. Artists as diverse as Joan Miró, Norman Rockwell, Jean Arp, and Andy Warhol have all been accorded this honor, as was Picasso in almost every city he set foot in.

Many of the most important collections of modern art were then and are now in the hands of artists themselves. Manet and Picasso famously collected and supported the work of their peers, and Andy Warhol, Dennis Hopper, and many others have stockpiled the best works of their generation. Sadly, few of these are open to the public, and many that are open remain geographically remote, as is Donald Judd's installation of his own work and those of others in a defunct military barracks at Marfa, Texas. When artists are showcased by other artists, as Dan Flavin and John Chamberlain are by Judd at Marfa, it's often challenging to sort out the creative labor of the artist from the "creative" capital that supports and preserves his or her work.

This increasingly incestuous ambiguity between author and steward of the work, and the *frisson* it confers on all parties involved in the traffic of contemporary art, has had the net effect of glorifying the buyer, and drawing more and more collectors into the fray of collecting and exhibiting new art. Many collectors now purchase the art of living artists with an eye to those that might someday merit specific museums of their own, while other collectors have become much more active patrons—commissioning and sometimes collaborating in the work they purchased to shape a museum-worthy inventory. The ubergalleries of impresarios like Larry Gagosian (who now has four vast locations) and "foundations" of career-making collectors such as Charles Saatchi are private fiefdoms, personal museums in all but name.[22]

The diversity of agendas and recognition that now typifies personal museums for art, whether they be named for a patron or an artist, has at least had the effect of radically diversifying the architectural expression of these institutions. Until the 1950s, almost all personal museums were housed in or adjoining the homes of their deceased benefactors. Since then, a vast array of structures have been imagined and realized for exhibiting collections. In fact, personal museums combine the exhibition space with the building type most commonly open to innovation since World War II, the single-family home. As a result (and no doubt for bet-ter *and* for worse), many of the most daring gambles in contemporary architec-ture are taken first in the housing of private art collections. Personal museums are by general consensus the Petri dishes of haute design.

While the Guggenheim and the Whitney—by Frank Lloyd Wright and Marcel Breuer, respectively—are emblematic of this trend and will be discussed in the context of New York, three other projects played equally powerful and more sub-tle roles in the spread of personal museum architecture: the Kimbell Museum in Fort Worth by Louis Kahn; the de Menil Collection, designed by Renzo Piano, in Houston; and Philip Johnson's Glass House and neighboring structures for art in New Canaan, Connecticut. All deal centrally with light and transparency, both as an issue of illumination and privacy, and all go to elaborate lengths to tailor and conceal their cultural cache. Importantly, all broker between traditions of high modern architecture and concurrent strains of minimalism in fine art.

Louis Kahn's Kimbell is a critical beachhead between minimalist art and late-modern architecture. Composed completely of nearly identical barrel vaults, run side-by-side and segmented to provide entry and a relief of small courtyards, the Kimbell neatly dispenses with both the radial logic of older museums and the gridded expanse of most modern ones. Donald Judd singled out the Kimbell as the only piece of American architecture worthy of the term, and the affinity that Kahn shares with Judd and his peers in terms of the orchestration of space through repetitive geometry is self-evident. For many art collectors, the Kimbell's synthesis of Roman forms and modern finishes made it possible to imagine dig-nified, privatized monuments for contemporary art. I.M. Pei, Tadao Ando, and Rafael Moneo head a long list of prolific international museum architects that have all expanded on the legacy of Kahn. Ando's recent Modern Art Museum of Fort Worth, catty-corner to the Kimbell, and his Pulitzer Collection in St. Louis read almost as inspired sequels to the Kahn original.

Renzo Piano's current popularity springs from two contradictory projects, his Centre Pompidou of 1975 and the de Menil Pavilion of 1981–86. In the latter he paid penance for many of the perceived sins of the former, working from inside out and focusing his attention on the display of art rather than the generation of spectacle. The wave-shaped reflectors that hover over and modulate the light entering the de Menil opened an entire cottage industry of skylight design for art (though they do not completely protect paintings from ultraviolet damage). In recent interviews, Piano claims that the de Menil rather than the Pompidou set the pattern for his career, a constant striving for better spaces of viewership. Museum trustees flock to him for this latter-day humility in the face of art, while architects remember him for rivaling art in the Pompidou.

A less likely but critical figure for U.S. collectors is Philip Johnson. Johnson's complex in New Canaan is often viewed exclusively through the scrim of his Glass House of 1949. While this vitrine-for-living foregrounds the relationship between exhibition and exhibitionism, the picture gallery and the sculpture gallery he built nearby in the 1970s are more original investigations, positing modest but new architectures for art. Each is precisely calibrated to the medium on display. The Picture Gallery takes its cloverleaf shape in plan from the three wall-height, radial rolodex used to rotate over thirty wall planes into a single gallery space. Naturally lit from above, the Sculpture Gallery steps down through multiple levels and terraces so that artworks of varying scale, orientation, and installation can be seen in the round and in relation to one another. As Francesco Dal Co describes, "Johnson's art collecting is united with architectural collecting. But it is, precisely, an encounter between two different tendencies. . . . The need to decodify is combined in Johnson's work with the eclectic experimentalism of his formal research, (and) with the autobiographical narcissism which is one with the innate penchant for collecting."[23]

Dal Co's essay concludes an issue of *Lotus International* devoted entirely to museums of architecture, one that begins with discussions of both John Soane's museum, completed in 1837, and the Isabella Stewart Gardner Museum of 1903. Like these earlier essays by enlightened "amateurs," Philip Johnson's New Canaan complex hinges vitally on his dilettantism, his willingness to borrow literally and figuratively across disciplines at no small cost to his credibility. While many have examined Johnson's likely sympathies for Mies, Nazi Germany, and various post–World War II "formalisms" in architecture, too little attention has been paid to the art collection he amassed with his partner David Whitney, and the more stringent formalism of art critic Clement Greenberg to which Johnson adhered in the medium specificity of his gallery architecture.

LA Apotheosis: Self-Sanctification, In-Name-Only Bailouts, and the Anti-Edifice

> And I liked the way history did not run loose here. They segregated visible history. They caged it, funded and bronzed it, they enshrined it carefully in museums and plazas and memorial parks. The rest was geography, all space and light and shadow and unspeakable hanging heat.
>
> —Don DeLillo[24]

With some noteworthy and recent exceptions, including the de Menil and Warhol museums mentioned above, and the Liberace Museum in Las Vegas and the Wolfsonian Museum of Decorative and Propaganda Art in Miami,[25] personal museums have taken root mostly in our two largest cities. Their competitive escalations in New York and Los Angeles could be construed as an arms race—one that Los Angeles perennially loses, often at Pyrrhic costs.[26] However, a closer look at both cities reveals very different terms and ambitions for these institutions. In New York, many single-name institutions have evolved into truly corporate polities, with multiple major donors, depersonalized but increasingly politicized in their scope. In the last twenty years, the Guggenheim has received at least two major transfusions of cash from nonfamilial trustees to stay open, and the Metropolitan Museum of Art and MoMA, linked for much of their histories to the Vanderbilt and Rockefeller fortunes respectively, have built extensive, named, and often stand-alone gallery space to house the work of other collectors.

In Los Angeles, by contrast, personal museums have remained intimately tied to their benefactors. While the Getty dwarfs them, the Armand Hammer and Norton Simon museums are formidable vaults in their own right, each indebted in very different ways to the Texas museums of Kahn and Piano. The blockwide, low arches of the Hammer Museum, supporting three-story-high blank facades

on all street sides, are most charitably understood as a misreading of Kahn's austere arcades and unadorned end walls at the Kimbell, somehow melded with the
urban mass of his British Art Center at Yale. (Though not a personal museum, the
BAC offered a template for mixing retail and exhibition space in a single structure
that the Hammer really should have stolen.) Frank Gehry's remodeling of the
Norton Simon, spearheaded by FOG partner Greg Walsh, takes much more sub-
tle advantage of the discoveries Kahn and Piano made in the baffling of natural
light, delving in from above and below the original structure to illuminate the Simon's superlative but polyglot trove of impressionist painting and Southeast
Asian statuary.

In the end, though, the Norton Simon and the Hammer both share with the
Getty Center a corporate travertine monumentality, a fixation on stone for
stone's sake borrowed from LACMA and continued in terracotta at MoCA. If, as
Mike Davis observed at its opening, the Getty resembles a "Nordstrom's in the
Sky" to some locals,[27] then the rest of LA's major museums—and here one should
also add the Pederson Automotive Museum, as well as nearby institutions dedicated to Tolerance and Television—offer little architecturally to compete with
the anchor tenant on high.

But not all Los Angeles personal museums are easily confused with big-box
mausoleums. Those operating in minor keys are less easily typecast, and some of
the majors deserve the benefit of the doubt for salvaging imperiled cultural institutions. The Norton Simon and the Geffen Contemporary at MoCA are both instances of single-benefactor bailouts of once independent museums.[28] At least by
the museum's current account of its history, industrialist Norton Simon rescued
the Pasadena Museum of Fine Art from near extinction, and while the "Temporary Contemporary," as the Geffen was previously known, might have persisted
as part of MoCA, it would no doubt have struggled for intrainstitutional autonomy
without David Geffen's $15-million infusion in 1998. (It's worth noting, however,
that some consider Geffen's naming opportunity a steal for that amount and a
civic disaster for downtown, and that Frank Gehry's much-touted conversion of a
storage garage into the Temporary long preceded Geffen's involvement.) ☒

The most recently and thoroughly publicized of these in-name-mostly bailouts is Eli Broad's ambitious restructuring of LACMA's campus around a new Broad Museum of Contemporary Art. After LACMA hosted a major competition, which Dutch architect Rem Koolhaas won with a brilliantly all-encompassing scheme that proved too ambitious and costly for LACMA's trustees, and after a county bond measure failed to garner any additional public funding, Broad resorted to his own architect, Renzo Piano, on his own dime. The results appear to "Citywalk" or to "Grove"[29] the parallel streetscape of Wilshire by closing off cross-streets and introducing an internal pedestrian "cul-de-sac" through LACMA, onto which all the existing and planned galleries will unfold.

Two less heralded personal collections deserve far larger audiences for grappling with conceptual art and for posing each of their "museums" as a kind of antiedifice. Though now based in Santa Fe, the Lannan Foundation resided in Los Angeles for eleven years as a lending museum with a small exhibition space in Mar Vista. The vast majority of their contemporary art collection was on constant loan, with just a few pieces—often difficult and incendiary work like Chris Burden's monument to the Vietnamese losses in the Vietnam War, a ten-foot-high bronze rolodex with hundreds of thousands of Vietnamese names, some generated by random syllabic combination for lack of actual records—shown in their base gallery. With a mission to bring as much contemporary art to as broad an audience as possible through all available venues, the Lannan poses one of the few easily defensible models for personal collecting made public.[30]

David Wilson's Museum of Jurassic Technology takes a very different, though equally selfless, tack to initiate visitors in the elliptical potential of conceptual art. As Lawrence Weschler has exhaustively explored in his monograph on the MJT, *Mr. Wilson's Cabinet of Wonder*, the Museum of Jurassic Technology inhabits a Culver City storefront only to pose a multitude of sometimes mundane, often paradoxical exhibits.[31] Armenian microminiatures that may or may not be to scale compete for one's attention with an elaborate installation documenting the complicated love triangle of Iguazu Falls, whose incommensurable plot lines, tortured geography, and pseudoscience are on par with the internal complexities of Marcel Duchamp's *Large Glass* or Matthew Barney's *Cremaster Cycle*. Robert Mangurian and Mary Ann Ray's multiple proposals for revamping the MJT, parts of which may or may not have been realized surreptitiously, only compound the institution's occult allure. Matt Colidge's nearby storefront, the Center for Land Use Interpretation, or CLUI, extends the MJT's charms as well.

In addition to the examples above, the massive personal collections of contemporary art currently held in private homes such as those of Michael Ovitz, Stanley and Elyse Grinstein, and Edythe and Eli Broad—to list only those on O.J. Simpson's former street in Brentwood—will provide ample fodder for new experiments in personal museology in Los Angeles over the coming decades.

The Concrete Stomach vs. the Kremlin of Modernism[32]

If Los Angeles extends the tradition of the personal museum both to new extremes of ostentation and to less easily quantified possibilities for the future, New York's personal museums respond to and exert other kinds of pressures in that city's continuing role as clearinghouse, if no longer sole arbiter, of the avant-garde. While art culture is less funereal in New York than elsewhere, it is also more socially competitive. Among patron-class New Yorkers, board seats for the living matter more than gallery real estate for the dead, and an attunement to the quality of works on display is still required. In all of these respects (and in at least their initial taste in architects), New Yorkers remain rather Dutch.

New York's dominance of the twentieth-century art market resulted in a network of vast, proactive galleries that often leave the experience of art in its museums feeling late and warmed-over. Many of the most compelling personal museums in New York, as well as some of its most dubious, follow a gallery model, and many New York galleries could plausibly call themselves museums.

The most important of these not-quite-for-profit experiments was Peggy Guggenheim's Art of this Century exhibition space, an intestinal circuit of curved display spaces designed by Fredrick Kiesler and opened in 1942. A niece of Solomon Guggenheim, whose museum was under discussion when she opened her own space, Peggy Guggenheim set a far more progressive agenda for Art of this Century, showcasing the latest work of the Surrealist émigrés during WWII and providing many of them with living stipends. Her championing of Jackson Pollock and the first wave of Abstract Expressionists guaranteed their survival.

Though Art of this Century only showed for a few years before being absorbed into the larger Guggenheim "mothership" uptown, it set a precedent for independent art exhibition that gallery owners, many of them also women like Ileana Sonnabend, Mary Boone, and Jeanie Greenberg, would take up in their retail spaces and extend quickly to installation and performance art.

Another art dynasty black sheep—the renegade daughter of Dominique de Menil, who commissioned Piano's Houston pavilion—Philippa de Menil converted to the Sufi faith and founded the Dia Art Foundation with curator Heiner Friedrich in the mid-1970s. Dia may be to the art of the 1960s and 70s what Art of this Century was to the 1940s and 50s.[33] Concentrating on a small stable of major artists, many "postgallery" in the siting and scale of their work, such as Walter de Maria and Michael Heizer, the Dia has enabled or preserved more land art and large-scale minimalist and postminimalist work than any other agency to date. In addition to the specific sites of works across the western United States, the Dia shows a wide array of contemporary art in an eight-story Chelsea warehouse, and recently opened Dia:Beacon in a half-million-square-foot former Nabisco factory in upstate New York, refurbished by Robert Irwin and OpenOffice. (The Chinati Foundation, a related nonprofit with shared board members, administers Judd's Marfa campus since his death in 1994.)

(If one were to look for more parallel institutions from generation to generation, the Dahesh Museum, founded to exhibit an extensive collection of decorative and symbolist art and housed on an anonymous floor of a midtown tower, runs the mannerist risk of reprising the kitsch Gallery of Modern Art at 2 Columbus Circle.)

Finally, the three major New York museums of twentieth-century art, however singular their origins, can only distantly be understood now as personal museums. The Museum of Modern Art, the Guggenheim, and the Whitney were all founded on a single collector's body of work,[34] but have grown and diversified more in the manner of private universities than other museums. All three are in the throes of major expansion plans, and those plans say a great deal about the futures of both art and architecture in the United States. Tellingly, Rem Koolhaas was in contention in every case, with schemes that either fell short in competition (the invitational MoMA charette), or were, like LACMA's, judged to be to expensive and abandoned (the NeWhitney), or were realized, only to be quickly shuttered (the Guggenheim Las Vegas). Koolhaas's common involvement, and his commitment to a "Metropolitanism" he coined in "Delirious New York" thirty years ago, suggests that as much as the current stewards of these institutions would like to raise (or raze) them to a uniform, if progressive, urbanity, the eccentricities of their founders persist, at least as obstacles to their homogenization by a single architect. (Architects blame philistinism and cowardice on the part of museum trustees for Koolhaas being denied all of them. None make this point with more bitter precision than Koolhaas himself.[35])

Of the three, the Whitney remains both the most mission-specific, concentrating on American art, and, largely for that reason, the most parochial. The Whitney's biennial survey of American art has become a regular excuse, at all points of the cultural spectrum, to grouse on the paltry offerings and/or offensive new directions of domestic art. Whether these cycles of hand-wringing improve U.S. artists' prospects—and for politically savvy artists of the "NEA 5" generation, they almost certainly did—they underscore a distinctly American friction between private taste and public edification. Expansion plans for the Whitney deserve a book of their own at this point, as does Breuer's original. The Whitney's stepped facade and cyclopean window facing Madison Avenue are enjoying a fashion revival, as was evident in Koolhaas's NeWhitney addition, a similarly faceted form that extended up from behind the original like a phantom of its host. A famously antithetical addition proposal by Michael Graves in the 1980s posed a collection of buildings like postmodern trinkets over and around Breuer's, reducing his to a scaleless toy. Less a response to Koolhaas's scheme, which it replaces, and more a diametrically understatement of Graves's, the current plans for a Whitney expansion by Renzo Piano are virtually invisible, with all design controversy reduced to whether one or two neighboring brownstones will be sacrificed to reach a characterless new entry.[36]

As with so much of the Rockefeller legacy, the Museum of Modern Art ad-

vances a Hamiltonian faith in American urbanity, a United States led not by popular will and Washington, but by an enlightened, autonomous New York City. For
all of the well-orchestrated "outrage" that early MoMA shows may have generated, there was never any real doubt or internal dispute regarding its agenda:
MoMA would bring the leading edge of European art to an American audience,
and over time ensure that Americans joined, and eventually led, that pantheon of
the New. The founders of MoMA—among them Alfred Barr, Philip Johnson, and
Nelson Rockefeller—could presume a broadly urbane and forward-looking consensus among moneyed New Yorkers, ready and willing to be shaped to new
ends. ✗

MoMA has rebuilt itself three or four times, and at every interval—from Abby
Rockefeller's apartment to the streamlined 53rd Street building, through Johnson's and Cesar Pelli's modifications—subtly redirected and narrowed its purview
on the canon of twentieth-century art. Its latest manifestation by Yoshio Tan-
iguchi poses an epic struggle between Cubism and Minimalism as the defining
drama of the last century, with a "push-pull" composition of volumes and spaces
redolent of the earlier vanguard, but rendered at the scale and in the palette of
the latter movement. Interestingly, the losers in this new configuration are the Expressionists, especially the gestural midcentury giants of AbEx that established
the museum, and by extension, the United States, as the post–World War II capital of the art world. The once epic canvases of Pollock, Rothko, and Rosenquist
read as mere accents in the cavernous voids of the new MoMA.

By contrast, the Guggenheim reflects the *arriviste* politics and aspirations of
Solomon Guggenheim, whose fortune was made in grocery chains supplying the
new suburbs of the Midwest. The Guggenheim's mission required interpretation
and translation, initially provided by Solomon's chief curator and likely mistress,
Hilla de Rebay. Though she was purged from the board of the Guggenheim by
Solomon's heirs before Wright's building was complete, Rebay's obsession with
what she termed "Non-Objective" art left an indelible mark on the inventory and
direction of the museum. In particular, "Non-Objectivity" was fruitfully inter-
preted in the 1960s to include almost all postpainterly abstraction, especially, Min-

imalist and Post-minimalist works that, while they could not have been imagined by the museum's founders, proved far better suited to its architecture.

Led currently by the controversial Thomas Krens, the Guggenheim has pioneered the global franchising of its collection and identity, at what many now feel was dire cost to the operational viability of the New York hub.[37] From the perspective of Solomon Guggenheim, however, Krens may well have ensured the Guggenheim name greater international notoriety, at least in the short term, than it would have had otherwise, simply on the basis of Krens's one broadly acknowledged success: the Guggenheim Bilbao. Though fewer tourists seem to be making the pilgrimage each year, and Basque separatists are again likely scheming to blow up the mammoth topiary puppy by Jeff Koons near its entrance (they tried the week of its opening), the Guggenheim Bilbao remains the benchmark against which all culturally based urban-renewal schemes are judged. Its near simultaneous opening with the Getty Center in 1997—a brutal coincidence for the stolid and far more costly Getty—will likely prove the high-water mark for personal museum construction.

MoMA and the Guggenheim are now vying, in partnerships with the Pompidou and the Hermitage, respectively, for their cut of the staggering sums earmarked for the redevelopment of Hong Kong's old airport island as Kowloon West. The scale of this development guarantees that Asia will enjoy its first comprehensive trove of Western art and artifacts, and, by the same token, that a huge portion of the patrimony of Europe and the United States will continue its westward migration off our shores. No matter the outcome, Kowloon West will broker the largest transfer of cultural wealth from Occident to Orient ever recorded.[38]

Whatever the outcome in Asia—and Kowloon West is only one of three sites on Krens's agenda for Guggenheim branches in Asia alone—it seems likely that the era of museum-by-plutocrat is winding down, or, in Guantanamo-speak, being "rendered quaint." The globally ranked museums, whether named for individuals or otherwise, now expand as brands rather than as sensibilities. The three big U.S. museum donors of the nineties—Eli Broad, Paul Allen, and Paul Lewis—

all avoided one-off structures in favor of influence and naming opportunities else-where.[39] Though he too serves on many museum boards, Mayor Michael Bloomberg learned from Nelson Rockefeller (who claimed all of his political skills were honed dealing with MoMA curators) that it's faster, cheaper, and less complicated to buy an office than an edifice. On this logic, we will likely see fewer new tombs for art, and more museums of celebrity and calamity, neither to be taken too personally.

Monastery Chic: The Ascetic Retreat in a Neoliberal Age

Sara Lipton

The most difficult room to book on the California coast is not in a luxury hotel or a resort spa, but in the Mount Calvary Monastery, an Episcopalian Benedictine retreat house in Santa Barbara, where there is a two-year-long waiting period for a weekend in a simply furnished cell. Rooms are in similar demand at the Benedictine New Camaldoli Hermitage in Big Sur, though here reservations are only accepted six months in advance.[1] Nor are lengthy waiting lists unique to monasteries with a Pacific view; they are repeated across the country, from Minnesota to Massachusetts, upstate New York, and the hills of Kentucky.[2] Although in 1978 a historian of religion declared that "migration into modernity may have finished off the hilltop gods of village, tribe, and monastic retreat,"[3] and a scant seven years ago a panel of theologians fretted that ritual and traditional religion were dying (in favor of a vague and ecumenical "spirituality"),[4] there is considerable evidence that the Christian monastery, the most rigidly structured and ritually formalistic of all Western religious institutions, has never been more popular.[5] According to *Publishers Weekly*, upward of 1.2 million Catholics and uncounted numbers of non-Catholics went on monastic retreat in 1997; Retreats International, an association of Catholic and Protestant retreat houses in the United

States and Canada, calculates that 2.5 million people went "on retreat" in the past year.[6] Even luxury hotels are jumping on the monastery bandwagon: advertisements for the four-star Hotel Monasterio de San Martin in Cadiz boast that the resort "maintains the original character and construction of an eighteenth-century monastery" (in spite of featuring a pool and a bar), and promise that visitors "may still feel the presence of the past" in a monastic atmosphere providing "an ideal place to relax."[7] And the press release announcing a forthcoming Rocco Forte luxury hotel to be built on the property of a still-working Augustinian monastery in Prague highlights the fact that "The Monastery will provide the hotel with a picturesque setting of established courtyards and elegant garden squares, while retaining certain areas for the practising Augustine [sic] monks who remain *in situ*."[8] These monks are apparently considered—along with the "key historic features" of cloistered terraces, wooden ceilings, wine vaults, and stone arches—to be a prime attraction, the kind of "signature" accent vaunted by Rocco Forte International.

In one sense, there is nothing new about this. Well-heeled lay folk have been staying in monastic guesthouses for as long as there have been monasteries. The sixth-century Rule of Saint Benedict enjoins the receiving of guests *tanquam Christus* (like Christ himself) as a central monastic duty, and most medieval houses accordingly ran hospices for pilgrims and travelers.[9] Some visitors came merely for convenience: since there was no such thing as a luxury hotel in premodern Europe: travelers who turned their noses up at rough-and-tumble inns had few other options.[10] But many others came for explicitly pious purposes: the poet Petrarch (d. 1374) sojourned several times in a Carthusian monastery in search of solitude,[11] and even the notoriously heretic-loving and loose-living Count Raymond of Toulouse (d. 1229) took a break from carousing and cleaving heads in twain to rest his own head on a hard convent cot.[12] Such gestures reflected the penitential value assigned asceticism in Catholic doctrine—denying the body was believed to cleanse the soul.

But there was a further theological logic to such monastic interludes, above and beyond self-mortification. In medieval Christendom, all of society was conceived as a single Body Christian, each limb of which supported the other and had

its assigned role to play. Monks' main work was to pray for the souls of their noble benefactors, whose main work was to fight. (Because desire for power and
fear of hell were equally prevalent among the lordly classes, the most generous
monastic patrons and the most ruthless and brutal killers were often one and the
same.[13]) Through stability, chastity, poverty, obedience, and various "supereroga-
tory acts" monks accrued surplus blessedness, which in turn could, via their
prayers, overflow onto the rest of society and confer spiritual benefit upon those
unable to earn it for themselves.[14] Establishing a personal connection with a
monastic foundation allowed one to tap into its surplus righteousness and sip its
grace.

None of this, though, does much to explain the current popularity of the
monastic retreat. According to some estimates, many, perhaps most, of the patrons of monastery guest houses are not Catholic, but Protestant, a faith that
rejects the doctrine of "surplus of merits," eschews the Catholic exaltation of
celibacy, and denies any role to "works" in salvation.[15] Other monastery visitors
are Jewish, unaffiliated, or agnostic, and so less likely still to be motivated by
Catholic doctrine or penitential practice.[16] Even those retreatants who are Catholic
must have a tenuous connection at best to Catholic salvation theology, the grim-
mer aspects of which have been downplayed by the Church in recent years.

So what *does* explain the current popularity of the monastic retreat? That
monks and nuns are considered "holy" or at least "spiritual" by most visitors
seems clear; what is less clear is what is to be gained by visiting them. Wherein
lies the attraction of the monastery, if it offers the visitor neither convenience nor
security, atonement nor salvation? Two different, contradictory explanations
dominate discussions of the trend. Some commentators classify the current popularity of the monastic retreat as simply the latest fad in that perennial American
pastime, "spiritual shopping."[17] In this reading, the Christian monastery of the
1990s and early 2000s is little different from the ashram of the 1970s or the Zen
health spa of the 1980s: each represents a spiritual "Other" whose primary appeal
is its romantic exoticism.[18] Other commentators, by contrast, locate the appeal of
the monastery in its very unfaddishness. They see the growing interest in traditional monasticism as a fundamental shift, a move away from the eclectic, self-

centered spirituality of the "Me-generation." Contemporary Americans, this theory goes, are attracted by the very incompatibility of current and monastic values: the monks' life of duty, ritual, rules, and self-denial contrasts with the perceived "emptiness" of modern life, devoid of tradition, structure, and obligation, and mired in meaningless consumption.[19] A religious book editor at Doubleday tells *Publishers Weekly* that this "longing for tradition" is "a backlash against the cafeteria-style Christianity" of the 1980s and 1990s: "I think we are just getting over millennial madness, and we want more of long-haul spirituality," he is quoted as saying, "We don't want a quick fix anymore."[20] Diane Weymouth, codirector of The Well, a Catholic religious retreat in Virginia, likewise notes: "Retreat is an old thing that's maybe being revived. . . . It's in our traditions. It's very ancient. Jesus went off. Moses went off. Solitude."[21] In either reading, whether exotic fad or return to roots, the monastery is seen as the antithesis of the current neoliberal world, and the monastic retreat as a flight from that world—the ultimate "antidote to twenty-first-century materialism."[22]

But a closer look at contemporary practice suggests that the twenty-first-century monastic retreat is more familiar than one might think. Indeed, if the attractions of the prototypical neoliberal neighborhood—the modern gated community—are security through fortification, order through homogeneity, exclusivity through selectivity, tradition through nostalgia, and beauty through carefully sculpted nature (all maintenance-free), then the contemporary version of the medieval monastery may well be the ultimate neoliberal paradise.[23] Far from facilitating a flight into either exotic otherness or a simpler past, monastic retreat as currently practiced replicates almost all the characteristics of the affluent, materialistic world from which the retreatants seek to flee.[24]

The setting, grounds, and architecture of many retreat centers, which can be stunningly beautiful, are described on Web sites that echo the tactics, if not the goals, of consumer advertisements, and in language redolent of the travel and real-estate industries. Casa Franciscan Renewal Center in Arizona boasts "twenty-three acres of a lush desert oasis set at the base of Camelback Mountain in the heart of the Scottsdale/Paradise Valley resort district."[25] La Casa de Maria (Santa Barbara), run by the Sisters of the Immaculate Heart, notes that the convent "can be found at the end of a winding lane canopied in dense foliage leading from the Upper Village in Montecito. Set in a secret garden, guarded by woodlands and the tumbling waters of the San Ysidro Creek, its ambience is that of a much-loved country house through which many generations have passed and left their mark."[26] The facilities of the Jesuit Retreat House of Cleveland include "57 acres of forest, meadows and pathways."[27] The Jesuit Spirituality Center in Louisiana is located in a 900-acre farmland setting "famous for its serenity, beautiful oak trees, azaleas, and flowering bushes."[28] Retreat destinations in eastern Canada include "a large French Gothic Revival abbey surrounded by forests, grazing cattle, and a serene lake; a priory in a three-story Queen Anne–style house with a wraparound porch and a corner tower . . . or an interdenominational retreat center . . . located on the dramatic Niagara escarpment."[29] Mater Dolorosa Passionist Retreat Center is located in Sierra Madre, California, "on 80 acres of foothills, open fields, [with] groves of trees surrounding the retreat facilities, the Stations of the Cross, and Monestary [sic] Gardens with a breathtaking view of the San Gabriel Valley."[30]

While guest rooms are generally simply though comfortably furnished, most monasteries offer such distinctly unascetic conveniences as private baths, lounges and/or living rooms that range from cozy to elegant, libraries, snack areas, and groomed grounds with walking and bicycling paths. Additional amenities at various monasteries include an oak solarium with fireplace; a manmade lake towered over by an imposing statue of Saint Benedict; a state-of-the-art computerized library and music-listening room; an outdoor pool and tennis court; garden labyrinths; a bubbling fountain; a tea garden complete with Chinese pagoda; tables overlooking ocean dunes; a bonsai collection; or a private bathing dock. And there is no need to quash one's consumer impulses while on retreat: souvenirs, generally in the form of books and tapes, images of saints, crafts, and jams and jellies produced at the monastery, are available for purchase in the near-ubiquitous gift shops.

Tasty meals seem to be the rule in the modern monastery. One retreatant raves that at the Abbey of Our Lady of the Holy Spirit in Conyers, Georgia, the "food was basic (baked chicken, iceberg lettuce salad, rice, and lemonade) but absolutely delicious!"[31] According to the Web site of a retreat center belonging to the Episcopal Diocese of Virginia, "Home-style cooking in the Southern tradition, served in abundance, is a hallmark of Shrine Mont's gracious hospitality."[32] A visitor to the Loretto Christian Life Centre near Niagara Falls recounts that she "enjoyed exceptionally good meals."[33] And another praises her monastery guest house's "tasty vegetarian food and freshly baked bread."[34]

The schedule and activities of the average weekend retreat are likewise a far cry from the stereotypical image of monastic labor and routine—this in spite of the fact that *Cloister Walk*, the book generally credited with sparking the current craze for monastic retreat, locates the monastery's spiritual value specifically in its structured daily liturgy and shared domestic duties. With a very few exceptions, no work is required of guests. Participation in prayers is strictly optional, and rules are generally few or nonexistent. At the Holy Cross Monastery in West Park, NY, the only rule posted is observation of the "quiet time," from 9:00 PM to 7:00 AM.[35] Andrea Braslavsky writes that her retreat experience was characterized by "no schedules, no expectations," and notes that "in another Catholic retreat house, a notice on the door of each retreatant's bedroom lists guidelines for participating in the community's common prayer. The last 'guideline' was not to take the guidelines too seriously."[36]

Most retreatants, while often attending at least one prayer service, prefer to spend the bulk of their time in less structured ways. "The idea was to go, and be free to read, think and reflect on whatever we wished, in the company of the monks. . . . And, it turns out, that the monks require recreation of their order: they believe that a person who fills every free moment with work is hiding from something (and the Brothers work and pray hard). So we figured it would be fine to work a couple hours a day of snowshoeing into the schedule."[37] An academic writes of her week at a monastery: "I lie on a bench and watch a hawk circle over the meadow. I sit at the base of a redwood tree and watch a spider hard at work. My monastery is close to the coast, and I usually take one day and go early to the beach." Another guest goes to "write poetry and take long walks beside a meandering creek."[38] And a writer explains his reading of choice during his monastic retreat: "Then I choose to walk, read *Architectural Digest* (I'm getting into place, here), and meditate."[39] The fairly widespread availability of double rooms suggests that celibacy is not necessarily expected of guests, and certainly cannot be enforced (in any case, a weekend's withdrawal hardly seems the stuff of epic struggle). All in all, the vast majority of the retreat testimonies describe the religious retreat in terms reminiscent of a combined vacation and therapy session.

Of course, there is nothing "evil" about this form of paradise. Most retreatants (and probably their families too) may well be better off for taking a few days' quiet reflection. Many seem to gain peace and a sense of sanctity. And the guest house fees support the monasteries, which often run charitable operations. But it is worth noting that there is nothing very monastic about any of this: the most fundamental ideals of monastic life play no part in the contemporary monastic retreat. In the words of one Benedictine monk, "In America, everyone wants to take a retreat at a monastery, but almost no one wants to become a monk."[40]

Why then, *do* people go on monastic retreat, if not even briefly or vicariously to experience monasticism? It would be easy to be cynical about "monastery chic," to accuse retreatants of hypocrisy in seeking sanctification without effort, or perhaps just stinginess in scoring a luxury vacation at a bargain-basement price.[41] But a 2-million-plus-person phenomenon seems significant enough to merit more thoughtful consideration; rather than ask why these retreatants go— for surely they go for a wide range of reasons, from the utterly selfish to the deeply soulful—we should perhaps examine what their image of sanctuary tells us about the current moment.

As has often been noted by both critics and proponents, visions of utopia are inherently ideological.[42] Although they tend to be structured by antithesis (the peace and plenty ascribed to the imaginary medieval land of Cockaigne, for example, directly contrasted with the reality of medieval life, plagued by war and famine), they inevitably reflect the logic of contemporary society and help reinforce its essence.[43] The medieval monastery, though consciously designed to represent heaven on earth, was not a negation of the medieval world but a recognizable, if improved, version of it: a fortress with spiritual rather than physical warriors, a city of order rather than disorder, which enshrined the fundamental hierarchical and agonistic assumptions of medieval Christendom. For Thomas Carlyle, the medieval monastery provided not an escape from nineteenth-

century modernization but a model for Victorian social reform and worker community.[44] The current fad for monastic retreat likewise arises from, confirms, and
consecrates contemporary neoliberal logic, in the process exposing its totalizing
nature. ✗

For there is, in fact, one form of physical deprivation imposed in most monastic retreats: the prohibition of television, radio, and Internet use, and the institution
of compulsory "quiet times."[45] Indeed, given that poverty, stability, obedience,
and chastity play almost no part in the contemporary monastic retreat, the sole
element of traditional monasticism experienced by most retreatants is (at least
occasional) silence. But far from constituting a hardship, this absence of electronic noise is almost universally cited as the main attraction of the monastery.
"Jim Wharton" reports that he went on a weekend retreat to the Holy Cross
Monastery because he wanted to escape "the electronic invasion"—to "break
through the noise of kids, TV, iPod, cell phone, and talk radio in the car."[46] *Travel
Girl* magazine touts the monastic retreat as an opportunity to "Leave behind the
job, the stress of daily living, the cell phone, the regular phone, the computer, the
TV" and find a "space to unplug" and to "get away from the noise."[47] Similar
comments abound in retreat testimonies: "I particularly like the quiet"; "What
lured me to the monastery was the prospect of being in a quiet, peaceful and
beautiful place for three whole days with nothing on my agenda"; "The most important component of my monastery experience is the silence"; and "[the best
part was being] away from television and ringing telephones."[48]

Such comments inevitably inspire the question: why, if the "electronic noise"
is so intrusive, cannot the subject simply *turn it off*? Why must one travel hours in
the car and spend days away from home to escape gadgets that are entirely under
our own control? The answer, of course, is that they are not. Information technology is central to contemporary society; integral to the goal of providing the
"comfortable" and "safe" family life that is our society's primary social value.[49]
Without e-mail, Internet, and telephone, few of us could teach our classes, do our
homework, write our reports, plan our meetings, contact our customers, track
our assets, pay our bills, or, for that matter, reach our friends and family. We bring
the globalized world and its expanded work demands into our family homes well

beyond work hours so as to be able to pay for those homes and yet still be "with" those families. The price we pay for our affluence-through-unfettered-exchange is allowing the outside world unfettered access into our lives. And, in turn, televisions and ever more elaborate media centers that generate still more noise have become the primary means by which our hard-acquired wealth is displayed, and through which it is enjoyed.

No wonder there is these days such a compulsion not just to flee this noise, if only temporarily, but to see that flight as a spiritual quest. If "the world" is constituted of electronic noise and external demands, then noiselessness and insulation from others' demands must be "unworldly." The need so many people feel for monastic retreat highlights the failures of our own neoliberal society to bring the promised happiness—the historicism of monasticism counters the rootlessness and novelty of contemporary life; its silence is a protest against the hegemony of information technology; and its solitude is mute witness to the insufficiency of "family values" to fully satisfy the soul. But this reading is *not* tantamount to endorsing the "retreat as antimaterialistic world-rejection" interpretation of the phenomenon. If monastic retreat is a fundamental expression of a neoliberal spiritual logic, it also echoes the cardinal neoliberal values: freedom and deregulation, comfort and isolation, individualism and lack of community, short-term commitment.[50] By going on this kind of retreat, modern Americans don't negate our current way of life, they replicate it in a "spiritual" setting. Retreatants are *not* remaking themselves, as some analyses of American spirituality would have it, but rather are sanctifying their own preferences by enacting them in a monastic context. This is essentially an updated, Debordian version of the Weberian Protestant ethic: our virtue is demonstrated by our desire to demonstrate our virtue.[51] Indeed, the visit to the monastery almost takes the place of watching television: the retreatants are largely passive spectators, outsiders peeking in; their experience of the monastery is aesthetic rather than participatory (whether the spectacle is the monks, or themselves gazing at the monks).

And the monastic retreat ultimately functions to legitimize that same neoliberal logic. The most telling snippets of the testimonies are the metaphors used to describe the effects of retreat: Laura S. wrote that it helped her to "recharge her batteries," and "Jim Wharton" compared his monastic weekend to "a spiritual power nap."[52] The need to "power nap"—to sleep if only for fifteen minutes in the middle of the workday—is created by the impossible schedules many Americans are forced to follow because of globalization and the incompatibility of family and work demands. And just as the "power nap" doesn't change these schedules, but permits them, the monastic retreat doesn't break the Faustian bargain we have made with neoliberalism, but allows us to live with it. Once we've assured ourselves of our ability to do without electronic noise, we no longer have to . . . and it remains on.[53]

Each generation sees heaven in its own image. This generation's idea of heaven is an aesthetically pleasing, falsely historicizing, socially isolated, and ethically undemanding version of the suburban lifestyle, lacking only the price normally extracted for that lifestyle. A weekend in a monastery offers a sanitized simulacrum of the Age of Faith: monks within, no starving peasants without. And values that are pure twenty-first century: freedom of choice, virtue via display, spirituality without social justice. It is surely this ability of the monastery to embody neoliberal hopes and dreams, to sanctify rather than threaten contemporary American values and lifestyles, and not any religious resurgence along Catholic lines, that underlies the current explosion of monastery chic. ✕

Floating Utopias:
Freedom and Unfreedom of the Seas

China Miéville

Ayn Rand Ahoy

Freedom is late.

Since 2003, a colossal barge called the *Freedom Ship*, of debatable tax status, should have been chugging with majestic aimlessness from port to port, a leviathan flâneur with more than 100,000 wealthy full-time residents living, working, and playing on-deck. That was the aim eight years ago when the project first made headlines,[1] confidently claiming that construction would start in 2000.

A visit to the "news" section of freedomship.com reveals a more sluggish pace. The most recent messages are more than a year old, forlornly explaining how "scam investors" are slowing things down but that "[t]hings are happening, and they are moving fast." Meanwhile the ship is not yet finished. Indeed, it is not started. Not a rivet has been hit nor a screw tightened. Despite this, Freedom Ship International Inc. has been startlingly successful in raising publicity for this "floating city." Much credulous journalistic cooing over "the biggest vessel in history," with its "hospitals, banks, sports centers, parks, theaters, and nightclubs,"[2] not to mention its airport, has ignored the vessel's stubborn nonexistence.

Freedom Ship's Web site claims that the vessel has not been conceived as a locus for tax avoidance, pointing out that as it will sail under a flag of convenience, residents may still be liable for taxes in their home countries. Nonetheless, whatever the ultimate tax status of those whom we will charitably pretend might one day set sail, much of the interest in Freedom Ship has revolved precisely around its perceived status as a tax haven.[3]

And despite the apparent corrective on the Web site, the project's officials have not been shy in purveying that impression. They have pushed promotional literature that, in the words of one journalist, "paints the picture of a luxurious tax haven," and stressed that the ship will levy "[n]o income tax, no real-estate tax, no sales tax, no business duties, no import duties."[4] Of course, as no cruise ship could ever levy income tax, to trumpet that fact is preposterous, except as a propaganda strategy to accrete some nebulous Hayekian kudos.

Freedom Ship's directors are canny enough to recognize tax hatred as a defining characteristic of the tradition of fantasies in which it sits. It is only one of countless recent dreams of a tax-free life on the ocean wave: advocates of "seasteading" are disproportionately adherents of one or other flavor of "libertarianism," that peculiarly American philosophy of venal petite-bourgeois dissidence.

Libertarianism, of course, is by no means a unified movement. As many of its advocates proudly stress, it comprises a taxonomy of bickering branches—minarchists, objectivists, paleo- and neolibertarians, agorists, et various al.—just like a real social theory. Claiming a lineage with postenlightenment classical liberalism, as well as in some cases with the resoundingly portentous blatherings of Ayn Rand, all its variants are characterized, to differing degrees, by fervent, even cultish, faith in what is quaintly termed the "free" market, and extreme antipathy to that vaguely conceived bogeyman "the state," with its regulatory and fiscal powers.

Above all, they recast their most banal avarice—the disinclination to pay tax—as a principled blow for political freedom. Not content with existing offshore tax shelters, multimillionaires and property developers have aspired to build their own. For each such rare project that sees (usually brief) life, there are many unfettered by actual existence, such as Laissez-Faire City, a proposed offshore tax haven which, inspired by a particularly crass and gung-ho libertarianism, generated press interest in the mid-1990s only to collapse in infighting and bad blood; or New Utopia, an intended sea-based libertarian micronation in the Caribbean, which degenerated with breathtaking lack of surprisingness into nonexistence and scandal.[5]

However, one senses in even their supporters' literature a dissatisfaction with these attempts not reducible to the fact of their abject failures. It is also psycho-geographical: there is something about the atolls, mounts, reefs, and miniature islets on which these pioneers have attempted to perch that is *infra dig*. By con-trast, whatever their stated politics, if any, there is something psychically appeal-ing about the free-floating pelagic cities dreamed up for the Venus Project, or the computer-rendered contours of the oceantop Seascape.[6]

A parable from seasteading's past goes some way to explaining. In 1971, mil-lionaire property developer Michael Oliver's attempted to announce the Republic of Minerva on a small South Pacific sand atoll. It was soon offhandedly annexed by Tonga, and, in a traumatic actualized metaphor, allowed to dissolve back into the sea. To defeat the predatory outreach of nations and tides, it is clearly not enough to be offshore: true freedom floats.

The Degradation of Utopia

Of course, visions of floating state evasion are not always reducible to a psychi-cally mediated hankering for tax evasion. There have been other precursors. Ships have allowed various groups ranging from cheerfully illicit pirate radio stations to socially committed abortion providers, like Women On Waves, to avoid prob-lematic local laws.[7] Unsurprisingly, this use for ships has been enthusiastically picked up on by business, concerned to avoid pesky labor and environmental laws by locating software engineers three miles off the U.S. coast.[8]

It is the less instrumentalist iterations that inspire the imagination. Occasion-ally in what seems a spirit of can-do contrarianism, some offshore spit or rig has been designated an independent country, such as Sealand, a sea-tower-based na-tion of dubious legality and no permanent inhabitants on Britain's Suffolk coast.[9] So startling a notion as the coagulated ship-city has unsurprisingly featured in fic-tion, as in Lloyd Kropp's Sargasso-based *The Drift* and Neal Stephenson's heterotopic "The Raft," in *Snow Crash*. It is a measure of how disastrous a film *Water-world* was that its floating homesteads manage not to hold our attention; the cultural fascination, though, remains.

Many of the various projects currently under discussion cite ecological concerns as their rationale. However, the more ambitious these projects are, the more vague their details and mechanics (the unbearably new-age habitat of Celestopea is to be built of the wincingly punning and hypothetical enviro-friendly Seament),[10] and the clearer the asymptotic rationale of seasteading becomes: sheer utopian exuberance.

Floating cities are dreamed because *how cool is that?*—an entirely legitimate, even admirable, reason. What criticisms follow are not some left-moralist injunction to be "realistic": the archives of seasteading are irresistible reading, the best of the utopias awesome, floating-city imaginings in themselves a delightful mental game.[11] The problem, rather, is precisely the crippling of that tradition by stunted free-market vulgarians.

In these times, utopian imagination for its own sake has a bad rap, so some unconvincing instrumental rationale must be tacked on—yeah, save the planet, whatever. Among the rather cautious purposes architect Eugene Tsui lists for his proposed floating city of Nexus are, for example, the development of mariculture, clean energy, and "experimental education programs":[12] reading these bullet points, one might almost forget that Nexus is a five-mile-long self-propelling mountainous island shaped like a horseshoe crab. Its sheer beautiful preposterousness should neither be an embarrassment: it is the point of the dream, whatever the design specs say, and that is no criticism.

Utopianism has always had two, usually though not always contradictory, aesthetic and avant-gardist gravitational pulls: toward a hallucinatory baroque, or, alternately, toward a post-Corbusier functionalism. In seasteading, their haute iterations are represented by Tsui's *ongapatchke* organicism on the one hand, and Buckminster Fuller's extraordinary floating ziggurat-like Triton City on the other.[13]

The libertarian seasteaders are the inheritors of this visionary tradition, but they betray their class politics by degrading it. They almost make their radical critic nostalgic for more grandiose enemy dreams. The uncompromising monoliths of fascist and Stalinist architecture expressed their paymasters' monstrous, massive ambitions. The wildest of the libertarian seasteaders, New Utopia, cross-fertilizes its drab Miami-ism with just enough candyfloss Las Vegaries to keep a crippled baroque very distantly in sight, but *Freedom Ship* is a floating shopping mall, a block like a midrange Mediterranean hotel. This collapse of utopian imagination is nowhere clearer than in the designs for the floating city of the long defunct but still influential Atlantis Project.[14]

It is a libertarian dream. Hexagonal neighborhoods of square apartments bob sedately by tiny coiffed parks and tastefully featureless marinas, a suburban Florida of the soul. It is the ultimate gated community, designed not by the very rich and certainly not by the very powerful, but by the middlingly so. As a utopia, the Atlantis Project is pitiful. Beyond the single one-trick fact of its watery location, it is tragically unambitious, crippled with class anxiety, nostalgic not even for a mythic glorious past but for the anonymous sanctimony of an invented Fifties. This is no ruling-class vision: this is, rather, the plaintive daydream of a frightened petite bourgeoisie, whose sulky solution to their perceived social problems is to *run away*, set sail into a tax-free sunset.

None of this is surprising: some of its adherents may be among the superrich, but libertarianism is not a ruling-class theory. It is indulged, certainly, for the useful ideas it can throw up: its prophets have at times had a major influence on dominant ideologies—witness the cack-handed depradations of the "Chicago boys" in Chile after Allende's bloody overthrow. But untempered by the *realpolitik* of Reaganism and Thatcherism, the antistatism of "pure" libertarianism is worse than useless to the ruling class.

It will support tax-lowering measures, of course, but big capital does not need to piss and moan about taxes with the tedious relentlessness of the libertarian: big capital, with its ranks of accountant-Houdinis, just gets on with not paying it. And why hate a state that pays so well? Big capital is big, after all, not only because of the generous contracts its state obligingly hands it, but because of the gunships with which its state opens up markets for it.

Libertarianism, by contrast, is a theory of and for those who find it hard to avoid their taxes, who are too small, incompetent, or insufficiently connected to win the Iraq-reconstruction contracts, or otherwise chow at the state trough. In its maundering about a mythical ideal-type capitalism, libertarianism betrays its fear of actually existing capitalism, at which it cannot quite succeed. It is a philosophy of capitalist inadequacy.

The Freedom of the Seas?

The "capitalism" it worships is not the only ideal-type in the libertarian schema: its nemesis, "the state," is no less abstract. This is particularly true for libertarianism's seasteading wing, for whom the political entity "the state" is bizarrely geographically literalized. Their intent is to slip the surly bonds of earth not up but sideways, beyond littoral borders. It is a lunatic syllogism: "I dislike the state: the state is made of land: therefore I dislike the land." Water is a solvent, dissolving "political" (state) power, leaving only "economics" behind.

Such magical thinking is not new. In the foundational, though usually uncited, bible of the libertarian seasteader, *Mare liberum*, by that seminal giant of international law, Hugo Grotius, a key reason for the sea's stateless nature is that water resists occupation and thus ownership, as it "can neither easily be built upon, nor enclosed." Water is free because it wobbles. The absurdity of this reasoning was pointed out four hundred years ago by Grotius's great interlocutor John Selden in *Mare clausum*, and seems to have been tacitly admitted by Grotius himself (who substantially revised his position, accepting many of Selden's corrections, in later work): still, though, it evades many latter-day Grotians.[15]

This is not the only inadequacy of today's vulgar Grotianism to undermine the predicates of seasteading libertarianism. Grotius's founding paean to supposed maritime liberty was commissioned by the Dutch East India Company in support of its state-sanctioned piracy and monopoly status. The contingency of any putative "freedom of the seas" and the primacy of political exigency and the state was made vividly clear in 1613, only a few years after the publication of *Mare liberum*. As part of a Dutch mission to England, Grotius cheerfully argued for monopoly and closed ports against English pleas for free seas. One can only imagine the irritation with which the English fruitlessly quoted *Mare liberum*, verbatim, against its author.[16]

Seasteaders, knowingly or not, base their utopia on a model of free seas that has been consistently repudiated, including by its own author, since it appeared in 1608. The range of territorial waters—unfree seas—have continually been extended over the centuries. Since Selden's riposte to Grotius, it has been more or less accepted that control can be—and regularly is—exercised by states over "international" waters in various ways. "There are today," as one modern commentator breezily puts it, "no more doubts that the cherished Grotian concept of the freedom of the seas [though clearly not, we can add, cherished by Grotius] does not apply."[17] By an act of petulant will, however—a Nietzschean pout—the seasteaders hope, or think they hope, to make it so.

"The Captain's Word Will Be Final"

There are cases when small communities *have* taken to the seas to escape oppressive state apparatuses. The historic miseries of refugee "boat people"— Indonesians, Haitians, Vietnamese, Cambodians, and others—have been grotesquely real, but this has not given middlebrow utopians pause, any more than the real life of the French peasant made Marie Antoinette hesitate in her games. The libertarian seasteader is a pollyanna of exile.

As well as such desperate anticommunities, there are examples of genuine countercultural maritime polities, shipboard societies in opposition to the despotism and exploitation of state power, that might provide a genuine inspiration. Since the publication of *The Many-Headed Hydra*,[18] no discussion of liberté-sur mer should proceed without reference to the grassroots democratic "hydrarchies" of the pirates that Peter Linebaugh and Marcus Rediker rescue, less from the enormous condescension of history than from the booing of its pantomime audience.

But libertarians are political dissidents only in attenuated and narrowly selfish directions. As respectful of "order" as the most polite bourgeois, pirates are inconceivable to them as antecedents, and can only be threats (which they might indeed be, if there were any seasteads to be plundered). By vehemently distancing themselves from the outlaw but freedom-seeking hydrarchy of buccaneers, in a not-very-surprising irony, the libertarian seasteaders unwittingly identify with the other hydrarchy that Linebaugh and Rediker discuss: the maritime empire. Just like such a state, coercive political apparatuses, operating internally and externally, are implicit, sometimes explicit, to the libertarian seasteading project. Good Brechtians, we ask: Who is to maintain New Utopia, Laissez-Faire City, the Freedom Ship? Who will cook the feasts and clean the heads? So many reports. So many questions. The fantasists of libertarian seasteading are vague or silent about labor standards on-ship, indeed about labor at all, preferring not to wonder who will wash the decks on which the offshore traders, speculators, and Web entrepreneurs will promenade.

They cannot, however, entirely forget the necessity that other people—nonpassengers, unpeople—would be present. And an attenuated anxiety for the ensuing social and class conflicts registers in the libertarian mind as anxiety about *crime* (of course it is beyond absurd to trust in the moral or legal rectitude of the passenger-citizens, but fear of *their* transgressions does not drive libertarian concern). Crime, the shibboleth of the petite bourgeoisie, is impossible to banish from the mind.

With crime, moreover, comes the police. In the case of *Freedom Ship*, as well as a jail and a "squad of intelligence officers," "[t]he ship's private security force of 2,000, led by a former FBI agent, will have access to weapons, both to maintain order within the vessel and to resist external threats."[19] And while technically the law applied would be that of whichever state lends its flag, official spokespeople make no bones that "the captain's word will be final."[20]

This is the authoritarianism at libertarianism's core, the symbiosis between the "free market" and tyranny. Seasteading libertarians flee the oppression of bourgeois democracy for the freedom of dictatorship. The necessity of internal repression, then, is admitted. The external repression is even less hypothetical: it is already here.

Seasteading as Empire

Speculation about *internal* labor conditions on these polities is anathema, raising as it does all sorts of unpleasant issues of working-class organization on the wrong side of the gate. *Externally*, there are no such conceptual constraints. Far from remaining vague, the usual charge levelled at utopians, Freedom Ship's board's insistence on their "realism" has made them gung-ho and explicit in detailing methods of economic imperialism to which they aspire.

Freedom Ship Inc. has ostentatiously arranged with Honduran authorities to construct the vessel in the port of Trujillo, citing geographical advantages and cheap labor from the 10–20,000 imaginary workers they imagine exploiting. Locals are deeply, justifiably skeptical that anything will ever be built, but the project, despite being less "speculative" than utterly fanciful, has achieved a critical mass of absent presence sufficient to throw up real socioeconomic effects— attacks on labor, speculative bubbles, and so on.[21] In the words of the great activist science-fiction writer Lucius Shepard, who knows the region well:

> [T]he Freedom Ship is scheduled to begin construction any day now in Trujillo. . . . Many, including myself, feel it is a scam, but others are believers. Either way, it's going to bring a whole new cast of characters into the place, grifters and entrepreneurs and so forth; and it testifies to the fact that foreigners—mostly Americans— believe they can come to Honduras and achieve wealth and power there, that they can work their hustles with impunity.[22]

Already, struggles against the *Freedom Ship* have begun. In April 2003, a protest march in Trujillo included farmers "protesting against the National Port Authority attempting to usurp their lands (for local elites, multinational tourism projects, and the huge American venture 'Freedom Ship')."[23] The protest was organized by the Comité de Emergencia Garifuna de Honduras, a grassroots organization to represent the country's Garifuna minority, descendents of African slaves and indigenous Caribs and Arawaks. The ship is a stated reason for one of the many landgrabs from the Garifuna, in an expropriatory project so unsubtly iniquitous as to be almost camp, as if *Freedom Ship*'s partisans are so keen to prove their "realism" that only an ostentatious performance of imperialist theft will do. Garifuna land is being jealously eyed with the government's active and official participation.

The most recent threat to Garifuna land rights emerged in September of 2002, in the protected reserve between the Caribbean Sea and the Guaymoreto Lagoon called Barranco Blanco. The National Port Company (ENP), a government body, began to conduct a topographical survey of Garifuna land, with the intention of renting out lands for the construction of "Freedom Ship.". . . The local Garifuna community has legal title to this land, but when they asserted their ownership in meetings with the National Port Company, the Port Company went so far as to cite the "international war on terror" at the meeting as a reason for their usurpation of lands, claiming they needed the land to protect the banana boats of Dole Fruit Company which dock at nearby Puerto Castilla.[24]

In one area at least, then, *Freedom Ship* has been admirably efficient and ahead of schedule. Its continuing nonexistence is no bar to it casting an imperial shadow. *Freedom Ship* is and will remain a castle in the air—or sea—but it has already laid foundations, on someone else's land.

Class Warfare as Bad Comedy

The era of the crassest globaldegook is over—the supposed imminent demise of the state, the perforation, dissolution, and evaporation of its sovereignty and borders under the onslaught of commerce and capital are asserted with considerably less vigor than during the boosterish early 1990s. The internationalization of capital was and remains real, however, and with such circuits, inevitably, comes the migration of labor.

One would think that an avowedly antistatist laissez-faire movement would support a free market in the particular commodity of labor power, and thus the free movement of labor, as well as capital. To its credit, the Libertarian Party of the United States has enough rigor to maintain the open-borders position its predicates demand. But as the ferocious debate on its Web site attests, alongside symposia in such journals as the *Journal of Libertarian Studies*, the question is hugely controversial even among the faithful.[25]

Much libertarianism has a love-hate relationship with borders. Despite the timidity of some unions on the issue, true freedom of labor would strengthen the working class, an unacceptable outcome to the right wing, and the cause of some intellectual gymnastics on the part of libertarian ideologues eager to justify the exclusion of foreign workers.

Usually this involves conceptualizing the state as the "private property" of its legal inhabitants. When, however, we read in the house journal of libertarianism that in a "natural order," due to the fact that "likes associate with other likes and live spatially separated from unlikes, . . . Whites live among Whites and separate from Asians and Blacks";[26] or see marshaled against an open-borders argument the question "Should we really be willing to see waves of diseased immigrants come in?";[27] or read the warnings of "illegals crossing the Tijuana border," and the lament for a Los Angeles with "crowds of immigrants, most of them probably illegal, roaming the streets in search of one knows not what,"[28] the despicable racial anxieties are blatant. For some libertarians, "liberty" is more negotiable than "Aryan."

Of course, big capital gains from borders less from the fact that they keep workers out than the manner in which they allow workers in: the economic benefits of "illegals" are enormous, both directly and as a wedge, because of their extreme vulnerability and availability for hyperexploitation. Realpolitikal big capital, then, and the hysterical wing of libertarianism unite in their predilection for borders, though for different reasons.

In the libertarian seastead, citizenship really *is* a ticket that must be purchased— not a right nor a privilege but a commodity. The claim that the state is private property is more believable in such a pretend place than in the real world, where citizenship is not reserved for paying passengers. Of course the political problem would be almost irrelevant in any case. Illegal immigration onto a floating city would be an impressive feat: another of the idea's charms. The dream is not of open borders but mobile ones, as ferociously exclusive as those of any other state, and more than most.

It is a small schadenfreude to know these dreams will never come true. There are dangerous enemies, and there are jokes thrown up by history. The libertarian seasteaders are a joke. The pitiful, incoherent, and cowardly utopia they pine for is a spoilt child's autarky, an imperialism of outsourcing, a very petty fascism played as maritime farce—Pinochet of Penzance.

Hives and Swarms:
On the "Nature" of Neoliberalism and the
Rise of the Ecological Insurgent

Daniel Bertrand Monk

If you're after getting the honey — hey
Then you don't go killing all the bees.
　　—Joe Strummer[1]

Vosotras, las familiares,
inevitables golosas,
vosotras, moscas vulgares,
me evocáis todas las cosas.

[You, the familiar.
Inevitable gluttons.
You, ordinary flies.
Remind me of all things.]
　　—Antonio Machado[2]

Life and Death

The most ambitious project of the neoliberal present is not to be found in the artificial archipelagoes and indoor ski slopes of Dubai. However ghastly, these ef-

forts to transform the shores of the Persian Gulf into an "evil paradise" pale in comparison with the changes taking place on the banks of the river Styx. Death, the last refuge from a world whose purpose is the creation of purposeless worlds, is itself now in danger of extinction. Not because we're becoming immortal, but because there is good reason to doubt whether we continue to live at all, in the sense of possessing an organic existence that is distinct from the abstract nature we ourselves make. In a historical moment when the difference between obsolescence and the end of life is becoming indistinguishable, death itself withers away.

First, because it loses its logical and ethical claims upon our actions as the contrary of an order that would make such things happen. (This is what Theodor Adorno meant when he suggested that after Auschwitz, and in the wake of the administered murder of millions, a "wrong life could not be lived rightly.")[3] Second, and no less important, death atrophies because when what is no longer useful is conceived in light of what is dead and what is dead is understood in terms of an expired utility (shelf life, for example), all of what has been permanently snuffed out from a world dominated by a principle of utility can then also be impressed into service. Then, senseless exterminations begin to make lots of sense, and purposeless slaughter becomes purposive—i.e., part of the natural order of things. To the degree that we "owe our life to the difference between the economic framework of capitalism, and its political facade," and to the extent that this slim difference is the basis for the "entire existence of countless multitudes" the maintenance of a distinction between life and death has now become a matter of life and death.[4]

None of this is pie in the sky. From the standpoint of death, the abstract character of contemporary existence is not only objective, but also self-evident. It pervades the way in which, under neoliberalism, we advance certain paradigms of killing as if they already confirmed a natural history of living. Most notably, today soldiers find it impossible to talk about the best ways to congregate for the purpose of killing without forming themselves into what Siegfried Kracauer once referred to as a "mass ornament," a term he relied on to describe the formation of masses into composite figures "whose closure is brought about by emptying all the substantial constructs of their contents."[5] (In things like the stadium patterns formed by thousands of people, Kracauer suggested, it was possible to divine the vain efforts of human beings to create a higher order of collective existence out of the same logic that robbed them of organic association to begin with.) Similarly, the forward-thinking soldiers of our own present no longer speak of battalions or divisions when contemplating the "nature" of their own society. Instead, they prefer to talk about *swarms* . . .

To the soldiers, this reversion to the mass ornament—that is, to second nature in the form of swarm talk—signals radical progress. This paradox—and its normalization—possesses their own history. Ever since the twilight of the Cold War, defense intellectuals and students of politics have been attempting to come to terms with what they describe as "the revolution in military affairs [RMA]." In the most general terms, the RMA refers to the anticipated transformation of combat demanded by the invention of increasingly complex and nearly cybernetic battle systems. The defense establishment's discussions concerning the RMA have persistently focused on the gap between its own grasp over actual or imminent technical capacities on one hand, and the effects those same capacities will have on strategy and tactics on the other. Because of this, the decade-long debate concerning the exact nature of the revolution in military affairs also marks the limits of reflexive insight into the historical status of the types of warfare we are actually advancing. Oddly enough, at those limits one often discovers an unreflexively materialist turn, as the futurologists of battle have attempted to explain the gap between the new means and their ends in terms of a time lag between consciousness and productive capacities.[6] Thus, for example, in an assessment of contemporary assessments of the RMA published in *Foreign Affairs* in 1996, Eliot Cohen suggested that the revolution in military affairs needed to be understood as the as-yet-unassimilated effects on warfare posed by two related historical transformations in the "civilian" sphere: the universalization of information technology on one hand, and what Cohen called "the efflorescence of capitalism"—i.e., the neoliberal economic order—on the other.[7] Construed in this fashion as the mode of fighting consonant with the information economy of postindustrial capitalism, normative accounts of the RMA regularly described it as the coming age of speedy, flexible, and smart deployment of "just-in-time" inventories of force . . . along with the forms of management necessary to make all of that happen. (In other words, what corporations like Wal-Mart could already do by Y2K with consumer goods, armies would have to do with strike capacity in the new millennium.)

The U.S. military's initial responses to the RMA privileged "standoff power," that is, it bargained on the belief that many military objectives could be achieved remotely with smart weaponry.[8] By giving priority to new platforms like cruise missiles, stealth technology, and smart munitions, the divisional force structures created to fight the Soviet Union could remain more or less in place after that particular enemy expired. (In this sense, all the talk about "smart" weapons during and after the first U.S. invasion of Iraq could actually be understood as an attempt to put the brakes on the RMA.) But as scholars like Eliot Cohen, among others, already understood, in the new world order of war it might be perfectly possible to attain operational success with inferior platforms if one's fighters have access to superior information.[9] (What good, for example, are complex satellites when— just like Hezbollah's field commanders in Lebanon—one's opponent can adjust the aim of crude "point 'n' shoot" Katyusha rockets by watching cable TV reports describing previous impacts?) By extension, when information in itself becomes "gear" as basic as an M-16 rifle, the RMA raises questions more proper to the concerns of labor history than tactics.

Indeed, now that jarheads in Falluja and generals in Florida can—and often do—view exactly the same information on exactly the same screen, students of war have begun to question the efficacy of traditional command structures.[10] In other words, as tactical and strategic orders of knowledge converge, those who observe this meeting of proximate and remote killing ask themselves how useful it is to maintain the rigidly hierarchical division of military labor that has been in place more or less since Frederick the Great. "Not very," is the response of a series of "complex systems" theorists, who suggest that the so-called smart battlefield presupposes a very different bureaucracy of carnage than the one now in place. Turning to logics of "flocking" and "swarming" to describe an alternative operational theory, a number of war intellectuals envision a kind of smart anarchy in the nearly present future battlefield. Here, the "self-organizing" and "adaptive" systems of movement characteristic of the birds and the bees are embraced by proponents of a new organicism in battle as the very archetype of nonlinear complex systems capable of existing "at the edge of chaos."[11]

Some soldiers have even added a philosophical dimension to the hi-tech organicism envisioned by the systems theorists. Most notably, in a series of interviews with architect Eyal Weizman, Brigadier Shimon Naveh of the Israeli Defense Forces [IDF] has given the new "swarm talk" a Deleuzian pedigree.[12] A member of the operational theory research group of the IDF's National Defense College, Naveh advances the view that in their various "Walking Through Walls" operations, the IDF's paratroopers have abandoned established conventions in favor of "nomadological" approaches to military operations in urban terrain [MOUT]. (In these assaults, troops eschew traditional lines of advance—the alleys and streets of refugee camps—and burrow through buildings instead. The most famous of these operations took place in April 2002, when the IDF invaded the Balata refugee camp and the Kasbah of Nablus.) Confusing the inversion of figure-ground relations in architecture for the attainment of the radical epistemological perspective characteristic of what Deleuze called the "War Machine," Naveh appears to find formal confirmation in reversed city plans—where voids are treated as solids and solids as voids—of his own enthrallment with the idea of a nonlinear sublime.[13] In consequence, he thinks it possible for the IDF to arrive at a radical operational theory capable of subverting the logic of Palestinian insurgency by negating the IDF's own normative tactical assumptions. ✗

Primal Swarming

Despite Naveh's philosophical ambitions, or perhaps because of them, it is difficult to escape the impression that the new Israeli swarm doctrines actually represent the latest chapter in the intellectual history of imperial war, which has always looked with real longing to the tactics of the insurgents against which it has directed its own slave hunts and hypostatized that longing into a theoretical principle. (In other words, there is a well-established tradition of venerating things like swarming, and of raising that veneration to the status of philosophy.) In this sense, Naveh's thought owes less to Deleuze or the poststructuralist cri-

tique of the Enlightenment than to an idealist tradition in modern military theory. To be sure, swarming first emerges as something approaching a regulative
ideal in the writings of T.E. Lawrence, who saw in the *faza'* (or pulsing) techniques of Arabian Bedouin irregulars during World War I, a tactic of abstraction
capable of defeating both the Turks and the norms of established trench warfare.[14] In an oft-cited passage, Lawrence described the implications of the desert
tactics of the Arabian campaign in the following way:

> suppose we were (as we might be) an influence, an idea, a thing intangible, invul-
> nerable, without front or back, drifting about like a gas? Armies were like plants,
> immobile, firm-rooted, nourished through long stems to the head. We might be a
> vapour, blowing where we listed. Our kingdoms lay in each man's mind; and as we
> wanted nothing material to live on, so we might offer nothing material to the kill-
> ing. It seemed a regular soldier might be helpless without a target, owning only
> what he sat on, and subjugating only what, by order, he could poke his rifle at.[15]

B.H. Liddell Hart adopted this assessment of maneuver combat, but suggested that Lawrence's musings about the desert campaigns of World War I actually confirmed an even broader principle, that he and other apostles of mobility
would eventually call "the strategy of the indirect approach."[16] In broad strokes,
this vision of strategy attempted to address the fundamental paradox of combat
in an age of total war: on one hand, since Clausewitz military thought had identified the aim of battle as the "overthrow of the enemy's means of resistance" by
destroying their armed forces; on the other hand, like J.F.C. Fuller before him,
Liddell Hart concluded that in an age of total or modern war, *that* same objective
was irrational.[17] Since the enemy's means of resistance, and one's own, were no
longer armies but the productive civilian populations that supply them, it became
imperative to avoid rather than reduce the enemy, if one aspired to achieve one's
strategic own aims. (As Fuller once noted: "to destroy a nation is to destroy the
very objective of peace.")[18] Avoidance, here, does not mean evasion, but something approaching a principle of *strategic* swarming that makes fighting an inferior choice to a kind of positional "checkmate" in which the enemy is left with no
military alternative:

the concentration of strength against weakness depends on the dispersion of your opponent's strength, which in turn is produced by a distribution of your own that gives the appearance, or the partial effect of dispersion. . . . True concentration is the fruit of calculated dispersion.[19]

In contemporary killing practices, the popularity of this positional ideal is attested to anecdotally by the fact that the latest U.S. Army operation in Samara, Iraq, was called "Operation Swarmer," and that the U.S. military is now the largest single consumer of the networked warfare systems that would help an army advance what Sean J.A. Edwards refers to as NLDOs, or "non-linear dispersed operations."[20] More importantly, however, in the U.S military swarm *talk* is more than anecdotal. Even if all of the top brass does not embrace swarming in fact, the concept nevertheless serves as the accepted shorthand for the problematic of the nation's strategic posture in the aftermath of a bipolar geopolitical order.[21]

And yet, contemporary visions of swarming differ substantially from the idealizations of organic dispersion and concentration presented by Lawrence and Liddell Hart, each of whom actually witnessed popular mobilizations to violence in colonial contexts.[22] (Liddell Hart was particularly interested in the Zionist followers of Orde Wingate in Palestine.) Today, theories of swarming presuppose a fearful asymmetry; they assume the warfare of established armies against irregulars that Mary Caldor calls "new wars" to be a given—that is, they believe asymmetry to characterize conflict per se, rather than viewing that lopsidedness as the historical consequence of a century of horrors during which civilian populations have progressively become the principal targets of the big guns looking for the *schwerpunkt*, or decisive lever, to victory. In a historical moment when the civilian-to-military casualty ratio is roughly 8:1 (an inversion of norms prior to WWI), theories of swarming may need to be understood not only as logical responses to new strategic threats, but also as the spasmodic conceptual reflex to a prevailing strategic-historical order that associates civilians with danger, and views anyone but soldiers as the principal threats to peace. It is almost as if the liberal internationalist concept of the "democratic peace" is now guaranteed solely to armies, which maintain their entente cordiale at the expense of anyone who is not in uniform.[23] Welcome to *their* evil paradise.

The Ecological Insurgent

Curiously, swarm talk participates in this vicious reorientation of the friend/enemy distinction by advancing in new and unexpected forms the image-ideal of an ecological insurgent, or archetypal swarmer. It's not just that that the current adepts of swarming continue a long-standing infatuation/fear with the image of a self-organized horde that is believed to be capable of winning wars in spontaneous coordinations attained by something resembling osmosis: but that in so doing, swarming's disciples conjure up forms of existence that history has, for all intents and purposes, already extinguished . . . if they ever existed at all. This is the conservative kernel at the heart of swarm theories: in them, the *demand* for an ecological insurgent who might serve as a tacit model and first cause for new military organizations serves, at the same time, as an unconscious call for an end to the logic that extinguishes the forms of collective political existence swarm talk presents as its own model. Little else can account, for example, for the priority given to the Mongol armies and the "Asiatic style of war" in Sean Edwards's *Swarming and the Future of Battle*, one of the most detailed of the recent studies on nonlinear tactics.[24] There, Edwards establishes a direct connection between nomadic pastoralism—an organic existence—and the origins of swarming. Following John Keegan's own observations concerning the "parallels between flock management skills and military tactics," Edwards suggests that "Mongol men essentially applied the same techniques they learned for survival, hunting, and herding to warfare."[25] In this fashion, Edwards explains, Mongol tactics conformed to what Keegan described as a style of "Oriental war making marked principally by traits of evasion, delay, indirectness."[26] Understood as the theoretical impulse of the prevailing conflictual order, swarming ratifies the realm of the merely existent as if it were already nature.

But this is a *nature morte*: swarming can only invoke natural history in the shape of extinction. This point is not as abstract as one might imagine. The philosopher Theodor Adorno once noted that in zoos humankind pays tribute to itself in the form of animals. Here, in other words, society redeems nature as something already societal—i.e., a *designated* contrary—according to much the same logic as Edwards redeems Mongol tactics as something already organic. But as a subsequent step in the natural history of "natural" fighting, Edwards's vision of swarming more closely resembles *a taxidermist's paradise* than the zoos and *volkenschauen* of the German Hagenbeck, whose faux naturalism betrayed "the ark by simulating the rescue that only Ararat can promise."[27] By giving privilege to what has already been wiped off the face of the earth, swarm theory recapitulates the need for "organic" exterminations to begin with.

Just as the concept of the ecological insurgent resurrects a familiar and perverse demand for a Nature that is already socially performed, the same ecological insurgent also speaks for the priority of a denatured Nature that is so completely identified with death that it becomes indistinguishable from history. By recalling the extinct species of its own imagination (the Arab nomads and Mongol hordes of the tacticians' imagination) as archetypes of swarming, natural histories of the natural warrior reveal how, in extinction itself, "the things that history has condemned are dragged along dead, neutralized and impotent as ignominious ballast."[28] Here, history exhumes death for its own purposes in much the same way as Edwards's Mongols sport with the carcasses of their charges in games of Buzkashi. In both instances, what is given up for dead actually possesses an afterlife: denied any status as an absolute, death is impressed into service as an eccentric "function of its own uniqueness."[29]

If the ecological insurgent presents a nature that is already historical, it also reveals the exact *nature* of the history regularly advanced in contemporary swarm theory. This is a definition of history that only appears obliquely in discussions concerning the properties of battle swarms across time and space. Something of this curious natural history suggests itself in John Arquilla and David Ronfeldt's *Swarming and the Future of Conflict*, where the ecological insurgent finds its place in a continuum between zoological genera and world history. Arguing that the study of swarming "derives insights from examples in nature and in history," the authors observe that "[b]oth areas are replete with instances of omnidirectional yet well-timed assaults. From ants and bees and wolf packs, to ancient Parthians and medieval Mongols, swarming in force or of fire, has often proven a very effective way of fighting."[30] Viewed as *genera*, the Parthian and Mongol swarms share with other species "network forms" of organization that are at once "seemingly amorphous" and "deliberately structured."[31] As civilizations, the Parthians and Mongols suggest a historical progression of swarming practice toward greater self-consciousness: in losing the unreflexive instincts that coordinated prior and more primitive battle swarms, the higher ones become aware of the need for swarming itself. Assessing the pulse tactics of contemporary Zapatistas, ICBL campaigners, activist hackers, and Chechen guerrillas—all of whom substitute the lost instincts with sophisticated communications networks—Arquilla and Ronfeldt imply that swarming's immanent progression ultimately necessitates the emergence of "swarm doctrine" itself. In other words, by reviewing the applied logic of "social netwar" and the other "people power" strategies in light of the swarming's historical and biological continuum, military thought becomes inductive, a doctrine to be applied rather than discovered. Swarming becomes swarm theory.

At that moment, swarming becomes something more than purely historical, presenting/insinuating itself as a mythic constant that more closely resembles the Nature swarm talk betrays in favor of society's own image than much else. In swarm theory, the ecological insurgent of the strategists' and generals' imagination appears solely as a *category* of thought/action, which they now believe themselves capable of apprehending independently of the *concrete* existence of the Zapatistas, Chechens, or any of the peoples whose political struggles take a backseat to what can be said about them in light of swarming to begin with. In this fashion, swarm doctrine exterminates the swarms it has kept around/alive only as an afterthought of other, forgotten, exterminations.

Having cheated death of its status as a logical absolute by rendering it usefully natural and historical at once, swarm theory asserts itself as a kind of necrophilia. And its invention, the ecological insurgent, reveals itself to be a kind of zombie, a creature that is animated on a tactical level but without *authentic* political volition. After all, what could the sophisticated politics of the Zapatistas have in com-

mon with Parthians to begin with, except, perhaps, for the fact that swarm studies have simultaneously acknowledged and dismissed them into oblivion as repositories of a certain logic, along with Mongols and wolves? To associate Attila the
Hun with the anti-landmine campaigner and Nobel peace laureate Jody Williams
is, effectively, to reduce contemporary social projects to their tactics/methods or
means, in the process resolving their political ends (such as a society's efforts to
curb its own repertoire of violence) into nothing more than the latest link in an
infinitely long chain of autonomous swarming—i.e., a series of instances in
which swarming engages with politics for the sake of more swarming, much like
Jerry Seinfeld's dentist converted to the Hebrew faith so he could continue to tell
Jewish jokes with impunity.

So total is this reduction of social movements to their tactics that even those
put on the wrong end of this equation/deal increasingly tend identify their own
aims—or more properly, identify themselves—in terms/light of their methods.
An instructive case in point is the International Center on Nonviolent Conflict,
which has concluded that the principal factor affecting the outcome of nonviolent direct action politics, or so-called people-power campaigns, is their members'
"strategic competence."[32] The ICNC has consequently created a PC-based strategy game called A Force More Powerful (AFMP), which introduces players to
techniques of strategic nonviolent conflict and brings these to bear on an array of
political scenarios abstracted from contemporary history. Assuming the role of
coordinator/strategist of a social justice campaign, the player organizes the actions of a series of avatars who are attempting to wrest concessions from a series
of Pierogi republics and theocratic absurdistans. What's at issue, in this instance,
is not the heuristic value of the initiative—which is as at least as considerable as
that of the shoot 'em up games with which the U.S. Army trains what it calls "digital natives" through its DARWARS program—but that (for all concerned) here,
ends are treated as first causes for the perpetuation of means.[33]

Nothing is more revealing about the actual historical status of swarming than
its own reflexive turn, which is, finally, an expression of its affirmative character.
However radical it might appear at the tactical level, swarm theory presupposes a
regressive mass psychology/politics. As opposed to T.E. Lawrence, who premised

much of his vision of guerrilla war on what he termed the "diathetics," or legitimate motivation of the mass, contemporary swarm theory betrays an underlying contempt for the ecological insurgent of its own manufacture. Contempt, not just in the sense that it refuses the ecological insurgent a political will by subordinating its imperatives to its tactics, but more importantly, in that what swarming gives with one hand, it takes away with the other: as it extols the dexterity of the ecological insurgent, swarm theory assumes swarming's end to be the demoralization of mindless hordes. What swarm theorists, like Arquilla and Ronfeldt, draw from the writings of Bakunin and Chairman Mao is chiefly a vision of victory premised on the moral deflation of the opponent. This is an understanding of morale war, according to which the effect that marauders may have on standing armies, as in Vietnam or Falluja, can, in turn be triggered in the behavior of ecological insurgents through the adoption of counter-swarming techniques. However, in a present that is for many people already uninhabitable to begin with, this reciprocity does not reflect the authentic state of affairs. For them, the macabre specter of the car bomber is less like a zombie than an angel—a plenipotentiary, in the form of death, of an authentic life that is nowhere on offer. Secure in the knowledge that there are things worse than death, they fight for the afterlife. And, in doing so, they confirm the worst suspicions raised by the popularity of swarming to begin with: that "only a humanity to whom death has become as indifferent as its members, that has itself died, can inflict it administratively on innumerable people."[34]

Notes

Introduction

1. "Diary Entries, 1938" (August 25), in Walter Benjamin, *Selected Writings: Volume 3 (1935–1938)* (Cambridge, MA: The Belknap Press/Harvard University Press, 2002), 340.

2. Arjay Kapur, Niall Macleod, and Narendra Singh, "Plutonomy: Buying Luxury, Explaining Global Imbalances," Citigroup Research, 16 October 2005, 2; Robert Reich, "The New Rich-Rich Gap," CommonDreams.org, 12 December 2005 (factory jobs); and Nick Mathiason, "Super-rich Hide Trillions Offshore," *The Observer*, 27 March 2005.

3. Pierre Bourdieu, "The Essence of Neoliberalism," *Le Monde Diplomatique*, December 1998.

4. Mike Davis, "The Political Economy of Late-Imperial America," *New Left Review* I, no. 143 (January–February 1984).

5. David Harvey, "Neo-liberalism and the Restoration of Class Power," in his *Spaces of Global Capitalism* (London: Verso, 2006), 43.

6. Kapur, Macleod, and Singh, "Plutonomy," 3, 6, 13.

7. Ibid. 13, 21; and "Revisiting Plutonomy: The Rich Getting Richer," Citigroup Research, 5 March 2006, 3.

8. "Revisiting Plutonomy," 3.

9. "Luxury," Special Christmas Report, *The Economist*, 34 December 2005, 67.

10. "Exchange with Theodore W. Adorno" in Benjamin, *Selected Writings: Volume 3*, 54–55.

Chapter 1: Dreamland

1. "State socialism" is an inadequate term for describing the multiple logics of the Soviet system, just as capitalism is for other systems. See the discussions in *What about the Workers? Workers and the Transition to Capitalism in Russia,* ed. Simon Clarke (London and New York: Verso, 1993), and David Stark, "Recombinant Property in East European Capitalism," in *The Laws of the Markets,* ed. Michel Callon, the *Sociological Review* monograph series (Oxford: Blackwell, 1998), 116–46.

2. International Monetary Fund (IMF), Middle Eastern Department, "The Egyptian Stabilization Experience: An Analytical Retrospective," prepared by Arvind Subramanian, *Working Papers of the International Monetary Fund,* WP/97/105, September 1997.

3. *Al-Ahram,* January 1, 1999, 40.

4. *Al-Wafd,* January 12, 1999, 1, 3.

5. The Toshka scheme, named after the depression 50 kilometers north of Abu Simbel through which the Nile waters were to be pumped, was budgeted to cost $86.5 billion over twenty years (1997–2017). United States, Department of State, *FY 2001 Country Commercial Guide: Egypt,* July 2000, available at http://www.state.gov/www/about_state/business/com_guides/2001.

6. Economist Intelligence Unit (EIU), *Country Report: Egypt,* 3rd quarter 1999, 25. Prince al-Walid bin Talal bin `Abd al-`Aziz Al Sa`ud's assets included ownership of 5 percent or more of Citigroup, Saks Fifth Avenue, TWA, Apple Computer, News Corporation, Disneyland, and Daewoo. He was also the principal investor in "New Cairo," in partnership with the Tal`at Mustafa Group. See *Middle East Times,* Egypt edition, January 19, 2001, available at http://www.metimes.com, and http://www.medea.be/en/index327.htm.

7. See the Cadiz Inc. quarterly report to the U.S. Securities and Exchange Commission at http://www.sec.gov/Archives/edgar/data/727273/0000727273-99-000018.txt, and http://www.sun-world.com. The parent company, Cadiz, was reorganizing itself along similar lines, moving away from agribusiness to earn rents from the groundwater storage basins beneath its agricultural properties in California. In Egypt, Cadiz agreed to a separate joint venture with Prince al-Walid to pursue a groundwater project in Sharq al-`Uwainat (East Oweinat), to the west of Toshka, where the government planned to irrigate 200,000 acres from deep wells. A third "Pharaonic" development project, involving extensive land reclamation in northern Sinai, was also under siege for the serious damage it threatened to the ecology of Sinai and the northern Nile Delta. See http://www.nile-river.org.

8. Beverly Hills was a 10.4 million-square-meter luxury housing development managed by a U.S.-Swiss joint venture, Turner-Steiner International S.A., and owned by Sixth of October Development and Investment Company, a venture formed by a group of Egypt's largest entrepreneurs. *Business Monthly,* December 1998, available at http://www.amcham.org.eg/HTML/news.publication/BusinessMonthly. On Media Production City see www.touregypt.net/mpc.htm.

9. Toshka was to divert 10 percent of Egypt's share of the Nile River into the desert. This was likely to have a serious impact on the ecology of the existing river valley, which already suffers from soil salinity, coastal erosion, and declining water quality. See http://www .nile-river.org.

10. Economist Intelligence Unit (EIU), *Country Report: Egypt*, 3rd quarter 1998, 10.

11. IMF, "Egyptian Stabilization," 59.

12. EIU, *Country Profile: Egypt, 1998–99*, table 28, 54.

13. Peter R. Odell, "Oil Price Fears Have No Strong Base," *Financial Times*, September 9, 1999, 12. The success was so great that less than a year later the United States was back negotiating oil price reductions with OPEC member governments again. Judith Miller, "Kuwait Is Said to Be Opposed to U.S. Effort to Cut Oil Prices," *New York Times*, February 24, 2000, C4.

14. The import restrictions included much tighter limits on credit, abolishing duty-free imports, and introducing new and onerous customs inspections requirements. Economist Intelligence Unit (EIU), *Country Report: Egypt*, 1st quarter 1999, 33; *Middle East Times*, August 27, 1999.

15. IMF, "Egyptian Stabilization," 5.

16. Ibid., 4.

17. For details of this illegal diversion of funds see chapter seven of my book, *Rule of Experts: Egypt, Techno-Politics, Modernity* (Berkeley: University of California Press, 2002).

18. Iraq was the major destination for Egyptian arms exports, which were valued at $1 billion in 1982 and $500 million in 1983/84. Library of Congress, Federal Research Division, *Egypt: A Country Study* (Washington, DC: Library of Congress, 1991), 408.

19. IMF, "Egyptian Stabilization," 47.

20. Howard Handy and Staff Team, *Egypt: Beyond Stabilization, Towards a Dynamic Market Economy*, IMF Occasional Paper, no. 163 (Washington, DC: IMF, 1998), table 21, 50. £ is the symbol for the Egyptian pound. For this chapter, the number of Egyptian pounds to the U.S. dollar is calculated at the average rate of 2.74 for 1989/90, 3.34 for 1991/92–93/94, and 3.39 for 1994/95–1997/98 (based on Handy et al., *Egypt: Beyond Stabilization*, table 1, 2). It is not clear whether the figures on the profitability of state-owned enterprises take full account of the cost of state subsidies and protections (just as they do not take account of the social benefit of the employment they provided). Clearly what triggered the crisis, however, was not the long-term problems of management and reinvestment in state enterprise, but the impending collapse of the banking sector.

21. Mahmoud Mohieldin, "Causes, Measures, and Impact of State Intervention in the Financial Sector: The Egyptian Example," *Working Papers of the Economic Research Forum for the Arab Countries, Iran and Turkey*, no. 9507 (Cairo, 1995), 20.

22. Robert Springborg, *Mubarak's Egypt: Fragmentation of the Political Order* (Boulder, CO: Westview, 1989).

23. Mohieldin, "State Intervention," 20–21.

24. Ibid., 17. On BCCI and the CIA, see United States Congress, Senate Committee on Foreign Relations, *The BCCI Affair: A Report to the Committee on Foreign Relations, United*

States Senate, by Senator John Kerry and Senator Hank Brown (Washington, DC: U. S. Government Printing Office, 1992).

25. On similar problems faced by the Indian state in the same period, and the importance of discipline, see Prabhat Patnaik and C.P. Chandrasekhar, "India: *Dirigisme*, Structural Adjustment, and the Radical Alternative," in *Globalization and Progressive Economic Policy*, ed. Dean Baker, Gerald Epstein, and Robert Pollin (Cambridge, UK: Cambridge University Press, 1998), 67–91.

26. The term "crony capitalism" came into vogue with the IMF during the global financial crisis. I prefer the term "indiscipline," for it points to the continuous difficulty in subjecting economic exchanges, within and outside the state, to law and regulation.

27. David Felix, "Asia and the Crisis of Financial Globalization," in Baker et al., *Globalization and Progressive Economic Policy*, table 1, 172.

28. The following is based on Yahya Sadowski, *Political Vegetables: Businessman and Bureaucrat in the Development of Egyptian Agriculture* (Washington, DC: Brookings Institution, 1991).

29. An UNCTAD report on the 1998/99 global financial crisis confirmed that the best predictor of economic crises in countries of the South was not state-led development but the deregulation of finances. United Nations Conference on Trade and Development, *Trade and Development Report 1998* (New York and Geneva: UNCTAD, 1999).

30. IMF, "Egyptian Stabilization," 31.

31. Ibid., 35; Economist Intelligence Unit, *Country Report: Egypt,* 3rd quarter 1998, 19–20. Other benefits were transferred to the banks in 1991, including a reduction in reserve requirements (a source of fiscal income) from 25 percent to 15 percent. Mohieldin, "State Intervention," 13.

32. Handy, *Egypt: Beyond Stabilization*, 62; IMF, "Egyptian Stabilization," 34.

33. Handy, *Egypt: Beyond Stabilization*, 59.

34. Ibid., 52.

35. Stark, "Recombinant Property in East European Capitalism," makes the same point in regard to Hungary, both before and after the collapse of "socialism."

36. On the Arab Contractors, see Sadowski, *Political Vegetables*, 105–26; on Eastern Tobacco, see Sophia Anninos, "Creating the Market: An Examination of Privatization Policies in Kazakhstan and Egypt" (Ph.D. dissertation, New York University, 2000).

37. Aida Seif El Dawla, "Egypt: The Eternal Pyramid," report of the New Woman Research Center, available at http://www.socwatch.org.uy/1998/english/reports/egypt.htm.

38. The government liquidated twenty-seven companies. Of the ninety-seven other companies in which the government sold shares, it retained a majority of the shares in eighteen, remained the largest single shareholder in a further twenty-five, retained significant share holdings in another twelve, and transferred twenty-eight more to "employee shareholder associations," which in practice allowed continued control by the same managers. Fourteen companies were said to have been sold directly to large "anchor investors." EIU, *Country Report: Egypt*, 3rd quarter 1998, 19; EIU, *Country Report: Egypt*, 3rd quarter 1999, 20.

39. Marat Terterov, "Is SOE Asset-swapping Privatization?" *Middle East Times*, August 9, 1998.

40. *Financial Times*, January 15, 1999, 36.

41. Sherine Abd Al-Razek, "Market in Overdrive," *Al-Ahram Weekly*, February 17–23, 2000, available at http://www.ahram.org.eg/weekly.

42. Stark, "Recombinant Property in East European Capitalism," 128–9.

43. EIU, *Country Report: Egypt*, 3rd quarter 1998, 21. *Business Today Egypt*, November 1988, 29. The EFG index is available at http://www.efg-hermes.com/docs/market/home.

44. Rafy Kourian, "Throwing Good Money after a Bad Market," *Middle East Times*, October 25, 1998.

45. Following the privatization of MobiNil—sold to the Orascom Group in consortium with Motorola of the U.S. and France Telecom—the government licensed a second mobile phone operator, Click GSM, to placate the powerful Alkan group, which had lost out in the bidding for MobiNil. See EIU, *Egypt: Country Report*, 3rd quarter 1999, 29–30.

46. The scramble also reflected a global reorganization of the cement industry. A decade earlier there had been no global cement makers. See EIU, *Egypt: Country Report*, 3rd quarter 1999, 20–21; *Business Monthly*, January 2000, 18; http://www.cemex.com; http://www.titan.gr/en/news; http://www.4m group. com.eg; http://www.holderbank.com; and http: www.lafarge.fr.

47. Another large industrialization project of the 1990s, described as a leading example of the new private-sector-funded, export-oriented investment (and the first big Egyptian-Israeli industrial venture), turned out to be relying on state funds and to be oriented, once again, to the domestic market. The Middle East Oil Refinery (Midor), a project to build a $1.5 billion oil refinery announced in 1996 by the Swiss-based Masaka company, owned by an Egyptian financier, Hussein Salem, and the Israeli Merhav Group, owned by Yosef Maiman, failed to attract private investment. So the Egyptian government increased its funding to 60 percent, the two private financiers reduced their shares to 20 percent each, and the Egyptian-Swiss partner passed on all except 2 percent out of this share to other, mostly state-owned Egyptian finance houses (16 percent to NBE Finance of the Cayman Islands, an offshore subsidiary of the National Bank of Egypt, and 2 percent to the local joint-sector Suez Canal Bank). Instead of refining petroleum products for export, the government announced, most of the production would be for the domestic market. EIU, *Egypt: Country Report*, 3rd quarter 1999, 27.

48. World Bank, *World Development Report 1999/2000*, table 13, 254–5.

49. World Bank, *World Development Report 1998/99*, table 11, 210–1.

50. Handy, *Egypt: Beyond Stabilization*, table 21, 50.

51. IMF, "Egyptian Stabilization," 12.

52. *Cairo Times*, December 10, 1998, 12.

53. See http://www.seoudi.com.

54. See "Arabian International Construction," at www.winne.com/Egypt.

55. See http://www.mmsons.com.

56. Nadine El Sherif, "Face of Business: Mohamed Mansour," *Business Today Egypt*, February 2001, 42–43.

57. Fariba Khorasanizadeh, "Sector Survey: Telecommunications," *Business Today Egypt*, February 2001, 51–61; "Egypt Supplement," *Forbes Magazine*, May 31, 1998, available at www.winne.com/Egypt.

58. See http://www.bahgat.com, and http://www.eief.org/bahgat.html.

59. See http://www.lakahgroup.com. On "cost-recovery" in medical care, see chapter eight of my book *Rule of Experts*.

60. *Business Today Egypt*, November 1998, 19.

61. In 1999 Egyptians purchased 68,609 new cars, 23,193 of them locally assembled and 45,416 imported. A significant proportion of these were sold for use as taxis rather than for private use. Dow Jones Newswires, December 17, 2000, quoted in *Cairo Times*, January 4–11, 2001.

62. Rehab El-Bakry, "Sweet Dreams," *Business Today Egypt*, February 2001, 41.

63. Osman M. Osman, "Development and Poverty-Reduction Strategies in Egypt," *Working Papers of the Economic Research Forum for the Arab Countries, Iran and Turkey*, no. 9813 (Cairo, 1998), 7–8.

64. IMF, "Egyptian Stabilization," 50.

65. *Al-Ahram*, January 1, 1999, supplement, 3.

66. Ulrich Bartsch, "Interpreting Household Budget Surveys: Estimates for Poverty and Income Distribution in Egypt," *Working Papers of the Economic Research Forum for the Arab Countries, Iran and Turkey*, no. 9714 (Cairo, 1997), 17–19.

67. "Indian Poverty and the Numbers Game," *The Economist*, April 29, 2000, 37–38. The discrepancy between national accounts and household surveys in India is also discussed in World Bank, *Global Economic Prospects and the Developing Countries: 2000* (Washington, DC: World Bank, 1999), 31.

68. Bartsch, "Interpreting Household Budget Surveys," 17–19.

69. Simon Kuznets, *National Income and Its Composition, 1919–1939*, vol. 1 (New York: National Bureau of Economic Research, 1941), xxvi.

70. Leading economists frequently acknowledge the difficulty of measuring the economy. Asking why "economists have not been very successful in explaining what has happened to the economy during the last two decades," Zvi Griliches, in his 1994 address as president of the American Economic Association (AEA), argued that whereas in the 1950s about half the overall economy was measurable, by 1990 the proportion had fallen to below one-third ("Productivity, R&D, and the Data Constraint," *American Economic Review* 14, no. 1 [1994]: 1–23, at 13). In an earlier AEA presidential address, Robert Eisner said that measures of the main macroeconomic variables—income, output, employment, prices, productivity, consumption, savings, investment, capital formation, wealth, debt, and deficits—were so unreliable that he and his fellow economists "have literally not known what we are talking about." "Divergences of Measurement and Theory and Some Implications for Economic Policy," *American Economic Review* 79, no. 1 (1989): 1–13, at 2.

71. Mahmoud Abdel-Fadil, "Informal Sector Employment in Egypt," in *Urban Research Strategies for Egypt*, ed. R. Lobbon, Cairo Papers in Social Science 6, monograph 2 (Cairo: American University in Cairo Press, 1983), 16–40.

72. The study defined informal dwellings as housing built since 1950 on land that was not formally subdivided or planned and not following regulatory regimes for construction. The total also included an estimate of those living in formal areas as squatters or other conditions of informality. Egyptian Center for Economic Studies and Institute for Liberty and Democracy, "Situational Analysis of Urban Real Estate in Egypt: Report," mimeo, Cairo, October 2000.

73. Sadowski, *Political Vegetables*, 233.

74. Ibid., 221, citing Midhat Hasanayn, "al-Iqtisad al-sirri fi misr," *al-Ahram al-iqtisadi*, December 15, 1985, 16. Nonpetroleum exports were worth $1.7 billion in 1988. Library of Congress, Federal Research Division, *Egypt: A Country Study*, 442.

75. See United Nations Office for Drug Control and Crime Prevention, Regional Office for the Middle East and North Africa, at http://www.undcp.org/egypt/country_profile_lebanon.html.

76. Yomna Kamel, "A Better Life with Bango," *Middle East Times*, July 18, 1999. Bango is more commonly known in the West as marijuana.

77. Sinai production was also facilitated by the 1979 Camp David agreement between Israel and Egypt, the terms of which excluded Egyptian military forces in the eastern part of Sinai after Israel withdrew. The government was thus prevented from using helicopters, for example, to search for hemp fields. The Egyptian Interior Ministry's Anti-Narcotic General Administration (established in 1929 and said to be the oldest drug control agency in the world) reported rapidly increasing seizures of cannabis herb (bango) in the later 1990s, reaching approximately 31 metric tons in 1998. Yet prices remained steady, according to the Cairo regional office of the U.N. Office for Drug Control, indicating increased cultivation rather than improved law enforcement. See http://www.undcp.org/egypt/country_profile_egypt.

78. IMF, "Egyptian Stabilization," 22.

79. International Institute for Strategic Studies, *The Military Balance 1989–90*, cited in Library of Congress, Federal Research Division, *Egypt: A Country Study*, 22–23, 399.

80. U.S. Department of State, *2001 Country Commercial Guide: Egypt*, 7–8.

81. My discussion of externalities and framing draws on Michel Callon, "An Essay on Framing and Overflowing: Economic Externalities Revisited by Sociology," in *The Laws of the Markets*, ed. Michel Callon, the *Sociological Review* monograph series (Oxford: Blackwell, 1998), 244–69.

82. Ibid.

83. For example, Douglas North, *Institutions, Institutional Change and Economic Performance* (Cambridge: Cambridge University Press, 1990).

84. The priority of the rule is reflected, and suppressed, in the forgotten history of economics. In eighteenth- and nineteenth-century Europe, before the rise of professional economics, the intellectual field that helped develop the regulations and understandings that

formatted and made possible modern forms of property, exchange, and profit was the field of law. In France and other parts of Europe the profession of economics developed as a branch of the study of law.

85. On the "constitutive outside," see the work of Jacques Derrida, for example, the essays in *Margins of Philosophy* (Chicago: University of Chicago Press, 1982), and "Structure, Sign and Play in the Discourse of the Human Sciences," in *Writing and Difference*, trans. Alan Bass (Chicago: University of Chicago Press, 1978), 278–93. I draw on this work in *Colonising Egypt* (Berkeley: University of California Press, 1991). See also the discussion in Ernesto Laclau, *New Reflections on the Revolution of Our Time* (London: Verso, 1990).

86. Callon, "An Essay on Framing and Overflowing," 254.

87. See my discussion of "enframing" in Mitchell, *Colonising Egypt*, and of the state as an effect of enframing in Mitchell, "Society, Economy, and the State Effect," in *State/Culture: State-Formation After the Cultural Turn*, ed. George Steinmetz (Ithaca, NY: Cornell University Press, 1999), 76–97.

88. Here is a simple example: before a foreign food product can be imported into Egypt, it must go through complex exchanges. At the Egyptian customs, it is inspected to ensure it complies with packaging and labeling regulations (language and placement of labels, production and expiration dates, ingredients, name of manufacturer and importer), local shelf-life standards (less than half the life must have expired by completion of customs inspection), and international and local product specifications. Samples of the product must be inspected in government laboratories to ensure compliance with Ministry of Health regulations on fitness for human consumption, contagious diseases, and prohibited coloring, additives, and preservatives, and international regulations on pesticide residues. See United States Department of Agriculture, Foreign Agricultural Service, "Egypt: Food and Agricultural Import Regulations and Standards, Country Report 2000," Global Agriculture Information Network, report no. EG0023, July 30, 2000.

89. In July 2000, thirty-one defendants were found guilty (the thirty-second had died). Three had fled the country and received sentences of fifteen years hard labor, fourteen received ten years hard labor, and the rest sentences of one to five years. Six months later the sentences were annulled and a retrial was ordered, because the investigation had violated banking secrecy laws. Tariq Hassan-Gordon, "Case of 31 Businessmen to Be Retried," *Middle East Times*, January 19, 2001.

90. Karl Marx, *Capital: A Critique of Political Economy*, vol. 1 (New York: The Modern Library, 1906), 809.

91. Sarah Anderson and John Cavanagh, with Thea Lee, *Field Guide to the Global Economy* (New York: The New Press, 2000), 29.

92. Karl Marx, *Capital*, vol. 3 (London: Penguin, 1981), 569.

93. Fernand Braudel's studies of the rise of capitalism formulate a distinction between markets, which tended to be places of local, small-scale exchange and difficult profits, and the large-scale monopolies out of which what came to be called capitalism emerged. *Af-*

terthoughts on Material Civilization and Capitalism, trans. Patricia Ranum (Baltimore: The Johns Hopkins University Press, 1977), 52, 111.

94. Adam Smith, *An Inquiry into the Origins and Nature of the Wealth of Nations*, ed. R.H. Campbell and A.S. Skinner, The Glasgow Edition of the Works and Correspondence of Adam Smith, vol. 2 (Oxford: The Clarendon Press, 1976). See also Ranajit Guha, *A Rule of Property for Bengal: An Essay on the Idea of Permanent Settlement* (Durham, NC: Duke University Press, 1996).

95. Erving Goffman, *Frame Analysis: An Essay on the Organization of Experience* (New York: Harper & Row, 1974).

96. The phrase is from Sir Philip Francis, quoted in Ranajit Guha, *A Rule of Property for Bengal: An Essay on the Idea of Permanent Settlement*, 2nd ed. (New Delhi: Orient Longman, 1981), 95.

97. Gamal Essam El-Din, "MPs Rage over Erosion of Parliamentary Power," *al-Ahram Weekly*, January 7–13, 1999, 3.

98. A 1993 law replaced the election of village heads and deans of university faculties with appointment by the government.

99. In May 1999 the United Nations Committee Against Torture recommended effective steps be taken against the use of torture in Egypt. Amnesty International, *Annual Report 2000: Egypt*, available at http://www.amnesty.org/web/ar2000web.nsf/countries.

100. Colonel Mohammed Ghanem, "The Tragedy of Administrative Detention," *Middle East Times*, June 3, 1999. The article was censored from the printed edition, but is available at http:metimes.com/issue99-24/opin/detention.htm. The author was previously the chairman of administration of legal research at the Ministry of Interior and a professor of criminal law at the Egyptian Police Academy. On prison conditions, see Amnesty International, *Annual Report 2000: Egypt*.

101. The government repressed the professional associations after board elections were won by members of the Muslim Brothers, an nonlegal political organization opposed to the regime. Fareed Ezz-Edine, "Egypt: An Emerging 'Market' of Double Repression," *Press Information Note no. 10*, Middle East Research and Information Project, November 18, 1999, available at http://www.merip.org.

102. Amnesty International, "Egypt: Muzzling Civil Society," September 19, 2000.

103. For a discussion of the U.S. democracy initiative, see Timothy Mitchell, "The 'Wrong Success': America's Fear of Democracy in the Middle East," [in Arabic], in Timothy Mitchell, *al-Dimuqratiya wa-'l-dawla fi al-`alam al-`arabi* (Damascus and Cyprus: Dar `Iybal, 1996).

104. Marx, *Capital*, 1:326.

105. Aidan Foster Carter, "The Modes of Production Controversy," *New Left Review* 107 (Jan.–Feb. 1978): 47–77, at 61–62, emphasis in original. For a reading of Marx that explores his understanding of violence in these terms, see Timothy Mitchell, "The Stage of Modernity," in *Questions of Modernity*, ed. Timothy Mitchell (Minneapolis: University of Minnesota Press, 2000), 1–34.

106. See Dahlia Reda, "La région dans la tourmente politique," *Al-Ahram Hebdo*, January 10–16, 2001, 11, and http://www.efg-hermes.com/docs/market/home.

107. An industry source reported that "larger developments such as Dreamland (Bahgat Group) and Beverly Hills (SODIC)" were effectively bankrupt. Hadia Mostafa, "Something to Build On," *Business Today Egypt*, February 2001, 22–27, at 25.

108. The Ministry of Finance agreed to pay E£1.5 billion of the debts of the Radio and Television Union (RTU) to the National Investment Bank over six years, in exchange for equity in the RTU, and the bank agreed to convert a further E£1 billion of debt into RTU equity. *Al-Ahram Hebdo*, January 10–16, 2001, 12.

109. The government put four bankers on the board of Arab Contractors, to increase its control of the company. *Business Monthly*, March 2001.

110. The British Embassy's quarterly economic report reported that banks had overextended credit to construction and other nonproductive projects leading to a large-scale default. Ibid., 23.

111. Lakah, who had French as well as Egyptian citizenship, had gone to Paris for a month, but threatened to sue anyone who claimed he had fled to avoid paying his debts. "Banks Put Squeeze on Businessmen," *Business Monthly*, November 2000; *Wall Street Journal*, November 30, 1999.

112. The two mobile phone operators claimed a total of 1.35 million subscribers, but many users subscribed to both services, since one or other network was frequently unavailable due to excess demand. *Business Today Egypt*, February 2001, 12, 20; EIU, *Egypt: Country Report*, 3rd quarter 1999, 29–30.

Chapter 3: Fear and Money in Dubai

1. *Business Week*, 13 March 2006.

2. "Dubai Overtakes Las Vegas as World's Hotel Capital," *Travel Weekly*, 3 May 2005.

3. "Ski in the Desert?," *Observer*, 20 November 2005; *Hydropolis: Project Description*, Dubai, August 2003 (www.conway.com).

4. See the *Mena Report 2005*, at www.menareport.com.

5. As a Dubai tourist official once complained to an American journalist about Egypt: "They have the pyramids and they do nothing with them. Can you imagine what we'd do with the pyramids?" Lee Smith, "The Road to Tech Mecca," *Wired Magazine*, July 2004.

6. Official Dubailand FAQs (from the marketing department). "It's as if a list of all known human pastimes have been collected on PowerPoint slides and then casually voted on by a show of hands." Ian Parker, "The Mirage," *The New Yorker*, 17 October 2005.

7. Parker, "Mirage."

8. The Maktoums also own Madame Tussaud's in London, the Helmsley Building and the Essex House in Manhattan, thousands of apartments in the Sunbelt states, enormous ranches in Kentucky, and what the *New York Times* describes as a "significant stake in Daim-

lerChrysler." See "Royal Family of Dubai Pays $1.1 Billion for 2 Pieces of New York Sky-line," 10 November 2005.

9. Saudi Arabia's "King Abdullah Economic City"—a projected $30-billion development on the Red Sea—will in fact be a satellite of Dubai, built by Emaar, the giant real-estate company owned by the Maktoum dynasty. See "OPEC Nations Temper the Extravagance," *New York Times*, 1 February 2006.

10. Rowan Moore, "Vertigo: The Strange New World of the Contemporary City," in *Vertigo*, ed. Rowan Moore (Corte Madera, CA, 1999).

11. "Emirate Rebrands Itself as a Global Melting Pot," *Financial Times*, 12 July 2005.

12. George Katodrytis, "Metropolitan Dubai and the Rise of Architectural Fantasy," *Bidoun* 4, spring 2005.

13. "In China, To Get Rich Is Glorious," *Business Week*, 6 February 2006.

14. Baruch Knei-Paz, *The Social and Political Thought of Leon Trotsky* (Oxford, 1978), 91.

15. "Oil Producers Gain Global Clout from Big Windfall," *Wall Street Journal*, 4 October 2005.

16. Joseph Kechichian, "Sociopolitical Origins of Emirati Leaders," in Kechichian, ed., *A Century in Thirty Years: Shaykh Zayed and the UAE*, ed. Joseph Kechichian (Washington, DC, 2000), 54.

17. Jack Lyne, "Disney Does the Desert?" 17 November 2003, online at *The Site Selection*.

18. Michael Pacione, "City Profile: Dubai," *Cities*, vol. 22, no. 3, 2005, 259–60.

19. "Young Iranians Follow Dreams to Dubai," *New York Times*, 4 December 2005. There is also a dramatic recent influx of wealthy Iranian Americans and "some Dubai streets are beginning to resemble parts of Los Angeles."

20. *Wall Street Journal*, 2 March 2006.

21. Gilbert King, *The Most Dangerous Man in the World: Dawood Ibrahim* (New York, 2004), 78; Douglas Farah, "Al Qaeda's Gold: Following the Trail to Dubai," *Washington Post*, 18 February 2002; and Sean Foley, "What Wealth Cannot Buy: UAE Security at the Turn of the 21st Century," in *Crises in the Contemporary Persian Gulf*, ed. Barry Rubin (London, 2002), 51–52.

22. Steve Coll, *Ghost Wars* (New York, 2004), 449.

23. Suketu Mehta, *Maximum City: Bombay Lost and Found* (New York, 2004), 135.

24. S. Hussain Zaidi, *Black Friday: The True Story of the Bombay Bomb Blasts* (Delhi, 2002), 25–27 and 41–44.

25. See "Dubai's Cooperation with the War on Terrorism Called into Question," *Transnational Threats Update*, Centre for Strategic and International Studies, February 2003, 2–3; and "Bin Laden's Operatives Still Using Freewheeling Dubai," *USA Today*, 2 September 2004.

26. Ira Chernus, 'Dubai: Home Base for Cold War,' 13 March 2006, Common Dreams News Centre.

27. Pratap Chatterjee, "Ports of Profit: Dubai Does Brisk War Business," 25 February 2006, Common Dreams News Centre.

28. Edward Chancellor, "Seven Pillars of Folly," *Wall Street Journal*, 8 March 2006; on Saudi repatriations, *AME Info*, 20 March 2005, www.ameinfo.com.

29. *AME Info*, 9 June 2005.

30. Chancellor, "Seven Pillars."

31. Stanley Reed, "The New Middle East Bonanza," *Business Week*, 13 March 2006.

32. Lyne, "Disney Does the Desert?"

33. Viewed from space, 1060 Water Homes at The Palm, Jebel Ali, will read: "Take wisdom from the wise people. Not everyone who rides is a jockey."

34. Peter Coy, "Oil Pricing," *Business Week*, 13 March 2006.

35. Tarek Atia, "Everybody's a Winner," *Al-Ahram Weekly*, 9 February 2005.

36. William Wallis, "Big Business: Intense Rivalry Among the Lieutenants," *Financial Times*, 12 July 2005.

37. Hari Sreenivasan, "Dubai: Build It and They Will Come," ABC News, 8 February 2005.

38. Pacione, "City Profile: Dubai," 257.

39. Smith, "The Road to Tech Mecca"; Stanley Reed, "A Bourse is Born in Dubai," *Business Week*, 3 October 2005; and Roula Khalaf, "Stock Exchanges: Chance to Tap into a Vast Pool of Capital," *Financial Times*, 12 July 2005.

40. Khalaf, "Stock Exchanges."

41. William McSheehy, "Financial Centre: A Three-way Race for Supremacy," *Financial Times*, 12 July 2005.

42. "A Short History of Dubai Property," *AME Info*, August 2004.

43. Lonely Planet, *Dubai: City Guide* (London, 2004), 9; and William Ridgeway, "Dubai, Dubai—The Scandal and the Vice," Social Affairs Unit, 4 April 2005.

44. William Wallis, "Demographics: Locals Swamped by a New Breed of Resident," *Financial Times*, 12 July 2005.

45. Nick Meo, "How Dubai, Playground of Business Men and Warlords, Is Built by Asian Wage Slaves," *Independent*, 1 March 2005.

46. Meo, "How Dubai."

47. Lucy Williamson, "Migrants' Woes in Dubai Worker Camps," BBC News, 10 February 2005.

48. See account posted on 15 February 2005, at secretdubai.blogspot.com.

49. On the jailing of rape victims, see Asia Pacific Mission for Migrants, *News Digest*, September 2003.

50. Meena Janardhan, "Welcome Mat Shrinking for Asian Workers in UAE," Inter Press Service, 2003.

51. See Ray Jureidini, *Migrant Workers and Xenophobia in the Middle East*, UN Research Institute for Social Development, Identities, Conflict and Cohesion: Programme Paper No. 2, Geneva, December 2003.

52. "UAE: Abuse of Migrant Workers," Human Rights Watch, 30 March 2006.

53. Anthony Shadid, "In UAE, Tales of Paradise Lost," *Washington Post*, 12 April 2006.

54. Hassan Fattah, "In Dubai, an Outcry from Asians for Workplace Rights," *New York Times*, 26 March 2006.

55. Julia Wheeler, "Workers' Safety Queried in Dubai," BBC News, 27 September 2004.

56. Fattah, "In Dubai"; Dan McDougall, "Tourists Become Targets as Dubai's Workers Take Revolt to the Beaches," *Observer*, 9 April 2006; and "Rioting in Dubai Labour Camp," *Arab News*, 4 July 2006.

57. Quoted in Lyne, "Disney Does the Desert?"

Chapter 4: Capital of Chaos

1. United Nations Security Council, *Report of the Secretary-General on the Situation in Afghanistan and Its Implications for International Peace and Security*, A/57/850-S/2003/754, July 23, 2003, 7.

2. John Sifton, "Afghanistan's Warlords Still Call the Shots," *Wall Street Journal Asia*, December 24, 2003.

3. Pierre-Arnaud Chouvy, "Afghan Opium Production Predicted to Reach New High," *Jane's Intelligence Review* 16, no. 10 (October 2004): 29–31.

4. United Nations Office on Drugs and Crime, *Statistical Annex to the Note "The Opium Situation in Afghanistan,"* August 29, 2005, 5.

5. President of the Islamic Republic of Afghanistan, *1384 Budget Decree*, http://www.af/resources/mof/nationalbudget/1384_National_Budget/1384NationalBudgetDecree Eng.pdf (accessed June 29, 2006).

6. Human Rights Watch, "Afghanistan: Human Rights Concerns for the 61st Session of the U.N. Commission," http://hrw.org/english/docs/2005/03/10/afghan10299.htm (accessed June 29, 2006).

7. President of the Islamic Republic of Afghanistan, *1384 Budget Decree*.

8. Revolutionary Association of the Women of Afghanistan (RAWA), "Crime and Barbarism in Shirpur by Afghan Ministers and High Authorities," September 16, 2003, http://www.rawa.org/land2.htm (accessed June 29, 2006).

9. "UN Accuses Top Afghan Ministers of Land Grab," *PakTribune*, September 12, 2003, can be read at http://www.rawa.org/land.htm (accessed June 29, 2006).

10. *CIA World Factbook, Afghanistan*, 2004 estimates, http://www.cia.gov/cia/publications/factbook/geos/af.html.

11. Agency Coordinating Body for Afghan Relief (ACBAR), "Concerns Related to Housing Rents in Afghanistan," May 12, 2002, www.care.org/newsroom/specialreports/afghanistan/05142002_afghanhousing.asp (accessed June 29, 2006).

12. "Minister Scorns NGOs' Work," Abdul Baseer Saeed, Institute for War and Peace Reporting, November 11, 2004, http://www.globalpolicy.org/ngos/state/2004/1111 scorn.htm.

13. Carlotta Gal, "Convoy Crash Sparks Kabul Riots," *New York Times*, May 31, 2006.

14. Ibid.

15. Fariba Nawa, "U.S. Security Companies Act As Kabul's Private Militias," *Albion Monitor* 147 (June 2006), http://www.albionmonitor.com/0606a/index.html (accessed June 29, 2006).

16. Office of the United Nations High Commissioner for Refugees, "Afghanistan: Repatriation from Pakistan Restarts after Winter Break," press briefing by UNHCR spokesperson Jennifer Pagonis, February 28, 2006, Palais des Nations, Geneva.

17. "Reconstruction and Development in Afghanistan—An Overview and Review of Opportunities for Economic Consultants," text prepared for a talk by Mark Wilson to the International Consulting Economists' Association, January 29, 2003 (www.icea.co.uk/archive/WatsonAfghanistan29_01_03.doc).

18. Joe Stephens and David B. Ottaway, "A Rebuilding Plan Full of Cracks," *Washington Post*, November 20, 2005.

19. Human Rights Watch, "Afghanistan: Human Rights Concerns."

20. Jason Burke, "Fear Battles Hope on the Road to Kandahar," *The Observer* (UK), June 25, 2006.

21. "A Call for Justice," a report by the Afghan Independent Human Rights Commission, January 29, 2005, can be read at http://www.aihrc.org.af (accessed July 02, 2006).

Chapter 5: Delirious Beijing

1. William Mellor and Allen Cheng, "Beijing Home to $160b Worth of Construction," *Vancouver Sun*, March 4, 2006.

2. Deyan Sudjic, "The City That Ate the World," *Guardian*, October 16, 2005.

3. Anne-Marie Broudehoux, "Learning from Chinatown: The Search for a Modern Architectural Identity, 1911–1998," in *Hybrid Urbanism: On the Identity Discourse and the Built Environment*, ed. Nezar Alsayyad (Westport, London: Praeger, 2001), 156–80.

4. For more on the role played by architecture in the new political economy of signs, see Steve Miles and Malcolm Miles, *Consuming Cities* (New York: Palgrave Macmillan, 2004), 45–201; Darrel Crilley, "Architecture as Advertising: Constructing the Image of Redevelopment," in *Selling Places: The City as Cultural Capital, Past and Present*, ed. Gerry Kearns and Chris Philo (Oxford, Pergamon Press, 1993); Graeme Evans, "Hard-Branding the Cultural City—From Prado to Prada," *International Journal of Urban and Regional Research* 27, 2 (June 2003): 417–40.

5. Guy Julier, "Urban Designscapes and the Production of Aesthetic Consent," *Urban Studies* 42, 5–6 (May 2005): 869–87.

6. For more on the National Theater controversy, see Anne-Marie Broudehoux, *The Making and Selling of Post-Mao Beijing* (London and New York: Routledge, 2004).

7. On Olympic projects, see Kieran Long, "The Greatest Show on Earth," *Guardian*, January 12, 2004; "Beijing Readies Facilities Plans," *China Daily*, July 12, 2003, 5; Zheng Shiling, "History Comes Crashing Down: Foreign Architectural Designs Are Swal-

lowing up China's History and Culture," *Beijing Review*, Aug. 31, 2004; Susan Jakes, "Soaring Ambitions: The World's Most Visionary Architects Are Rebuilding China," *Times Asia*, April 26 2004; "Beijing's Olympic Gateway," *Straits Times* (Singapore), November 18, 2003.

8. "Kool enough for Beijing," *China Daily*, Mar. 2, 2004; "Koolhaas as Seen by the Architectural World," *China Daily*, Mar. 2, 2004, 13; and Chistopher Hawthorne, "China Pulls Up the Drawbridge," *New York Times*, September 19, 2004.

9. The average GNP was US$1,090 in 2003. Li Yongyan, "China's Economic Miracle Hasn't Reached the Poor," *Asia Times*, August 26, 2004.

10. Companies will pay $62 million for the right to be an official partner of the 2008 Olympics. Coca-Cola alone will reportedly give $1 billion to Beijing, double its usual sponsorship commitment. Mark Godfrey, *Going for Gold*, www.sinomedia.net/eurobiz/v200406/story0406.html, June 2004.

11. For example, the National Stadium will be built by the CITIC group, a transnational conglomerate that raised 42 percent of the construction funds, while the remaining 58 percent were funded by the Beijing municipal government, through the state-owned Assets Management Company. The two companies jointly established the National Stadium Company, which will responsible for the investment, design, construction, operation, and management aspects of the venue for the Games and will then own the rights to operate the stadium for the next thirty years. See "Consortium Wins Bid for National Stadium," *China Daily*, August 11, 2003.

12. Ryan Ong, "New Beijing, Great Olympics: Beijing and Its Unfolding Legacy," *Stanford Journal of East-Asian Affairs*, vol. 14, no. 2 (2004): 35–49.

13. See David Whitson and Donald Macintosh, "The Global Circus: International Sport, Tourism and the Marketing of Cities," *Journal of Sport and Social Issues* 20(3) (August 1996): 278–95; John D. Horne and Wolfram Manzenreiter, "Accounting for Mega-Events," *International Review for the Sociology of Sports* 39(2) (2004): 187–203; and Matthew Burbank, *Olympic Dreams: The Impact of Mega-Events on Local Politics* (Boulder, CO: Lynne Rienner Publishers, 2001).

14. Mary-Anne Toy, "New China Rises on the Backs of Unpaid Migrant Workers," *The Age*, January 30, 2006.

15. Given the state's notoriously unreliable statistics, this estimate must be seen as a conservative figure. Mark Magnier, "China's Migrant Workers Ask for Little and Receive Nothing," *Los Angeles Times*, January 21, 2004, A-4.

16. In October 2005, migrant worker Wang Binyu was executed after killing four people in a rampage over unpaid wages. Mary-Anne Toy, "New China Rises."

17. Freda Wan, "Rights Group Urges Eviction Safeguards," *South China Morning Post*, March 25, 2004, 8.

18. Ke Fang and Yan Zhang, "Plan and Market Mismatch: Urban Redevelopment in Beijing During a Period of Transition," *Asia Pacific Viewpoint*, vol. 44, no. 2 (August 2003): 149–62.

19. Sam Howe Verhovek, "Rebellion of the Displaced," *Los Angeles Times*, Sept. 5, 2003, A-1;

and Francis Markus, "Chinese Eviction Lawyer Jailed," BBC News, October 28, 2003, http://news.bbc.co.uk/1/hi/world/asia-pacific/3220643.stm.

20. Louisa Lim, "China Detains Demolition Gang," BBC News, October 31, 2003, http://news.bbc.co.uk/go/pr/fr/-/1/hi/world/asia-pacific/3229583.stm; and Louisa Lim, "China to Defuse Property Unrest," BBC News, June 15, 2004, http:news.bbc.co.uk/go/pr/fr/-/1/hi/world/asia-pacific/3807627.stm.

21. Jane Macartney, "Thousands of Homes Destroyed to Make Way for Olympic Tourists," *Times Online*, May 26, 2005, http://www.timesonline.co.uk/article/0,,3-1628199,00.html.

22. Jehangir Pocha, "Demolitions Straining Families In China," *Boston Globe*, July 9, 2004, A6.

23. Louisa Lim, "China's Middle Class Rebels," BBC News, June 23, 2004, http://news.bbc.co.uk/go/pr/fr/-/1/hi/world/asia-pacific/3829935.stm; Pocha, "Demolitions Straining Families."

24. "China Eviction Protester 'Jailed,'" BBC News, December 18, 2004, http://news.bbc.co.uk/1/hi/world/asia-pacific/4107609.stm.

25. In December 2005, the United Nations Development Programme declared that China's growing income gap should be seen as one of the most pressing issues faced by the Chinese leadership, which could threaten its stability, and pressed China to increase social spending. Mure Dickie, "UN Calls for Reform in China to Narrow Growing Income Gap and Aid Stability," *Financial Times*, December 17, 2005.

26. Caolin Gu and Jianafa Shen, "Transformation of Urban Socio-spatial Structure in Socialist Market Economies: The Case of Beijing," *Habitat International* 27 (2003): 107–22.

27. Peter S. Goodman, "Rural Poor Aren't Sharing In Spoils of China's Changes—Costs of Goods Rise, Standard of Living Falls," *Washington Post*, July 12, 2005, A1.

28. Goodman, "Rural Poor"; and "China's Urban Income Gap Widens to Alarming Level," www.chinaview.cn, February 6, 2006; "Experts: China's Urban Poverty Worsens," www.chinaview.cn, February 12, 2006.

29. Xinhua News Agency, in Goodman, "Rural Poor."

30. Joseph Kahn, "In Beijing, a Little Piece of France Embodies a World of Change," *New York Times*, December 27, 2004, 11.

31. Joseph Kahn, "China's Elite Learn to Flaunt It While the New Landless Weep," *New York Times*, December 25, 2004.

32. See Jim Yardley, "Down on the Farm, by the Golf Course and Subdivision," *New York Times*, November 8, 2005.

33. Jehangir S. Pocha, "China's Inequities Energize New Left—Failures of Reform Buoy New Thinking," *San Francisco Chronicle*, June 19, 2005, F1. See also Minxin Pei, "The Dark Side of China's Rise," *Foreign Policy* (March–April 2006).

34. Edward Cody, "A Chinese City's Rage At the Rich And Powerful—Beating of Student Sparks Riot, Looting," *Washington Post*, August 1, 2005, A1.

35. Fulong Wu and Klaire Webber, "The Rise of 'Foreign Gated Communities' in Beijing: Between Economic Globalization and Local Institutions," *Cities*, vol. 21, no. 3 (2004): 203–13.

36. A process that Chinese scholar Fulong Wu describes as "imagined globalization." Fu-long Wu, "Transplanting Cityscapes: The Use of Imagined Globalization in Housing Commodification in Beijing," *Area* 36(3) (2004): 227–34.

37. Wu, "Transplanting Cityscapes."

38. These observations are based on a series of informal interviews with residents of La Firenza gated community, south of Beijing, in October 2005.

39. Pei, "The Dark Side of China's Rise."

40. For example, on August 20, 2004, hundreds of disgruntled farmers lined up bicycles and rickshaws to block traffic in a Beijing suburb to protest land seizure. Edward Cody, "China's Land Grabs Raise Specter of Popular Unrest," *Washington Post*, October 5, 2004, A1.

41. In December 2005, Chinese police killed twenty protesters near Hong Kong who were demanding adequate compensation for land taken to build a power plant. Sam Crane, "In China, It's Powerlessness to the People," *Los Angeles Times*, December 18, 2005.

42. Elaine Kurtenbach, "Chinese Lose Homes, Farms in New Land Grab," *Los Angeles Times*, March 6, 2005, A-3; and Edward Cody, "China's Land Grabs."

43. Edward Cody, "A Chinese City's Rage," Howard W. French, "Alarm and Disarray on Rise in China," *New York Times*, August 24, 2005.

44. Mark Magnier, "Letting Passions Burn May Backfire on China," *Los Angeles Times*, April 25, 2005, A-1; Jehangir S. Pocha, "China's inequities"; and Robert Marquand, "In China, Stresses Spill over into Riots," *Christian Science Monitor*, November 22, 2004, World, 1.

45. Nearly half of *Forbes* magazine's list of the one hundred richest individuals in China in 2004 were real-estate developers. See Pei, "The Dark Side of China's Rise."

46. Marquand, "In China, Stresses Spill over into Riots."

47. The party's Central Committee also disciplined several officials involved in illegal land deals and expelled the former land and resources minister for taking more than $600,000 in bribes. Cody, "China's Land Grabs." See also Kurtenbach, "Chinese Lose Homes, Farms."

48. Robert Marquand, "In China, stresses spill over into riots." *Christian Science Monitor*, November 22, 2004, World, 1.

49. For example, the architects of the National Stadium were told to reduce steel consumption and to omit the planned retractable roof. But the project otherwise remained essentially the same.

50. Chistopher Hawthorne, "China Pulls Up the Drawbridge," *New York Times*, September 19, 2004; Chen Wen, "Dear Prudence: Beijing Olympic Planners Discussing Financing and the Long-term Goals of 2008," *Beijing Review*, http://www.bjreview.com.cn/200436/Cover-200436(C).htm; Jonathan Watts, "Beijing-baiting Is Latest Sport as Olympic Focus Shifts to China," *Guardian Weekly*, September 3–9, 2004, 28; Li Gang, "Beijing Tries to Rein in Costs for 2008," *CRI News*, Aug. 31, 2004; and Ulf Meyer, "Will the 2008 Olympics Be a Boon or Boondoggle for Beijing? Suspense Is Building," *San Francisco Chronicle*, August 28, 2004.

51. The state also continues to play the nationalist card in its attempt to convert pent-up frustrations into patriotic fervor by redirecting popular resentment toward peripheral issues. In April 2005, Chinese authorities endorsed a series of anti-Japanese public demon-

strations throughout China, allowing people to voice their anger after the publication of a Japanese history textbook that played down Japan's wartime atrocities. The ten-thousand-strong rally that took place on the streets of Beijing was the largest protest since 1999, when a series of similarly state-sanctioned demonstrations against the U.S. bombing of the Chinese embassy in Belgrade were held. But as the anti-Japanese protests began to gain momentum over a period of several days, the state discovered the important risks carried by such diversion tactics, and realized that public discontent, once unleashed, can be difficult to contain. Mark Magnier, "Letting Passions Burn May Backfire on China," *Los Angeles Times*, April 25, 2005, A-1; and Robert A. Manning, "Beijing Rules, But It's Got A Host of Problems," *Washington Post*, July 15, 2001, B1.

52. Guy Debord demonstrated in the 1960s how the spectacle can act as a tool of social control, which distracts people from politics, anesthetizes their critical judgment, and erodes their capacity to react. Guy Debord, *La société du spectacle* (Paris: Gallimard, 1992 [1967]); and *Commentaires sur la société du spectacle* (Paris: Gallimard, 1992 [1988]).

53. Weeks before the Mexico City Summer Games of 1968, thousands of students demonstrated to protest the wasting of public funds on Olympic preparations rather than spending them on social welfare. The Mexican government, fearing that the Games would be canceled, replied with the infamous Tlatelolco Massacre. The Games proceeded with little protest from the international community. John M. Hoberman, *The Olympic Crisis: Sport, Politics and the Moral Order* (Austin: University of Texas Press, 1986).

In Seoul, Korean students and opposition groups deftly used the international media focus generated by the Olympic Games to further the fragile transition from a military dictatorship to a pluralist democracy. In June 1987, fifteen months before the Olympics, a massive popular mobilization erupted all over South Korea. In the face of this political crisis, the international community threatened to move the Olympics to a new location if a quick resolution was not found. Under such international pressure, the South Korean government finally conceded to the demonstrators' demands, and put forward a package of important democratic reforms in June 1987, which ultimately forced General Chun to step down. As a result, the first democratic presidential elections in sixteen years were held in December 1987. James F. Larson and Heung-Soo Park, *Global Television and the Politics of the Seoul Olympic Games* (Boulder, CO: Westview Press, 1993); and Pieter de Lange, *The Games Cities Play* (Pretoria: Sigma Press, 1998).

54. At the time of writing in March 2006, several human rights organizations had called for a boycott of the 2008 Olympics in protest against the state's human rights violations.

55. Even as the fastest-growing economy in the world, and now the world's fourth-largest economy (after its gross domestic product exceeded that of Britain and France in January 2006), China has freed itself from its previous socialist obligations regarding social security and continues to underinvest in crucial social services, especially housing, education, and public health.

Chapter 6: "Palm Springs"

1. Lev Manovich, *The Language of New Media* (Cambridge, MA: MIT Press, 2001).

2. Edward Soja, "Taking Los Angeles Apart: Towards a Postmodern Geography," in Richard LeGates and Frederic Stout (eds.), *The City Reader* (London: Routledge, 1996), 191.

3. Kim Dovey, *Framing Places: Mediating Power in Built Form* (London: Routledge, 1999), 153.

4. Mike Davis, *City of Quartz: Excavating the Future in Los Angeles* (New York: Verso, 1990), 224.

5. Gordon Mathews, *Global Culture/Individual Identity: Searching for Home in the Cultural Supermarket* (London: Routledge, 2000), 172.

Chapter 7: Johannesburg

1. P. Ngonyama, "Oscar-Winning Film Exposes South African Capitalism," *GreenLeft Weekly*, 22 March 2006.

2. For Human Development Index comparisons that combine income, education, and mortality, Johannesburg's white residents rate 44, just below the average of rich countries (45); the city's black residents rate 32, just above South Africa as a whole. In the world rankings, South Africa fell from 86th to 120th place out of 177 countries during the early 2000s. Greater Johannesburg Metropolitan Council (2003), *Johannesburg 2030*, 12.

3. B. Ludman, "JoBurg Gains a Brand and Loses an Apostrophe," *Mail and Guardian*, 6 June 2002.

4. J. Robinson, "Global and World Cities: A View from Off the Map," *International Journal of Urban and Regional Research* 26 (2002), 3.

5. From 1999 to at least 2009, Gauteng's premier is Mbhazima Shilowa, a high-profile former Congress of SA Trade Unions (Cosatu) general secretary and South African Communist Party (SACP) central committee member known for his love of fine cigars. The Gautrain project was termed the "Shilowa Express' and in late 2005 was opposed—belatedly, halfheartedly, and unsuccessfully—by Cosatu and the SACP.

6. International Monetary Fund "South Africa: Selected Issues," IMF Country Report No. 05/345 (Washington, 2005), 48. In South Africa, the contribution of manufacturing to GDP fell from 21.2% in 1994 to 18.8% in 2002, while the category of "financial intermediation" (including insurance and real estate) rose from 16.4% of GDP in 1994 to 19.5% in 2002.

7. P. Bond and R. Dada, *Trouble in the Air: Global Warming and the Privatized Atmosphere* (Durban: University of KwaZulu-Natal Centre for Civil Society, 2005).

8. The combined class/race/gendered system that "articulated" the capitalist and non-capitalist modes of production is reviewed in H. Wolpe, "Capitalism and Cheap Labour Power," *Economy and Society*, (1972) 1; M. Legassick, "South Africa: Capital Accumulation

and Violence," *Economy and Society*, (1974) 3; and D. O'Meara, *Forty Lost Years* (Blooming-ton: Indiana University Press, 1996).

9. Johannesburg's major black townships—Soweto, Alexandra, Ivory Park, and Orange Farm—are host to 192,000 formal dwellings. In addition to preexisting "matchbox" houses, most post-1994 state-financed houses include a small plot of land and a low-cost permanent structure often half as big as a matchbox (typically costing $2,300). There are also 83 informal shack settlements in greater Johannesburg, with 189,000 dwellings. Most lack piped water/sanitation, electricity, and other municipal services.

10. The average Johannesburg resident takes fifty minutes to get to work, while 48 percent spend more than 10 percent of income on their work transport (although racial break-downs are not available, these statistics are likely highly significant when correlated against race). See A. Boraine, "Can We Avert an Urban Crisis?" South African Cities Network Pre-sentation to Institute for Justice and Reconciliation Public Debate, Cape Town, 22 Sep-tember 2004, http://www.ijr.org.za/pastevents/Boraine%20presentation.ppt.

11. See ongoing documentation of these problems at the Municipal Services Project web-site at http://www.queensu.ca/msp.

12. *Sunday Times*, Gauteng Metro, 19 May 2002.

13. *The Star*, 14 May 2001.

14. E. Harvey, "A Critical Analysis of the Decision to Corporatize the Water and Wastewater Services in the City of Johannesburg" (masters dissertation, University of the Witwater-srand Graduate School of Public and Development Management, Johannesburg, 2003).

15. Financial and Fiscal Commission, "Local Government in a System of Intergovern-mental Fiscal Relations in South Africa: A Discussion Document," Midrand (1997).

16. P. Bond, "Redlining Cuts off Jo'burg's Lifeblood," *Weekly Mail*, 17–23 April 1992.

17. G. Thomson, "Water Tap Often Shut to South Africa Poor," *New York Times*, 29 May 2003.

18. M. Mayekiso, *Township Politics: Civic Struggles for a New South Africa* (New York: Monthly Review 1996); M. Murray, *The Revolution Deferred* (London: Verso, 1995); H. Marais, *South Africa: Political Economy of Change* (London: Zed Press; and Cape Town: University of Cape Town Press, 2000); and G. Adler and J. Steinberg (eds.), *The South African Civics Movement and the Transition to Democracy* (London: Macmillan, 2000).

19. E. Zuern, "Democracy from the Grassroots? Civic Participation and the Decline of Participatory Democracy in South Africa's Transformation Process, 1979–1999" (Ph.D. dissertation, Columbia University, 2000).

20. J. Jeter, "For South Africa's Poor, a New Power Struggle," *Washington Post*, 6 Novem-ber 2001.

21. T. Ngwane, "Sparks in Soweto," interview, *New Left Review*, July–August 2003.

22. Thomson, "Water Tap Often Shut to South Africa Poor."

23. P. Kingsnorth, *One No, Many Yeses: A Journey to the Heart of the Global Resistance Move-ment* (London: The Free Press, 2003); and N. Klein, *Fences and Windows* (London: Flamingo Press, 2002).

Chapter 8: "Nueva Managua"

1. I thank Claire La Hovary, Caroline Moser, José Luis Rocha, and Peter Solis for useful comments on an earlier version, which appeared in *Environment and Urbanisation* 16(2): 113–23, as well as Peter-Jan Vermeij for excellent photographic support.

2. See *Instituto Nicaragüense de Estadísticas y Censos* (INEC–Nicaraguan Statistics and Census Institute) Website, http://www.inec.gob.ni/estadisticas/proyeccion2003.htm, accessed 20 July 2004.

3. See G. Black, *Triumph of the People: The Sandinista Revolution in Nicaragua* (London: Zed Books, 1981), 57.

4. See J. C. Godoy Blanco, *El Proceso de Estructuración Urbana de Managua: 1950–1979* (PhD dissertation, Universidad de Costa Rica, Ciudad Universitaria "Rodrigo Faccio," Costa Rica, 1983).

5. See P. Drewe, "Integrated Upgrading of Marginal Areas in Managua," *Cities* 3:4 (1986): 333–49.

6. D. L. Wall, "City Profile: Managua," *Cities* 13:1 (1996): 48–49.

7. R. Leonardi, *Nicaragua Handbook* (Bath: Footprint Handbooks, 2001), 57.

8. D. Harvey, *The Condition of Postmodernity: An Enquiry into the Origins of Cultural Change* (Oxford: Blackwell, 1990), 66.

9. D. E. Whisnant, *Rascally Signs in Sacred Places: The Politics of Culture in Nicaragua* (Chapel Hill: University of North Carolina Press, 1995), 447.

10. F. E. Babb, *After Revolution: Mapping Gender and Cultural Politics in Neoliberal Nicaragua* (Austin: University of Texas Press, 2001), 61.

11. Nicaragua is brutally polarized between rich and poor, and has a Gini coefficient that is the fifth most unequal in the world according to the World Bank (*World Development Indicators 2001* (Washington, DC: World Bank, 2001), 70–72, table 2.8). This situation is compounded by the fact that the country is extremely poor, meaning that "not only is the cake badly divided, but in addition there is almost no cake at all, just a small cookie," according to J. L. Rocha ("Microsalarios y megasalarios: Megadesigualdad y microdesarrollo," *Envío* 240 (2002: 25). The population is therefore divided into an overwhelming majority of poor on the one hand, and a small minority of comparative—albeit variable—affluence on the other. This latter group includes not only traditionally powerful notable families but also a hotchpotch mix of professionals, businessmen, intelligentsia, and returned exiles, as well as foreigners working principally for NGOs and international development agencies. It is difficult to estimate the numerical weight of these groups, but none of them are very big, either in relation to each other or compared to the impoverished, and it makes sense to consider them as a single socioeconomic group. The relatively small number of new bars, restaurants, and malls in Managua are arenas where these different subgroups very much intermingle.

12. See A. Serbin and D. Ferreyra (eds.), *Gobernabilidad Democrática y Seguridad Ciudadana en Centroamérica: El caso de Nicaragua* (Managua: CRIES, 2000), 185–87.

13. See A. Díaz Lacayo, "Nicaragua Briefs," *Envío in English* 204 (July 1998): 31.

14. See INIFOM (Instituto Nicaragüense de Fomento Municipal—Nicaraguan Institute for the Promotion of Municipal Affairs), "Ficha Municipal: Managua" (n.d.), http://www.inifom.gob.ni/ArchivosPDF/Managua2.pdf.

15. See *Confidencial*, 5–11 May 2002, http://www.confidencial.com.ni/2002=288/depotadal288.html, accessed 26 July 2004.

16. See D. Rodgers, "Living in the Shadow of Death: Gangs, Violence, and Social Order in Urban Nicaragua, 1996–2002," *Journal of Latin American Studies* 38:2 (2006).

17. See R. J. Cajina, "Nicaragua: De la seguridad del Estado a la inseguridad ciudadana," in A. Serbin and D. Ferreyra (eds.), *Gobernabilidad Democráticay Seguridad Ciudadana en Centroamérica: El caso de Nicaragua* (Managua: CRIES, 2000), 174.

18. See R. J. Cajina, "Nicaragua," 169.

19. See *La Prensa*, 3 March 2003, http://www.laprensa.com.ni/cronologico/2003/marzo/03/nacionales/nacionales-20030303-18.html, accessed 18 July 2004.

20. See http://www.policia.gob.ni/estadisticas/dosier2003/dosier9.htm, accessed 18 July 2004.

21. *La Prensa*, 3 March 2003, http://www.laprensa.com.ni/cronologico/2003/marzo/03/nacionales/nacionales-20030303-18.html, accessed 18 July 2004.

22. *La Prensa*, 14 August 2000, http://www.laprensa.com.ni/cronologico/2000/agosto/14/nacionales/nacionales-20000814-05.html, accessed 20 July 2004.

23. See Rodgers, "Living in the Shadow of Death."

24. T.P.R. Caldeira, *City of Walls: Crime, Segregation and Citizenship in Sao Paulo* (Berkeley: University of California Press, 2000).

25. Babb, *After Revolution*, 67–68.

26. A pseudonym, as are all the names of barrio inhabitants mentioned in this article.

27. See *El Nuevo Diario*, 29 January 2000, http://wwwni.elnuevodiario.com.ni/archivo/2000/enero/29–enero-2000/opinion/opinion6.html, accessed 23 June 2004.

28. See http://www.managua.gob.ni/managua/rv.html, accessed 26 July 2004; *La Prensa*, 11 October 2001, http://wwwni.laprensa.com.ni/archivo/2001/octubre/11/nacionales/nacionales-20011011–07.html, accessed 18 May 2004; and *La Prensa*, 31 May 2004, http://www.laprensa.com.ni/archivo/2004/mayo/31/nacionales/nacionales-20040531–02.html, accessed 1 June 2004.

29. See INIFOM, "Ficha Municipal: Managua."

30. F. Wilson, "Towards a Political Economy of Roads: Experiences from Peru," *Development and Change* 35:3 (2004): 529.

31. See http://www.inec.gob.ni/estadisticas/sociodemografico/parqueautomotor.pdf, accessed 1 March 2006; PNUD (Programa de las Naciones Unidas para el Desarrollo–United Nations Development Programme), *El Desarrollo Humano en Nicaragua* (Managua:

PNUD, 2000), 173; and *El Nuevo Diario*, 4 June 2000, http://www-ni.elnuevodiario. com.ni/ archivo/2000/junio/04–junio–2000/variedades/variedades1.html, accessed 23 June 2004.

32. See http://www.euram.com.ni/pverdes/Entrevista/carlos_bendana.htm, accessed 23 June 2004.

33. *La Presna*, 29 January 2004, http://wwwni.laprensa.com.ni/cronologico/2004/enero/ 29/sucesos/sucesos–20040129–04.html, accessed 18 May 2004; *La Prensa*, 19 October 2000, http://wwwni.laprensa.com.ni/cronologico/2000/octubre/19/sucesos/sucesos– 20001019–01.html, accessed 18 May 2004; and INFOM, "Ficha Municipal: Managua." 34. *La Prensa*, 16 April 2004, http:wwwni.laprensa.com.ni/cronologico/2004/abril/16/ sucesos/sucesos–20040416–01.html, accessed 18 May 2004.

35. A. Smart, "Unruly Places: Urban Governance and the Persistence of Illegality in Hong Kong's Urban Squatter Areas," *American Anthropologist* 103:1 (2001): 30.

36. See S.E. Merry, "Spatial Governmentality and the New Urban Social Order: Controlling Gender Violence through Law," *American Anthropologist* 103:1 (2001): 16–29.

37. See M. Davis, *City of Quartz: Excavating the Future of Los Angeles* (London: Verso, 1990).

38. See A. Giddens, *The Consequences of Modernity* (Cambridge: Polity Press, 1990), and *Modernity and Self-identity: Self and Society in the Late Modern Age* (Palo Alto, CA: Stanford University Press, 1991).

39. M. Hess, "Spatial Relationships? Towards a Reconceptualization of Embeddedness," *Progress in Human Geography* 28:2 (2004): 177.

40. Caldeira, *City of Walls*, 213.

41. See C. Lasch, *The Revolt of the Elites and the Betrayal of Democracy* (New York: Norton, 1995).

42. See M. Davis, "Planet of Slums: Urban Involution and the Informal Proletariat," *New Left Review* 26 (March–April 2004): 5–24.

43. D. Harvey, "The Right to the City," *International Journal of Urban and Regional Research* 27:4 (2003): 941.

Chapter 9: Becoming Bourgeois

*Special thanks to Istvan Adorjan and Norma Moruzzi for lovingly being aware of the collective and material foundations of "individual creative work" and making this paper possible.

1. Iván Tosics, "Lakáspolitika—szociális várospolitika," *Budapesti Negyed* 8, no. 2 (2002): 143.

2. Ibid.

3. *Ingatlanpiac*.

4. János Ladányi, "Residential Segregation among Social and Ethnic Groups in Budapest during the Post-Communist Transition," in *Of States and Cities: The Partitioning of Urban Space*, ed. Peter Marcuse and Ronald van Kempen (Oxford, 2002), 170.

5. Ibid.

6. Judit Bodnár, "Dual Cities and the Manufacturing of Unity" (paper, International Sociological Association, Paris, June 30–July 2, 2005).

7. Judit Bodnár, "Shamed by Comparison: Eastern Europe and the 'Rest,'" in *Europe's Symbolic Geographies*, ed. Sorin Antohi and Larry Wolff (New York: CEU Press, forthcoming).

8. Susan Gal, "Bartok's Funeral: Representations of Europe in Hungarian Political Rhetoric," *American Ethnologist* 16, no. 3 (1991): 440–58; József Böröcz, "Goodness Is Elsewhere: The Rule of European Difference," *Comparative Studies in Society and History* 48, no. 1 (January 2006): 110–38.

9. Sharon Zukin, "Mimesis in the Origins of Bourgeois Culture," *Theory and Society* 4, no. 3 (1977): 333–58.

10. The thesis concerning interrupted embourgeoisement and the resuming of the process under state socialism by Ivan Szelenyi refers specifically to the life trajectories of peasant families and their expanding economic autonomization in the second economy. Ivan Szelenyi et al., *Socialist Entrepreneurs: Embourgeoisement in Rural Hungary* (Madison: University of Wisconsin Press, 1988).

11. Krisztina Fehérváry, "American Kitchens, Luxury Bathrooms, and the Search for a 'Normal' Life in Postsocialist Hungary," *Ethnos* 67, no. 3 (2002): 369–400.

12. For lack of space I cannot outline even the basics of class analysis, its classic or contemporary debates. I still need to make a few clarifications on the shifting use of related concepts, such as "bourgeois," "middle-class," "citizen," and "elite" for the purpose of this essay:

- The Hungarian term *polgár* merges the meaning of "citizen" and "bourgeois." Gil Eyal, Ivan Szelenyi, and Eleanor Townsley, *Making Capitalism without Capitalists: Class Formation and Elite Struggles in Post-Communist Central Europe* (London: Verso, 1998).

- Historians tend to use "bourgeois" and "middle-class" interchangeably due to the historical origins of the bourgeoisie. In sociological class analysis, however, it predominantly designates in-between, sometimes contradictory, class positions. Nicos Poulantzas, *Classes in Contemporary Capitalism* (London: New Left Books, 1975); Erik Olin Wright, *Classes* (London: Verso, 1986); Erik Olin Wright et al., *The Debate on Classes* (London: Verso, 1989).

- Analysts of postsocialist social change tend to refer to "elites," partly and understandably to avoid opening debates about the legacy of class analysis.

13. In contemporary politics the term has assumed a new meaning: especially in center-right discourses it is used to signal a supposedly nonideological position that is to transcend party politics—with special regards to oppositional ones—and encompass the entire nation, conveniently bracketing the class-base of the term.

14. Interview with E.N.

15. Other than slavishly following fashion, the "American" kitchen is usually the sign of less cooking and signals the disappearance of hired labor in the family, the housewife doing the cooking rather than an employee.

16. *Szép Házak* 6 (2005): 44–45.

17. Ibid., 188–9.

18. Interview with E.V.

19. Being a newcomer to a class is a no-win game. Aspiring bourgeois are bound to make mistakes since they lack the most bourgeois of bourgeois virtues: a sense of proportion.

20. *Élet és Irodalom*, January 14, 2005, 7.

21. Interview with E.V.

22. Werner Sombart, *The Quintessence of Capitalism: A Study of the History and Psychology of the Modern Business Man*, trans. M. Epstein (1915; New York: Howard Fertig, 1967); Zukin, "Mimesis."

23. Neil Brenner and Nik Theodore, "Cities and the Geogrpahies of 'Actually Existing Neoliberalism,'" in *Spaces of Neoliberalism: Urban Restructuring in North America and Western Europe*, ed. Neil Brenner and Nik Theodore, 2-32 (Oxford: Blackwell, 2002).

24. Edward J. Blakely and Mary Gail Snyder, *Fortress America: Gated Communities in the United States* (Washington, DC: Brookings Institution, 1997).

25. Robert Fishman, *Bourgeois Utopias: The Rise and Fall of Suburbia* (New York: Basic Books, 1987).

26. Ibid., 4.

27. David Harvey, *Spaces of Hope* (Berkeley: University of California Press, 2000).

28. Ibid., after Louis Marin.

29. Evan McKenzie, *Privatopia: Homeowner Associations and the Rise of Residential Private Government* (New Haven: Yale University Press, 1994).

30. Harvey, *Spaces of Hope*, 152.

31. Interview with E.V.

32. Gábor Csanádi and János Ladányi, "Budapest—a városszerkezet törénetének és a különbözö társadalmi csoportok városszerkezeti elhelyezkedésének vizsgálata," in *Szociológiai Mühelytanulmányok* (Budapest: MKKE, 1987).

33. Partha Chatterjee, "Are Indian Cities Becoming Bourgeois?" in *The Politics of the Governed: Reflections of Popular Politics in Most Parts of the World* (New York: Columbia University Press, 2004).

34. Ibid.

35. Endre Sik, "Emberpiac a Moszkva téren [Men's Market in Moscow Square], 1995–2005" (manuscript).

36. Rakesh Kochhar, *Latino Labor Report, 2004: More Jobs to New Immigrants but at Lower Wages* (Washington, DC: Pew Hispanic Center, 2005).

37. Interview with E.V.

38. Gábor Gyáni, *Család, háztartás és városi cselédség* (Budapest: Magvetö, 1983).

39. Ethnic households are more directly connected to networks of labor migration. Although domestic labor of other ethnic origins may be comparatively cheaper and just as reliable, the existence of Hungarian diasporas and the uneven development of the region makes it possible to draw domestic laborers from Hungarian-speaking communities, pri-

marily in Romania. It is also a necessity: with Hungarian an insignificant world language, the crowd of ambitious student babysitters flocking into the UK and the United States from abroad to learn English is entirely missing in Hungary. The argument that many parents gave in a prestigious Chicago private school when choosing Spanish as a foreign language for their children, however encouraging, is completely unimaginable in Hungary: "We chose Spanish so that the kids can talk to the maid and the nanny."

40. Jürgen Kocka, "The Middle Classes in Europe," *Journal of Modern History* 67, no. 4 (1995): 787.

41. Interestingly, it is the nonfeminist and non-Marxist—sometimes confessedly anti-Marxist—Hannah Arendt who thematizes the unacknowledged foundations of the acclaimed sphere of the public and politics in her simultaneous analysis of labor, work, and action (Norma Claire Moruzzi, *Speaking through the Mask: Hannah Arendt and the Politics of Social Identity* [Ithaca: Cornell University Press, 2000]). The private realm of the household contains labor, the drudgery of necessity, repetition, sweat and the body, and reproduction that do not bring lasting results yet are needed for the higher registers of both the *vita activa* and *contemplativa* (Hannah Arendt, *The Human Condition* [Garden City, NY: Doubleday, 1959]).

42. See Erik Olin Wright's work to make Marxian class analysis more operationalizable and more accommodating to "non-classy" class positions that balance domination and exploitation as foundations of class relations, including control over the operation of production as well as the labor of workers. His work problematizes the gender-blindness of class analysis but does not mention control over domestic paid labor (Wright, *Classes*; Wright, *Debate on Classes*). This is partly due to the fact that domestic workers, even though predominantly paid by the "men of the house," tend to fall under the control of women—housewives or wage earners—whose class position is already ambiguous in the shadow of their husbands.

43. Gyáni, 1994.

44. Kocka, "Middle Classes," 805.

45. Ibid., 787.

46. Saskia Sassen, "Global Cities and Survival Circuits," in *Global Women: Nannies, Maids, and Sex Workers in the New Economy*, ed. Barbara Ehrenreich and Arlie Russell Hochschild, 254–74 (New York, 2003).

47. Bridget Anderson, *Doing the Dirty Work? The Global Politics of Domestic Labour* (London: Zed Books, 2000); Barbara Ehrenreich and Arlie Russell Hochschild, eds., *Global Women: Nannies, Maids, and Sex Workers in the New Economy* (New York, 2003); and Rhacel Salazar Parreñas, *Servants of Globalization: Women, Migration and Domestic Work* (Palo Alto, CA: Stanford University Press, 2001).

48. Ehrenreich and Hochschild, *Global Women*.

Chapter 10: "Extreme Makeover"

1. Thanks to the long-defunct Grupo de Investigación de la Conflictividad Urbana, as well as Sandra Ocampo. This essay is written in memory of Sandra's mother, Eva Kohn, who would likely have disagreed with its thrust.

2. Alonso Salazar, *La Parábola de Pablo: Auge y caída de un gran capo del narcotráfico* (Bogotá: Planeta, 2002). Scare quotes are used around "cartel" because the group of cocaine entrepreneurs organized under that rubric worked in small, overlapping circles; hardly consonant with general usage of the term.

3. Mario Arango Jaramillo, *Los funerales de Antioquia la grande: La bancarrota del modelo económico antioqueño* (Medellín: Ed. J.M. Arango, 1990), 25. See also Marleny Cardona et al., "Escenarios de homicidios en Medellín (Colombia) entre 1990–2002," *Revista Cubana Salud Pública* 31:3 (online) (July–September 2005), scielo.sld.cu. For annual homicide figures from 1981 to 1996, see Ana Jaramillo et al., *En la encrucijada: Conflicto y cultura política en los noventa* (Medellín: Corporación Región, 1998), 110–11.

4. Quoted in *El Colombiano*, 20 August 2005, www.elcolombiano.com/proyectos/Colom biamoda2005/historias/general.htm.

5. "Medellín, ciudad para los negocios," 12 May 2005, www.descifrado.org.

6. The distinction is T.H. Marshall's, but I follow Alan Knight, "Democratic and Revolutionary Traditions in Latin America," *Bulletin of Latin American Research* 20:2 (2001): 147–86.

7. Ann Farnsworth-Alvear, *Dulcinea in the Factory: Myths, Morals, Men, and Women in Colombia's Industrial Experiment, 1905–1960* (Durham, NC: Duke University Press, 2000), xii, 39.

8. Marco Palacios, *Entre la legitimidad y la violenceia: Colombia, 1875–1994* (Bogotá: Norma, 1995), 298.

9. Mike Davis, *Planet of Slums* (New York: Verso, 2006), 16–17.

10. David Bushnell, *The Making of Modern Colombia: A Nation in Spite of Itself* (Berkeley: University of California Press, 1993), 277.

11. Alonso Salazar, *No nacimos pa' semilla* (Bogotá: CINEP, 1990), 86–87; Ramiro Ceballos Melguizo, "The Evolution of Armed Conflict in Medellín: An Analysis of Major Actors," *Latin American Perspectives* 28:1 (January 2001): 120–21.

12. Although Steven Dudley's *Walking Ghosts: Murder and Guerrilla Politics in Colombia* (New York: Routledge, 2004) argues the opposite, it offers evidence to support more nuanced interpretations, like Mauricio Romero's in *Paramilitares y autodefensas, 1982–2003* (Bogotá: IEPRI, 2003).

13. Ana Carrigan, *The Palace of Justice: A Colombian Tragedy* (New York: Four Walls Eight Windows, 1993).

14. Mary Roldán, "Cocaine and the 'Miracle' of Modernity in Medellín," in Paul Gootenberg, ed., *Cocaine: Global Histories* (London: Routledge, 1999), 165–83.

15. Melguizo, "The Evolution of Armed Conflict in Medellín," 113. Interviews with lawyers, journalists, community activists, and former militia leaders, Medellín, Colombia, August 2000. See also William Estrada and Adriana Gómez, eds., *Somos historia: Comuna nororiental* (Medellín, n.d.), 65–88, 106–7, 128–33.

16. Interviews with militia members, Medellín, June 1999; May 2000; July 2002.

17. Cited in Ana Jaramillo et al., *En la encrucijada: Conflicto y cultura política en los noventa*, 65, n.9.

18. Arango Jaramillo, *Los funerales de Antioquia la grande*, 280; Daniel Pécaut, *Guerra contra la sociedad* (Bogotá: Espesa, 2001), 173.

19. Interview with former members of *La Ramada*, Medellín, May 2000.

20. Roldán, "Cocaine and the "Miracle" of Modernity," 175.

21. Alonso Salazar, *La Parábola de Pablo: Auge y caída de un gran capo del narcotráfico* (Bogotá: Planeta, 2002), 307–14.

22. Gonzalo Sánchez, "Introduction: Problems of Violence, Prospects for Peace," in Charles Bergquist et al., eds., *Violence in Colombia, 1990–2000: Waging War and Negotiating Peace* (Wilmington, DE: Scholarly Resources, 2001), 11.

23. Astrid Mireya Téllez Ardilla, *Milicias Populares: Otra expresión de la violencia social en Colombia* (Bogotá: Rodriguez Quito, 1995), 107. See also Fernando Cubides, "From Private to Public Violence: The Paramilitaries," in Charles Bergquist et al., eds., *Violence in Colombia, 1990–2000: Waging War and Negotiating Peace* (Wilmington, DE: Scholarly Resources, 2001), 131.

24. Roldán, "Cocaine and the 'Miracle' of Modernity," 178. See also Joseph Conteras, *Biografía no autorizada de Álvaro Uribe Vélez: El señor de las Sombras* (Bogotá: Editorial Oveja Negra, 2002), 120–46.

25. Though said "office" does not officially exist, interviews with traffickers in Medellín in December 2004, April and August 2005, and June 2006, revealed business as usual.

26. Quoted in Amnesty International, "The Paramilitaries in Medellín: Demobilization or Legalization?" September 2005, 35: www.amnesty.org.

27. Quoted in Javier Sulé, "Medellín Orgulloso," *El País* (Madrid), 17 May 2006.

28. James Parsons, *Antioquia's Corridor to the Sea: An Historical Geography of the Settlement of Urabá* (Berkeley: University of California Press, 1967).

29. Greg Grandin, *The Last Colonial Massacre: Latin America in the Cold War* (Chicago: University of Chicago Press, 2004), 14.

Chapter 12: Bunkering in Paradise

1. *Wall Street Journal*, October 3, 2003, A18.

2. Data supplied by ICSC (International Council of Shopping Centers) in the cover story of its May 2003 bulletin "Lifestyle Centers: Do They Work?," available from http://icsc.org/srch/sct/sct0503/?region=. Last consultation March 20, 2006.

3. Mike Davis, *City of Quartz: Excavating the Future in Los Angeles* (New York: Random House, 1992), 240–44.

4. On the reintroduction of nature to the city, see the review *Communications* (no. 74, 2003), in particular Isabelle Auricoste, "Urbaniste moderne et symbolique du gazon," 19–32.

5. Michel Ragon, *Histoire de l'architecture et de l'urbanisme modernes*, 3 vol. (Paris: Casterman, 1986), vol. 1, "Idéologie et pionniers (1800–1910)," 123.

6. On the birth of the gridiron and its modifications: Kenneth T. Jackson, *Crabgrass Frontier: The Suburbanization of the United States* (Oxford: Oxford University Press, 1985), ch. 4.

7. Joel Garreau, *Edge City: Life on the New Frontier* (New York: Doubleday, 1991), glossary, 443, 453, 458.

8. Franco Moretti, "Homo Palpitans: Balzac's Novels and Urban Personalità," in *Signs Taken for Wonders*, 3rd ed. (London: Verso, 1987), 127.

9. Lewis Mumford, *The City in History: Its Origins, Transformations, and Its Prospect* (New York: Harcourt Brace, 1961), 494.

10. ". . . Fuggitive beauté . . . / Ne te verrai-je plus que dans l'éternité? / Ailleurs, bien loin d'ici / Trop tard! *Jamais* peut-être! / Car j'ignore où tu fuis, tu ne sais où je vais": Charles Baudelaire, *A une passante*, in *Les fleurs du mal* (1857) (Paris: Librairie Générale Française, Livres de Poche, 1972), 232.

11. For a fuller discussion of the emptying of the street, see Marco d'Eramo, *The Pig and the Skyscraper: Chicago: A History of Our Future* (London: Verso, 2003), 117–18.

12. A process analogous to that which occurred in late antiquity when the emptying of cities led to a decline in the genres of drama and theater, which were performed in public spaces, and the rise of the novel, which could be read in the intimacy of the home: see Franz Altheim, *Gesicht vom Abend zum Morgen. Von de Antike zur Mittelalter* (Frankfurt am Mein: Fischer Bücherei, 1955) and *Dall'antichità al Medioevo* (Florence: Sansoni, 1961), 16–24.

13. CNN / Money, Jan. 12, 2005.

14. Theboxtank [a collaborative Weblog focused on big urbanism], Aug. 7, 2005: www.theboxtank.com / walmartbox / lifestyle_centers /, last visited Mar. 20, 2006.

15. Kate Jacobs, "The Manchurian Main Street," in *Metropolitan Magazine* [e-newsletter], May 16, 2005: www.metropolismag.com / cda / story.php?artid=1296, last visited Mar. 20, 2006.

16. Cited in Garreau, *Edge City*, 232 (my emphasis).

17. Robert E. Park, Ernest W. Burgess, Roderick D. McKenzie, *The City* (Chicago: University of Chicago Press, 1967), 40–41.

18. Davis, *City of Quartz*, 246–48; and Teresa P. R. Caldeira, *City of Walls: Crime, Segregation, and Citizenship in Saõ Paulo* (Berkeley: University of California Press, 2000).

19. Edward J. Blakeley and Mary Gail Snyder, *Fortress America: Gated Communities in the United States* (Washington DC: Brookings Institute Press, 1997).

20. Evan McKenzie, "Common-Interest Housing in the Communities of Tomorrow," *Housing Policy Debate*, vol. 14, I, issues 1 and 2 (2003): 204.

21. Ibid., 220.

22. Robert Nozick, *Anarchy, State and Utopia* (New York: Basic Books, 2000), 168–69.

23. *Amarillo Globe News*, June 29, 2001.

24. Garreau, *Edge City*, 190–91.

25. McKenzie, "Common Interest Housing," 207, and Community Association Institute 1998.

26. Cited by Evan McKenzie, *Privatopia: Homeowner Associations and the Rise of Residential Private Government* (New Haven: Yale University Press, 1996), 186.

27. Michael E. Hunt (ed.), *Retirement Communities: An American Original* (New York: Haworth Press, 1984), 1.

28. Lewis Mumford, "For Older People: Not Segregation but Integration," *Architectural Record* 119 (May 1956): 191–94.

29. Emil Bloch, "Ein Platz an der Sonne," *Die Zeit*, June 26, 2003; and the documentary *Sun City*, by Herbert Fell, produced by Arte.

30. Worth mentioning in this regard—other than Hunt, *Retirement Communities*—is Katherine McMillan Heintz, *Retirement Communities, for Adults Only* (New Brunswick, NJ: Center for Urban Policy Research, Rutgers University, 1976), and—from the human geography and urban studies perspective—Hubert B. Stroud's extensive overview, *The Promise of Paradise: Recreational and Retirement Communities in the United States since 1950* (Baltimore: Johns Hopkins University Press, 1995). For bibliographic material and references on retirement communities, see also Raymond J. Burby and Shirley Weiss et al., *New Communities U.S.A.* (Lexington, MA: D.C. Health and Company, Lexington Books, 1976).

31. *New York Times*, October 5, 1986.

32. Joel Garreau, *Edge City*, 190.

Chapter 14: "Hell Is Other People"

1. "The 400 Richest Americans," *Forbes*, Sept. 22, 2005, www.forbes.com/lists/2005/54/ETX7.html.

2. "Ecologically sensitive": from Ted Turner's Web site, www.tedturner.com/enterprises_properties.html.

3. Susan Gallagher, "Learning Montana's Lay of the Land," *Southern Oregon Mail Tribune*, March 27, 2005, www.mailtribune.com/archive/2005/0327/biz/stories/02biz.htm; lwww.hallhall.com/ranches/mt/index.html.

4. Ken Auletta, "The Lost Tycoon," *New Yorker*, April 23, 2001, www.kenauletta.com/2001_04_23_thelosttycoon.html.

5. Gail Schontzler, "Indian Leaders Honor Turner During Historic Meeting On The Flying D," *Bozeman Daily Chronicle*, August 17, 2002, http://bozemandailychronicle.com/articles/ 2002/08/17/news407.txt.

6. Menu at www.tedsmontanagrill.com/menu.html.

7. Jane Fonda's recipe for bison osso buco: http://evaamurri.com/members/recipes/recipes33.html.

8. Auletta, "The Lost Tycoon."

9. At Turner's Web site, http://www.tedturner.com/legacy_interview.html.

10. Turner Endangered Species Fund 2004 Annual Report, www.tesf.org/turner/tesf/reports/.

11. Scott McMillion, "Poisoning Begins on Cherry Creek," *Bozeman Daily Chronicle*, August 5, 2003, http://bozemandailychronicle.com/articles/2003/08/05/news/003cherry ckbzbigs.txt; McMillion, "Court Rules In Favor Of Cherry Creek Fish Poisoning Project," *Bozeman Daily Chronicle,* March 26, 2004, http://bozemandailychronicle.com/articles/2004/03/26/news/cherrybzbigs.txt.

12. McMillion, "Poisoning Begins."

13. Jack Hitt, "One Nation, Under Ted." *Outside*, December 2001, http:// outside.away.com/outside/environment/200112/200112under_ted.html; also at www.tedturner.com/download/Articles/OutsideMagazineOneNationUnderTed_12_01.pdf; U.S. Fish and Wildlife Service, Endangered Species Program, "Westslope Cutthroat Trout," http://mountain-prairie.fws.gov/species/fish/wct/.

14. McMillion, "Poisoning Begins"; Hitt, "One Nation."

15. Scott McMillion, "Work on Cherry Creek Reaches Third Year," *Bozeman Daily Chronicle,* August 17, 2005, http://bozemandailychronicle.com/articles/2005/08/17/news/cherrycreek.txt.

16. "Vermejo Park Ranch Elk Hunting," www.vermejoparkranch.com/Elk.php.

17. "Vermejo Park Ranch Rates for 2005 Hunting Season," www.vermejopark ranch.com/HuntRates.php.

18. Gail Schontzler, "Hunting Season Ends," *Bozeman Daily Chronicle*, Dec. 12, 2002, http://bozemandailychronicle.com/articles/2002/12/02/news/huntingbzbigs.txt.

19. Paul Tharp, "Ted Sacrifices Green Goals For Greenbacks," *New York Post*, April 29, 2004.

20. Mark Matthews, "Ted Turner Makes a Deal," *High Country News* (Paonia, CO), November 25, 1996, www.hcn.org/servlets/hcn.Article?article_id=2920.

21. Ibid.

22. Nick Gevock, "Landowner Sues County, Turner over Access to Property," *Bozeman Daily Chronicle*, Jan. 16, 2004, http://bozemandailychronicle.com/articles/2004/01/16/news/roadlawsuitbzbigs.txt.

23. www.vermejoparkranch.com/Corporate.php.

24. Monte Burke and William P. Barrett, "This Land Is My Land," *Forbes*, Oct. 6, 2003, www.forbes.com/forbes/2003/1006/050_print.html.

25. Mark Bixler, "Turner to Stump for DMZ Ecology," *Atlanta Journal Constitution,* July 23, 2005, www.ajc.com/search/content/auto/epaper/editions/today/news_241efd2e96662 19f0035.html.

Chapter 15: People Like Hicks

All Briefs and the Joint Appendix are catalogued under 2002 U.S. 371 *and are available through* LexisNexis.

1. A more detailed analysis of the case of Kevin Hicks as it traveled the lower courts into the Supreme Court can be found in Don Mitchell, "Property Rights, the First Amendment, and Judicial Anti-Urbanism: The Strange Case of *Hicks v. Virginia,*" *Urban Geography* (forthcoming). This chapter is drawn from that analysis.

2. See *Hicks v. Commonwealth* 36 Va. App. 49 (2001), 251; *Virginia v. Hicks* 123 S. Ct. 2191(2003), 2,195.

3. Brief of the American Civil Liberties Union (ACLU) and the National Association of Criminal Defense Lawyers, 2002, 7.

4. The Council of Large Public Housing Authorities declares trespass-barment rules to be "a crucial . . . tool . . . to prevent wrongdoers from gaining access to public housing grounds." It was a tool that allowed PHAs to "act as landlords" and better control who could and could not be on their property (Brief of Council of Large Public Housing Authorities et al., 2002, 4–5).

5. Brief of City of Richmond and Richmond Redevelopment and Housing Authority, 2002, 8.

6. ACLU, Brief, 2002, 7, n.5.

7. Sentencing statement of Judge Nance, Joint Appendix, 2002, 68–72.

8. For a review of public forum doctrine as it relates to the geography of political protest, see Don Mitchell, *The Right to the City: Social Justice and the Fight for Public Space* (New York: Guilford, 2003), chapter 2.

9. *Hague v. CIO* 307 U.S. 496 (1939).

10. *Hicks v. Commonwealth* 33 Va. App. 561 (2000), in Joint Appendix, 2002.

11. Ibid., 2002, 111.

12. Ibid.

13. *Hicks v. Commonwealth* 36 Va. App. 49 (2001), in Joint Appendix, 2002, 131.

14. Ibid., 136.

15. Brief of the States of Alabama, Alaska, Delaware, Florida, Hawaii, Indiana, Mississippi, Missouri, Ohio, Oklahoma, Oregon, South Dakota, Tennessee, Texas, Utah, and the Commonwealth of Puerto Rico; and Brief for the United States.

16. See e.g., ACLU Brief and Brief of the Richmond Tenants Organization, Charlottesville Public Housing Association of Residents, ENPHRONT, and Massachusetts Union of Public Housing Tenants.

17. *Virginia v. Hicks* 123 S. Ct. 2191 (2003), 2,197.

18. Ibid., 2,197–98.

19. Ibid., 2,198, original emphasis.

20. Ibid.

21. Ibid.

22. Henri Lefebvre, "The Right to the City," in *Writings on Cities* (Oxford: Blackwell, 1996 [1968], edited and translated by E. Kofman and E. Lebas).

23. "A Trio of Good Rulings," *New York Times*, 17 June 2003, 26.

24. "Curfew What a Stinker," *Private Eye* 1138, 5 August 2005, 27.

25. Quoted in "Curfew What a Stinker."

26. "Blair v. the Yobs," *Independent*, 10 January 2006, 1.

27. Quoted in "Curfew What a Stinker."

28. "Soothing the Savage Breast," *Economist*, 14 January 2006, 57.

29. "Court Lifts Begging ASBO," *Nottingham Evening Post*, 29 December 2005, 21.

30. "The Supreme Court, 2002 Term: Leading Cases: I. Constitutional Law: 3. Trespass Policies," *Harvard Law Review* 117 (2003): 359–69.

Chapter 16: Hubrispace

1. J.G. Ballard, *Highrise* (New York: Popular Library, 1978).

2. Colin Joyce, "On Top of Tokyo, Views of Modern Art," *Los Angeles Times*, Oct. 18, 2003, E1. See also the Mori's Web site: http://www.mori.art.museum/html/eng/architecture .html.

3. http://www.mori.art.museum/html/eng/mission.html: The Mori's mission is pointedly agnostic between the East and West, and stipulates no permanent collection at least for a period after opening: "15. DECIDE WHAT KIND OF COLLECTION WOULD BE MOST APPROPRIATE ONCE IT HAS BEEN OPERATING FOR TWO YEARS."

4. To extend the comparison, I imagine "Sleepless in Translation": Tragedy would beget farce in a Mori sequel to *Highrise*. Fueled by news coverage of sensationally offensive art, a mob storms the penthouse museum, only to find it evacuated, save for a few predictably offensive works—maybe some Mapplethorpe nudes, the dung Madonna by Chris Ofili, or Andres Serrano's *Piss Christ*. The crowd, however, is hushed by the gallery's pristine silence, quickly sated by sushi and sake, then hopelessly distracted by the view. Romance ensues, saccharine but superstylized, rather than apocalypse.

5. Joan Didion, "The Getty," in *The White Album* (New York: Simon & Schuster: 1979), 78.

6. For a quantitative approach to comparing the major New York museums, see Diane Crane, *The Transformation of the Avant-Garde: The New York Art World, 1940–1985* (Chicago: University of Chicago Press, 1987).

7. See Hugh Eakins, "Museums Under Fire on Ancient Artifacts," *New York Times*, Nov. 17, 2005, B1, B8; and Jason Felch, "Munitz Steps Down as Head of Getty," *Los Angeles Times*, Feb. 10, 2006.

8. Eileen Hooper-Greenhill, *Museums and the Shaping of Knowledge* (London: Routledge, 1992).

9. Thomas A. Markus, *Buildings + Power: Freedom and Control in the Origin of Modern Building Types* (London: Routledge, 1993).

10. Hooper-Greenhill, *Museums*, 69–71.

11. http://www.recentpast.org/types/skyscraper/2columbus/: "Designed by Edward Durell Stone and completed in 1964, Huntington Hartford's Gallery of Modern Art at 2 Columbus Circle has been loved, loathed, and continues to be at the center of heated debate concerning modern architecture and its preservation."

12. Steven Conn, *Museums and American Intellectual Life, 1876–1926* (Chicago: University of Chicago Press, 1998), 187.

13. The Peale has been the object of much recent scholarship. Among the most thorough is Susan Stewart, "Death and Life, in That Order, in the Works of Charles Willson Peale," in *Visual Display: Culture Beyond Appearances*, ed. Lynne Cook and Peter Wollen (Seattle: Bay Press, 1995), 30–53.

14. For the Mütter's history, see http://www.collphyphil.org/mutthist.htm.

15. Jonathan Franzen introduced me to the Mercer Museum in his collection of essays, *How to Be Alone* (New York: Farrar, Straus and Giroux, 2002). Steven Conn offers a much more thoroughgoing assessment of both the Mercer and Ford Museums in *Museums and American Intellectual Life, 1876–1926.* (Chicago: University of Chicago, 1998). Basic facts available at: http://www.mercermuseum.org/mercermuseum/mm-facts.htm.

16. John Steele Gordon, *An Empire of Wealth: The Epic History of American Economic Power* (New York: HarperCollins, 2004), 245–55.

17. http://www.frick.org/collection/history.htm.

18. For more on the Barnes Collection see Roberta Smith, "Does It Matter Where This Painting Hangs?" *New York Times*, December 15, 2004, B1, 7; Ralph Blumenthal, "Release of Audit Roils Trust Fight at the Barnes," *New York Times*, May 5, 2003, B1, 8. The Barnes collection, with its 353 Renoirs, Cézannes, Matisses and Picassos alone, has been valued at more than $6 billion, but costly lawsuits and management problems have left the foundation broke and its treasures "captive to the roiling crosscurrents of race and politics, ego and greed," wrote John Anderson, the author of "Art Held Hostage" and a contributing editor to the *American Lawyer*. "The litigation tangle had its origins 90 years ago, when Barnes, an anti-elitist and art-besotted patent-medicine multimillionaire, began assembling a trove of French Post-Impressionist masterpieces and African, medieval and American folk art that became widely regarded as the finest private collection in the nation."

19. Emma Barker, ed., *Contemporary Cultures of Display* (New Haven: Yale/Open University, 1999), 179.

20. *The Field of Cultural Production* (New York: Columbia University Press, 1993), 257.

21. Museums for historical figures outside the fine arts are common as well, e.g., museums for presidents, writers, sport figures, war heroes, local personalities. Arguably, the discussion of museums for specific artists should be viewed in this same light. They have been included in this discussion because of their recent effect on single-patron institutions.

22. For a sense of scale, see http://www.gagosian.com/exhibitions/?gid=5 and http://www.saatchi-gallery.co.uk/virtual-tour.htm.

23. Francesco Dal Co, "House of Dreams and Memories," in *Lotus International 35*, (Venice: Electa, 1982), 122–28.

24. *Underworld* (New York: Scribner, 1997), 86.

25. Paula Harper, "Wolfsonian Redux—Miami, Florida, Museum Makes an Alliance with the State University System," *Art in America*, Jan. 1997.

26. In part because major individual collectors were long-spurned by LACMA and other established museums, Los Angeles has lost a lot of great art, most painfully, in hindsight, the Arensberg and Annenberg collections. See Suzanne Muchnic's "Coralling the Collectors," *Los Angeles Times*, Nov. 27, 2005. She writes, "L.A. galleries are filled with masterworks. Then there are the great ones that got away."

27. Mike Davis interview.

28. For the evolution of the Norton Simon, see http://www.nortonsimon.org/aboutnsm/nsmhistory.asp.

29. Two self-encapsulated local mall projects by Jon Jerde that have become verbs in their own right, meaning roughly to displace urban realities with nearby enclaves—usually a piazza-ring of disguised chain stores.

30. http://www.lannan.org/lf/about/history/.

31. Lawrence Weschler, *Mr. Wilson's Cabinet Of Wonder: Pronged Ants, Horned Humans, Mice on Toast, and Other Marvels of Jurassic Technology* (New York: Vintage, 1995).

32. Robert Smithson dubbed the Guggenheim the "Concrete Stomache" in his 1968 essay, "Quasi-Infinities"; Robert Hughes, refered to MoMA as the "Kremlin of Modernism" recently in the *Guardian* (Feb. 2005), though its coinage may be earlier: http://www.guardian.co.uk/arts/features/story/0,,1337482,00.html.

33. An heir to the Schlumberger fortune, Dominique de Menil (1908–1997) emigrated to the United States in 1941 and began collecting art. Together with her husband, she established the Menil Foundation in Houston. Her daughter Philippa founded Dia in the mid-1970s with Heiner Friedrich and Helen Winkler. http://www.diacenter.org/exhibs_b/warhol-patronage/.

34. Benefactors Solomon Guggenheim and Nelson Rockefeller were both rumored to have died in the throes of passion: see http://www.hedyobeil.com/hilla_rebay.html and http://home.earthlink.net/~zkkatz/page67.html.

35. See Koolhaas et al., *CONTENT* (New York: Taschen, 2004).

36. Kevin Pratt, "Player Piano," *ArtForum*, Sept. 2004, 77: "a recent readjustment of architectural priorities within the tightly knit world of museum trustees and directors had had one obvious consequence: Rem Koolhaas is out; Renzo Piano is in."

37. See Paul Werner, *Museum, Inc.: Inside the Global Art World* (Chicago: Prickly Paradigm, 2005).

38. The development is currently imperiled. "The Hong Kong Government retreated from plans to build one of the world's largest cultural centers after real-estate developers

refused to participate, complaining that the financial terms had become too onerous." They were asked to ante up US$3.87 billion for a trust fund to operate the complex after construction. (Keith Bradsher, *New York Times*, February 22, 2006, B1.)

39. Paul Allen's Music Experience in Seattle, originally titled the Jimi Hendrix Museum, may be naiveté writ large, and Paul Lewis's $70-million bailout of the Guggenheim now looks rash in the wake of his leaving the board, but Broad found ways to leverage his collection, gifts, and directorships on an alphabet soup of institutions (MoCA, LACMA, MoMA) into an unprecedented sphere of influence over the reception of contemporary art—as well as vastly increasing the value of his own collection.

Chapter 17: Monastery Chic

1. For Mount Calvary, see http://www.vcn.bc.ca/ims-hq/pilgrim20.htm (accessed 4/7/2006); confirmed in a telephone call on April 7, 2006. The six-month wait for a room at New Camaldoli Hermitage was confirmed in a telephone inquiry on Feb. 27, 2006.

2. According to Tamala M. Edwards, "Get Thee To a Monastery," *Time* 152.5 (Aug. 3, 1998): 52–54, the wait at the Abbey of Gethsemani in Kentucky (popularized by Thomas Merton) is one year, as is that for a room at an unnamed Vermont monastery. An article in *Commonweal* notes that at a Trappist monastery in Spencer, Mass., one must reserve a room six months in advance: Vincent P. Stanton, "The Last Word—Be Still—Experiences at Religious Retreat," *Commonweal* 127.2 (Jan. 28, 2000): 31.

3. Timothy L. Smith, "Religion and Ethnicity in America," *American Historical Review* 83.5 (1978): 1,155–85; here 1,181.

4. Wade Clark Roof, Anne E. Patrick, Ronald L. Grimes, and Bill J. Leonard, "Forum: American Spirituality," *Religion and American Culture* 9.2 (1999): 131–57.

5. See Edwards, "Get Thee to a Monastery"; Nancy Shute, "Into and out of the Mystic (Religious Retreats in Northern California)," *U.S. News & World Report* 126.15 (April 19, 1999): 86; Robert Nelson, "Advancing Retreats: The Spirituality Minded Seek a Respite from Daily Life," *Omaha World Herald* (Nebraska), March 13, 1999, 57; Maja Beckstrom, "Retreats Gaining Ground; People Seek Renewal in Spiritual Getaways," *Plain Dealer* (Cleveland, OH), July 15, 1995, 6E; and Janice Shumake, "Retreat Offers Rest, Relaxation, Renewal," *Post and Courier* (Charleston, SC), Jan. 1, 1998, 1.

6. Kimberly Winston, "Get Thee to a Monastery," *Publishers Weekly* 247:15 (April 10, 2000): 37–9.

7. http://www.charming-spain-hotels.com/en/321/ANDALUCIA/Cadiz/San-Martin-del-Tesorillo/Hotel-Monasterio-de-San-Martin (accessed 1/17/2006) and http://www.lodging-in-spain/hotel_San_Martin_del_Tesorillo/228809/Hotel_Monasterio_de_San_ Martin_ 1.htm (accessed 1/17/2006).

8. Press release, undated, "Rocco Forte Hotels Expands Into Prague." I thank Susan Heady of Rocco Forte Hotels for sending me the release and answering my questions.

9. Benedictine Rule, chapter 53: "Concerning the Reception of Guests." For an accessible English translation, see Timothy Fry, *The Rule of Saint Benedict in English* (Collegeville, MN: 1981), 73. For a description of the customs associated with the receiving of guests in a monastery, see Léo Moulin, *La vie quotidienne des religieux au moyen âge, X–XV siècle* (Paris, 1978), 220–22. For an overview of the history of monastic hospitality, see Christine Pohl, *Making Room: Recovering Hospitality as a Christian Tradition* (Grand Rapids, MI, 1999), 36–60.

10. On medieval travel, see Olivia Remie Constable, *Housing the Stranger in the Mediterranean World: Lodging, Trade, and Travel in Late Antiquity and the Middle Ages* (Cambridge, 2003).

11. W. Scott Blanchard, "Petrarch and the Genealogy of Asceticism," *Journal of the History of Ideas* 62.3 (2001): 413.

12. Guillaume de Puylaurens, *Historia Albigensium*, in M. Bouquet et al., eds. *Recueil des historiens des Gaules et de la France* (Paris, 1737–1904), 19:214–15. Count Raymond, the main target of the antiheretical Albigensian Crusade (1209–29), was not himself accused of unorthodox belief, but was excommunicated for being "soft" on heresy. Caroline A. Bruzelius, "Hearing Is Believing: Clarissan Architecture, ca. 1213–1340," *Gesta* 31.2 (1992): 86, notes that in the thirteenth and fourteenth centuries retreat to the Convent of Santa Maria Donnaregina was a fashionable form of devotion among noble Neapolitan ladies.

13. In the foundation charter of the monastery of Cluny (910), the notoriously brutal Duke William of Acquitaine acknowledged this quite explicitly: "the providence of God has so provided for certain rich men that, by means of their transitory possessions, if they use them well, they may be able to merit everlasting rewards. . . . although I myself am unable to despise all things, nevertheless by receiving despisers of this world, whom I believe to be righteous, I may receive the reward of the righteous." (E.F. Henderson, *Select Historical Documents of the Middle Ages* (London, 1910), 329–333 (http://www.fordham.edu/HALSALL/source/chart-cluny.html).

14. For a survey of the history of this doctrine, see David Heyd, *Supererogation* (Cambridge, 1982).

15. Edwards, "Get Thee to a Monastery." Kathleen Norris, whose book, *Cloister Walk*, is credited by many with starting the fad for monastic retreat, is Presbyterian. Sara Hopkins-Powell, "A College President Finds Silence for a Week," *Chronicle of Higher Education* 47:42 (June 29, 2001), B5, writes that "I am not Catholic and have not been a churchgoer for much of my adult life." According to Linda McNatt ("A Search for Serenity: The Well, A Religious Retreat, Offers Peace and Solitude in a Pastoral Setting," *The Virginian Pilot*, October 11, 1995, 6), although The Well, a religious retreat in Suffolk, Virginia, is owned by the Catholic Diocese of Richmond, "only about half the people and churches it now serves are Catholic." On the salvific economy of the Puritans, see the still-influential work of Edmund S. Morgan, *Visible Saints: The History of a Puritan Idea* (Ithaca, NY, 1963).

16. Edwards, "Get Thee to a Monastery;" Winston, "Get Thee to a Monastery" ("'The retreat market has gone way beyond the Catholic Church,' Bauer noted.").

17. "Forum: American Spirituality," 156; Edwards, "Get Thee to a Monastery;" Winston,

"Get Thee to a Monastery." On "spiritual shopping," see Wade Clark Roof, A *Generation of Seekers: The Spiritual Journeys of the Baby Boom Generation* (New York and San Francisco, 1993).

18. In 1967 Martin E. Marty lumped "Trappist monasteries" together with southern Californian cults in "The Spirit's Holy Errand: The Search for a Spiritual Style in Secular America," *Daedalus* 96:1 (1967): 99–115.

19. For example, a publisher of religious books asserts of the turn toward monasticism, "It is not as ephemeral as books on angels. It is a recovery of a major tradition in Christianity that was long lost." Quoted in Winston, "Get Thee to a Monastery." A Presbyterian visitor to the Abbey of the Genesee interviewed by *Time* magazine remarked of the monastic routine: "This has an authenticity to it. It was not manufactured 15 weeks ago." (Quoted in Edwards, "Get Thee to a Monastery.")

20. Winston, "Get Thee to a Monastery."

21. McNatt, "A Search for Serenity." See also Nelson, "Advancing Retreats": "[monastic retreat represents] a return to some fundamental spiritual ideals."

22. Melissa Jones, "Desert Monks: A Unique Hermit Community in the Colorado Wilderness Offers an Antidote to 21st Century Materialism," *National Catholic Reporter* 39.16 (Feb. 21, 2003): 34. The testimonials of individuals who have gone on monastic retreat seem (initially) to support this assumption: they are redolent with the language of anti-modernity and world rejection. A *Travel Girl* article bills the retreat as an opportunity to "get away from it all." Andrea Braslavsky, "Making a Journey Within: Monastic Retreats Can Be a Salve for the Soul," *Travel Girl* 2.2 (July/August 2004): 71–77, 152.

23. This characterization of the gated community is from Kirstin D. Maxwell, "Gated Communities: Selling the Good Life," *Plan Canada*, 44.4 (winter 2004): 20–22.

24. It is worth noting that the retreatants quoted in this article come not from major urban centers but from such prosperous and physically attractive localities as an Oregon college town; Simi Valley, CA; Beverly, MA; Setauket, Long Island; and Menlo Park, CA.

25. http://www.spiritsite.com/centers/centers1.shtml (accessed 4/4/2006).

26. http://www.lacasademaria-elbosque.org/aboutus.html (accessed 4/4/2006).

27. http://www.jrh-cleveland.org/facilities3.html (accessed 4/4/2006.)

28. http://home.centurytel.net/spiritualitycenter/index.html (accessed 4/4/2006).

29. Sandi Tarling, "Unwind at a Monastic Retreat," at www.vitalitymagazine.com/node/299 (accessed 4/4/2006).

30. http://www.materdolorosa.org/retreats.html (accessed 4/4/2006).

31. Laura S., "Retreat Reflections: Her View," http://www.trappist.net/newweb/enews_01_12_05.html (accessed 4/4/2006).

32. http://www.shrinemont.com/ (accessed 4/4/2006).

33. Tarling, "Unwind at a Monastic Retreat."

34. Hopkins-Powell, "A College President Finds Silence for a Week."

35. "Jim Wharton" (a pseudonym, at the request of the subject), personal interview, 3/11/2006.

36. Quoted in Patricia Wittberg, "Deep Structure in Community Cultures: The Revival of Religious Orders in Roman Catholicism," *Sociology of Religion* 58:3 (1997): 239–60.

37. Chris Gulker, "Blog: Retreat to Emery House in West Newbury," February 21, 2003, http://www.gulker.com/2003/02/21.html (accessed 4/4/2006).

38. Beckstrom, "Retreats Gaining Ground."

39. Penelope McCain, "Monastic Retreat: A Visit," *Spirituality & Health: The Soul/Body Connection* (fall 1999).

40. "Forum: American Spirituality," 153.

41. See the concluding paragraph of Edwards, "Get Thee to a Monastery": "But not everyone begging for reservations at the Abbey of Gethsemani, Kentucky (wait: one year), or New Camaldoli Hermitage, California (wait: six months, only because they refuse to book any further), is so sincere. The problem is not an entirely new one. The earliest monasteries were founded in the 4th century in the Egyptian desert. As Christianity became legalized and then haute, the Desert Fathers and Mothers found themselves overrun by hipsters from Alexandria and Rome. Father Robert of New Camaldoli, where the spare rooms offer a heart-stopping view of the Pacific—for $30 a night—can relate. A hard call? 'Sometimes,' he sighs, 'the first question is about the pool or the tennis courts.'"

42. For a recent overview of utopian writing and its critics, see Fredric Jameson, *Archeologies of the Future: The Desire Called Utopia and Other Science Fictions* (London and New York, 2005).

43. See Herman Pleij, *Dreaming of Cockaigne: Medieval Fantasies of the Perfect Life*, trans. by Diane Webb (New York, 2001).

44. Thomas Carlyle, *Past and Present* (1843), ed. Richard D. Altick (New York: New York University Press, 1965). On this work, see John M. Ulrich, *Signs of Their Times: History, Labour and the Body in Cobbett, Carlyle, and Disraeli* (Athens, OH, 2002). I thank Dan Monk for directing my attention to Carlyle's text.

45. McCain, "Monastic Retreat: A Visit."

46. "Jim Wharton" (a pseudonym, at the request of the subject), personal interview, 3/11/2006.

47. Braslavsky, "Making a Journey Within."

48. James K., "Retreat Reflections: His View," http://www.trappist.net/newweb/enews_01_12_05.html (accessed 4/4/2006); Laura S., "Retreat Reflections: Her View," http://www.trappist.net/newweb/enews_01_12_05.html (accessed 4/4/2006); Hopkins-Powell, "A College President Finds Silence for a Week;" and Beckstrom, "Retreats Gaining Ground."

49. This observation has become a truism of contemporary social analysis. See, for example, David Harvey, A *Brief History of Neoliberalism* (Oxford, 2005), 4.

50. Jean-Francois Lyotard, *The Postmodern Condition: A Report on Knowledge*, trans. by Geoff Bennington and Brian Massumi (Minneapolis, 1984), identified the short-term contract as characteristic of the postmodern condition, "[supplanting] permanent institutions in the professional, emotional, sexual, cultural, family, and international domains, as well as in political affairs." I would add in religion too.

51. See the epigram to Guy Debord, *Society of the Spectacle*, trans. Ken Knabb (London, 2005), 6 (quoting Ludwig Feuerbach, preface to the 2nd ed. of *The Essence of Christianity*): "But certainly for the present age, which prefers the sign to the thing signified, the copy to the original, representation to reality, the appearance to the essence . . . illusion only is sacred, truth profane. Nay, sacredness is held to be enhanced in proportion as truth decreases and illusion increases, so that the highest degree of illusion comes to be the highest degree of sacredness."

52. Laura S., "Retreat Reflections: Her View," http://www.trappist.net/newweb/enews_01_12_05.html (accessed 4/4/2006); and "Jim Wharton" (a pseudonym, at the request of the subject), personal interview, 3/11/2006.

53. See Terry Eagleton, "Making a Break" (review of Jameson, *Archeologies of the Future*), *London Review of Books* 28.5 (9 March 2006), quoting Karus: "utopias are part of the problem to which they pose as a solution."

Chapter 18: Floating Utopias

1. See http://www.popularmechanics.com/science/transportation/1289186.html.

2. http://news.bbc.co.uk/1/hi/world/americas/532259.stm.

3. See "And Now for Something Completely Different . . . Freedom Ship. The World's Biggest Ship—The World's Newest Tax Haven?" www.escapeartist.com/efam17/Freedom_Shift.html.

4. Jason Burke, "Freedom Ship 'Will Be Target For Terrorists,'" *Observer*, 28 May 2000.

5. The forlorn remnants of Laissez-Faire City's Website is at http://www.lfcity.com/, an outline of the scandal at www.scamdog.com/freedom_projects/?view=laissez_faire_city. For New Utopia, see http://www.carbonfusion.com/utopia/, and a denunciation from a fellow traveller at http://patrifriedman.com/projects/independence/newutopia.html.

6. See http://www.thevenusproject.com/city_think/city_sea.htm, and http://www.seascapel.com.

7. For Women On Waves, see http://www.womenonwaves.org.

8. http://www.sea-code.com.

9. http://www.sealandgov.org.

10. http://www.celestopea.com.

11. See in particular http://seastead.org/commented/paper/review.html, and "Castles in the Sea: A Survey of Artificial Islands and Floating Utopias," by James H. Lee, 2003, at http://www.seastead.org/localres/floating-utopias.

12. http://www.tdrinc.com/nexus.html.

13. Triton Foundation, Inc., *Triton City: A Prototype Floating Community*, prepared for the Department of Housing and Urban Development (Cambridge, MA); reproduced by the Clearinghouse for Federal Scientific and Technical Information, Springfield, VA, 1968.

14. http://www.oceania.org.

15. Hugo Grotius, *The Free Sea* [*Mare liberum*, 1604], trans. by Richard Hakluyt (Indianapolis: Liberty Fund, 2004); and John Selden, *Of the Dominion: or, Ownership of the Sea* [*Mare clausum*, 1635], 2 vols. (New York: Arno, 1972).

16. See China Miéville, *Between Equal Rights: A Marxist Theory of International Law* (Boston: Brill, 2005), 208–14.

17. Francis Ngantcha, *The Right of Innocent Passage and the Evolution of the International Law of the Sea* (New York: Pinter Publishers, 1990), 6.

18. Peter Linebaugh and Marcus Rediker, *The Many-Headed Hydra: Sailors, Slaves, Commoners, and the Hidden History of the Revolutionary Atlantic* (Boston: Beacon Press, 2000).

19. Burke, "Freedom Ship."

20. http://www.guardian.co.uk/international/story/0, ,217795,00.html.

21. http://www.marrder.com/htw/aug99/national.htm http://nolassf.dev.advance.net/businessstory/ship12.html.

22. Lucius Shepard interviewed by Nick Gevers, 2003: http://www.scifi.com/sfw.issue314/interview.html.

23. Details from the collective of grassroots organizations, "Groots": http://www.groots.org/newsflash.htm.

24. http://www.witness.org/option,com_rightsalert/Itemid,178/task,story/alert_id,14/. See also http://www.marrder.com/htw.2003Apr/cultural.htm.

25. See the contributions to issue 13.2, 1998.

26. Hans-Hermann Hoppe, "Natural Order, the State, and the Immigration Problem," *Journal of Libertarian Studies* 16:1 (2002): 75–97, 78, 77.

27. John Hospers, "A Libertarian Argument Against Open Borders," *Journal of Libertarian Studies* 13:2 (1998): 153–65.

28. Ibid., 164–5.

Chapter 19: Hives and Swarms

1. Joe Strummer and the Mescaleros, "Johnny Appleseed," *Global A Go-Go*, 2001, Hellcat Records.

2. Antonio Machado, "Las Moscas," in *Soledades; Galerias, Otros Poemas* (Barcelona: Editorial Labor, 1975), author's translation.

3. Theodor W. Adorno, *Minima Moralia* (NLB, 1974), 39.

4. Ibid., 112–13.

5. Siegfried Kracauer, "The Mass Ornament," in *The Mass Ornament, Weimar Essays*, trans. Thomas Y. Levin (Cambridge, MA: Harvard University Press, 1995), 79.

6. In this connection, see Azar Gat, *A History of Military Thought*, Oxford Historical Monographs (Oxford: Clarendon Press, 1989): 521–608.

7. Eliot A. Cohen, "A Revolution in Warfare," *Foreign Affairs*, vol. 75, issue 2 (March–April 1996): 37–54.

8. John Arquilla and David Ronfeldt, *Swarming and the Future of Conflict* (Santa Monica, CA: Rand, 2000), p.vii and p.1.

9. Cohen, "A Revolution," 45.

10. One of the most fascinating and comprehensive analyses of the changes on the ground can be found in Caroline Croser, "Networking Security in the Space of the City: Event-Ful Battlespaces and the Contingency of the Encounter," Forthcoming, in *Theory and Event* (http://muse.jhu.edu/journals/theory_and_event/toc/index.html).

11. Thomas K. Adams, "The Real Military Revolution," *Parameters*, U.S. Army War College, vol. 30, issue 3 (autumn 2000), 12.

12. Eyal Weizman, "Walking Through Walls," *Theory and Event*, forthcoming.

13. On "nomadology," see: Gilles Deleuze and Félix Guattari, *A Thousand Plateaus: Capitalism and Schizophrenia*, trans. Brian Massumi (Minneapolis: University of Minnesota Press, 1987), 351–474. For my own skepticism concerning the reification of Deleuze and Guattari's epistemology into a practical politics of space, see "The Art of Castramentation," *Assemblage* 36 (Aug. 1998): 64–83. Naveh's own contributions to military science are to be found in Shimon Naveh, *In Pursuit of Military Excellence: The Evolution of Operational Theory* (London: Frank Cass Publishers, 1997). See also Shimon Naveh's "Rhizomic Manoeuver," in *The Dictionary of War*, http://dictionaryofwar.org/en-dict/taxonomy/term/12.

14. Although the Arabic term *faza'* generally refers to surprise or alarm, the term has also referred to modes of combat that closely approximate "pulse tactics" in English.

15. T.E. Lawrence, *The Seven Pillars of Wisdom: A Triumph* (New York: Anchor Books, 1991), 133–4.

16. J.F.C. Fuller advances this view in his *Armament and History : The Influence of Armament on History from the Dawn of Classical Warfare to the End of the Second World War* (New York: Da Capo Press, 1998).

17. Gat, "A History of Military Thought," 676.

18. Fuller, as cited in ibid., 665.

19. Liddell Hart, *Strategy of the Indirect Approach* (London: Faber Ltd., 1941), 339–40.

20. Sean J.A. Edwards, *Swarming and the Future of Warfare* (Santa Monica, CA: Rand, 2005), 133.

21. "Iraqi Security Forces, Coalition Launch Operation Swarmer," 3/16/2006 Release Number: 06-03-01P, http://www.globalsecurity.org/military/library/news/2006/03/mil-060316-centcom01.htm.

22. Even though they regularly invoke them as precursors.

23. On the democratic peace, see: "Democracy, Liberalism, and War: Rethinking the Democratic Peace Debate," *Peace Research Abstracts* 41, no. 3 (2004); Christopher Layne, "Kant or Cant: The Myth of the Democratic Peace," *International Security* 19, no. 2 (1994): 5–49; Hilde Ravlo, Nils Gleditsch, and Han Dorussen, "Colonial War and the Democratic Peace," *Peace Research Abstracts* 41, no. 1 (2004); Michael Williams, "The Discipline of the

Democratic Peace: Kant, Liberalism and the Social Construction of Security Communities," *European Journal of International Relations* 7, no. 4 (2001): 525–53.

24. Edwards notes: "the Eastern and Central Asian art of war, to the extent that it is written down, reflects a philosophy geared to fluid, deceptive, and evasive tactics." Edwards, *Swarming*, 74. Edwards credits John Keegan for these observations, citing the latter's *A History of Warfare* in support for his description of the origins of swarming in "An Asiatic Style of War."

25. Edwards, *Swarming*, 74–75.

26. Keegan, *A History of Warfare*, 387, as cited in Edwards, 175.

27. Adorno, *Minima Moralia*, 115.

28. Ibid., 135. Adorno is referring to the fate of the individual in mass society. But the link between those concerns and the ones expressed here are implicit, to the degree that what appears to attain collective singularity in concepts like swarming, is in reality the victim of a private regression.

29. Ibid., 135.

30. John Arquilla and David Ronfeldt, *Swarming and the Future of Conflict* (Santa Monica, CA: Rand, National Defense Research Institute, 2000), vii–viii.

31. Ibid.

32. See Peter Ackerman, *Strategic Nonviolent Conflict: The Dynamics of People Power in the Twentieth Century* (Westport, CT: Praeger, 1994).

33. "They love it," says Colonel Casey Wardynski, the director of the America's Army video game, which he developed at West Point. Young men and women are "used to thinking about the world this way," he says. "You can call them 'digital natives.'" "Cutting edge: Serious Wargames," *Daily Telegraph*, March 1, 2006, 14. For America's Army see: http://www.americasarmy.com/.

34. Adorno, *Minima Moralia*, 231.

Contributors

Judit Bodnár is a U.S.-trained sociologist who is now based in Budapest and teaches at the Central European University. The author of *Fin-de-Millennaire Budapest: Metamorphoses of Urban Life* (University of Minnesota Press, 2001), she is working on a book that interrogates local histories of global urban restructuring through a comparative analysis of new genres of socially exclusive middle-class housing in the United States, Germany, and Hungary.

Patrick Bond is Director of the Centre for Civil Society at the University of KwaZulu-Natal in Durban. He is the author of several dozen books and working papers, including most recently, *Looting Africa: The Economics of Exploitation* (Zed, 2006) and (with Ashwin Desai) *Crony Neoliberalism and Paranoid Nationalism: Debating South Africa's "Developmental State"* (UKZN Press, 2006).

Anne-Marie Broudehoux is a professor in the School of Design at the University of Quebec at Montreal. She has studied urban renewal, tourist development, and "city branding" in India, Brazil, and China. *The Making and Selling of Post-Mao Beijing* was published by Routledge in 2004.

Mike Davis lives in San Diego. He is most recently the author of *In Praise of Barbarians* (Haymarket, 2007), *Buda's Wagon: a Brief History of the Car Bomb* (Verso,

2007), *Planet of Slums* (Verso, 2006), and *The Monster at Our Door* (The New Press, 2006). He is a longtime member of the editorial collective of the *New Left Review.*

Joe Day is a Los Angeles architect, clothing designer, and design historian. On the board of the Southern California Institute of Architecture, he edited an AIA Award–winning monograph on Frank Israel (Rizzoli, 1992) and is currently assembling the *LA Forum Reader* and a study of the roles played by prisons and museums in urban renewal.

Marco d'Eramo is a former theoretical physicist who studied sociology with Pierre Bourdieu in Paris and has become one of Italy's leading urbanists. A regular contributor to the newspaper *Il Manifesto*, he frequently reports on life and politics in the United States. *The Pig and the Skyscraper: Chicago, a History of Our Future* was published by Verso in 2002.

Anthony Fontenot is a New Orleans–based architect, sometimes at Princeton, who has worked on-site in Kabul. A former member of the Office for Metropolitan Architecture/Rem Koolhaas, he writes frequently for architectural journals and has contributed firsthand accounts of the aftermath of Hurricane Katrina to *The Nation.*

Marina Forti is a foreign correspondent for Italian daily newspaper *Il Manifesto*. Her beat ranges from Iran to South and Southeast Asia, and she writes a regular column on environmental conflicts in Asia—the subject of her latest book, *La Signora di Narmada* (Feltrinelli, 2004), awarded the Elsa Morante Prize for Communication 2004.

Forrest Hylton now resides in Brooklyn, but lived in Colombia and Bolivia from 2002 to 2005. He is the author of *Evil Hour in Colombia* (Verso, 2006) and co-author of *Revolutionary Horizons: Popular Politics in Bolivia* (Verso, forthcoming).

Sara Lipton teaches medieval history at SUNY Stony Brook and writes about the politics of art and visual representation in the Middle Ages. *Images of Intolerance: The Representation of Jews and Judaism in the Bible Moralisee* (California, 1999) won the John Nicolas Brown Prize for Best First Book.

Ajmal Maiwandi is an Afghan-born, American architect based in London. He is currently working with an international organization in Kabul on the reconstruction of some of the Afghan capital's most important public buildings.

China Miéville stood for the British House of Commons in 2001 as a Socialist Alliance candidate from London. Twice winner of the coveted Arthur C. Clarke Award, he is a bestselling writer of fantastic fiction (*King Rat, Perdido Street Station, The Scar,* and *Iron Council*) as well as the author of a pioneering Marxist study of international law (*Between Equal Rights*). His latest novel is *Un Lun Dun* (Del Rey Books, 2007).

Don Mitchell is the chair of the department of geography at Syracuse University. His books include *The Lie of the Land: Migrant Workers and the California Landscape* (Minnesota, 1996) and *The Right to the City: Social Justice and the Fight for Public Space* (Guildford, 2003).

Timothy Mitchell is professor of politics at NYU and is a leading authority on the politics of modernization and expertise in the Middle East. His books include *Questions of Modernity* (Minnesota, 2000) and *Rule of Experts: Egypt, Techno-Politics, Modernity* (California, 2002).

Daniel Bertrand Monk directs the program in Peace and Conflict Studies at Colgate University and is the co-organizer of a new Web-based international research consortium called The Conflict-Lab. He is the author of *An Aesthetic Occupation: The Immediacy of Architecture and the Palestine Conflict* (Duke University Press, 2002), as well as a number of other studies concerning the cultural and historical logic of the Israel–Palestine conflict. He is currently completing a book on Israel's era of euphoria after the Six-Day War of 1967.

Dennis Rodgers teaches at the London School of Economics. He has worked and published on urban violence, especially youth gangs, in Nicaragua, and local governance and politics in postcrisis Argentina. He is writing a book on Managua.

Laura Ruggeri teaches theory of design at the Hong Kong Polytechnic University. A video and installation artist, she co-edited *HK Lab2* and is currently studying Hong Kong's infraspaces. Her essays have appeared in a number of international publications.

Emir Sader is one of Latin America's most well-known public intellectuals. Director of the Laboratory of Public Studies at the State University of Rio de Janeiro, he is also a popular newspaper columnist and was one of the founders of the Brazilian Workers Party (PT) and, later, of the World Social Forum.

Rebecca Schoenkopf was senior editor at *OC Weekly* in Orange County, California, until its takeover by the conservative *New Times* chain. She has written for *Teen* and *Newsday*, and won the Association of Alternative Newsweeklies award for Best Political Column of 2006 for her column "Commie Girl." She lives with her son, Jimmy.

Jon Wiener teaches history at UC Irvine and is a contributing editor of *The Nation*. His most recent book is *Historians in Trouble: Plagiarism, Fraud and Politics in the Ivory Tower* (The New Press, 2005).

Index